The Comprehensive Guide for PMP® Certification

PMP Preparation Made Easy

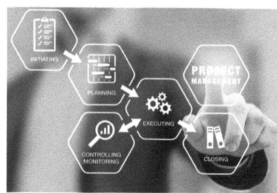

A guide for passing the PMP® Exam on your first attempt.

Aligned with PMBOK 6th Edition

For PMP Exams after March 2018

What's inside: *10 Knowledge Areas *Solved examples
*ITTO diagrams for all 49 Processes *400+ practice questions

Kal Jayaswal, PMP and
Archana Jayaswal, PMP, CSM

The Comprehensive Guide for PMP® Certification
PMP Preparation Made Easy
A Crash Guide for Passing the PMP on Your First Attempt
Aligned with PMBOK 6th Edition
For PMP Exams after March 2018
All Rights Reserved.
Copyright © 2019 Kal Jayaswal, PMP and Archana Jayaswal, PMP, CSM
v5.0

Outskirts Press, Inc.
http://www.outskirtspress.com

ISBN: 978-1-4787-9949-8

PRINTED IN THE UNITED STATES OF AMERICA

COPYRIGHT NOTICE

About the Authors

About Kal Jayaswal

Kal Jayaswal, PMP, is an internationally-recognized and expert project manager, author and speaker with more than 30 years of industry experience. He has provided project management and consulting services to global organizations such as Caterpillar, Cisco, Gilead Sciences, IBM, Pacific Gas and Electric (PG&E), Roche Bioscience, Symantec, University of California and Yahoo.

He is the author of a book titled "Administering Data centers" published by John Wiley and Sons, New York and another titled "Cloud Computing Black Book" published by Dreamtech Press in 2014.

About Archana Jayaswal

Archana Jayaswal, PMP and CSM, is a technical writer, software developer, entrepreneur and project manager.

She has more than 20 years of experience in managing large-scale projects and has provided consulting and project management services to organizations such as IBM, Caterpillar and Google. She has been co-founder of an IT services firm, where she managed a number of software application development and fiber-optic deployment projects for global telecom service providers.

Table of Contents

Advantages of this PMP® Exam Guide

This guide is based on the PMBOK 6ᵗʰ Edition® and is meant for PMP® Exams starting March, 2018. We have tried to incorporate various elements that we have found to be missing in the leading books in the market and online tutorials for PMP.

The intention of this book is to make exam preparation efficient, quick and without needing to refer to multiple sources of information. In this book, you will find:

- Figures with text that is built-in for easy reference and quick reading
- Tables, instead of lengthy paragraphs
- Step-by-step instructions on various tools and techniques
- Solved examples to help you quickly understand difficult concepts
- Workbook-style exercises for number-based questions
- ITTO (input, tools and techniques and outputs) diagrams for all 49 processes with built-in text to make it easier to remember
- Exam tips, based on our experience in taking the PMP exam and managing projects
- Full-length practice test (200 questions) with answers and detailed explanations

This book is a companion guide (and not a substitute) for the PMBOK® 6ᵗʰ Edition. In various places, we have cross-referenced page numbers in the PMBOK®, where you have detailed descriptions. This guide complements the PMBOK® and has brief explanations but the focus is on applications of concepts, exercises, solved examples and case studies, all of which are meant to prepare you for questions in the PMP® Exam.

Each chapter has Knowledge Area-specific points for the Exam and a set of practice questions. There is a full-length mock exam at the end of the book. Besides, we have various tips on preparing for and taking the Exam.

About PMI® and PMP® Exams

Over the last 20+ years, there has been a steady increase in the popularity and number of PMP®-certified professionals, around the world. This is because PMP® certification:

- demonstrates a commitment to a career in project management,
- establishes certification-holders as an authority in project management,
- serves as a trusted credential, and
- helps project managers in career advancement.

The PMP certification has gained credibility in more than 150 countries. Various jobs advertised for project managers utilize the PMP® certification as an application criterion to screen job candidates.

About Project Management Institute® (PMI)

PMI® (www.pmi.org) is the world's leading organization for project, program, and portfolio management professionals. It was founded in 1969 with its headquarters in Newtown Square, Pennsylvania and offers the following certifications:

1. Certified Associate in Project Management (CAPM)
2. Project Management Professional (PMP)
3. Program Management Professional (PgMP)
4. Portfolio Management Professional (PfMP)
5. PMI Risk Management Professional (PMI-RMP)
6. PMI Scheduling Professional (PMI-SP)
7. PMI Agile Certified Practitioner (PMI-ACP)
8. PMI Professional in Business Analysis (PMI-PBA)

About the 6th Edition of PMBOK® Guide

The acronym PMBOK® stands for Project Management Body of Knowledge. It is published by the PMI. PMP® Exams, starting from March, 2018 are based on the PMBOK® 6th Edition, which contains:

- 5 Process Groups, as mentioned in Table A-1
- 10 Knowledge Areas (covered in chapters 4 through 13)
- 49 processes, each having a set of inputs, tools and techniques and outputs (ITTO).

The 10 Knowledge Areas are:

1. Project Integration Management
2. Project Scope Management
3. Project Schedule Management
4. Project Cost Management
5. Project Quality Management

6. Project Resource Management
7. Project Communications Management
8. Project Risk Management
9. Project Procurement Management
10. Project Stakeholder Management

Each of the 10 Knowledge Areas has various processes and a dedicated chapter in the PMBOK®.

Chapter	Ten Knowledge Areas	Five Process Groups				
		Initiating	Planning	Executing	Monitoring and Controlling	Closing
4	**Integration Management**	4.1) Develop Project Charter	4.2) Develop Project Management Plan	4.3) Direct and Manage Work 4.4) Manage Project Knowledge	4.5) Monitor and Control Project Work 4.6) Perform Integrated Change Control	4.7) Close Project or Phase
5	**Scope Management**		5.1) Plan Scope Management 5.2) Collect Requirements 5.3) Define Scope 5.4) Create WBS		5.5) Validate Scope 5.6) Control Scope	
6	**Schedule Management**		6.1) Plan Schedule Management 6.2) Define Activities 6.3) Sequence Activities 6.4) Estimate Activity Durations 6.5) Develop Schedule		6.6) Control Schedule	
7	**Cost Management**		7.1) Plan Cost Management 7.2) Estimate Costs 7.3) Determine Budget		7.4) Control Costs	
8	**Quality Management**		8.1) Plan Quality Management	8.2) Manage Quality	8.3) Control Quality	
9	**Resource Management**		9.1) Plan Resource Management 9.2) Estimate Activity Resources	9.3) Acquire Resources 9.4) Develop Team 9.5) Manage Team	9.6) Control Resources	
10	**Communications Management**		10.1) Plan Communications Management	10.2) Manage Communications	10.3) Monitor Communications	

No.					
11	**Risk Management**		11.1) Plan Risk Management 11.2) Identify Risks 11.3) Perform Qualitative Risk Analysis 11.4) Perform Quantitative Risk Analysis 11.5) Plan Risk Responses	11.6) Implement Risk Responses	11.7) Monitor Risks	
12	**Procurement Management**		12.1) Plan Procurement Management	12.2) Conduct Procurements	12.3) Control Procurements	
13	**Stakeholder Management**	13.1) Identify Stakeholders	13.2) Plan Stakeholder Management	13.3) Manage Stakeholder Engagement	13.4) Monitor Stakeholder Engagement	

Table A-1: 10 Knowledge Areas, 5 Process Groups and 49 Processes

About the PMP Exam

Here are a few quick facts about the Exam:

- There are 200 multiple-choice questions.
- Each question has four choices, out of which only one is correct.
- There is no negative marking for wrong answers.
- The allocated time is four hours, including breaks. You can take as many breaks as you want, but time for breaks count towards the 4 hours.
- Out of 200 questions, 25 are experiential (or pre-test) questions. Answers you provide for those 25 do not count towards your score. They are used by PMI to assess whether those should be included in the future exams. Experiential questions that are too easy or too difficult are discarded.
- Most of the questions in the PMP exam are short case studies or scenarios.

The 200 questions and the choices are decided the moment you start the exam. These 200 do not change or adapt to the way you are answering questions. Think of it as receiving a printed set of multiple-choice questions. Table A-2 has the distribution (approximate) of questions amongst the Process Groups.

No.	Process Group	Approx. Percentage of Questions	Approx. Number of Questions
1	Initiating	13%	26
2	Planning	24%	48
3	Executing	31%	62
4	Monitoring and Controlling	25%	50
5	Closing	7%	14
	Total number of questions	**100%**	**200 questions**

Table A-2: Approximate Distribution of 200 questions in the PMP® Exam

Out of the 10 Knowledge Areas, test-takers commonly find questions from the following four knowledge areas listed below to be the most difficult. Those are listed in the order of difficulty (that we perceive), with the first one being the most challenging:

- Risk Management, Chapter 11
- Procurement Management, Chapter 12
- Integration Management, Chapter 4
- Quality Management, Chapter 8

The Process Groups are listed below in the order of most-difficult to most-easy:

- Executing
- Monitoring and Controlling
- Initiating
- Planning
- Closing

There is a full-length exam with 200 questions at the end of this book. Besides taking the full exam, you should also practice questions that are at the end of each chapter.

How to register for the PMP® Exam?

You need to create an account at www.pmi.org. This gives you access to filling out the PMP application form.

You can opt to be a PMI member for an annual fee. But you do not have to be a PMI member or a local chapter member to take the exam. However, the PMP fee is lower for PMI members. If you pay for one year of PMI® membership plus the exam fee, the total cost would be less than the exam fee for a non-member.

Table A-3 shows the qualifying requirements for the PMP® exam.

No.	Education	Required project management experience	Required number of hours spent on projects	Project management training requirements
1	High school diploma or associate degree	Five years of project management experience	7,500 hours	35 hours of formal education
2	Four-year bachelor's degree	Three years of project management experience	4,500 hours	35 hours of formal education

Table A-3: Qualifications and Experience Required for PMP Registration

Figure A-1 shows the steps to enroll for the PMP® exam. Once you have filled and submitted the application, PMI will take about one week to review and approve or reject the application.

Some applications are selected for audit. If your application is not selected for audit and is approved, you can pay the exam fee and block a date and time for the exam. If your application is selected for audit, you will need to submit proof of degrees and experience that you have claimed. You may also need to provide a copy of the diploma or degree and letters from your supervisor or program manager, attesting to the projects you have done, etc.

What is the pass mark for the Exam?

PMI does not publish the percentage required to pass the exam. You need to do as many mock tests as possible. The time limit and pressure are not easy for most test-takers. Our suggestion is for you to get more than 80% in most of the practice tests before going for the exam. Most of the successful candidates take at least 20 mock tests and score above 80% in those mock tests.

Can I pass the PMP® exam by just reading the PMBOK®?

For most project managers with even 10+ years of project management experience, the PMBOK guide is by itself, not enough to pass the exam. The content in the PMBOK is abstract and often terse. The abstract style is intentional because the content is intended to be industry-neutral and relevant to various business sectors.

Most of the questions in the exam are not theoretical, but situational applications of the concepts in the PMBOK. You need a thorough understanding of how to apply the PMBOK concepts. There are very few examples in the PMBOK, and those do not prepare you for the various situational (case-study) questions in the exam.

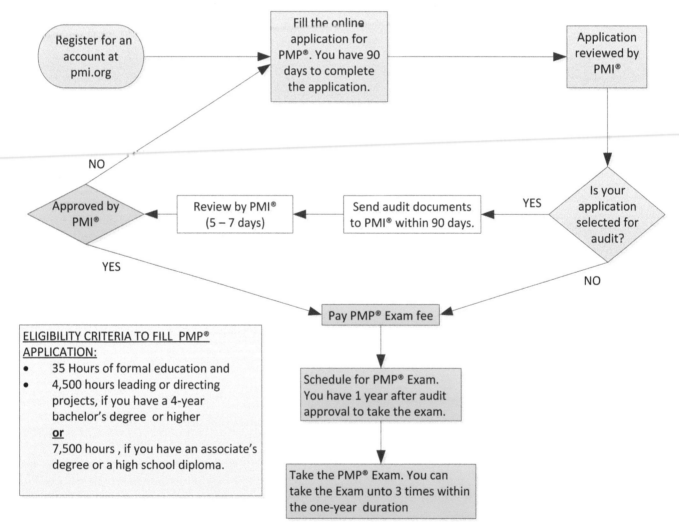

Figure A-1: Steps to Register for the PMP® Exam

Most of the PMBOK content is also tedious and difficult to comprehend or remember. Some content in the PMBOK may appear easy, but again the questions are not straightforward either. To pass the exam, just reading the PMBOK® is not enough. A guide, for example this book, is required.

Can I pass the PMP exam based on my extensive experience in project management?

Project managers with many years of extensive project management experience may ask if that is enough to pass the exam. But they may not be following the PMBOK methodology and processes at their workplace. They may not be applying the PMBOK concepts. For the exam, you need to know the terms and concepts in the PMBOK and how to apply those.

The second reason is that your experience may not cover all the 10 Knowledge Areas required for the exam. You may have successfully completed many projects, but there could be various gaps in your knowledge. Many project managers may have little or no experience in Knowledge Areas such as quality, risk, or procurement management. They may not have applied concepts such as earned value analysis, critical path methods, etc.

The reason for failing the exam could be one or more of the following:

- Lack of understanding of the terms and concepts in the PMBOK.
- Preparation that is generic and not focused on exam questions.
- Insufficient time spent on the PMBOK and guide books.
- Inadequate practice of sample questions. You need to be getting 80% or more in the mock tests because the pressure is less during mock tests than in the exam.
- Poor time and stress management during the exam.

When you are trying to select the correct answer out of the four choices, you need to think in the following order:

1. Think of how the *PMBOK* author wants you to answer the question. For this, you need to thoroughly know the terms and concepts in the PMBOK.
2. Think of how the content in *this guide book*, would have you answer the question.
3. If you have taken an online or instructor-led training, think of how the instructor would have answered the question.
4. If all the above approaches fail, use your real-world *work experience* to select the correct answer.

To pass the exam, you need to have a thorough understanding of the concepts described in the PMBOK and its applications in real life.

What are the various types of questions in the PMP® Exam?

Most of the questions will be case studies or situation-based questions. There will be a few with pure numbers, for example from procurement, risk, or cost knowledge areas. Some questions will be difficult, for which even expert project managers could select the wrong answer. Some questions will seem to take more than two or three minutes during the exam. In that case, mark those questions for later review and move on to the next. Some questions will have vague or confusing choices. Some will have two or more choices that appear to be correct, in which case you need to select the *best* or *most correct* choice.

Below is a list of *question types* that you can expect in the exam.

Question type 1: Questions based on ITTO (input, tools and techniques, outputs)
Sample question: Cost baseline is an output of:
- A. Plan Cost Management
- B. Estimate Costs
- C. Determine Budget
- D. Develop Project Management Plan.

Correct answer: C

There will be questions directly from the ITTO for the 49 processes, but the questions will usually be for common documents and techniques.

Here are a few more ITTO-related questions:

1. Which process has the project charter as an output?
2. Which process has the lessons learned document as an output? (The answer is Manage Project Knowledge process. The "Close Project or Phase" process has "updates to lessons learned" as an output.)
3. Which process has the baselines (scope, cost or schedule) as an output?
4. Which processes have change requests as an output?
5. Which processes have change requests as an input?
6. Which process has approved change requests as an output?
7. Which process has deliverables as an output?
8. Which process has accepted deliverables as an output?
9. Which processes have work performance reports as an output?

It may be too early to answer the above questions. But after, understanding Chapters 4 through 13, you should be able to answer the above.

Question type 2: Questions that require a deep understanding of a Knowledge Area
Sample Question: You have categorized the project activities into control accounts and planning packages. Which of the following is not true about work and planning packages and control accounts within a work breakdown structure?
- A. A control account consists of planning and/or work packages.
- B. A control account is a management control point where performance is measured by comparing planned scope, expenses, and schedule to the actual outcome, at any point in time, during the project lifecycle.
- C. A work package can be shared by multiple control accounts.
- D. A planning package consists of known work content but without detailed schedule or activities.

Correct answer: C

C is false. A work package cannot be shared by multiple control accounts. Note the keyword, **not**, in the question.

You need to know the levels of work breakdown into control accounts, planning packages, and work packages. A work package is the lowest level where the required cost and time can be estimated, and the activities can be executed, monitored, and controlled.

To answer these types of questions, you need a good understanding of the terms in the PMBOK.

Question type 3: Questions that seem to have two or more correct answers, where you need to select the "most correct" or best answer
Sample Question: You are developing a list of activities for an international office relocation project. The stakeholders are in various time zones. About 100 employees will be relocated from North America to Asia. You have also defined the activity attributes such as relationships, labels, imposed dates, constraints, and assumptions, etc. for each activity. What can you use the activity attributes for?
 A. Sequence the activities.
 B. Identify the location where the activity must be done.
 C. Prepare the project calendar.
 D. Develop project schedule and schedule baseline.

Correct answer: D

All the stated choices require activity attributes, but the best answer is "develop project schedule" since that includes the other choices.

In the exam, you will have questions where two or more choices will seem to be correct. In that case, eliminate the choices that are sometimes true and sometimes false. Select the choice that is true most of the time.

Question type 4: Situational questions (Case Studies)
Sample Question: You have got approvals for your project baselines, but now the customer wants changes to the requirements and scope. What would be the first thing to do?
 A. Get buy-in from the project sponsor.
 B. Assess the changes to the project such as a need for skills, funds and time and then estimate the impact of the changes on baselines, constraints, risks, customer satisfaction, etc.
 C. Develop options to accommodate the change such as fast tracking, crashing the schedule, getting additional funding, etc.
 D. Develop change requests and get approvals.

Correct answer: B

All choices are good things to do, but the **first thing** to do would be Choice B.

Situational questions are the most common of all question types in the exam. These are real-world applications of concepts in the PMBOK. Think about how the PMBOK and this guide book would have you answer the question. If that does not help, feel free to use learnings from your work experience.

Question type 5: Questions with irrelevant information
Sample Question: Alex Andersen is s senior program manager working for a global office and facilities management firm. The firm has recently acquired several new customers in various countries in Asia, Africa, and South America. To meet the needs of the expanded client base, Alex needs to hire more project managers, coordinators, and expeditors in various countries.

The new hires need to work with customers and partners around the world. They will also need to travel to other countries where the need for project management resources is higher. The employees get travel allowances as well as per-diem allowances, but they must be willing to travel at short notice and stay for several months at client sites. They need to manage temporary staff sourced from the local regions. They must also be willing to work in countries where the culture and work practices are different and unfamiliar to them.

Which of these skills should Alex look for when interviewing the applicants?
   A. Written communication skills especially for writing e-mails and project plans
   B. Technical skills and prior experience in the same business vertical
   C. Ability to influence senior management within the organization
   D. Ability to communicate effectively with stakeholders, project team members, customers and partners

Correct answer: D

These categories of questions have lots of unnecessary information. Do not get lost in the details. Follow these three steps:

   (1) First, identify the question that is being asked. In this case, the question is "which key skills should Alex look for in the applicants?"
   (2) Go back to the description and pay attention to the relevant points only. Ignore the rest.
   (3) Read the four choices and select the best answer.

Question type 6: Questions that relate to multiple knowledge areas
Sample Question: You have prepared the scope baseline, list of activities, work breakdown structure, and schedule baseline. You now need to estimate the budget required for the project, including contingencies (management and contingency). Which of the following would be required to develop the budget?
   A. Project scope statement
   B. Project schedule along with a list of activities and their attributes
   C. Project risks
   D. All of the above

Correct answer: D

Preparing the budget requires that you know the scope, risks, time, and skills needed for each activity.

The various knowledge areas contribute to each other. Preparing plans or documents such as the resource management plan, stakeholder management plan, or team performance assessment necessitate that you know the project scope, constraints, schedule, risks, quality requirements, etc.

Questions like this will require you to integrate your understanding of multiple Knowledge Areas.

Question type 7: Questions where you need to watch out for keywords
Sample Question: Alex Anderson is completing the project charter. He is working with the stakeholders to develop the schedule, scope statements, WBS, and budget. Which of the following is not true for the work underway?
   A. Stakeholder engagement is higher toward the beginning of the project.
   B. Cost for introducing changes is lower toward the beginning of the project.
   C. Monitoring and controlling are done mainly after the project execution has started.
   D. Engagement of project team members is lower during project initiation.

Correct answer: C

Notice the word **not.** Monitoring and controlling are done across the project and during all processes.

Watch out for words such as **never, always, first, last, best, worst**, in the question. If you are in a rush, missing these terms is certain to lead you to pick a wrong answer. These words may sometimes appear in the choices as well. Beware!

Question type 8: Questions that require formulas!
Sample Question: Your project has a baseline of $50,000. Halfway down the project duration, you see that you have completed only 20 percent of the work and spent $20,000 so far. What is the schedule variance (SV)?
   A. -$20,000
   B. -$10,000
   C. -$25,000
   D. -$15,000

Correct answer: D

In these problems, you need to first note the information that is provided:

   ▪ The BAC (budget at completion) is $50,000
   ▪ PV (planned value) so far is 50% (halfway) of $50,000 = $25,000
   ▪ EV (earned value) is however only 20% of $50,000 = $10,000
   ▪ AC (actual cost) so far = $20,000
   ▪ The question asks for SV = EV – PV = $10,000 - $25,000 = -$15,000.

Appendix C in this book has a list of formulas required for the exam.

Question type 9: Questions with terms that are not in the PMBOK!
Sample Question: Samuel Simpson is a project manager for a QA team and has selected 20 samples of the engineering drawings for manual inspection. This is referred to as:

A. Selective sampling
B. Optimized sampling
C. Statistical sampling
D. Random Sampling

Correct answer: C

Statistical sampling is selecting a part of the population to verify quality. This is done because verifying quality for all the units (100% of the population) would be too expensive, time-consuming or unnecessary. See Page 303 of the PMBOK for more on statistical sampling. All the other terms in the choices are not in the PMBOK!

CHAPTER 1
Introduction

This chapter provides concepts about **projects**, **programs,** and **portfolios** and how they are different from operational work. Although most of the content in this chapter is outside the Knowledge Areas, you will have questions from this chapter, as well, in the exam.

What is a Project?

PMBOK®: Page 4

A project is a **temporary** effort which results in a **unique** product, service, or outcome. Table 1-1 shows the distinguishing features of a project.

	Features of a Project	Details
1	It is temporary	A project has definite start and end dates.
2	It has unique outcome(s)	The outcome or result of a project could be: ■ a new service, ■ a new product, ■ change(s) in an existing service, or ■ change(s) or new feature(s) in an existing product. *Example:* Two shopping complexes in the same neighborhood with similar architecture and built by the same builder using the same set of vendors will have several processes that are common. But they are still two different projects. Why? Because the location, schedule, duration, issues faced, risks, resources, changes, etc. are different for the two projects.

Table 1-1: Features of a Project

> *** For the Exam ***
> As mentioned in the above table, projects have a definite end. Is it required that you complete the planned scope and work before you can close a project? No! A project can be terminated by the sponsor or stakeholder if, after project initiation, the project timing does not seem proper, or the goals are no longer relevant or worth the expenses.

Valid outcomes of a project are:

- A new product that is complete by itself
- A new product that is used as an input to another product (such as a battery or cylinder for a car)
- A new feature for an existing product
- A new service
- An improvement to a service or product
- A document such as a new research paper or response to a Request for Proposal (RFP)
- A change in an organizational process.

Projects and Operations

Projects are temporary and have unique outcomes. Operational work is ongoing (such as technical support, equipment maintenance, assembly line work in a factory), has no end date and all the outcomes are similar. Table 1-2 lists the differences between projects and operational work.

#	Feature	Projects	Operations
1	**Duration**	Projects have a start and end date.	Ongoing and continuous work—it has a start date but no end-date. Example of a start date would be a date that the users started using an application
2	**Uniqueness of the outcome**	The outcome of a project is a unique product or service.	The outcome of an operational work is not unique.
3	**Primary concern**	Optimizing resources and time necessary to complete the assigned scope is critical to managing projects.	High efficiency of the processes used for the ongoing production of goods or services is essential for successful operations.

Table 1-2: Distinction between Projects and Operations

The exam could have questions that describe a task and ask you to identify if it is a project or operational work. To answer questions of this type, you need to understand the difference between projects and operational work. For example, for a year-long project, you may conduct daily 15-minute status calls, and it might seem like an operational activity, but it is project work because it has an end-date.

Life of a Project

Projects vary in duration, budget, complexity, etc. Each project can, in general, be divided into the following stages:

1. Starting the project
2. Preparing the project plans
3. Doing the project work
4. Closing the project

The amount of work accomplished, resources involved, actual money spent, and the issues encountered, are not evenly spread across the project duration. Some of these are higher at the beginning of the project. Some are higher in the middle of the project and others towards the close of the project.

Here are some generalizations about projects:

- **Influence** of the project sponsor and senior stakeholders (or management) are highest toward the beginning of the project. Once the project has been planned and work has started, they spend less time on the project and they usually get involved for only a few activities such as managing fund approvals, change requests, etc.
- **Risks and uncertainties** are highest at the beginning of a project. These factors become less threatening further down the project as more work is completed and more is known about the project.
- **Costs incurred** (due to man-hours and resources utilized) are highest towards the middle of the project (that is when the project work is being done). It is lower toward the beginning and closing of the project.
- **Cost of changes** is highest towards the end of the project. Changes are easier and less expensive if made during the initiating or planning stages.

---
* For the Exam *
Unless otherwise mentioned in the question, you can assume that the generalizations mentioned above apply to all projects especially for those with a predictive or waterfall (see Figure 1-4) life cycle.

The above generalizations may not apply to all projects but are true for most projects with predictive life cycle.

For projects with an adaptive life cycle, stakeholder influence is high and the cost of making changes is low throughout the project duration.

Portfolios, Program, and Projects

PMBOK®: Page 11

A **portfolio** is a collection of programs and projects that are grouped for effective management of the work and aim to achieve strategic organizational goals. Attaining these organizational goals require that the work is divided and organized as programs and projects.

A **program** consists of projects that are managed together to achieve benefits which would otherwise not be possible, if those projects were managed separately. A program also helps coordinate and optimize the use of resources shared by the projects. Note that certain projects can be standalone and not part of any program, as shown in Figure 1-1.

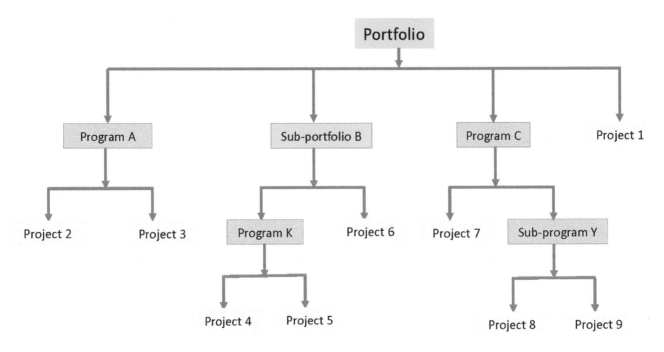

Figure 1-1: Portfolio, Programs, and Projects

---

* For the Exam *
- A portfolio contains programs, but it can also have sub-portfolios and projects.
- A program contains projects, but it can also have sub-programs.

Figure 1-2 is an example of a portfolio and programs.

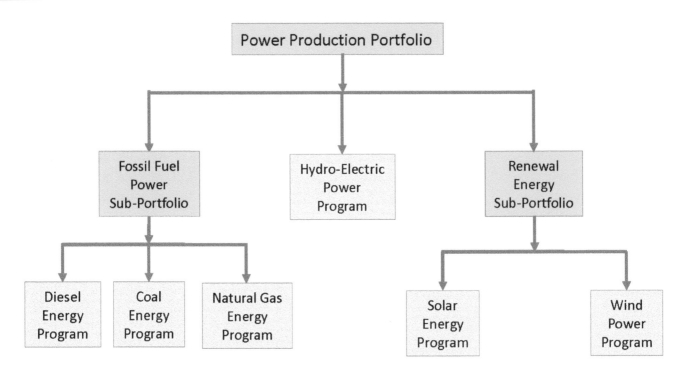

Figure 1-2: Example of portfolio and programs

Salient features of a portfolio, program and project are:

- A **portfolio** consists of sub-portfolios, programs, projects, and operational work, all grouped together for effectively managing the work, undertaken to meet an organizational goal. The success of the goal is usually quantified as a return on the amount invested for the portfolio. Should all the components of a portfolio be inter-related? No. The only relationship is that all the components contribute to meeting the organizational goal.
- A **program** consists of sub-programs and projects that are related and have a common outcome or objective. The focus is to manage the interdependencies between the projects and optimize the utilization of resources that are shared by the projects and sub-programs.
- A **project** is a temporary endeavor and has specific deliverables and outcomes. The focus is to manage the interdependence of activities. Note that project-related activities are temporary and have start and end dates.

What is Organizational Project Management (OPM)?

OPM is a framework that provides overall direction and guidance for prioritizing and managing portfolios, programs, projects, and other work with a goal of achieving the strategic objectives of the organization, as illustrated in Figure 1-3.

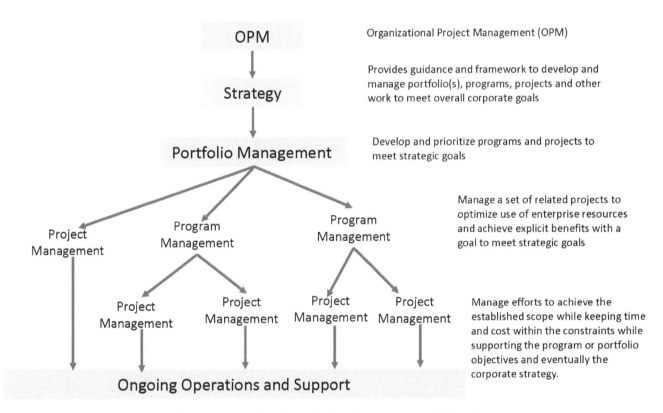

Figure 1-3: Components of Organizational Project Management (OPM)

What is OPM3?

The acronym OPM3 stands for Organizational Project Management Maturity Model. It examines an organization's processes and capabilities for project management to establish a rating for the organization (high, medium or low).

Project Life Cycle Management Methodologies

There are two broad methodologies for managing project lifecycles:

- **predictive** and
- **adaptive**

In a **predictive** (plan-driven) methodology, the requirements, scope, and deliverables are firmed and defined at the beginning of the project. The requirements `scope are known at the beginning of the project and the schedule and budget are developed to meet the requirements. Execution is started according to the plan. Changes to the scope are methodically managed.

Sometimes, predictive lifecycles may use a **rolling wave plan**, where an overall, high-level plan is developed at the start of the project. Activity details are added to the schedule after the execution has started and there is additional clarity and information on what must be done.

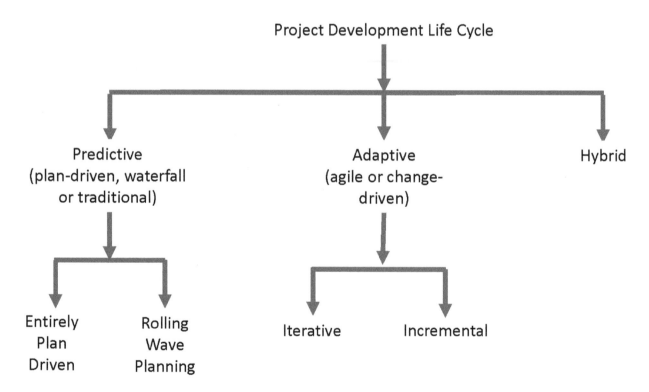

Figure 1-4: Methodologies for Project Life Cycle Management

For an **adaptive (change-driven** or **agile)** life cycle, the scope and requirements cannot be entirely established at the beginning of the project and changes must be quickly accommodated throughout the project. As the project progresses, the requirements and scope are continuously updated and fine-tuned. This lifecycle must be adopted when the following are true:

- The end-product cannot be fully defined at the start of the project.
- There is continuous stakeholder involvement to update requirements and scope.
- You must include frequent and multiple changes and lessons learned from ongoing work into the scope and requirements.
- You are expected to provide intermediate (work-in-progress) deliverables to stakeholders for feedback.

For an **iterative life cycle**, the project or phase starts with an overall project vision. But the final product cannot be completed in the first attempt. As soon as an initial scope and deliverables are developed, work is started to produce the deliverables. The initial focus is on completing a simplified implementation. As the work progresses, the scope and deliverables for the subsequent iterations are further developed. Once a particular iteration has started, it has a fixed duration (usually two to four weeks) and modifications to its scope are usually not allowed. All modifications are pushed to the next iteration. In subsequent iterations, more features and functionality are added until the final product is ready.

An **incremental life cycle** is one where the scope (as for iterative life cycles) is not completely known at the beginning. The initial scope is decided and later developed in a series of increments (small steps), until the product is ready.

Projects with Single and Multiple Phases

A project can be divided into multiple phases. Each phase has a set of activities from each of the five processes groups (Figure 1-5). Each phase provides one or more project deliverables, which must be approved and accepted before those can be used by the subsequent phases.

The end of each phase serves as a logical point to reassess whether to terminate the project or continue to the next phase. The end of each phase is also known as a stage gate, phase gate, milestone, phase review or a kill point.

The multiple phases (with a project) can be either sequential or overlapping.

- If the phases are sequential, the risks and uncertainty are lower, but the overall schedule is longer.
- If the phases are overlapping, part of the work is done in parallel. It helps reduce the project duration, but the risks of rework and poor quality could be higher.

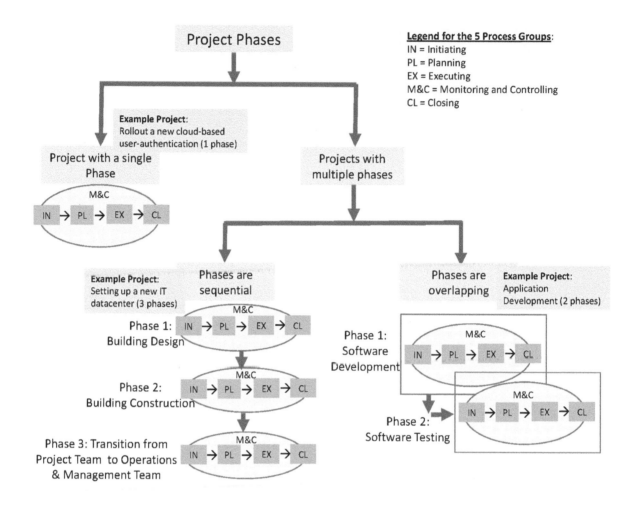

Figure 1-5: Projects with single and multiple phases (each phase has all five process groups)

Project and Product Processes

Every project is different and has varying objectives, end-products, etc. Yet, there are various common aspects in terms of "how it is done", processes, planning, etc. These common aspects of projects can be grouped together into project management processes and product-oriented processes (Figure 1-6).

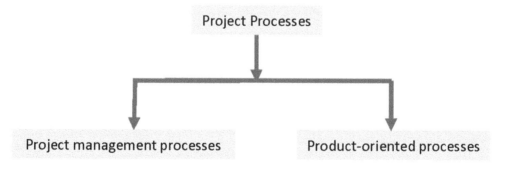

Figure 1-6: Project and Product-oriented Processes performed by the project team

There are certain areas of specialization or professional fields that are necessary components in a typical project. These are grouped into knowledge areas.

When you are managing projects, everything that the project team does can be grouped as project management processes. Various tasks are related to the deliverables (products or services) of the project. The processes can be grouped into two sets:

(a) **Project management processes**: These are processes that enable the progress of a project. They include work for preparing the project charter, schedule, budget, etc., analyzing risks, preparing a plan to mitigate the risks, developing requirements documents and comparing the work done and money spent with the approved baselines. It may sound like a lot of work for the project manager! But for small projects, a project manager may not require all of these. For large projects, there would be others in the project management team and project team who are responsible for various. For example:

- Business analysts are usually responsible for the requirements documents.
- Financial analysts are responsible for the budget and earned value analysis.
- Functional managers would be responsible for assigning resources.
- Deployment (cutover) leads would be responsible for certain execution tasks and handover to the operations teams.
- Change analysts or communications leads would be responsible for letting the users know of the new services or products.

(b) **Product-oriented processes**: These processes specify and implement tasks to meet the requirements and details of the product. For example, if a project is to construct a shopping complex, you will need an architect team to develop a detailed layout for each floor and dimensions of each unit. You will need various teams such as for construction, electricals, and landscaping. They will help prepare the end-results for the project.

Process Groups

PMBOK®: Page 23

The project management processes are grouped into process groups (Figure 1-7). They are:

1. Initiating
2. Planning
3. Executing
4. Monitoring and Controlling
5. Closing

A process group is **not** a phase. A phase is like a project and it includes all or most of the processes within the five process groups.

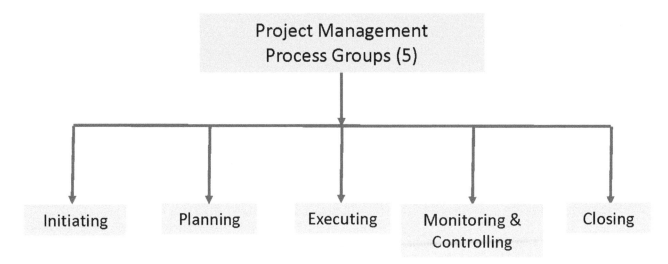

Figure 1-7: Five Process Groups

A large project is divided into phases.

Certain tasks are done before the start of the project and after the end of the project as shown in Figure 1-8. This includes:

- developing the business case
- doing a cost-benefit analysis (CBA) and return on investment (ROI) estimation.

The objective is to decide whether the organization should go ahead with the project. On the other hand, certain tasks such as archiving the project documents and providing the deliverables to the clients or users can be done after project-end boundary.

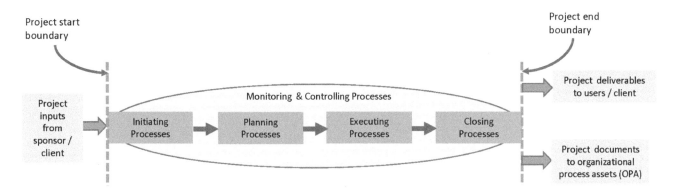

Figure 1-8: Project Boundaries within a Project or Phase

1 of 5: Initiating Process Group

This process group includes processes that pertain to starting a new project and preparing and getting approvals for the project charter. The project charter is a document which contains a high-level description of the project scope, constraints, approximate timelines, key stakeholders, budget estimates, etc. Besides the project charter, you also prepare the stakeholder register that contains details about the stakeholders, their expectations from the project and their roles in the project.

2 of 5: Planning Process Group

In this process group, various details related to the project scope, objectives and the actions needed to achieve those are established and documented. Plans pertaining to all knowledge areas (scope, schedule, cost, quality, resources, communications, risks, procurement and stakeholders) are developed.

What is the benefit of all the planning work? It keeps all the stakeholders (including project team) updated on plans and status and promotes a common understanding of the project. It makes it easier to get buy-in and support from the stakeholders. Another key benefit of the planning process group is the establishment of baselines (scope, schedule, and cost), against which project progress is measured. As we will see later, this is part of earned value analysis (EVA) and done during the monitoring and controlling Process Group.

All of this certainly sounds like a lot of work for the project manager. But as a project manager, you do not have the onus of developing the plans alone. You need to leverage the expertise and help of the project team. A key benefit of involving the project team is that it instills, within the team, a sense of ownership towards the project. During execution, the team does not see it as a set of tasks imposed on them. Rather, they view it as something they helped create and now must own.

3 of 5: Executing Process Group

This process group is about getting the project work done according to the project scope, schedule and cost baselines.

Will the project manager encounter unanticipated roadblocks? Will some of the identified risks become a reality during project execution? Yes! If the project manager is unable to keep the schedule or costs at the current baselines, change requests will need to be written and approved, leading to changes in the baselines.

Usually, most of the allocated time and funds are utilized during this process group.

4 of 5: Monitoring and Controlling Process Group

The processes in this process group are used to track and manage the progress and performance of project work against the planned baselines. What are the benefits of using the processes in this group?

- It helps identify deviations of actual work from the baselines so that corrective and/or preventive actions can be undertaken to bring the project back on track.
- It helps in the identification of changes to the plans. The changes requested go through "Integrated Change Control" for approvals and baselines updates.
- It helps gain insights into the health of the project and identifies areas that need attention.

5 of 5: Closing Process Group

This processes in Closing Process group help with formally closing the project. The key objectives and activities are:

- Close all contracts.
- Communicate the completion to all stakeholders.
- Finalize the lessons learned, planning documents and other project documents and get those ready to be archived in the organizational process assets.
- Finalize and handover the deliverables to the client or users.

Knowledge Areas

Knowledge areas are domains that help with the progress of projects. PMBOK has classified this into ten sets, shown in the table below.

Chapter	Knowledge Area	Description
4	Integration Management	Here you are concerned with establishing processes to combine various project activities. The goal is to make sure that the activities are coordinated and move smoothly while working around limitations and constraints posed by other projects and/or operational work. Each project can be divided into tracks that could initially be independent but must later be integrated.
5	Scope Management	This is concerned with defining the work that is included and excluded from the project. The goal is to prevent gold-plating and scope creep, which are common reasons for missing the established project baselines.
6	Schedule Management	This is concerned with developing a project timeline or schedule and making sure that the project is completed within the established schedule. You need to identify the critical path which is the longest track of activities in the project. In case, certain activities are delayed, there are techniques, such as fast-tracking and crashing other activates to make up for the delays.
7	Cost Management	Here you are concerned with establishing a budget for your project. Once the work starts, you need to estimate variances between the actual incurred expenses and the planned expenses.
8	Quality Management	Here you establish quality objectives and a continuous improvement plan to meet the objectives. Remember, the quality applies to the project as well as the product deliverables.
9	Resource Management	This includes processes to put together a project team from various groups in the organization and then get them to work together during all the processes, but especially for the planning and execution tasks.
10	Communications Management	Communications is about timely and appropriate planning, documentation, and distribution of status and information related to your project. Of the 10 knowledge areas, communications take the most time from a project manager. Why? Because a project manager deals with team members and stakeholders who have varying levels of interest and influence in and demands from the project. The project manager needs to make sure that the stakeholders provide the resources and support required for project success.

11	Risks Management	Your project will have positive and negative risks. The goal of risk management is to increase the possibility and impact of positive risks and decrease those for negative risks. In this knowledge area, you think of and document the risks, their impact on the project, and how you will deal with those, should they turn out to be an issue.
12	Procurement Management	This Knowledge Area is about the various types of contracts and the procedures to select a vendor, prepare a contract or purchase order, and get the work done by the vendor. For your project, you need to work with vendors and internal divisions to buy various products or services. You will involve the procurement and finance teams, but the project manager needs to be the interface with the vendor.
13	Stakeholder Management	There are various stakeholders for your project. They are interested in your project because they are impacted, either positively or negatively, by your project. But it is not all one-way. They too can positively or negatively affect your project. It is a project manager's job to identify and document their expectations and involvement with the project, provide updates as needed, and manage conflicting interests, if any!

Table 1-3: Knowledge Areas (10) and Descriptions

Chapters 4 through 13 in the PMBOK® are dedicated to these ten knowledge areas. The sections in these chapters are numbered in a particular way, as shown in Figure 1-9. It shows an example section 4.3.1.2. The first digit 4 refers to Chapter 4 (Integration Knowledge Area). The digit 3 refers to the third process in that Knowledge Area, which is Direct and Manage Project Work. The digit 1 refers to Inputs for the particular process and the last digit, which is 2, refers to the second input, which is Project Documents in this case.

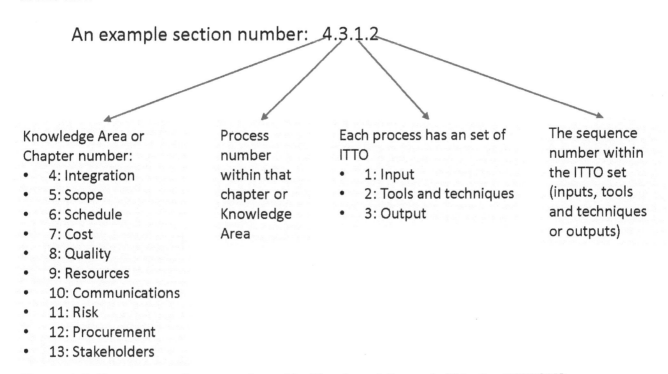

An example section number: 4.3.1.2

Knowledge Area or Chapter number:
- 4: Integration
- 5: Scope
- 6: Schedule
- 7: Cost
- 8: Quality
- 9: Resources
- 10: Communications
- 11: Risk
- 12: Procurement
- 13: Stakeholders

Process number within that chapter or Knowledge Area

Each process has an set of ITTO
- 1: Input
- 2: Tools and techniques
- 3: Output

The sequence number within the ITTO set (inputs, tools and techniques or outputs)

Figure 1-9: How are sections numbered in Chapters 4 through 13 in the PMBOK?

Project Information

PMBOK®: Page 26

As the project work progresses, a large amount of information are collected, analyzed, and reported. This information is associated with incurred costs, tasks completed, quality of project deliverables, and other work done during the execution processes. The unorganized raw measurements are called **work performance data**. The data is organized, categorized, analyzed, and presented in a context which is called **work performance information**. Later, these are further formatted as a report and distributed (via emails or handouts), presented to stakeholders, or stored as **work performance reports.** These are shown in Figure 1-10 and Table 1-4. The reports are an electronic or physical representation of the information.

Work performance data, information, and reports sound similar, but there are differences between the three. An understanding of these differences is important to answer questions during the exam.

- **Data** is the building block or raw observation of the work-in-progress.
- **Information** is meaning and context that you get once you have analyzed the data.
- **Report** is what you can prepare and provide to stakeholders or use as part of a project document or presentation.

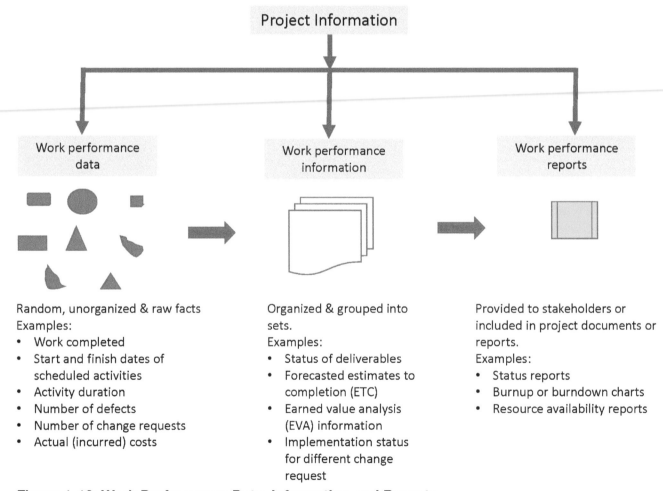

Figure 1-10: Work Performance Data, Information and Reports

You will also see that work performance data, information, and reports are inputs and outputs for various processes in the **Executing** and **Monitoring and Controlling** Process Groups.

	Type of project data	Description	Example	Output of the following processes (where it comes from)	Input to the following processes (where it is needed)
1	Work performance data	These are raw measurements or observations of the project work that is in-progress. It is the "as of today" project status.	Examples: • Amount of time or money utilized so far. • List of completed activities. • Measurements of product dimensions. • The number of approved, rejected, or deferred change requests.	• Direct and Manage Project Work	• Validate Scope • Control Scope • Control Schedule • Control Costs • Control Quality • Control Communications • Control Risks • Control Procurements • Control Stakeholder Engagement
2	Work performance information	This is the collected data that is analyzed and represented in context, as to what is needed by the stakeholders. This is a comparison of actual performance versus what was planned.	Examples: • Status of deliverables. • Output of earned value analysis (EVA) calculations such as to-complete performance index (TCPI), cost variance (CV), etc.	• Validate Scope • Control Scope • Control Schedule • Control Costs • Control Quality • Control Communications • Control Risks • Control Procurements • Control Stakeholder Engagement	• Monitor and Control Project Work
3	Work performance reports	These are representations (electronic or physical) of the work performance information compiled in project documents. The goals are to improve project awareness amongst the stakeholders, generate discussions, and create action items.	Examples: • Status reports for the project. • Recommendations. • Reports posted on electronic dashboards.	• Monitor and Control Project Work	• Manage Project Team • Manage Communications • Perform Integrated Change Control • Control Risks • Control Procurements

Table 1-4: Work Performance Data, Information and Reports

What Is Tailoring?

PMBOK®: Page 28

The 6th Edition of the PMI PMBOK Guide has 49 processes categorized into 10 knowledge areas and 5 process groups. Each process has several inputs, tools and techniques, and outputs (ITTO). Do you need to perform all the processes for each project? No!

The project manager needs to tailor or customize the number of processes and ITTOs to be used for the project. Tailoring is about identifying processes that are applicable for a project. Once you have selected the processes, the next step is to identify the relevant ITTO documents and techniques.

A section on tailoring is included toward the beginning of chapters 4 through 13. This section contains guidance and steps to develop a customized plan for a project.

What Are Project Management Business Documents?

PMBOK®: Page 29

The project goals and justification are described in two documents, namely:

- Project business case.
- Project benefits management plan.

These two documents may be prepared and maintained at the program level and are used as inputs for the project charter. These are developed from details in the "needs assessment" document, which contains the existing issues, opportunities, and recommendations. This is shown in Figure 1-11.

The business case and benefits management plan are used to develop the project charter. The charter, in turn, authorizes the project manager to request for and utilize required resources for the project.

The project management plan describes how the project will be executed, monitored, controlled, and finally closed. There are several plan documents including one for each of the ten Knowledge Areas.

Another business-level document is the "project success measures." It contains quantitative and qualitative criteria to determine if the project has been successful. The quantitative measures are meeting the pre-determined targets of:

- Benefit-cost ratio (BCR)
- Internal Rate of Return (IRR).
- Net Present Value (NPV).
- Payback period.
- Return on Investment (RoI).

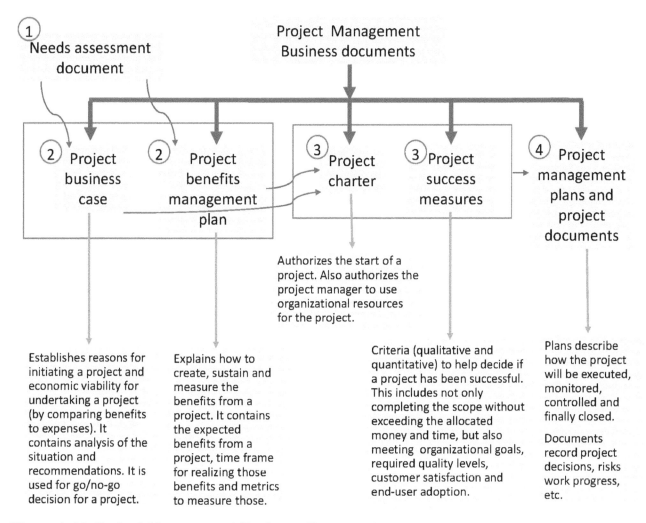

Figure 1-11: Project Management Business Documents

The qualitative measures are:

- Meeting the quality levels.
- Achieving customer satisfaction.
- Adoption of the products by the end-users.
- Completing the assigned scope while keeping within the limits of the assigned budget and time.
- Fulfilling contract terms and conditions.
- Meeting compliance criteria.
- Meeting organizational objectives.

Project Success and Constraints

PMBOK®: Page 34

Finally, remember that the expectation from and responsibility of a project manager is to complete the project successfully. But what is a successful project? A project which meets the project objectives upon completion while staying within the project constraints is deemed successful. The project constraints are typically the following:

- scope of the project,
- allocated time,
- allocated budget and resources
- required quality, and
- expected benefits (the value that the project delivers to the stakeholders).

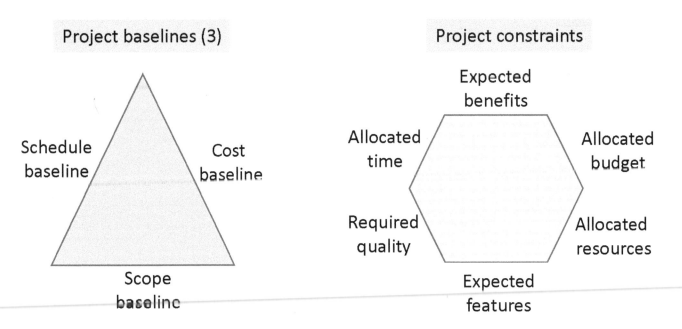

Figure 1-12: Project Baselines and Constraints

Note that an unsuccessful but completed project is one that has fulfilled all scope requirements but did not fulfill one or more of the specified constraints (see Figure 1-12), such as the quality requirements, allocated budget, timelines, etc.

More points for the exam:

- For the PMP Exam, assume that you are managing a project (not a program or operations).
- Each project is part of a program or portfolio and this relationship impacts how the project is planned and executed.
- When answering questions in the PMP® Exam, unless otherwise specified in the question, assume that you are a managing a large project with features such as:
    - o   A schedule of about one year,
    - o   About 100 resources spread in 10+ countries,
    - o   About 50 stakeholders,
    - o   Approved budget of about $10+ million,
    - o   Currently in Executing Process group,
    - o   Project charter, plans and baselines that are ready and approved for the project.
- Also, assume that updates to the baselines require a change request that has been approved by the Change Control Board (CCB) and your organization is matrixed and has a PMO.
- There are 49 processes in the PMBOK. All the 49 are not relevant for each project. Tailoring is selecting a subset of processes and tools and techniques that are relevant for a project.
- The project business case is maintained by the project sponsor (not the project manager).
- The following are not part of the project documents:
    - o   Needs assessment document
    - o   Project business case
    - o   Benefits management plan

Practice Questions for Chapter 1

1. Which of the following is not one of the key constraints within a project?
    A. Scope of the project
    B. Resources committed for the project
    C. Team members assigned to the project
    D. Approved budget

2. Which of the following is a project?
    A. Managing the schedule for a team of construction workers.
    B. Developing a priority order of issues that need to be mitigated.
    C. Constructing a set of units for an apartment complex, where the layout and material used for each unit are identical.
    D. Developing a daily status report with cost and schedule variances for a two-year construction project.

3. Which of these is true for a program?
    A. It is a control process to meet government regulations.
    B. It is a group of unrelated projects that are managed together to meet a common corporate objective.
    C. It is a group of projects that have a common corporate objective.
    D. It is a group of projects that are managed in a coordinated way, thus providing greater benefits and optimized resource utilization.

4. You have just completed determining the details of the budget and schedule constraints. Which of the following process group are you in now?
    A. Planning
    B. Monitoring and Controlling
    C. Executing
    D. Initiating

5. Who manages all the efforts that have a common outcome or goal?
    A. Project Management Office (PMO)
    B. Program manager
    C. Portfolio manager
    D. Project manager

6. Jamie has completed a phase and she has sent an invite for a meeting to her project sponsor and senior stakeholders. They now need to collectively decide on a go/no-go to the subsequent phase. This meeting is referred to as:
    A. Kill point
    B. Project success check
    C. Go/No-Go meeting
    D. Lessons learned meeting

7. Gary Gilbert has joined a large business with several portfolios and profit centers. He is explaining the need for proper organizational project management (OPM). What would you advise Gary Gilbert to tell the management about OPM?
   A. He should emphasize that OPM will help align the various business goals by systematic management of portfolios, program, and projects.
   B. He should emphasize that hierarchical relationship of portfolios, programs and projects.
   C. He should sell how OPM helps integrate strategy and operations.
   D. He should discuss the relationship between portfolio and programs.

8. There are 5 process groups. Which of the following is not a Process Group?
   A. Project Closing
   B. Project Initiating
   C. Project Monitoring and Controlling
   D. Project Intaking

9. Bob Simpson is managing construction of four similar multiplex theaters in a city. He is working with the same project team for all the theaters. Most of the construction work is outsourced to the same set of vendors. Which of the following is true for Bob's work?
   A. Bob is doing operational work since the work is similar and has the same project team and vendors.
   B. Each multiplex theater is a unique effort or project.
   C. The work is somewhere in between operational and project work.
   D. The entire effort for all four theaters should be bundled into a single project to reduce administrative work and documentation.

10. Jill Jackson has joined an IT consulting organization as a senior project manager. Which of the following is most likely to be a project?
    A. Preparing and submitting a Request for Proposal (RFP) for a large disaster recovery (DR) datacenter.
    B. Helping the functional manager with annual performance review for the project team members.
    C. Getting a vendor to setup fax services for new MFD (multi-function devices) that are being installed in the office.
    D. Helping the procurement team select a vendor for a 24x7 customer service center.

11. Jeremy Jacobson has recently joined a pharmaceutical firm and been assigned to initiate a 10-month project with 20 project resources in Europe and Asia. Which of these could Jeremey expect not to happen at the beginning of the project?
    A. Expenses and project resource involvement are likely to be low at the beginning of the project.
    B. Cost of making changes will be low at the beginning of a project.
    C. Issues and change requests will be low at the beginning of a project.
    D. Stakeholder interest and involvement are likely to be low at the beginning of the project.

12. Rick Rodriguez has been recruited for a new project. He is told that the high-level scope has been determined, but the product will have developed in repeated cycles and cost and time estimates will be updated or revised after each cycle. Such a development life cycle is called:
    A. Change-driven
    B. Agile
    C. Adaptive
    D. Iterative

13. Jessica Mason has been appointed as a project coordinator. Her program manager, Richard Roxon, explains to her that the project scope and product functionality are not completely defined. However, those will evolve in stages and in an incremental manner. This is referred to as:
    A. Change-driven development
    B. Progressive elaboration
    C. Incremental elaboration
    D. Rolling wave planning

14. Which of the following is true about project phases?
    A. Project phases can be sequential or overlapping.
    B. Each project phase can have processes from all five Process Groups.
    C. Project phases are part of a project life-cycle.
    D. All the above choices are true about project phases.

15. Edwards Ellington is managing several small and large projects. He uses the PMBOK® 6th Edition, as a guide. However, Edwards along with his project team, reviews the various processes and their tools and techniques to decide and select the ones that are applicable for each of the projects. This approach is called:
    A. Tailoring
    B. Effort Optimization
    C. Defining scope
    D. Defining activities

16. Which one of the following choices, is not an objective of organizational project management (OPM)?
    A. OPM helps ensure that the organization undertakes suitable projects and allocates the critical resources appropriately.
    B. It helps the management team understand and appreciate the strategic visions, project objectives and use of corporate resources.
    C. It helps in building a partnership between the project and functional teams and operations.
    D. It helps ensure that the various business units work in harmony with the vendors and customers.

17. A collection of logically-related project activities, that together provide one or more deliverables is called:
    A. Project phase
    B. Program
    C. Project task
    D. Process

18. PMI PMBOK® does not describe or provide details about:
    A. Project integration
    B. Project management office
    C. Organizational structure
    D. Operations management

19. Which of the following precedes the development of the business case for a project?
    A. Needs assessment
    B. Project charter
    C. Project management plan
    D. Benefits management plan

20. What of these is a key differentiator between work performance data and work performance information?
    A. Work performance data is about the number and details of change requests which work performance information is about the implementation status of the change requests.
    B. Work performance data contains raw measurements and observation, but work performance information has been analyzed and integrated across relevant project areas and is, therefore, more useful.
    C. Work performance data contains schedule activity dates and cost, but work performance information consists of schedule and cost baselines.
    D. Work performance data is collected during project execution, but performance information is created during project monitoring and controlling.

ANSWERS

Question Number	Correct Answer	Explanation
1	C	Team members are not a key constraint, because any particular member can be replaced by someone else. This is one example where all the four choices are correct. For such questions, you need to choose the best out of the four choices. The key constraints are scope, schedule, and cost.
2	C	Constructing a set of units for an apartment complex is a project because the resources, time and effort needed to construct the units would be different. Also, the work has a beginning and end date, which a project characteristic. All other mentioned choices are operational work or activities in a project.
3	D	A program consists of projects that are managed in a coordinated manner to obtain benefits that would not be possible if the projects were managed individually. See Table 1-2, **Comparative Overview of Portfolios, Programs and Projects** on Page 13 of PMBOK® Guide.
4	A	You are in **Planning** Process Group and have just finished processes such as **Develop Schedule** and **Determine Budget**. However, if the question says that you have completed only a high-level budget or schedule, then you would be in **Initiating** Process Group where these are needed for the project charter.
5	B	The answer is program manager. Notice how the question says " .. manage all efforts .." and not " .. manage all projects ..", which would have made the answer "program manager", very obvious. Also, can a program manager manage multiple programs with dissimilar outcome? Yes. But still, Choice B is the best answer.
6	A	This stage is known as kill point. It is also known as phase review, stage gate, phase exit or entrance. See Page 21 of the PMBOK® Guide.
7	A	OPM is about using portfolios, program and projects in a systematic manner to achieve the corporate goals. See Page 17 of the PMBOK®.
8	D	Intaking is not a Process Group. But it is an activity that provides business justification and approval to start a project. It happens before the **Initiating** Process Group.
9	B	Each theater is a unique project. The four theaters should be separate projects because there are differences in schedule, budget, duration, work start and stop dates, quality of workmanship, resources involved, location, etc.
10	A	Each of these seem like a project since they have a definite beginning and end and lead to a unique outcome. But A is the best answer. In the exam, you will have questions, where you will need to eliminate the wrong answers to end up with the right choice. Practice this approach! In Choice B and C, Jill is just helping someone. In Choice C., Jill is arranging for a vendor to do the work. But preparing an RFP (Choice A) for a Datacenter is a project. Jill needs to work with stakeholders and a project team to prepare the business and technical requirements, evaluation criteria for vendor selection, draft design and other sections of the RFP.

11	D	Note the keyword **not**, in the last sentence in the question. In the exam, when time is short, watch for keywords. Stakeholder involvement is not low towards the start of any project, when the charter and planning documents are being developed and approved. The other aspects such as expenses, cost of making changes, issues, change requests and resource utilization are likely to be low towards the start of any project.
12	D	The development lifecycle is iterative because the product will be developed in cycles, and estimates (for cost, time, needed skills) will be updated after each cycle. Also remember, that adaptive, change-driven and agile are synonyms. Adaptive methodologies are of two types: ▪ Iterative methodology, where the features and functionalities are updated in each cycle. ▪ Incremental methodology, where new features and functionalities are added in each cycle. See Page 19 of the PMBOK®.
13	B	Progressive elaboration is a methodology where there is limited visibility at the stat of the project. Further product and project details evolve as the project progresses.
14	D	A project lifecycle is made of project phases. Within each phase, you can expect processes from all the 5 process groups.
15	A	The answer is tailoring. Efforts optimization is not described in the PMBOK. Also, defining scope and activities are processes and not used to select processes that are applicable. See Page 28 in the PMBOK®.
16	D	OPM is about understanding the organizational strategy and goals and then coming up with portfolios, programs and projects to meet the strategy and goals. It is not essentially about vendors or customers.
17	A	A project phase is a collection of related activities that ends up in one or more deliverables. A phase could be treated as an entire project and have processes from all the five Process Groups. Also, a project can be divided into phases such as concept development phase, customer requirement collection phase, design phase, build phase, testing phase and deployment phase.
18	D	There are no details about operations management in the PMBOK. There is only a brief mention of how an operation is different from project management. There are no comprehensive sections on operations management.
19	A	The 'needs assessment' helps establish and precedes the business case. The correct sequence of developing the documents is: needs assessment document → business case → benefits management plan → project charter (output of **Initiating** Process Group) → project management plans (output of **Planning** Process group).
20	B	Work performance data is about raw project data and measurements. These are analyzed and integrated to create work performance information. Later the work performance information is compiled to create work performance reports (such as status reports, dashboards, memos and updates). Note that Choice A is also true but it is just an example and not the best answer.

CHAPTER 2
Organizational Influences on Projects

Success or failure of a project is determined, not only by the work done by the project manager, but to a large extent, by the relationships that the project manager has developed over the course of time with the stakeholders.

Other factors, such as organizational policies, commitments for other projects and operational tasks required to run the business could impact project progress. Also, the perceived benefits, market conditions and need to complete a project may decline with time, which can lead to unexpected project closure. Some of these conditions could be outside the influence or control of the project manager.

In this chapter, we will look at how various organizational factors contribute to project progress and influence project management.

What Does the Organization Have to Offer to Projects?

Over the years, organizations have developed a set of internal policies, best practices, and recommendations that project managers can take advantage of. Figure 2-1 shows the resources and assets that an organization can contribute to projects. You will see that Enterprise Environmental Factors (EEF) and Organizational Process Assets (OPA) are inputs for various processes.

It is the organization's responsibility to develop and maintain a corporate knowledge base of documents from previous projects. In return, it is the project manager's responsibility to know about and use the knowledge base.

The interaction between the enterprise and the project is not a one-way street. Each project (in-progress or completed) contributes to and helps grow the existing knowledge base of resources and documents. You will see that "updates to EEF and OPA" are outputs of various processes.

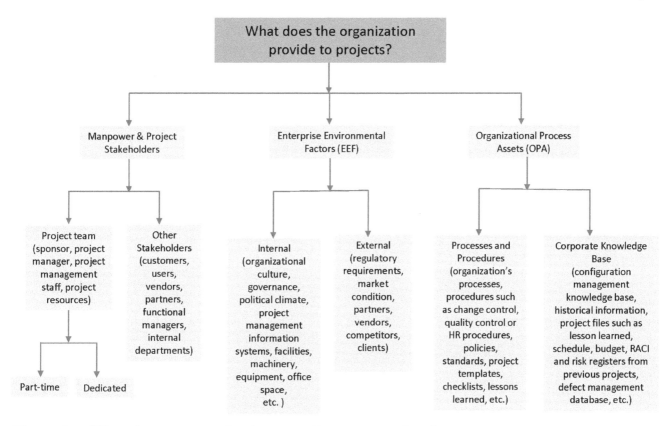

Figure 2-1: What does an organization contribute to a project?

Manpower and Project Stakeholders

Project stakeholders (Figure 2-2) are a group of people who are interested in and impacted (positively or negatively) by the activities and outcome of a project.

Will all the stakeholders have the same expectations from and involvement in the project? No! There will also be conflicting and competing expectations. Few will support and help the project manager and others may not support the project. More on this is discussed in Chapter 10 (Communications Management) and Chapter 13 (Stakeholder Management).

For now, you need to know that the stakeholders are a bigger group than what you may imagine! As you can see in Figure 2-2, stakeholders comprise of project team members and those not in the project team.

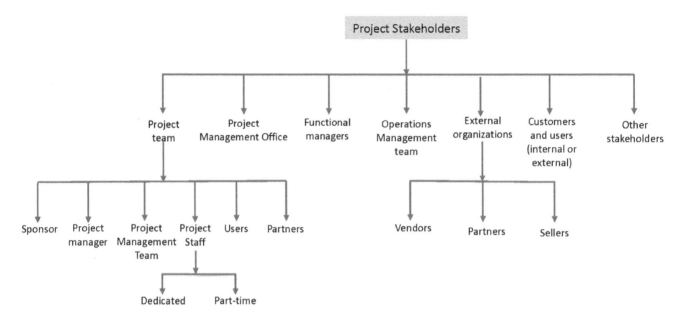

Figure 2-2: Stakeholders within a project

The **project team** consists of those who are involved almost throughout the project life cycle. They work together to plan and execute the project and are responsible for project execution and outcomes. They attend most of the meetings. The project team includes:

- Project manager: Every project team has one project manager, regardless of his or her authority or power.
- Project sponsor: The project sponsor is usually involved throughout the project and is part of the project team. In some cases, he or she may only help with key aspects such as project initiation, change requests, approval of contingency funds, and acceptance of final deliverables by the client.
- Project management team: This team is responsible for managing the project. It includes the sponsor, functional members such as a business analyst who helps with developing the requirements and traceability matrix document, a financial analyst who helps with financial tracking and reports, and project scheduler, who helps develop the project plan or schedule. These members and tasks they do may be supported by the Project Management Office (PMO). In some cases, and especially for small-scope projects, the project manager could be responsible for developing and getting approvals for all deliverables, related to requirements and financial planning.

Depending on project scope, there may be other stakeholders in the project team, such as external vendors, customers, PMO, function managers and operational team members.

What is EEF?

PMBOK®: Page 38

Enterprise environment factors (EEF)) are causes that arise from the enterprise or the working conditions. These factors influence and place constraints on projects and are considered as inputs to various processes. Usually, these factors are not within the control of the project manager and could have a positive or negative impact on the project

EEFs could be internal or external to the organization. A few examples of **internal** EEFs are:

- The reporting hierarchy within the organization,
- The HR policies related to recruitment of new staff members for the project, training, retention, employee performance evaluation, time tracking, overtime, etc.,
- Risk tolerance of the stakeholders,
- Project management information system (PMIS), which includes software tools to improve automation and document sharing such as:
  - o project scheduling software (examples: Microsoft Project, Oracle Primavera)
  - o Storage space for sharing project documents (example: Microsoft SharePoint)
  - o Time-tracking application
  - o Software to compute earned value management
  - o Procurement management applications
- The geographic location of the project staff members,
- The laws and rules of the country or state where the project is being executed,
- The organizational culture, and
- The political climate in the organization.

Examples of **external** EEFs are:

- Government regulations.
- Industry standards that must be adopted for the projects or products.
- Marketplace conditions
- Contribution from partners, clients, and vendors.

---

* For the Exam *
Remember that EEF are factors or constraints over which the project manager has little or no control but within which the project manager needs to function. These factors or resources could be owned by the enterprise, suppliers or partners. These could be shared by various projects.

What is OPA?

PMBOK®: Page 39

Organizational process assets (OPA) are plans, policies, and knowledge bases that are provided by the organization for project use. It includes:

- Artifacts from completed and in-progress projects, and
- Documents created by various departments within the organization.

OPA can be divided into two broad categories (Figure 2-1):

- Process and procedures.
- Corporate knowledge base.

Processes and Procedures

These are organizational processes that need to be followed by the project. These include:

1. Guidelines for tailoring the standard set of procedures to meet the requirements of specific projects.
2. Templates for project plans, project charter, RACI matrix, WBS, schedule network diagram, risk register, etc.
3. Sample project documents from previously-completed projects
4. Policy standards mandated by HR, finance, procurement, quality control or another division. An example would be quality checklists and quality procedures for reducing defects.
5. Established procedures for projects, for example, change control procedures, communication procedures, etc.
6. Vendor management procedures for obtaining quotes from vendors, gaining approvals for the quotes, issuing purchase orders and payments to the vendors, etc.

Corporate Knowledge Base

These are historical records and documents that are developed and stored in a pre-defined manner in a corporate database.

	Corporate Knowledge Base	What It Contains
1	Configuration management database (CMDB)	Repository of documents that contains versions and baselines of project documents, corporate policies, established procedures, details of corporate equipment and assets, adopted standards, etc.
2	Financial databases	Contain project budgets, cost overruns, insurred and expected costs, and other financial documents related to projects and to the organization.
3	Historical information.	Contains project documents, interim status reports, lessons learned from previous projects, etc.
4	Issue and defect management database	Contains information about issues and defects, such as their status, associated risks, impact, planned action, and items for resolution.
5	Process measurement database	Contains available measurement data for products and processes.

Table 2-1: Examples of Corporate Knowledge Base

Organizational Structure Types and Their Influence on Projects

PMBOK®: Page 45

Organizational structure is the setup and reporting hierarchy for the staff and project team.

It influences the way that projects are managed such as getting commitment for project team. Figure 2-3 shows various organizational structures.

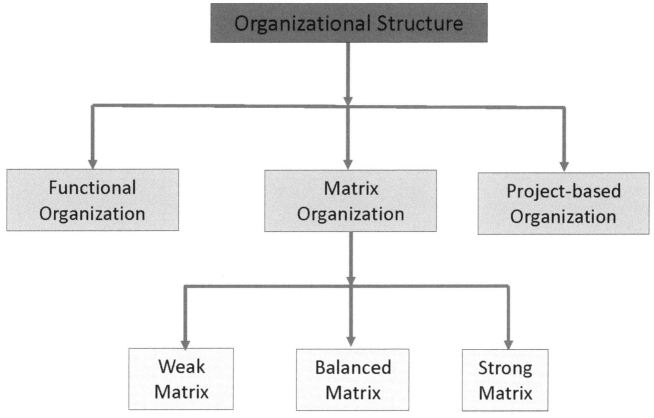

Figure 2-3: Types of Organizational Structures

Functional organizations: In functional organizations, staff members are grouped according to their specialty. They report to a functional manager or department head. Project managers report to a functional manager or department head. The functional manager usually controls the scope and budget of projects. Some projects may be contained within the department and may require minor involvement of other departments.

Project-based (projectized) organizations: On the other hand, project-based organizations are those where the project team reports to the project manager. An example of this could be an organization that constructs residential buildings or business complexes. Before a new construction project is started, project manager(s) and project resources are brought in for planning and execution. A new project team is formed that reports to the project manager. When the residential complex is completed and handed over to operations and maintenance staff, the project team members are moved to other active projects or let go.

Matrixed organizations: Most of the organizations today are matrixed. The staff members have hardline reporting to the functional managers and dotted line reporting to the project managers. The project team is usually engaged in normal day-to-day operational (run-the-business) tasks as well as project activities.

There are three forms of matrixed organizations: **weak, balanced** and **strong**, based on the authority and power that lies with the project managers. In a weak matrix, most of the authority and power lies with the functional managers. In a balanced matrix, the power is shared by the functional and the project managers. In a strong matrix, it lies mostly with the project managers.

Table 2-2 describes the types of organizational structure and their influence on projects.

Organizational structure	Functional organizations	Matrix Organizations			Project-based organizations
		Weak	**Balanced**	**Strong**	
Definition	Staff members are grouped by their specialty and report to the functional manager.	These have a blend of characteristics from functional and project-based organizations. The classification of weak, balanced, and strong reflects the level of power and influence that the project manager has over the budget, resources and project management.			Staff members are grouped by the projects they work on and they report to the project manager.
Who does the project manager report to?	Functional manager	Functional manager	Functional manager	PMO (or manager of project managers)	PMO (sometimes to the CEO or project sponsor)
Who does the project team report to?	Functional manager	Functional manager	Functional manager	Functional manager	Project manager
Role of a project manager	Project expeditor	Project expeditor or coordinator	Project coordinator	Project manager	Project manager
Who controls the project budget?	Functional manager	Functional manager	Functional and project manager	Project manager	Project manager

Table 2-2: Organization Structure and Their Influence on Projects

> *** For the Exam ***
> In the exam, if a question does not specify a functional or a project-based organization, you can assume that the question is related to a matrixed organization.

Project Coordinators and Expeditors

A **project coordinator** usually does not make key project decisions. Some of the responsibilities of a project coordinator would be to help with team communications and updates project artifacts. They also help in monitoring and controlling project progress.

Project expeditors act as a staff assistant and cannot make or enforce decisions. They can provide input to the decision-making process and communicate the decisions to the relevant stakeholders. They also communicate with the project team and suppliers to ensure timely completion or activities or delivery of materials.

Project managers have more authority and decision-making power than project coordinators. Project coordinators have more authority than project expeditors.

Project Management Office (PMO)

PMBOK®: Page 48

A **project management office (PMO)** is a management structure that helps establish governance for projects and facilitate the sharing of resources, methodologies, tools, and processes across all projects.

Table 2-3 describes the three types of PMO structures that can exist in an organization. A PMO can also be a hybrid of any two of these three types.

	Type of PMO structure	Degree of control	Role	What do they provide?
1	Supportive	Low	Consultative role	The PMO provides templates, training, best practices, lessons learned, etc. for project managers. But these are not forced upon the project managers; they are provided on demand and when asked for.
2	Controlling	Medium	Guiding and Auditing	The PMO requires the project managers to conform to the established corporate methodologies and regulatory requirements by the government. They provide tools, templates, forms, and processes that the project managers must use. In some organizations, the PMO conducts reviews at certain project milestones before the project can continue with the next set of activities. For example, the PMO will review and sign off on the planning documents before the project manager can start execution activities.
3	Directive	High	Governing	The PMO controls projects by directly managing the projects. They select and hire project managers.

Table 2-3: The three types of PMO Structures

The most suitable PMO structure depends on the planned goals for the PMO, the existing corporate culture and the intended future culture that the organization must move towards. For example, if the goal is to comply with the government and regulatory requirements, the PMO must make sure that the project managers conform to certain regulations and requirements. The PMO might mandate that project managers prepare and maintain certain regulatory documents required for compliance audits. In this case, the best choice could be to establish a controlling PMO structure.

Can the PMO manage one or more set of related projects? Yes. The responsibilities of the PMO can range from providing governance and support for the projects to directly managing the projects.

What are the differences between the PMO and the program manager? The PMO is responsible for all projects across the organization. The projects could be unrelated to each other. But a program manager, on the other hand, is responsible for a set of related projects.

EXERCISE TIME:

Question:

Identify the most suitable PMO structure for the following situations.

	Requirements for the PMO	Most suitable PMO structure (Supportive, Controlling, or Directive)
1	The PMO sets a priority for completing projects and assigns project managers to different projects across the organization	
2	The PMO makes sure that progress, documents, and project processes are audited at various milestones before the project manager can move on to the subsequent set of activities.	
3	Project managers have a hardline reporting to the PMO.	
4	The PMO strives to promote standardization across the organization by recommending common templates and procedures.	

Solution:

	Most suitable PMO structure
1	Directive
2	Controlling
3	Directive
4	Supportive

More points for the exam:

- Projects are planned with input from the project team and stakeholders (and not alone by the project manager or sponsor).
- Each organization has project-related policies and procedures and the project manager must make sure that those are followed for the project.
- Organizations have records (knowledge bases) from previous projects and the project manager can use those to plan for future projects.
- The project manager maintains the project artifacts, plans, documents, lessons learned, etc. and provides those back to the organizational knowledge bases.
- For the exam, assume that the organization being described has a PMO office and provides governance and support for all projects.

Practice Questions for Chapter 2

1. You are a project manager. But you have almost no direct control over your project staff members. They are from Test and Engineering divisions and report to managers in those divisions. What type of organization are you in?
   A. Strong matrix organization
   B. Projectized (project-based) organization
   C. Functional organization
   D. Weak matrix organization.

2. As a project manager, you have the most authority in which type of organizational structure?
   A. Strong matrix organization
   B. Balanced matrix organization
   C. Weak matrix organization
   D. The amount of authority depends on the organizational structure, work culture and the project manager's ability to influence the functional managers.

3. You have joined a new organization as a project manager. The organization is structured as a projectized (project-based) organization. You have been assigned to manage six projects. These projects have the same project team from the engineering department, but the project team is not sure on the priority of the six projects and which one is most urgent. Who do you consult with to get the project priority?
   A. You work with the project team members to decide the priority.
   B. You refer to the company mission and vision.
   C. You consult your peer project managers.
   D. You consult the project management office (PMO).

4. Configuration management knowledge base contains the versions and baselines of various standards, software versions and project documents, and are part of:
   A. Enterprise environmental factors
   B. Organizational process assets
   C. Work performance information
   D. Historical information

5. You have joined an organization where the PMO plays a consultative role and provides the best practices and project templates. What is the PMO structure?
   A. Directive
   B. Controlling
   C. Supportive
   D. Moderate

6. Sue has started work as a project coordinator. She has been assigned to lead the communications for a program manager. She has been told that the organizational structure is primarily matrixed. She can expect that the communications will be:
   A. Simple and will not take much time.
   B. Mainly done by the program manager.
   C. Across various verticals and hence complex.
   D. Primarily done by the functional managers.

7. Jim Johnson has joined a cruise company as a senior engineer to refurbish and renovate older ships. Jim reports to a functional manager, but he works for almost 100% of his time under the supervision of a project manager, who is responsible for the renovation of ships. Whose job is it to manage the dual-reporting relationship?
   A. Jim needs to take responsibility for managing the dual reporting relationship. He must keep both managers updated on his progress.
   B. Project manager
   C. Functional manager
   D. It is the combined ownership of Jim and the two managers.

8. Gary Garcia, a senior project manager has provided a set of completed deliverables to the clients. However, the client has found defects and has returned some of the deliverables, with a defect list. Gary needs to log the defect descriptions, issues and action items for resolution in a defects database. Where should Gary look for to get the defects database?
   A. Gary should consult with the program or portfolio manager or his lead project manager
   B. Enterprise environment factors (EEF)
   C. Organizational process assets (OPA)
   D. Gary should open a new change request and log all the findings and action items there.

9. Which of the following activities could a project management office (PMO) do?
   A. Act as an integral stakeholder and decision-maker throughout the project lifecycle.
   B. Keep projects aligned with the business objectives.
   C. Conduct project success checks (PSCs) or audits to make sure that the various project activities are in compliance with the project management standards, policies and regulatory requirements.
   D. All of the above.

10. Max Maloney has joined a pharmaceutical firm, along with three other project managers for a new program. Max reports to a program manager but he has almost no control over the project budget. The reporting hierarchy of the project team members is arranged according to their job functions. What is this type of organizational structure called?
    A. Hybrid
    B. Functional
    C. Project-based
    D. Moderate or balanced matrix

ANSWERS

Question Number	Correct Answer	Explanation
1	C	In a functional organization, the project manager has almost no direct control over the project team.
2	A	In a strong matrix organization, the project manager administers the project budget and has moderate to high authority.
3	D	The PMO has the project priority in a projectized (project-based) organization. You need to consult the PMO.
4	B	Configuration management knowledge bases (repositories) are part of organizational process assets (OPA). Note there will be questions in the exam that will require you to be familiar with the PMBOK terminology and concepts.
5	C	The type of PMO, that is described, is supportive and its role is limited to training, maintaining templates, sharing best practices, etc. Moderate is not a type of PMO structure.
6	C	Communications in a matrix organization is complex and happens across various reporting lines.
7	B	The answer is project manager. Why can the functional manager not do the coordination? Because he/she is usually not aware of the project tasks being done by Jim. Choice D appears to be correct but it is not the best answer.
8	C	Issue and defects management database are part of organizational process assets (OPA).
9	D	Depending on the PMO structure (supportive, controlling or directive) the PMO could be involved in all of the activities listed in the four choices.

PMO acts as a key decision-maker and makes sure that the project and organizational objectives are aligned. The PMO also conducts project success checks (also called gate reviews) to make sure that the deliverables are in compliance with government regulations. |
| 10 | B | A functional organization is one where the reporting hierarchy of the project team is based on the job and the functional manager controls the project budget. |

CHAPTER 3

Skills and Required Competencies of a Project Manager

Can a project manager's skills and experience be a reason for the failure or success of a project? Usually yes! Effective leaders believe in the "people first, strategy second" policy. They know that with the right person, leading from the front, strategy and processes become secondary factors for the project outcome. Effective leaders implement that belief. They first get the right people on a project; then they move some to the front of the project and others into supporting roles; only then do they proceed to develop a roadmap and plans!

Failing to follow processes or lack of technical skills are usually not the leading reasons for project failures. Project failures are commonly due to people reasons. Stakeholder support is crucial for project progress and success. Improving and maintaining the support of the stakeholders is one of the key responsibilities of the project manager. A project manager must collaborate with other managers (program, operations, and functional managers) and stakeholders to ensure project success.

Before discussing soft skills needed for managing projects and stakeholders, let us differentiate between the roles of a project, program, functional and operations manager:

- A project manager leads the team to achieve project objectives and ensures that any decision made by the team steers the project toward its objective.
- A program manager oversees a set of related projects that together meet certain objectives(s) for the organization.
- A functional manager provides oversight for a business unit or a functional group such as HR, payroll, procurement, IT, engineering, etc.
- An operations manager is responsible for running the business, which usually takes priority over projects for resource commitments.

Project Manager's Sphere of Influence

PMBOK®: Page 52

A project manager must have the necessary level of influence on the project stakeholders and to some extent over the organization and industry.

Influence on the Project

A project manager needs to establish and maintain adequate communications with project team and stakeholders. Will all stakeholders always support a project manager's view or decision? No. However, as a project manager, if you and the project team are convinced that a proposed decision is in the best interests of the project, you must work to gain support and consensus for the decision. A consensus is not about getting everyone to believe that a decision is in the best interests of the project, but it is about getting a commitment from the stakeholders that they will support the decision, if implemented.

Project success depends to a large extent, on the interpersonal, communication and soft skills of the project manager. It is, therefore, necessary to develop good verbal, nonverbal, and written communication skills.

Project communications must be consistent and transparent. The content must be complete, relevant and tailored to the audience. There must also be a way for the recipients to provide feedback.

Influence within the Organization

A project manager also needs to develop formal and informal relationships with a large network of people. These relationships could later help resolve issues with projects.

Organizational resources and funding are often shared by various projects. A supportive network of people within the organization would help a project manager with quicker decision-making and smooth progress for the project.

The project manager must work with functional and other managers to make sure that resources are committed to projects, especially for projects with urgent objectives.

Influence within the Industry

The project manager must know about the current industry trends and apply those to projects, as needed. These trends could be related to technical advancement, emerging market conditions, new regulatory requirements, etc. It is the responsibility of the project manager to ensure that the processes and deliverables comply with required government regulations. At the same time, the project manager must make sure that the project is able to take advantage of the industry advancements, as much as possible.

Influence within the Professional Discipline

A project manager needs to keep learning. Project management is always evolving to keep pace with the continuous changes in the industry and business sectors. Project managers need to participate in trainings and knowledge-transfer sessions with professionals in project management as well as in industry sectors that are related to the project.

Project Manager's Competencies and Skills

PMBOK®: Page 56

A project manager must develop technical and soft skills to maintain an influence on the project stakeholders, organization and industry.

Technical Skills

A project manager must have the know-how of the various project procedures and knowledge areas (such as cost, schedule, quality, procurement, risks, communications, etc.). A project manager must have the technical skills to develop and maintain project documents such as project schedule, communications plan, budget, risk register, etc.

Relevant information about the industry or business sector is important but subject matter expertise is usually not required.

Strategic Skills

As a project manager, do you understand and are you able to explain how the project deliverables meet the strategic goals of the organization? For this, you need to know the mission, strategy, offered products and services, and priorities of the organization. Also, as a project manager, you need the ability to apply the knowledge in order to maximize the business value of the project. You also need to make sure the project objectives are relevant and aligned to the organizational mission.

Business Management Skills

Business skills are about adequate know-how of the key corporate functions, such as finance, quality, sales, IT, and marketing. It is also about aligning the project planning and activities to the way work is performed within the organization.

Leadership Skills

Leadership skills refer to the ability to guide a team along the right track and keep them motivated so, they stay committed to the project work and the organization.

Part of the project management work is about developing status reports, schedules, cost forecast and variance reports. However, leading the team and keeping them motivated is a far more essential responsibility. The team must be motivated to contribute and develop the documents and reports.

Leadership qualities include developing trust, demonstrating integrity (you do what is right even though no one is observing you), developing consensus, collaborating to resolve issues, being optimistic, developing personal and professional networks and cultivating political acumen.

People Skills

A common resource for all projects is people and therefore, managing relationships with the project team and stakeholders are critical for project success. This includes asking and listening, caring for how others are doing, helping others being successful, building trust, and communicating proactively.

Ability to Manage Organizational Politics

As a project manager, you need to acknowledge that workplace politics is a matter of fact. It will not go away. There are various factors at play within the organizational landscape and all is not in anyone's control. There are various forms of power (as shown in Figure 3-1) prevalent within the organization and impacting progress for all projects and operations.

As a project manager, you need to know who has what power within the organizational hierarchy. You need to be aware of your relationships with people. You also need to proactively work to acquire the power and authority within the organizational protocols. This will enable you to resolve project issues and problems, should any arise later.

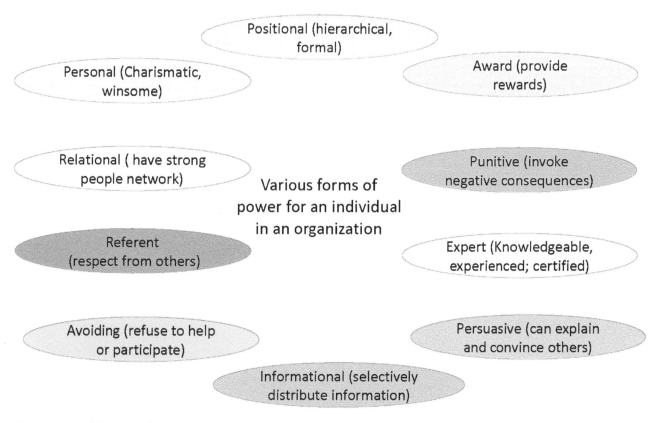

Figure 3-1: Various forms of power within an organization

Management and Leadership Skills

PMBOK®: Page 64

First, we need to differentiate between **management** and **leadership** skills. This content may not be new to you. But you will have situational questions in the exam, for which you will be asked to select the skills that would be most suitable for the described situation.

How do you distinguish between the two? Management is about getting the work done, by following the prescribed process! Leadership, on the other hand, is about collaboration to make sure, that the processes are effective and efficient, and then guiding the team through the processes. Figure 3-2 has the management and leadership skills.

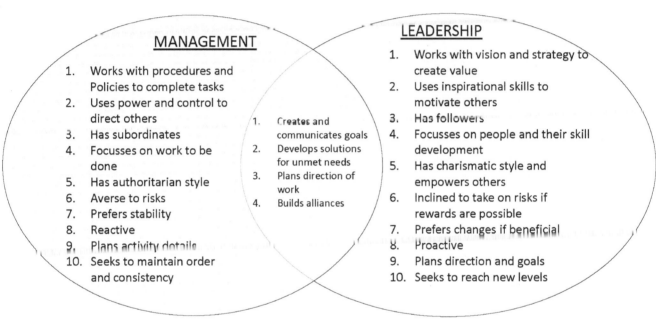

Figure 3-2: Management and leadership skills

Given a particular situation, should you use your management or leadership skills? It depends on the situation! In some cases, you need to follow the processes or prepare documents in a prescribed format. This is management skills. In other situations, you may need to motivate the project team to quickly complete the work, although they have other commitments and projects. Figure 3-3 shows the various leadership styles.

Figure 3-3: Various leadership styles in use at workplaces

Which of these leadership styles should you use? Again, it depends! Given a situation, any of the methods or styles in Figure 3-3, can be a suitable choice. You need to consider various factors, such as the people involved, the urgency of completing the task, motivation level within the team, etc.

You need to pick a leadership style that will deliver the right outcome and inspire the project team or resource, where he or she gets enough guidance and feels motivated to move ahead. However, there should not be too much guidance or telling. Too much advice may make the person seem undervalued and create a feeling that he or she is being "told to do things." Striking a balance requires tact, soft skills and making on-the-spot decisions.

Performing Project Integration

PMBOK®: Page 66

Integration (like communications) is a key activity for a project manager. Project integration is done at distinct two levels (see Figure 3-4):

  A. Integration of project objectives and deliverables with the portfolio and business goals and organizational vision, and
  B. Integration of project activities and teams to enable smooth progress, which is further categorized into three sets, as shown in Figure 3-4.

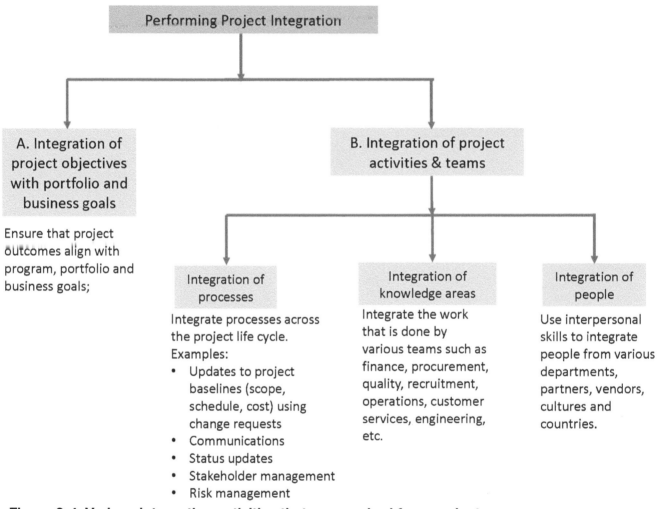

Figure 3-4: Various integration activities that are required for a project

Project integration is complex. Each project is unique, the likes of which may not have been done earlier by the team. There is often limited visibility on how the project will progress.

At a high level, projects are often planned using predictive or waterfall methodology. But the planning for activity details is usually adaptive or iterative. As the work starts and progresses, various portions of the scope and requirements become clearer. It may then be necessary to modify the scope, schedule, assigned budget, etc. Change requests must be initiated to accommodate the new understanding.

> **More points for the exam:**
>
> - As a project manager, you need managerial as well as leadership skills to effectively manage a project.
> - Skills (management, leadership or both) that is suitable for a situation depends on the problem at hand.
> - As a project manager, you have authority and responsibility to control the assigned resources, expenses, and schedule for the benefit of the organization and client.

Practice Questions for Chapter 3

1. Greg Garcia is managing a complex project. Greg and his program and portfolio managers are part of the project management office (PMO). Which of the following would not be a valid process for Greg to ensure project progress?
   A. Work closely with the portfolio manager and keep him proactively informed of all project activities.
   B. Provide status reports to functional managers who have committed resources for the project.
   C. Keep the project sponsor updated on risks and issues.
   D. Address internal stakeholder-related issues that may impact the project progress.

2. Which of the following is not a competency in the PMI Talent Triangle?
   A. Technical project management skills
   B. Leadership skills
   C. Strategic and business management skills
   D. Strong oratory and speaking skills

3. Which of the following is a recent trend that is impacting the processes used to plan and execute projects?
   A. Virtual teams
   B. Multicultural teams
   C. Social networks
   D. All of the above

4. Alex is managing a project that has a team of 20 resources and his project staff and stakeholders are in Asia, Europe and Canada. The project has several elements of complexity. But which of the following is not a dimension of complexity?
   A. System behavior
   B. Complexity in establishing effective communications and bonding since the resources and stakeholders are in different time zones.
   C. Human behavior
   D. Ambiguity

5. Susan Ramirez is looking for a job and interviewing for a role as an application migration project manager at an IT product firm. The interviewer asks her to differentiate between various first-line managers such as operations manager, project manager, functional manager and product manager. Which of the following would be an incorrect response for her?
   A. Operations managers are responsible for efficiency and effectiveness of the business operations.
   B. Project managers are concerned about leading a cross-functional team to deliver certain business objectives.
   C. Product managers are primarily responsible for making sure that the features of a product or project deliverables can be supported by the operations team.
   D. Functional managers are responsible for a certain business unit or function such as procurement, training, engineering, manufacturing, etc.

6. Albert Ramirez has joined a manufacturing firm as a project manager. He is taking over four projects from another project manager, who is leaving the firm. Albert needs to make sure that the project deliverables meet the organizational mission and goals. Which of the following should he first learn about the firm?
   A. Products offered by the firm
   B. Organizational objectives
   C. Strategy for meeting product requirements
   D. All of the above

7. Which of the following is the furthest for the project managers to influence?
   A. Resource managers in the organization
   B. Project Management Office (PMO)
   C. Suppliers
   D. Project sponsor

8. Kristine Johnson needs to get approval for a change request from the Change Control Board (CCB). The change is to extend the project duration by 4 weeks. The project sponsor supports the extension. However, a few of the CCB members want to stop the project. They say, "The deliverables will not be worth the required resources and effort. The need for the deliverables does not exist anymore". Kristine wants to get consensus for the extension. What should she aim to achieve?
   A. She must make sure that 100% of the members in the CCB agree to extend the completion date.
   B. She needs to make sure at least 50% of the members in the CCB agree to the new completion date.
   C. She must make sure that all members agree to support the increase in project duration and commit resources to the project, even if they do not entirely agree that the deliverables are worth pursuing.
   D. She must make sure that the impacted and key members in the CCB support the increase in project duration, even if it does not have support from 100% of the members.

9. Which of the following actions is not essential for successful project management?
   A. Develop and maintain a good relationship with the project stakeholders.
   B. Demonstrate good verbal, non-verbal and written communication skills.
   C. Maintain a positive attitude towards the project scope.
   D. Make sure your documentation is always updated since stakeholders and project team members can download and review the documents from the shared project folders.

10. Rodney Roxon has been promoted to a senior project manager and given a project with 100 team members spread across 10 countries and having project duration of 10 months. He has reviewed the signed project charter. He meets with the project sponsor and says, "This project is way too complex for me to manage!" The sponsor realizes that Rodney needs more time to get familiar with the project scope and team. How should the project sponsor respond?
    A. "Rodney, give yourself some time! You will understand this."
    B. "I agree! This project has certain elements of complexity. Once you break the scope or other parts that appear complex to you, you can then develop a better plan for execution!"
    C. "Rodney, this is a good opportunity for you! This project will help you develop and grow."
    D. "Take your time and try to learn the scope! If you are still not comfortable, we can talk to the program manager and try and have someone else take over this project."

ANSWERS

Question Number	Correct Answer	Explanation
1	A	There is no need to inform the portfolio manager of all project activities. The portfolio manager is involved primarily during the project intake, initiation and for critical changes. See the section titled "THE ORGANIZATION" on Pages 54 and 55 in the PMBOK®.
2	D	Oratory and speaking skills are essential, but they are not one of the three skills in the PMI Talent Triangle. The first three choices mentioned in the above list are skill sets in the PMI Talent Triangle.
3	D	All these are new factors and components of projects. Refer to the section titled "INTEGRATION AT THE CONTEXT LEVEL" on Page 67 in the PMBOK®.
4	B	The three dimensions of complexity are system behavior, human behavior, and ambiguity (uncertainty within the organization or environment). Issues related to time zone differences or lack of in-person meetings do not add to the complexity. However, they add to the need for closer collaboration, frequent status updates, phone or video meetings, shared repository for project documents, etc. See Page 68 in the PMBOK.
5	C	A product manager is responsible for delivering a product that meets the user requirements and its integration with other products, offered by the organization. See Page 52 in the PMBOK®.
6	D	He should know all of these to align the project objectives with the organizational goals. See Page 59 in the PMBOK®.
7	C	The correct answer is suppliers. Suppliers have a statement of work or purchase order. They do the work or supply the product, which could be a small portion of the entire project. Suppliers may be unaware of the overall scope or goals of the project. See Figure 3-1 on Page 52 in the PMBOK®. The furthest ones from the project manager's influence are stakeholders, suppliers, customers, and end-users.
8	D	She needs to get a consensus. The project sponsor supports the extension. Now all she needs to do is make sure relevant and key stakeholders provide their support and resources to increase the project duration.
9	D	Communication skills and stakeholder relationships are crucial for project success. Notice the keyword, **not**, in the question. Watch for such keywords in the question. If any of the choices have words such as NEVER, ALWAYS or MUST, it is a clue that the choice is not a correct answer.
10	B	Complexity is a perception. Projects by themselves are not entirely complex. Rather they contain elements or certain parts that appear complex. What is difficult now could later appear simple. See Page 68 in the PMBOK®.

CHAPTER 4

Integration Management

As a project manager, you will be working with various teams such as procurement, human resources, finance, quality control, operations, etc. Figure 4-1 shows the functional areas that contribute towards a project. The project manager is required to integrate the work done by various teams into a cohesive whole. The assortment of teams and tasks is what makes the job of a project manager unique.

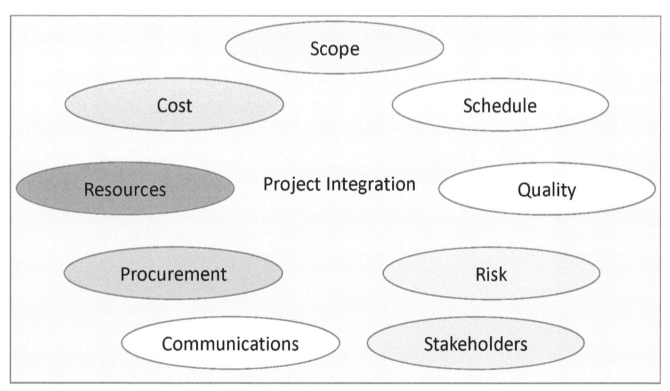

Figure 4-1: Project integration is about combining efforts by various teams

Certain tasks such as developing a project schedule, aggregating activity costs, estimating earned value parameters etc. can be automated. You can have software to help you with some tasks. Also, other functional teams such as finance, procurement, quality, HR, corporate communications, etc. can help in certain project tasks.

The integration of the work done by the internal departments, vendors, customers, etc. cannot be automated. It will continue to be a manual process, to a large extent. Soft skills such as team-building, conflict-resolution and interpersonal skills are critical for project progress and success. Managing projects, therefore, cannot be categorized or labelled as commodity work.

Project management has been practiced for thousands of years. Ever since pyramids were built in Egypt and the Great Wall of China was built in the 3rd century BC, managing projects have been an important profession. The triple constraints of cost (including resources), time and scope have been key considerations for project managers for thousands of years.

Project management techniques have certainly evolved since then. But the core tasks of determining work scope, budgeting, motivating teams using interpersonal skills, optimizing resource utilization and completing the scope within the committed budget and time are still important and will remain critical constraints for projects for centuries to come.

There are 7 processes in the **Integration Management** Knowledge Area.

Initiating Process Group	Planning Process Group	Executing Process Group	Monitoring and Controlling Process Group	Closing Process Group
4.1) Develop Project Charter	4.2) Develop Project Management Plan	4.3) Direct and Manage Project Work 4.4) Manage Project Knowledge	4.5) Monitor and Control Project Work 4.6) Perform Integrated Change Control	4.7) Close Project or Phase

Trends and Emerging Practices

Automation tools are increasingly being used to help the project manager in the integration of various project tasks. These tools can be used to create visual illustrations of the project status and variances, which help stakeholders to understand the project trends, risks, and issues.

Use of these tools is the choice and responsibility of the project manager.

There is a growing trend that project managers have begun to be engaged on a contract basis (instead of being hired as full-time employees). Projects have a finite life. That sometimes, makes the job duration or contract of a project manager tied to the project duration, especially in functional or weak matrix organizations. It has also increased the need for thorough and detailed documentation of project artifacts, plans and status reports to help during reviews and audits, after the project is closed.

There is a trend that project plans are initially made at a high-level, showing only the key milestones and deliverables. As the project progresses, detailed activity lists and duration for each deliverable are developed and revised. Practices followed by agile, iterative and incremental project methodologies, are being included for fine-tuning projects that are initially developed on waterfall methodology.

Project governance has become important due to an increase in regulatory and compliance requirements required by government agencies. There are various sector-specific compliance requirements, especially for companies in the pharmaceutical, finance or utility sectors.

Tailoring Considerations

It is important to tailor the processes within the **Integration Management** Knowledge Area to meet the unique nature and requirements of each project.

The key factors for tailoring are:

- The selected methodology (agile, waterfall, or hybrid) for managing the project life cycle
- The knowledge management process to encourage collaboration between the project team, customers, etc.
- The process used to control changes to requirements and scope
- Compliance and regulatory requirements that must be followed by the project
- The process to realize benefits at the end of each phase or iteration

Considerations for Agile/Adaptive Environments

In an agile/adaptive environment, the project staff members have the responsibility to determine the details of the project plan and how different activities from various teams must be integrated. The project staff members, who have a broad cross-functional knowledge of other divisions, can provide the needed help with integration.

The primary responsibility of the project manager is to provide an environment where the project team can freely collaborate and develop the right plans. At the same time, the project must have the ability to quickly respond to changes in requirements, schedule, budget, etc.

Process 1: Develop Project Charter

PMBOK®: Page 75
Process Group: Initiating

In this process, you develop a project charter and get formal approvals.

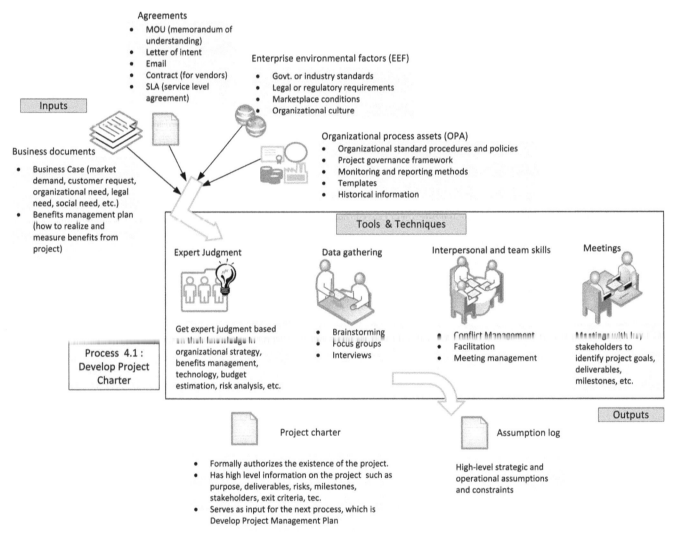

Figure 4-2: ITTO for Develop Project Charter process

* For the exam *
About 13% of the questions (26 out of 200) in the PMP exam will be from the **Initiating** Process Group which consists of two processes:
  ▪ **Develop Project Charter** process
  ▪ **Identify Stakeholders** process
Understanding these two processes well is important for the Exam.

But how is the project charter important for you and the organization? The benefits of the project charter are that it:

- signifies the start of a new project within the organization,
- provides authority to the project manager to ask for and use corporate resources for the project, and
- authorizes the functional managers to commit resources for the project.

Why would you need to initiate a project? The need for a project is usually to solve a business problem or meet a user need. This need can arise from internal or external sources. For example, there could be an internal need to upgrade an existing application or infrastructure. There can be external sources, such as a new regulatory requirement that must be met by the products or internal processes. There could be a technical advancement in the industry which must be implemented internally to meet market demands.

What are the inputs to developing a project charter? The key inputs are:

- **Business case document**: It describes the need and driving reason for initiating the project. It could be due to new market demand, technical advancements, legal requirements, a social need or an organizational demand. For example, a new regulatory requirement could be to develop guidelines and train employees in a pharmaceutical manufacturing factory.
- **Business management plan:** This contains how and when the project benefits will be delivered to the organization, how the benefits will be measured and how the project benefits will transition to become part of ongoing operations. One example is the cost-benefit analysis (CBA) which compares the project cost and benefits. It helps justify the project.
- **Agreements**: These are used to define intentions and need for a project. For internal agreements, less formal documentation such as an email, letter of intent, and memorandum of understanding (MoU) or even a verbal agreement would be sufficient. However, for external clients, you will need formal documentation such as a contract or a service level agreement (SLA).
- **Enterprise environmental factors (EEF)** such as industry standards, regulatory requirements, governance framework within the organization and stakeholder expectations of the project that are needed input for the charter
- **Organizational process assets (OPA)** such as procedures, policies, reporting methods, templates and lessons learned from previous similar projects are also an input for the charter.

If some part of the work needs to be contracted to a vendor or partner, there needs to be a statement of work (SOW). It contains the description of service. The SOW can sometimes come from a client in the form of a bid document, such as a request for information (RFI) or request for proposal (RFP). The SOW can also come from an internal project initiator or sponsor, in which case it contains the required objectives and how it aligns with the organization's strategic plan.

How would you develop a business case and justification for a project? Or if you have two or more projects at hand, but need to select one, which project would you select? Table 4-1 shows quantitative techniques to build a business case or justification for a proposed project.

	Technique for measurement	Definition	Example
1	Opportunity cost	When you have two or more (mutually exclusive) alternatives and you select and take up one, there is a loss from not having taken up the next best alternative. That loss is the opportunity cost.	Working professionals who take up evening or weekend classes, do so because they cannot bear the loss or opportunity cost of a salary (for example $120,000 each year). On the other hand, for those who move from a full-time job to be a full-time student, the opportunity cost = tuition fees + lost salary. If annual fee is $50,000, the opportunity cost is therefore $50,000 + $120,000 = $170,000 each year.
2	Lifecycle costing	Sum of all one-time and recurring costs over the lifespan of a particular service or product.	You are the project manager responsible for set up and go-live of a new factory to assemble cars. There 3 components of the factory lifecycle cost are: 1. The one-time cost to buy machinery and set up the factory. 2. The recurring expenses for operations and maintenance (O&M) of the factory. 3. Later if you need to close the factory, there could be another **project** to shut down and salvage all the equipment and the building.
3	Present Value (PV)	It is also known as present discounted value. It is the value of a future amount (income or expense) that has been discounted to today's value.	Let us say that you expect to receive $1,000 one year from now. But what is that worth today? In other words, what is the PV of that $1,000? Assume an annual interest rate of 10%. Answer: PV= $1000/(1 +0.1) = $909.09
4	Net Present Value (NPV)	NPV for a project is the PV of all benefits (incoming cash flow) minus the PV of all expenses (cash outflows) over a period of time. Projects that have a positive NPV are suitable for investment. Projects that have zero or negative NPV should be avoided.	Step 1: You identify the amount of all cash inflows (income) and cash outflows (expenses) and when they occur. Step 2: You compute the PV of all the inflows and outflows using a standard interest rate (for example 5%). Step 3: NPV = (sum of PV of all cash inflows or income) – (sum of PV of all cash outflows or expenses). Remember that the higher the NPV, the better the investment in the project.
5	Benefit-Cost ratio (BCR)	This is the ratio of the benefits of a project (or product or proposal) relative to the costs required as expressed in present value (PV).	If the PV for benefits is $300,000 and the PV for expenses is $200,000, BCR = 300,000/200,000 = 1.5 Remember that the higher the BCR, the better the investment in the project.

6	Internal rate of rerun (IRR)	It is the interest rate at which the net present value (PV of incoming cash flow or profits minus PV of all outgoing cash flows or expenses) is zero over a period of time.	For the PMP exam, you will not be required to estimate IRR. But you just need to remember that the higher the IRR, the better the investment in the project (as for BCR and NPV).
7	Discounted Cash Flow (DCF)	It is a cash flow summary (of income or expenses) where the amount has been changed to reflect the time value of money. DCF is a process that is used to calculate the PV of a project or investments future cash flows (income and expenses) in order to arrive at today's fair value for the project or investment. The adjustment is done using a standard or preset interest rate.	NPV is part of and used to estimate DCF. DCF = $CF_1/(1+r)^1 + CF_2/(1+r)^2 + CF_3/(1+r)^3 ...+ CF_n/(1+r)^n$ Where: CF_1 = cash flow in Period 1, CF_2 = cash flow in Period 2, CF_3 = cash flow in Period 3, CF_n = cash flow in Period n, and r = discount rate (or required rate of return) .
8	Depreciation	Accounting method used to allocate the cost of a tangible asset over its useful life. It is done to show the reduction in the value of an asset with the passage of time.	You have built a cloud-based storage system with a capital expense of $30,000, which has a salvage value of zero dollars after 3 years. Accounting department depreciates the asset over 3 years using straight-line depreciation at $10,000 each year for 3 years. At the end of 3 years, the hardware is fully depreciated.

Table 4-1: Quantitative measurement techniques to compare project costs and benefits

Let us review some examples based on the techniques in Table 4-1.

EXERCISE TIME 1: PV

Question: What would be the **present value** (PV) of an income of $10,000 that is due two years from now? Assume an annual interest rate of 5%.

Solution:
- Value at the end of 2 years from now; $10,000
- Value at the end of 1 year from now: $10,000/ (1+0.05) = $10,000/1.05 = $9,524
- Present value = $9524/(1+0.05) = $9,070

Answer: PV = $9,070 This also shows that $9,070 will grow to $10,000 in 2 years at a simple interest rate of 5% per year.

Questions on present value (PV) and future value (FV) could be in the exam.

Remember **Present Value = (Future Value) / (1 +r) ^n**
where
- **r** is the interest rate for the period (e.g. 4% each year which is written as 0.04), and
- **n** is the number of periods (e.g. 5 years).

FV = PV * (1 +r) ^n

Note that the FV of money is always higher than its PV.

Here is an example on **net present value** (NPV). Remember that a PV is for a future revenue, sales or expense. But an NPV is for future income which is revenue (or sales) minus expenses.

EXERCISE TIME 2: NPV

Question:
What would be the net present value (NPV) of a project with an expected income of $10,000 that is due two years from now? The project has an initial capital expense of $2,000 and maintenance expense of $1,000 at the end of first and second years. Assume an annual interest rate of 10%.

Solution:
Step 1: Identify cash inflows (income) and outflows (expenses) and when they occur.
    Cash inflow = $10,000 after 2 years
    Cash outflows= $2,000 (initial), $1,000 after Year 1 and again $1,000 after Year 2

Step 2: Compute the PV of all the inflows and outflows using an interest rate=10%
    PV of inflow = $10,000 /(1+0.1)^2
            = $10,000/(1.1*1.1)
            = $ 8,264
    PV of outflow = $2,000 + $1,000 /(1+0.1) + $1,000/(1+0.1)^2
            = $2,000 + $909 + $826
            = $3,735

Step 3: NPV = (sum of PV of all cash inflows or income) – (sum of PV of all cash outflows or expenses) = $ 8,264 - $3,735 = $4,529

Answer: NPV = $4,529. The higher the NPV, the better the investment in the project.

Here is an example of **benefit-cost ratio** (BCR) technique, part of cost-benefit analysis (CBA).

EXERCISE TIME 3: BCR

Question A:
What does a BCR of 2.1 mean?

Solution: It means that the benefit or revenue is 2.1 times the cost. Note that we have benefit or revenue (not the profits which are a smaller amount).

Question B:
If you have two projects X and Y. Project X has a BCR of 1.3 and Project Y has a BCR of 2.3. Which should be selected?

Solution: Project Y should be selected because it has a higher BCR.

Here is an example of opportunity cost.

EXERCISE TIME 4: Opportunity cost

Question:
What would be your opportunity cost, if you spend your time to develop a new facility for $800,000, instead of operating an existing business that could earn a profit of $400,000?

Solution:
Your opportunity cost = $0.8M + $0.4M = $1.2M.

This is because you spent $0.8M and also lost the opportunity to earn $0.4M.

Here is an example of an **internal rate of return** (IRR). In the PMP Exam, you may not have problems requiring you to compute IRR. But you could be asked to select between projects based solely on IRR values. In that case, the project with the highest IRR must be selected.

EXERCISE TIME 5: Two questions on IRR

Question A:
What do you mean by an IRR of 20%?

Solution:
At an interest rate of 20%, for the project duration, the project outflows will be equal to the inflows. The rate of growth of the invested money is 20% over the life of the project. It is like putting money in a bank account that earns interest at 20%.

Question B:
If you must choose between Project A that has a potential IRR of 11% and Project B that has a potential IRR of 18%, which would you choose?

Solution:
The answer is Project B because it has a higher IRR.

The objective of all these calculations is to identify the most beneficial project for initiation. These calculations are part of the project business case.

Another parameter to develop a business case is the **payback period**. It is the time that it takes to recover the investment in a project. It is also called the breakeven point, after which the project is profitable. If you are considering between two projects A and B, where Project A has a payback period of 20 months and Project B of 15 months, it is wise to select Project B since it has a shorter payback period. Other factors since as IRR, NPV, life-cycle cost, DCF and BCR must also be considered when selecting a project for initiation.

As a project manager, you will purchase equipment such as computer, furniture, or even real estate for your project. Building an airport or a shopping complex is also a project. There are project managers who have managed that, although many of you may not have managed such a project yet! All the cost incurred for capital purchase cannot be used by your accounting team as a deductible expense in the first year (although they may sometimes want to!). The cost needs to be spread over the life of the asset, for example over 3 or 10 years. This is called depreciation.

There are two methods for estimating depreciation, as shown in Figure 4-3:

- **Straight-line method,** and
- **Accelerated method**

Straight-line uses the same amount each year. This is used for assets that have a uniform loss in value for example for real estate or furniture. The accelerated method uses a reducing depreciation amount. It is used for assets whose loss in value is higher in the earlier years of use such as for computer equipment or machinery in a factory. In the later years, the loss in value is lower.

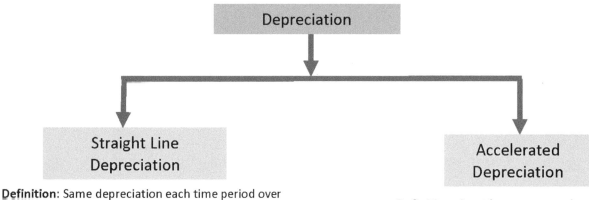

Depreciation

Straight Line Depreciation

Definition: Same depreciation each time period over the life of the asset.
Formula:
Depreciation = (Initial value– Salvage value)/years
Example: Initial Asset value= $2,000
　　　　Salvage value= $500 after 5 years
Depreciation = ($2,000-$500)/5=$300 each year

Year	Depreciation	Book Value
Initial value	$0	$2,000
After year 1	$300	$1,700
After year 2	$300	$1,400
After year 3	$300	$1,100
After year 4	$300	$800
After year 5	$300	$500

Accelerated Depreciation

Definition: Asset looses more value in earlier years of the life of the asset. It can be estimated using double-declining balance method or another specified technique.
Example: Initial Asset value= $2,000
　　　　Salvage value= $500 after 5 years

Year	Depreciation	Book Value
Initial value	$0	$2,000
After year 1	$500	$1,500
After year 2	$400	$1,100
After year 3	$300	$800
After year 4	$200	$600
After year 5	$100	$500

Figure 4-3: Example of straight-line and accelerated depreciation

For projects that are in-progress, you will need to assess, at different checkpoints or milestones, whether to continue the project or kill it. The **law of diminishing returns** can be used to assess if adding resources for an existing project is worth the expense or not. If you continue to add more resources, after a certain point, the benefit per resource starts reducing. For example, if you have an optimal team size but you nevertheless go ahead and triple the team size, the amount of work done per person will reduce.

A project charter document is a key output of the **Develop Project Charter** process. Table 4-2 has a sample project charter.

Project Title: Upgrade the existing online surveillance and monitoring system across all corporate offices

Background: The existing surveillance recording system was installed in 2014. Since then we have added office premises, which are not covered by our existing surveillance monitoring system. The current system stores motion recordings for 30 days. It is also not in compliance with the regulatory requirements for the medical and drug development industry.

Project Scope: Design and deploy a surveillance system that covers all critical office areas and meets regulatory requirements for the next three years.

Justification for the project: There are serious gaps in our security coverage due to the absence of monitoring for various critical areas and entrances. We need a surveillance system that meets the regulatory requirements for our industry vertical.

Out of scope items: The following are out of scope:
- Adding more personnel to the existing physical security staff
- Upgrade the surveillance system that is now in-place for the parking areas and other locations outside the office premises

Project Steering Committee:

Name	Role
Albert Ricker	Business owner
Victor Gonzalez	Director, IT operations
Andrew Moore	Senior Manager. Engineering and Development

Project Core Team:

Name	Role
Victor Gonzalez	Director, IT operations
Bill Grover	Senior Architect
Sue Johnson	Test Lead
Joe Clarkson	Senior Project Manager

Project budget: The assigned budget is $600,000 and an contingency amount of $50,000.

Project timeline: The project will start in January 2019 and end by November 2019. Here are the key project phases and completion deadlines:
- Project planning and solution development: March 2019
- Vendor selection and equipment purchase: June 2019
- Deployment and setup: September 2019
- Training for the physical security staff member: October 2019
- Transition maintenance to operational staff: November 2019

Project Risks:

Risk Description	Probability of occurrence (High / Medium / Low)	Impact (High / Medium / Low)
Delay for design approvals from City	Low	Medium
Conflict of interest amongst partners and internal stakeholders	Medium	High

Project Constraints:

Constraint Description	Impact (High / Medium / Low)
Lack of experience in delivering a similar scope by the project resources	Medium
No prior working relationship with enlisted vendors	Medium

Project Assumptions:

Assumption Description	Impact (High / Medium / Low)
All IT equipment will be delivered by vendor within planned lead time.	Medium
Currency fluctuations between US dollars and Yen will be within +/- 2% over the next 9 months.	Medium

Project deliverables: The project is expected to deliver the following:
- 24x7 video recording at all critical areas, all entrance/exit points and common areas for employees.
- Ability to store and easily access recordings for the last 24 months.
- Provide a system that is in compliance with regulatory requirements applicable to the pharmaceutical industry.

Project manager, assigned for this project: Mr. Joe Clarkson

Project sponsor: Mr. George Jones
Signed: _____ , Mr. George Jones, Project Sponsor Date:_____
Signed: _____ , Mr. Kevin Clarkson, Project Manager Date:_____
Signed: _____ , Mr. Tony Thompson, SVP, IT Operations Date:_____

Table 4-2: Sample Project Charter

An important section in the project charter is the scope description. It should be made in consultation with the sponsor and key stakeholders. Some tasks or deliverables that could be interpreted as being in-scope but are actually out-of-scope should be listed in the out-of-scope section (Figure 4-4).

Another output is the assumption log document, which contains a list of assumptions used to develop the charter.

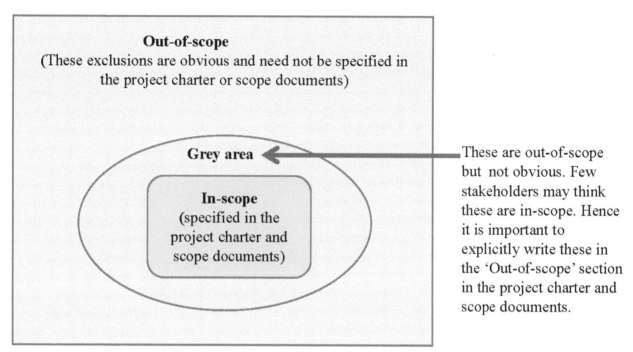

Figure 4-4: Certain out-of-scope items must be specified in a project charter and scope documents

The project is used within the organization for different divisions such as the PMO, engineering, finance, etc. But can it be used to establish agreements with vendors or partners? No! Because the project charter is not developed, agreed upon or signed by vendors. For them, the project team is the seller. The vendor needs a contract or statement of work (SOW).

Process 2: Develop Project Management Plan

PMBOK®: Page 82
Process Group: Planning

This process defines, prepares and coordinates all plans into a comprehensive project management plan. This defines how the project work will be executed, monitored, controlled and closed.

Figure 4-5 shows the inputs, tools and techniques and outputs for this process.

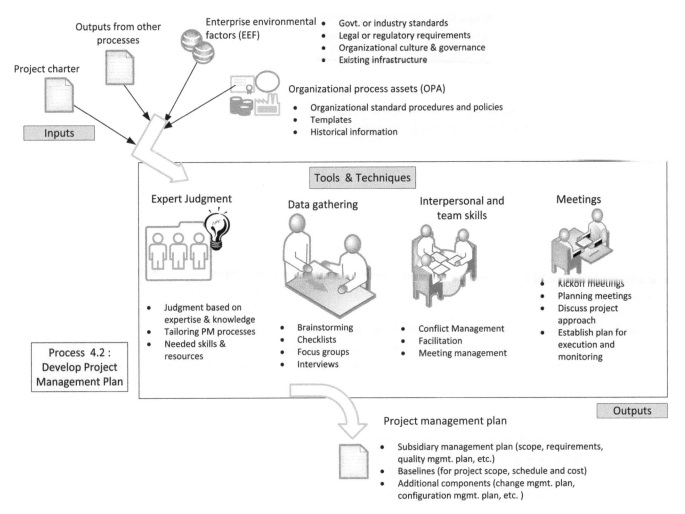

Figure 4-5: ITTO for Develop Project Management Plan process

Figure 4-6 has a list of project management plans and project documents.

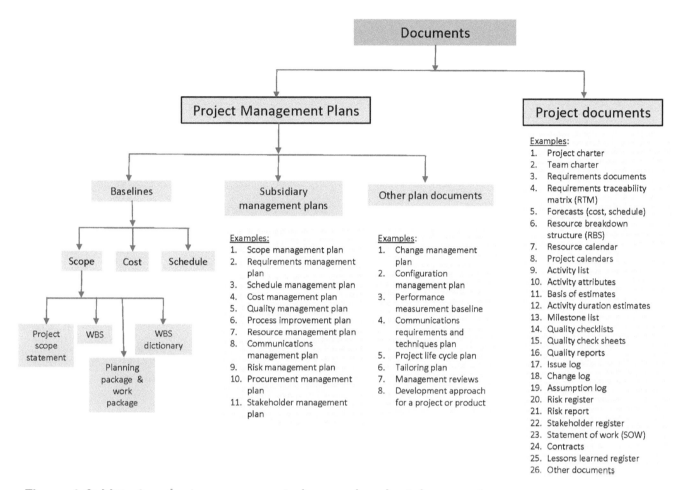

Figure 4-6: List of project management plans and project documents

The project management plan documents are developed by the project manager with help from the project team and then approved by the stakeholders (if needed). Here are a few key points to remember for the exam:

1. Project management plans are created during the planning process group and later updated during project execution.
2. Project management plans contain how you will conduct the rest of the project work namely execution, monitoring, controlling and closing.
3. There is one project management plan for each other **nine** knowledge areas. In addition, there are other project management plans such as:
   - Requirements management plan,
   - Process improvement plan,
   - Change management plan, and
   - Configuration management plan.
4. Baselines (for scope, cost, and schedule) are also part of the project management plan. The project manager uses the baselines to measure project progress and establish variance (such as by earned value analysis or EVA). That is why the baselines are also called performance measurement baselines. Measurements (such as cost variance and schedule variance) are part

of work performance information. They point to the performance of the project as well as the project team. A project manager's performance is tied to the project performance. He or she must ensure that the project progresses as agreed to in the baselines.

5. Then there are project documents as shown in Figure 4-6. Unlike project management plans, project documents are created during any of the process groups. For example, the project charter is created during the **Initiating** Process Group, and the lessons learned document is created during the **Executing** Process Group.

Once the project management plans are prepared, you are ready to start the **Executing** process group. There are a few activities (Figure 4-7) that are required for the transition from planning to execution:

1. **Sign off on the project management plan**: This can be done by electronically signing the softcopies or by sending an approval by email. Alternatively, the documents can be uploaded on a shared folder or portal for online approval by the required stakeholders.

2. **Project success check (PSC)** or **Gate Reviews**: This is a meeting with the PMO or an audit group, entitled to review the project documents and provide approval or disapproval. If approved, you go on to subsequent project tasks or **Process Group**. If disapproved, you need to revise the plan documents and schedule another review meeting.

3. **Kickoff meeting**: This is a meeting with the project team and stakeholders. The goals are to announce that the project planning has begun and discuss the salient points in the charter, milestones, anticipated risks, governance requirements, expected timelines, etc. In some projects, the kickoff meeting can be held immediately after the charter is signed and before project planning is started.

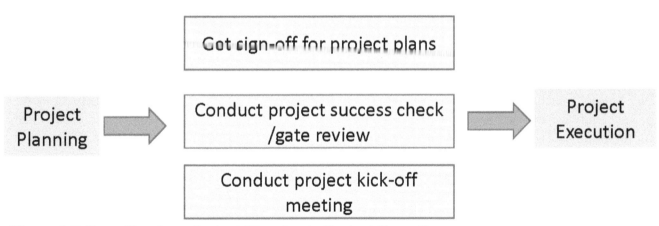

Figure 4-7: Transition from Project Planning to Project Execution

Process 3: Direct and Manage Project Work

> PMBOK®: Page 90
> Process Group: Executing

This process group is concerned with doing the project work. The project manager along with the project team conducts the activities, listed in the project plan or schedule.

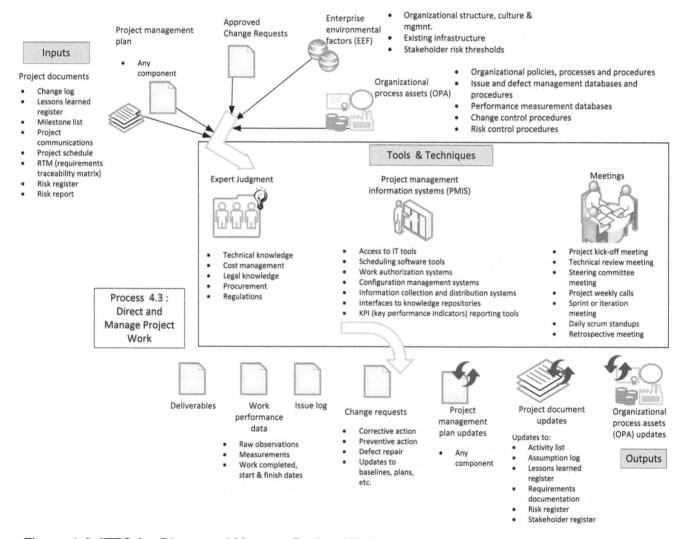

Figure 4-8: ITTO for Direct and Manage Project Work process

This process involves the following key activities:

1. Provide overall management of the project work.
2. Perform the work as outlined in the project management plan to meet the project objectives.
3. Obtain and use the project resources including tools and facilities.
4. Train and manage the project members assigned to the work.
5. Create the project deliverables as listed in the scope baseline and project charter.

6. Create and distribute project communication reports.
7. Create new change requests and get approvals.
8. Implement approved changes.

As a project manager, you do not just do the project as a whole. Instead, you need to give attention and time to each knowledge area. You need to manage the timeline, cost, risks, communication, quality and vendors. You need to see how risks in one knowledge area affect risks in other areas. For example, if there is a change request for an increase in work scope, you may require an additional budget, time, and resources. Integration management is about combining the work related to various knowledge areas.

Project management information systems (PMIS) provide access to various software tools, as shown in Figure 4-9.

One of the key outputs of this process is the deliverables. Each deliverable is a unique and verifiable product or a capability to perform a service. It is also an essential component needed to complete the project or process.

Another key output is the work performance data, which comprises of the lowest level of details, raw observations and measurements collected while the project work is in-progress.

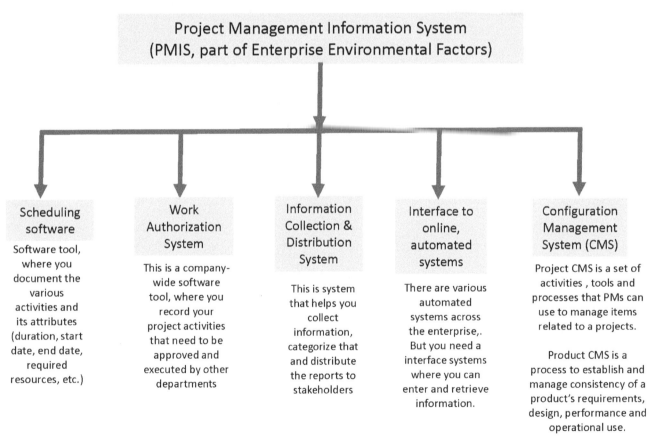

Figure 4-9: PMIS provides access to various software tools

** For the exam **
Note that the **Direct and Manage Project Work** is the only process that has work performance data as an output.

Process 4: Manage Project Knowledge

PMBOK®: Page 98
Process Group: Executing

The organization has various sources of knowledge and trainings that can help the project, such as

- Documents from previous projects
- Organizational procedures that can help the project progress
- Experts within the organization and from partner organizations
- Training programs offered by the organization on general topics or project-specific details
- Knowledge-sharing sessions to discuss information relevant to the project

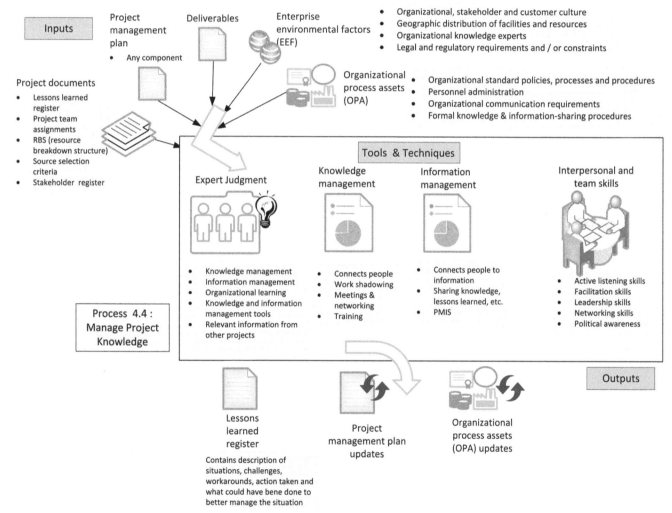

Figure 4-10: ITTO for Manage Project Knowledge Process

All these knowledge bodies within and outside the organization can help make significant progress for the project. The two types of project knowledge are explained in Figure 4-11.

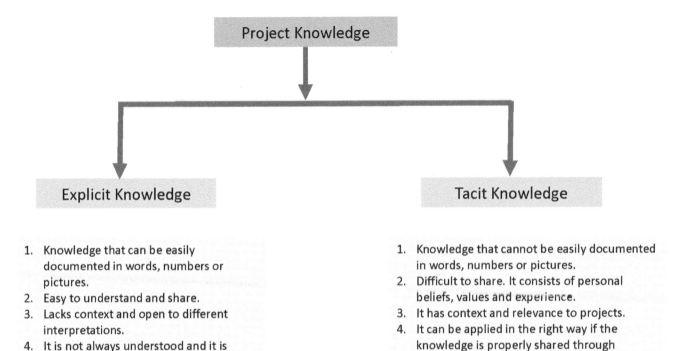

Figure 4-11: Explicit and Tacit Project Knowledge

Help from the organization is not one-way from the organization to the project. The project team creates new documents and processes and updates existing ones, which in-turn helps other active and future projects, especially those with a similar scope.

What are the techniques to create and manage project knowledge? To create new knowledge documents, the project manager must work with the project team, subject matter experts, other departments in the organization, special interest groups and focus groups to develop processes and documents required for the project. You can use existing project documents (from previous projects) to serve as a template and get a jumpstart.

It takes good team-building and interpersonal skills to conduct productive meetings between members from diverse fields or organizations, establish an open and non-threatening environment, overcome bias, discuss disagreements and reach a consensus or decision that can be implemented by the project team.

The key output of this process is the lessons learned register, developed primarily from feedback given by the project team. When the project is closed, the lessons learned are transferred to the lessons learned repository, part of the organization process assets (OPA). In case a similar project is initiated, in the future, the lessons learned can be used by the new project.

Process 5: Monitor and Control Project Work

> **PMBOK®: Page 105**
> Process Group: Monitoring and Controlling

In this process, you track and review the project status and if needed, take corrective actions and preventive actions (CAPA) to bring the project back on track, improve existing processes to prevent issues, and (if needed) make updates to the baselines.

The words monitoring and controlling appear to be redundant and seem like synonyms. But there are differences between the two. **Monitoring** is concerned with collecting and distributing project information. The benefit is that it allows the stakeholders to know and understand the project status and if there should be changes to the project direction and progress. It provides insight into project health and areas that need attention. It also compares actual performance with the approved baselines.

On the other hand, **controlling** uses the information from project monitoring, to come up with corrective actions, if required, to bring the project back on track. It later assesses whether the implemented actions were effective. It also determines whether the preventive actions were able to reduce and the probability of occurrence of negative risks and the impact of issues.

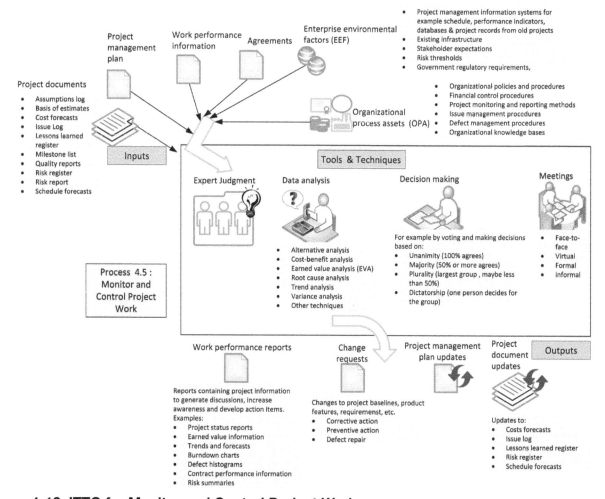

Figure 4-12: ITTO for Monitor and Control Project Work

---

* For the Exam *

Notice the difference between **Monitor and Control Project Work** process and **Monitoring and Controlling** process group:

- ▪ **Monitor and Control Project Work** process is about measuring the progress against the planned baselines and then trying to bring the project on track (for example by fast tracking or compressing).
- ▪ **Monitoring and Controlling** process group refers to and includes the 12 processes in the group.

Inputs to this process are the project plans, baselines (for scope, cost and schedule) and forecasts (for cost and schedule), a list of validated changes and work performance information.

Table 4-3 describes the various analytical techniques. Most of these use performance data for work completed so far in the project, to identify patterns, prepare work performance information and predict potential risks. Once you identify potential risks, you can develop a plan to mitigate those risks.

In the exam, you could be asked to select the name of an analytical technique, when its description is provided in the question. You will need to know the technique name and description (but usually not the mathematical details of the techniques).

	Analytical techniques	Description
1	Alternatives Analysis	Many activities have several ways those can be accomplished. Alternatives analysis is an approach to evaluate the various options and identify the most optimum option to perform the project activity, given the various constraints. For example, if you need to use a software application, the various options are to develop, purchase, lease, or use a cloud-based service on a pay-per-use model.
2	Regression analysis	This is a forecasting method that looks at the relationship between one or more independent variables (predictors or X) that causes changes in a dependent variable (Y). It shows how the dependent variable varies, if one of the independent variables, changes while others are kept fixed. For example, resource availability, hourly rate and skills are independent variables and budget is the dependent variable. You can make changes to one of the independent variables at a time and see if you can meet the budgetary goals.
3	Grouping techniques	A common implementation is the **Nominal Group Technique** (NGT) which is a group process to discuss the problem and allow time for each person in the group to present their proposed solution. Each person gets to vote and rank the presented solutions. The steps are: 1. The group discusses the problem 2. Each person generates and presents his or her solution to the group 3. Each person then votes on the proposed solutions 4. The group as a whole uses the individual votes to rank the solutions and decide on the winning solution.
4	Causal analysis	Here you develop a statistical relationship between a dependent variable (what you are trying to forecast) and a number of independent variables (factors that affect the forecast).
5	Root cause analysis	You understand the root cause and factors that led to success or failure of the past performance. Then you identify which of those would be relevant for the future and use those to predict future performance.

6	Forecasting methods (such as time series, scenario building or simulation)	Forecasting is about predicting the future. It helps develop project plans and empowers the people to control what will happen in the future by modifying input variables. Forecasting methods in project management, utilize the available information (for example to-date performance, available resources, etc.) to calculate the future status (for example, estimate to complete or ETC for a project). The forecasting techniques are: ▪ **Time-series method**: here you extract meaningful statistics from recent performance and use that to predict near-term future performance. This method is less accurate if used for the far future. ▪ **Scenario-building technique**: The forecaster develops various sets of assumptions and an outcome for each set. The business team or decision-maker reviews the outcomes and selects one that is most likely to happen. ▪ **Simulation techniques**: This is a technique to create a model that will help understand the factors that control the project and predict the future status. For this, one needs to be able to quantitatively describe the behavior using rules and equations. Monte Carlo simulation technique uses randomness to solve problems that may be deterministic. It first defines a domain of possible input numbers and then obtains a set of input numbers randomly from the domain using a probability distribution. These input numbers are used in a deterministic computation to obtain results that are later aggregated to create a model to predict future status.
7	Failure Mode and Effect Analysis (FMEA)	FMEA is a proactive method where you evaluate the different parts of a process, identify where and how each part might fail and then assess the effect of those failures on the project. You then identify the critical parts that must be enhanced or upgraded to avoid failures.
8	Fault Tree Analysis (FTA)	This is a top-down deductive, failure analysis where the faulty state is analyzed using Boolean logic to combine a series of detailed events. This helps to understand how a process or product has failed and identify ways to reduce the risk. It is also used in software engineering to identify and troubleshoot bugs. This technique was developed in 1962 at Bell laboratories under a US government contract and used to evaluate inter-continental ballistic missiles.
9	Reserve analysis	Reserve analysis is a technique used to determine the amount of time or money to be added as contingency and management reserves. These are for cost overruns and to mitigate problems. Take a minute to understand what a reserve is for! It is an amount of time or money set aside by management, to be used in case the project encounters problems (known and unknown problems) during execution. Distinguish between contingency and management reserves: ▪ Contingency reserves are part of the cost baseline as well as project budget. It is allocated by the project manager to mitigate **known** risks, if and when the risks turn into issues. The project manager can authorize use of this amount. ▪ Management reserves are **not** part of the cost baseline, but part of the project budget. It is allocated by management. It is used to mitigate **unknown** risks as they turn into issues. A project manager cannot authorize use of management reserves.
10	Earned Value Analysis (EVA)	You compare the actual project performance with the baselines. For each work package or control account, you estimate the planned value (PV), Earned value (EV) and Actual Cost (AC)

11	Variance analysis	Variance is the difference between actual performance and the baseline. In other words, it is the quantitative delta between what has happened and what was expected to happen. Variance analysis consists of: ▪ identifying the variance, ▪ identifying the cause of the variance, and ▪ finding how you can change processes or activities to avoid negative variances in the future. You estimate the cost and schedule variance (CV and SV), cost and schedule performance index (CPI and SPI), estimate to completion (ETC), Variance at completion (VAC), etc. This is discussed in the chapter on **Cost** Knowledge Area. Other variances are: ▪ Purchase price variance: Actual price paid minus the standard price for a product ▪ Variable overhead variance: the difference between the standard variable overhead and actual (incurred) cost. **Example**: If your year-to-date project budget was supposed to be $50,000, however, the actual expense has been $65,000, the cost variance is, therefore, negative $15,000 and you need to identify the root cause and mitigation steps.
12	Trend analysis	This is a forecasting technique where you plot the performance for the past reporting periods and use that to project future performance. This assumes that the performance trend does not change.

Table 4-3: Analytical techniques used to predict project status and progress

The outputs of this process are work performance reports, change requests and update to the project documents and plans.

The change requests could be for:

- corrective actions (to realign the project performance to the plan)
- preventive actions (to make sure that future performance is aligned to the project plan) and
- defect repairs (to modify or correct a product feature that does not meet the requirements).

But are these change requests ready to be implemented? No! Why? Because change requests must be first reviewed and approved by the Change Control Board (CCB). This is explained in the next process, **Perform Integrated Change Control**.

---

* For the Exam *
- Note that the **Monitor and Control Project Work** is the only process that has work performance information as an input.
- It is also the only process that has work performance reports as an output.

Process 6: Perform Integrated Change Control

PMBOK®: Page 113
Process Group: Monitoring and Controlling

This process is concerned with reviewing the change requests, approving or rejecting the change requests and communicating the decisions. Approved change requests lead to updates for various documents such as project plans, baselines, change log, etc.

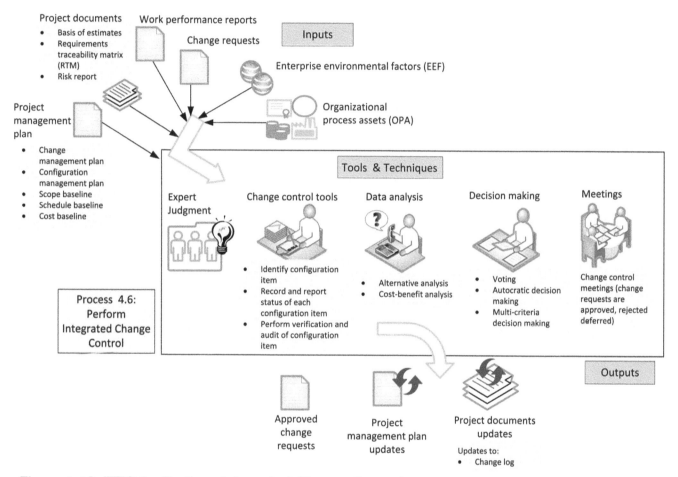

Figure 4-13: ITTO for Perform Integrated Change Control process

For the PMP exam, understand the difference between change control and configuration control. Change control (Figure 4-14) has the steps from identification of the change, approval or rejection by the change control board (CCB) and if approved, consequent modifications to the project baselines, deliverables and logs.

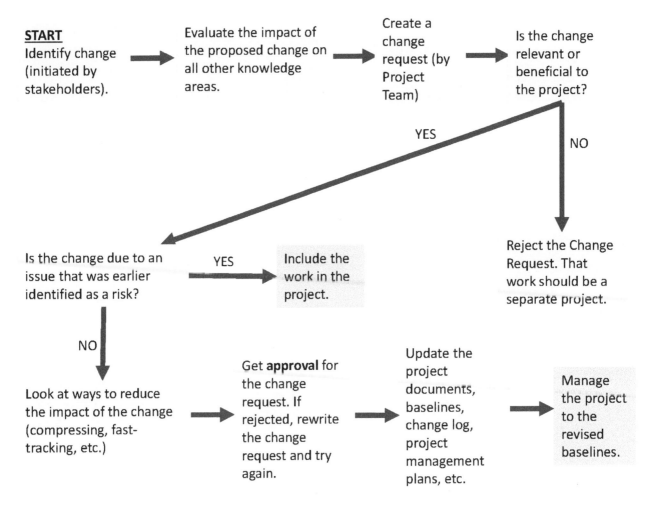

Figure 4-14: Steps to create and get approvals for a change request

On the other hand, configuration management (Figure 4-15) is concerned with the specifications and features of the products and deliverables of the project.

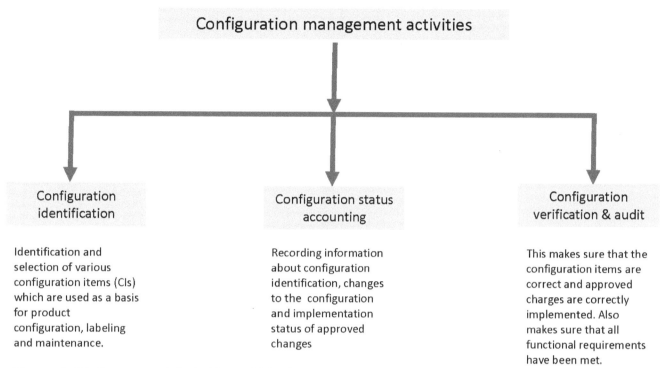

Figure 4-15: Scope and Activities within Configuration Management

Key inputs to this process are:

- project management plans,
- project documents,
- work performance reports, and
- change requests.

In this process, you work experts and the change control board (CCB) to seek approval for the change requests. The techniques used to review change requests are:

- change control tools, that can help you to identify the status of the configuration items (CI) and also, verify that the changes have been correctly implemented,
- change control meetings with the change control board (CCB),
- alternatives analysis – where you evaluate other options to accomplish the objective of the change request and judge if the action plan is the optimum method,
- cost-benefit analysis – where you evaluate if the benefits of the change request are worth the expenses incurred, and
- decision-making techniques to approve or reject the change request or defer the decision to a future meeting. The techniques are:
  - o voting, where the decision is based unanimity (has support from 100% of the group), majority (has support from more than 50% agree) or plurality (has support from the largest group),
  - o autocratic decision-making, where one person decides for the group, and
  - o multicriteria decision-making, where you use a decision matrix and a set of predefined criteria to approve or reject change requests.

The main outputs are approved change requests and updates to the project documents (especially the three baselines and change log).

Change requests can be approved, rejected or deferred for later review. The decision is recorded in the change log. Figure 4-16 describes the activities that could result from an approved change request. Note that only approved change requests can be used to update baselines.

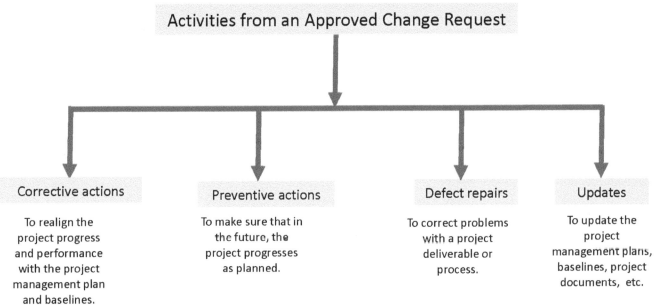

Figure 4-16: Consequences of an Approved Change Request

> * For the Exam
> Note that the **Perform Integrated Change Control** is the only process that has approved change requests as an output.

Process 7: Close Project or Phase

PMBOK®: Page 121
Process Group: Closing

This process is concerned with completing various activities to close a project or phase. After this process, the project staff members that were committed to the project are free to take up other projects or assignments.

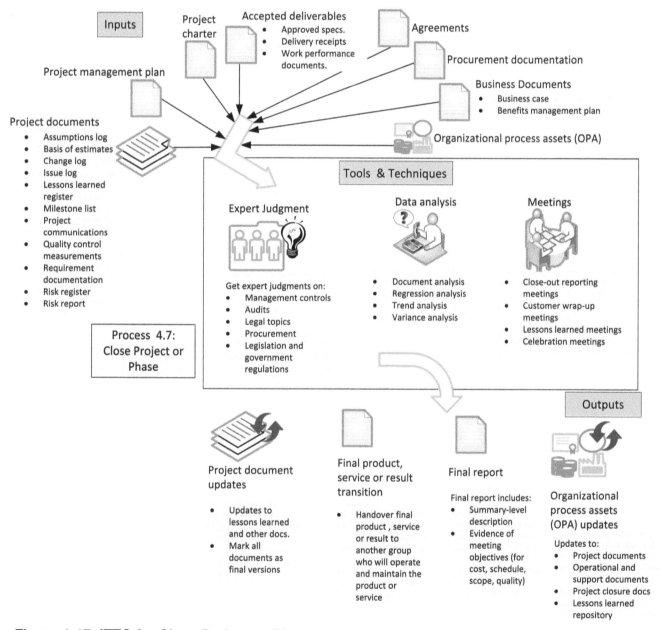

Figure 4-17: ITTO for Close Project or Phase

Here are key tasks for the **Close Project or Phase** process:

- Provide the project deliverables to the user group or client.
- Transition the deliverables from the project team to the operations team.
- Provide training to the operation team as needed.
- Announce that the project is formally closed, and the project deliverables are ready for use.
- Close the statements of work (SoWs) and contracts with vendors and provide the final payments to them.
- Develop a lesson learned register, to help the project teams in the future who may be undertaking a similar project.
- Update the project management plans, baselines, risk register, project calendar, change log, etc., to reflect the project closure.

The above list assumes that the project team has successfully completed the objectives and deliverables. But is that true for all projects? No! A project can be terminated at any time, prior to completion.

If terminated early, are you required to formally close the project? Yes! You must update the project documents with the reasons for early termination. You must transfer the deliverables (completely or partially finished) to others. You can also prepare a lesson learned document that includes reasons for termination of the project.

More points for the exam:

- A project is rejected or selected for initiation based on how well the project meets the strategic goals of the organization.
- As a PM, you know why the project was selected and you must make sure that the business case and goals are met.
- A PM is assigned during project initiation.
- Each project has an approved charter, which authorizes the use of organizational resources for the project.
- Each project has management plans, developed during the planning stage of the project.
- Each project has required project documents, including project charter and the three baselines (scope, cost, and schedule).
- After change requests to the baselines are reviewed and approved by the change control board (CCB), you can update the baseline(s).
- All project documents are updated throughout the project life.
- Monitoring and controlling happen throughout the project.
- Lessons learned document is created during the **Manage Project Knowledge** process and updated throughout the project life.
- Final acceptance of the project deliverables and approval by the stakeholders to close the project, are required before a project can be closed.
- Even if a project is canceled or terminated before scope completion, you must close it formally, get closure signoff from the stakeholders and archive project documents.

Practice Questions for Chapter 4

1. What is the key significance of an approved project charter?
   A. It authorizes the project manager to request and use corporate resources for the project.
   B. It serves as a reference for developing baselines for scope, cost, and schedule.
   C. It provides details of various risks, assumptions, and constraints for the project.
   D. It contains a list of all stakeholders that need to be managed throughout the project.

2. Which of the following is a key output of the Perform Integrated Change Control process?
   A. Lessons learned register
   B. Change requests
   C. Approved change requests
   D. Updates to the scope baseline

3. Rick Reinert is a senior project manager for a cloud services provider. After reviewing the project charter and benefits management plan for a new disaster recovery (DR) datacenter, he finds certain points in the business benefits management plan that he does not agree with. He wants to get those changed. He has earlier helped execute several DR datacenter setups as an engineer and is familiar with DR benefits. Which of the following should he do to introduce the changes that he wants?
   A. Rick needs to open change requests and get change control board (CCB) to approve those.
   B. Rick should escalate the suggestions he has to the program or portfolio manager.
   C. Rick is not supposed to initiate any changes to the benefits management plan since these are not part of the project.
   D. Rick must find out the author or team who created the benefits management plan and make recommendations for the change. He cannot change the benefits management plan since it is not a project document.

4. Which of the following is not a part of the Integration Management Knowledge Area?
   A. Develop project management plans to achieve the project objectives.
   B. Make sure that the outcome and benefits described in the benefits management plan are aligned with the project goals
   C. Manage and monitor performance and changes to the project tasks
   D. All of the above are a part of the Integration Management.

5. Which of the following is not true about accepted deliverables?
   A. They are completed work that meets the acceptance criteria and are approved by the customer and/or sponsor.
   B. They are an output of the Validate Scope process.
   C. They are an input to the Close Project or Phase process.
   D. They are an output of the Close Project or Phase process.

6. Which one of the following is not a consideration for tailoring processes in the Integration Management Knowledge Area?
   A. Project management methodology (predictive, adaptive or hybrid) adopted for the project and whether the entire scope is known or not at project initiation.
   B. Governance needed for the project.
   C. Change management system for the project.
   D. The amount of funds and time needed for the project.

7. Alex Anderson has joined an iron ore mining company as a project manager. Alex has developed a weighted score criteria to select and initiate one out of four candidate projects. The criteria and their weights are in the first two columns in the table below. For each project, the ratings (out of 10) for those criteria are listed in the project columns.

Criteria	Weight	Rating (out of 10) for each criterion			
		Project A	Project B	Project C	Project D
Ease of completion	10%	5	2	1	3
Demand in the market	30%	6	4	6	2
Funding required	20%	2	4	2	6
Availability of skills	40%	5	5	3	6
Total	100%				

Which project should Alex select?

A. Project A
B. Project B
C. Project C
D. Project D

8. Which of the following is usually not included in the project charter?
   A. Success criteria
   B. Project risks
   C. Functional and non-functional requirements
   D. Project assumptions

9. You are managing a project life-cycle, which has several phases. What can you expect about the various phases?
   A. Your phases will essentially be sequential.
   B. Since the phases are part of the same bigger goal, you can expect that the work in various phases will be similar.
   C. The closure of each phase has a transfer or handoff and it is a natural point to reassess the activities and change or terminate the entire project.
   D. All the above choices are true about project phases.

10. A project to develop a water treatment plant is expected to cost $300,000. The initial investment is supposed to generate $5,000 each month for the first year and $10,000 each month after that. What is the payback period?
   A. 40 months
   B. 36 months
   C. 30 months
   D. 42 months

11. Vivian Vixen is a project manager responsible for setting up a new IT helpdesk process for a global telecom operator. He is documenting various requirements to be later used for a solution. Which of the following is a business requirement for him?
   A. Need to resolve trouble tickets within 2 days.
   B. Need to escalate user problems from Level 2 to Level 3 support within 4 hours.
   C. Ability to have a real-time view of all trouble tickets that are in different stages such as new, in-progress, escalated, on-hold or closed.
   D. Need to reduce the number of customer calls to the helpdesk, quickly resolve issues and improve user morale.

12. Which of these is part of the project management plan?
   A. Project schedule
   B. Milestone list
   C. Schedule baseline
   D. Project schedule network diagram

13. Which one of the following processes, does not have the project charter as an input?
   A. Develop Project Management Plan
   B. Direct and Manage Project Work
   C. Collect Requirements
   D. Define Scope

14. Which of the following is not a project document?
   A. Change log
   B. Risk report
   C. Document containing test results
   D. Benefits management plan

ANSWERS

Question Number	Correct Answer	Explanation
1	A	The key significance of an approved charter is that it formally authorizes the project manager to request and use resources for the project.
2	C	Change requests are an input and approved change requests are an output to the **Perform Integrated Change Control** process. The change requests can be approved, deferred or rejected.
3	D	The benefits management plan is not a project document (a list of project documents is on Page 89 of the PMBOK®). A project manager cannot update the benefits management plan but can make suggestions for the changes. The benefits management plan is part of the business documents. See Page 78 of the PMBOK® Guide.
4	D	All the choices (A, B and C) are part of the **Integration Management**, which is concerned with defining, combining and coordinating the various processes and project management activities within the five Process Groups.
5	D	Accepted deliverables are not an output of the **Close Project or Phase** process. They are an output of the **Validate Scope** process and an input for the **Close Project or Phase** process.
6	D	Again, notice the keyword, **not**, in the question! The amount of funds or time needed is not a factor for tailoring. See Page 74 in the PMBOK® Guide.
7	A	For each project, you need to compute the total weighted score, which is sum of products of weight and rating for each criterion. The project with the highest weighted score is selected. For Project A: The weighted score = 10*5 + 30*6 + 20*2 + 40*5 = 50 + 180 + 40 + 200 = 470 For Project B: The weighted score = 10*2 + 30*4 + 20*4 + 40*5 = 20 + 120 + 80 + 200 = 420 For Project C: The weighted score = 10*1 + 30*6 + 20*2 + 40*3 = 10 + 180 + 40 + 120 = 360 For Project D: The weighted score = 10*3 + 30*2 + 20*6 + 40*6 = 30 + 60 + 120 + 240 = 450 The highest weighted score is for Project A and hence that is the correct answer.
8	C	Functional and non-functional requirements are not included in the charter. Those are in the requirements documentation.
9	C	Choice C is correct. The end of each phase is a kill point or phase review, where you can assess and decide whether to continue or kill the project lifecycle Choice A is wrong since phases need not be sequential and can be overlapping. Choice B is also wrong since the work and objectives in each phase are different.
10	B	For the first year, the recovered amount is $5,000 x 12 months = $60,000. The remaining amount of $300,000 - $60,000 = $240,000 will take 24 months to recover. The total payback period is therefore 12 + 24 = 36 months.

11	D	A business requirement is a high-level or executive need. In this question, the business requirement is to reduce the number of customer calls, quickly resolve issues and improve user morale. Here are the requirement types:

No.	Requirement type	Definition
1	Business requirements	Strategic vision or objective that is used to initiate a project or product.
2	Solution requirements	What needs to be in the solution or system. These are of 2 types: ▪ Functional requirements: these are features of the solution or product. ▪ Non-functional requirements: These are conditions for the solution to be effective. Examples are security features, 24x7 service availability, application response time, and ease-of-use.
3	Quality requirements	Requirements that must be met for successful completion of the project or product.
4	Stakeholder requirements	Requirements that come from one stakeholder or a group of stakeholders.
5	Transition requirements	Short-term requirements that help transition a project stage or solution to another team. Examples are: ▪ escalation ▪ training for the operations team to take over product support
6	Project requirements	Requirements to successfully meet the project objectives. Examples are: ▪ a detailed communications plan for transitioning users to the new application ▪ weekly cost variance report that must be prepared and posted on the project portal.

In the provided choices:
- Choice A is a functional requirement
- Choice B is a transition requirement
- Choice C is a stakeholder requirement
- Choice D is a business requirement

12	C	Schedule baseline (like cost and scope baselines) is part of the project management plan. The other choices are part of project documents. Page 89 in the PMBOK® has a list of project management plans and project documents.

13	B	The **Direct and Manage Project Work** process is part of the **Executing** Process Group and does not have project charter as its input.
		
		Project charter is usually an input for processes in the **Planning** Process Group. In this case, all the processes except for the **Direct and Manage Project Work** are part of the **Planning** and have project charter as an input.
		
		There are 2 other processes that are not in the **Planning** Process Group but have project charter as an input:
		   ▪ The **Identify Stakeholders** process (part of the **Initiating** Process Group) and
		   ▪ The **Close Project or Phase** process (part of the **Closing** Process Group).

14	D	Business documents (such as business case and benefits management plan) are not part of the project documents. The business documents are used to select a project for initiation and later used as an input for the project charter. The project manager does not have ownership of these but can make recommendations for updates to the business documents.

CHAPTER 5
Scope Management

Have you wondered what you are supposed to accomplish within a project? The answer is in the project scope. In addition, a brief version of the proposed scope is also in the project charter. But the details are in the project scope statement, an output of the **Define Scope** process.

Scope Management is about defining the work and deliverables that must be included for project success. Project scope is different from product scope, which is about the functionality and features of a product or deliverable (see Figure 5-1).

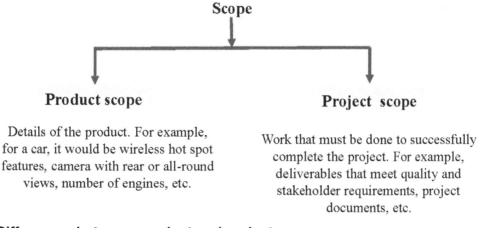

Scope

Product scope

Details of the product. For example, for a car, it would be wireless hot spot features, camera with rear or all-round views, number of engines, etc.

Project scope

Work that must be done to successfully complete the project. For example, deliverables that meet quality and stakeholder requirements, project documents, etc.

Figure 5-1: Differences between product and project scope

There are 6 processes in the **Scope Management** Knowledge Area:

Planning Process Group	Monitoring and Controlling Process Group
5.1) Plan Scope Management 5.2) Collect Requirements 5.3) Define Scope 5.4) Create WBS	5.5) Validate Scope 5.6) Control Scope

One of the key outputs in this knowledge area is the scope baseline, which is an approved version of the project scope. Scope baseline consists of:

1. Work breakdown structure (WBS), and
2. WBS dictionary

We will discuss more on this in the **Create WBS** process.

Trends and Emerging Practices

There is a trend to adopt business analysis procedures to improve the discovery and refinement of project requirements. Organizations have business analysts, who work with stakeholders to identify, refine and document the requirements. They also develop test scenarios to verify that the requirements are met by the deliverables. The business analysts along with the project manager must own and manage requirement-related activities and deliverables.

The project manager must make sure that all work related to requirements, are included in the project scope and completed on time. The project manager needs to collaborate with the business analyst to help with successful completion of project objectives.

Tailoring Considerations

Processes in the **Scope Management** knowledge area must be tailored or customized to meet the project needs.

The tailoring is based on:

- requirements management system used within the organization,
- selected project management methodology (waterfall, agile, hybrid, iterative, etc.) for the project,
- whether the requirements are expected to change during the project life cycle,
- governance and audit-related guidelines for collecting requirements, and
- procedures used for validation of the requirements.

Considerations for Agile/Adaptive Environments

For some projects, it may be difficult to accurately capture and document all the requirements, towards the start of the projects. For such projects, the initial focus should be to decide on the process that will be used to discover and refine changes to the requirements.

Changes in project or product requirements will impact the project scope and schedule. The project team must develop prototypes that will help the stakeholders update the project requirements and scope, across the project life.

Process 1: Plan Scope Management

PMBOK®: Page 134
Process Group: Planning

This process helps develop a plan on how the project scope will be defined, validated and controlled. The inputs are the project charter and project management plans as shown in Figure 5-2. The project charter contains the intention and objectives of the project, as provided by the stakeholders.

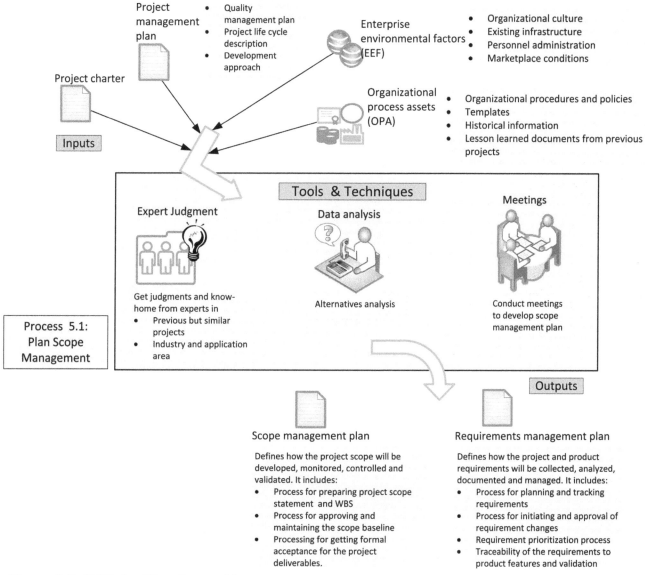

Figure 5-2: ITTO for Plan Scope Management process

Table 5-1 shows the two outputs of this process: the scope management plan and the requirements management plan.

	Outputs of the **Plan Scope Management** process	Description
1	Scope management plan document	This document defines how the project scope will be defined, validated, monitored and controlled. As we have seen earlier, it is a component of the program or project management plan. It is a key input for the **Develop Project Management Plan** process in the **Integration** knowledge area. The scope management plan includes: ▪ details on how you will create the project scope statement, ▪ procedures on using the scope statement to create the WBS, ▪ plans for managing and controlling the WBS, ▪ plans for creating and getting approvals for change requests, ▪ plans for baseline updates.
2	Requirements management plan document	This document describes, how you will: ▪ Identify, analyze and control the requirements, ▪ Initiate and approve changes to the requirements, ▪ Prioritize and group the requirements into high, medium and low categories, ▪ Develop the requirements traceability matrix. Like the scope management plan, this is also a component of the program or project management plan. It could be for the project itself and/or for the product (created by the project)

Table 5-1: Key outputs of the Plan Scope Management process

How does the scope management plan help the project?

- It provides guidance on how scope will be managed throughout the project.
- It helps reduce the risk of scope creep.
- It helps identify gold-plating and provides ways to avoid that.

Process 2: Collect Requirements

PMBOK®: Page 138
Process Group: Planning

Do you collect and document requirements for your projects? If you are working in a small company or on a small project, the requirements possibly come from the project sponsor or the stakeholder who provides the funding. If you are working for a large organization or have business analysts in your project, they possibly prepare the requirements documents. You may not have spent too much time collecting or documenting project requirements. However, for the exam, you need to know this process.

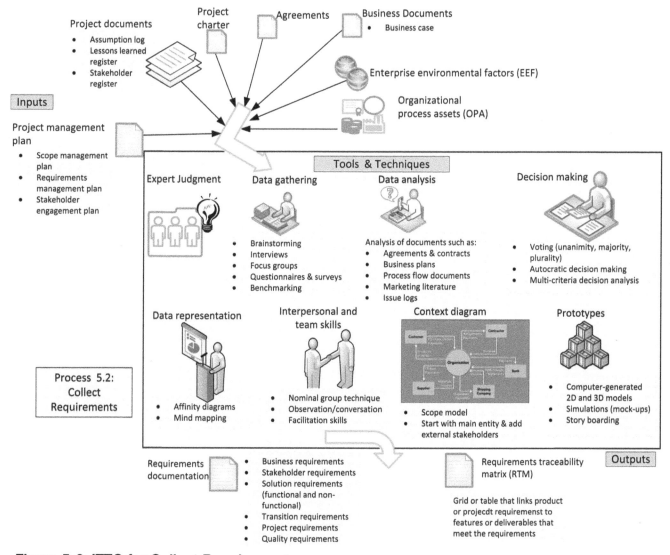

Figure 5-3: ITTO for Collect Requirements process

What is **Collect Requirements** process about? In this process, you work with the stakeholders to identify, document and get signoff for the project and product requirements. These requirements are used by the **Define Scope** process to develop the project and product scope.

Who do you get the requirements from? They come from the stakeholders, but primarily from the customers, sponsors, and users of the product. Table 5-2 describes the tools and techniques used to collect requirements.

#	Group creativity techniques	Description
1	Affinity diagram technique	Here the participants come up with various ideas or project requirements and then group those into sets. The sets are named such as "performance requirements", "ease-of-use requirements", etc.
2	Benchmarking	You first identify another project (internal or external) that had a similar scope and closed successfully. You then compare your project plan to that of the identified project with a goal to identify areas of improvement and best practices for your new project.
3	Brainstorming sessions	You organize a group where you solicit and collect the project requirements. This is not a meeting to decide if an idea is good or bad. There is no evaluation or ranking of the ideas. The objective is to generate and collect ideas and requirements.
4	Context diagrams (CD)	A context diagram (CD) is a figure that shows a system (deliverable, equipment or process) and how other systems, stakeholders or departments interact with it. It is a visual display of the interactions between various people and systems.
5	Delphi technique	You identify a panel of experts from inside and/or outside the organization. Usually, the participants remain anonymous. This frees the participants from their personal biases and minimizes the groupthink or 'halo' effect. Also, this can be done as a virtual meeting. There is a facilitator that transfers messages back and forth. Each participant is given a questionnaire and asked for answers. The facilitator or leader collects and shares all the answers with the entire team and asks the members for another revised set of answers. This is iterated until you reach a predefined stop criterion (number of rounds, the stability of results, consensus, etc.). The answers in the final round are considered as an outcome (result) of the session.
6	Facilitation technique	Facilitation is used during workshops and focused sessions, where you bring in stakeholders from different divisions to define the project requirements. Since the stakeholders are together they can quickly identify and resolve issues in real-time. This saves you from trying to resolve disagreements and differences over emails or during 1:1 meetings. In this focused session, you: ▪ discuss and list all cross-functional requirements, ▪ reconcile the differences of opinions between the stakeholders, ▪ discover issues and resolve those in real-time during the session and ▪ foster open relationships between the stakeholders with a goal to get consensus for the project requirements.
7	Idea or Mind mapping technique	A mind map is a technique used to capture key thoughts and depict those in a visual manner. It illustrates the relationships between the various ideas. In this technique, you draw the primary idea or image in the center of a page. Secondary (major) ideas are drawn close to the center and connected to the primary (central) image. All tertiary (supporting) ideas branch out from the major ideas, using radial lines.
8	Multi-criteria decision analysis technique	Here the meeting participants use a matrix containing several criteria to come up with a quantitative ranking of the ideas. The criteria could be the benefit-cost ratio, time spent on the project, expected risks, expenses incurred, etc.

9	Nominal group technique (NGT, Figure 5-4)	NGT is a useful technique to generate and prioritize ideas. It combines brainstorming and multi-voting. It provides a fair inclusion of all members and ideas and avoids conflicts and criticisms. How do you do an NGT session? You ask all the participants to write their ideas or requirements anonymously on paper. Then you discuss each idea and prioritize those (by a simple show of hands) and based on pre-decided selection criteria. You can use the ranked list for the next process, **Define Scope**.
10	Prototyping	A prototype is a model of the actual, final product. In this technique, you develop a model (or prototype) based on requirements you have collected earlier using brainstorming, workshop or interview sessions. You then use the model to update your initial requirements. Since the model is tangible, stakeholders can view and use it and provide the project team with a revised and firm set of requirements. This is an example of progressive elaboration and an iterative technique, where you update the project requirements. Another prototyping example is storyboarding, which is a sequence of images or illustrations that show the benefits of a required feature in a product.

11	Questionnaires and surveys	This is a technique where you prepare and send out a set of written questions to a large audience to seek their requirements for the project. This technique is preferred if:
		  ▪ the audience is geographically-dispersed,
		  ▪ you need a quick turnaround, and
		  ▪ a statistical analysis of the input data is necessary..

Table 5-2: Techniques used to collect requirements

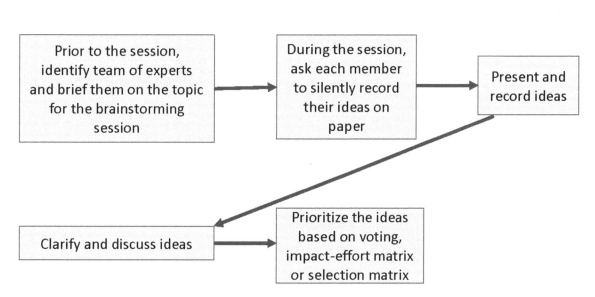

Figure 5-4: Steps during a Nominal Group Technique (NGT) session

When you are collecting requirements, conducting group discussions and brainstorming sessions, you could come to an impasse. You will have multiple options and you will need to rank (prioritize) the options or select the best one. Table 5-3 has voting techniques that can be used to select one of the options.

#	Techniques for selecting an option	The selected option must have support from...
1	Unanimity	All members (100%) must agree to an option for it to be selected.
2	Majority	More than 50% must agree on an option for it to be selected.
3	Plurality	The biggest group (could be more or less than 50%) must agree on an option.
4	Dictatorship or autocratic decision-making	One person, who decides for everyone in the group.

Table 5-3: Voting Techniques to select an option or solution

The different types of requirements are listed below:

1. Business requirements: These are related to how the organization would benefit from the project or product. These typically come from the sponsor, customer and the senior management in the organization.
2. Solution requirements: These are related to the technical needs of the project or product. There are two categories of solution requirements:
   - Functional requirements - about features and functionality of a product.
   - Non-functional requirements - about the quality of the product.
   There will be questions in the exam that will state a requirement (for example, need to harden the network and application security), and ask you to select the type of requirement (technical, functional, non-functional, etc.). Remember, that supporting features such as availability, reliability and security are non-functional requirements.
3. Stakeholder requirements. These are not about the product or solution, but these are needed to meet the requirements of some stakeholders.
4. Transition requirements: These requirements are needed to transition (partially or entirely) the product or project from one team to another. For example, after a product is setup and deployed for production use, the day-to-day administration of the product is transitioned to the operations and support teams.
5. Project requirements: These are needed to make sure that the project has been successfully completed and gain 'project closure' signoff from stakeholders.
6. Quality requirements: These are related to the quality of the product or project deliverables.

---

* For the Exam *
Remember the difference between functional and non-functional requirements. If a question states a condition, that the user needs and it seems like a feature or functionality, it is a functional requirement. If the requirement (such as improved security, 24x7 availability or faster performance) supports a feature, it is a non-functional requirement.

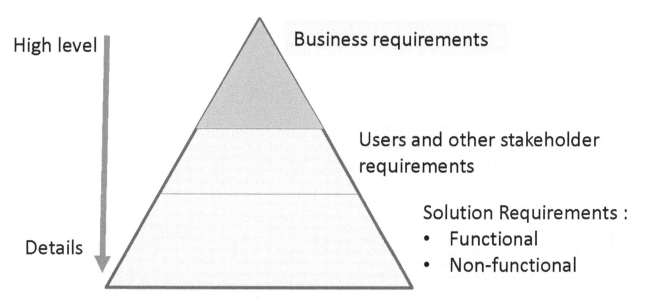

Requirements for a Project or Product

Functional requirements	Non-functional requirements
Come from the users	Come from developers or architects
Relate to what the product or solution does and its features	Relate to qualities of the solution that could help in supporting or managing the solution over its lifetime

Figure 5-5: Types of Requirements

EXERCISE TIME:

Question:
Identify if the following are functional or non-functional requirements.

	Requirement	Is the requirement functional or non-functional?
1	Improve the service uptime from 99% to 99.99%	
2	Add capability for clients to change their date of birth and address in their profile page	
3	Add ability to prevent users from copying data to their USB drives	
4	Add a feature that the instrument would automatically shut off when running above 1200 RPM to prevent damage to the instrument	

Solution:

	Answer
1	Non-functional requirement
2	Functional requirement
3	Non-functional requirement
4	Non-functional requirement

These are examples of functional and non-functional requirements for a product or service.

Requirements Traceability Matrix (RTM)

An RTM is a document that helps track requirements throughout the project life. It links the business requirements from the origin (when those are collected from stakeholders) to design features in the deliverables and test scenarios (to validate that the built features satisfy the requirements).

Figure 5-6 has the key components of an RTM, which are:

- the business goals,
- requirement description with Requirement ID number, the source of requirement, the type of requirement, etc.
- risk(s) associated with the business goals and requirements, and
- features, proposed to meet the requirements.

Test scenarios are developed to validate the various requirements. The RTM links the requirements, WBS, work packages and the test scenarios.

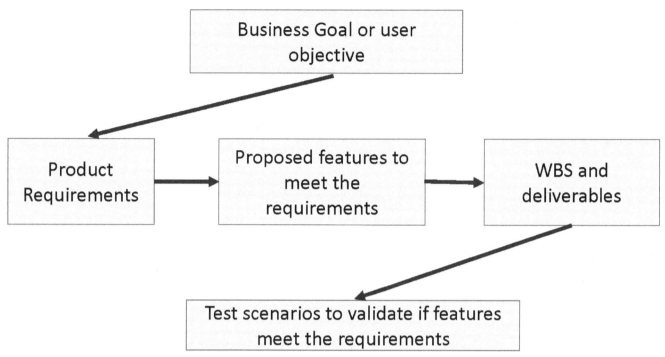

Figure 5-6: Requirements Traceability Matrix (RTM) provides relationship and traceability from goals to validation of features.

Table 5-4 is an example of a simple RTM.

RTM ID	Business requirement number (This comes from the Business Requirement document or BRD)	Technical requirement number (This comes from the Technical Requirement document or TRD)	Test case ID number (This comes from the Test Scenarios document)
1	B1	T1	Test Case 1
2	B1	T2	Test Case 2
3	B2	T3	Test Case 3
4	B3	T4	Test Case 4
5	B3	T5	Test Case 5

Table 5-4: An example of a Requirements Traceability Matrix (RTM)

It is possible that your workplace has business analysts (BAs) who develop and provide you the business requirements document (BRD), technical requirements documents (TRD), functional and non-functional requirements documents (FRD and N-FRD), test documents and RTM.

But you need to know about the RTM for the exam. Many project managers complete a project without ever needing or creating an RTM.

Here are the benefits of an RTM:

- It helps you track all the requirements.
- You can link requirements with product design and project scope.
- In case you later need to change a requirement, it tells you what project deliverables, features and test scenarios must be modified (forward traceability).
- It helps you develop and test the features to make sure that the features meet the requirements (backward traceability).
- It helps you identify scope creep. If someone suggests adding features that do not link to any requirements, then the suggested features are not needed (backward traceability).
- Defects or test failures can be traced back to the project WBS, design, feature, code or deliverable that must be fixed.
- It helps you identify requirements that could be violated (or be in jeopardy) in case a feature or deliverable is modified.

Process 3: Define Scope

> **PMBOK®: Page 150**
> Process Group: Planning

In this process, you will develop the project scope statement, using the requirements documents. But do you need to include all the stated requirements as part of your project? No. At this stage, you need to assess each of the requirements and decide if they should be in-scope or out-of-scope. The scope statement is an important input for developing the scope baseline, which helps develop the other two baselines (schedule and cost).

It is important to note the sequence: requirements → scope statement → scope baseline including WBS → schedule and cost baselines. Project managers often spend an inordinate amount of time during project execution, trying to interpret and explain the scope to meet the established schedule and budget. That is working backward! Instead, the scope should dictate the schedule and budget.

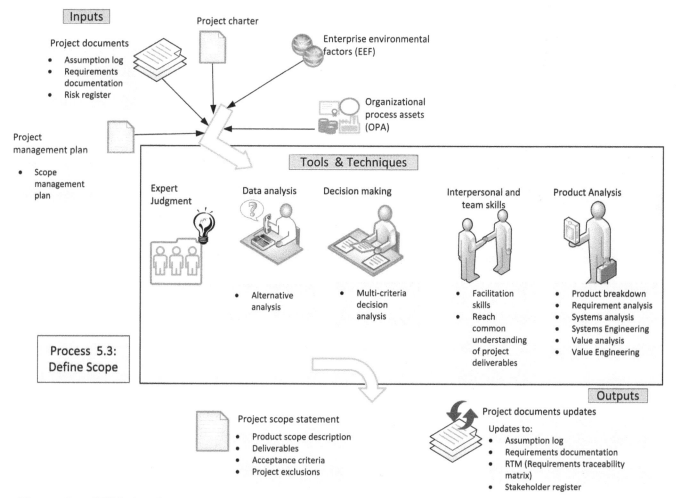

Figure 5-7: ITTO for Define Scope process

Project scope statement includes:

- Product scope description (characteristics of the product, service, or deliverables)
- Project scope description (to meet the requirements)
- List of deliverables (product, service, outcomes, project reports, documents, etc.)
- Assumptions, that form the basis of the proposed scope
- Constraints, that could limit the project progress
- Acceptance criteria (conditions that must be met for signoff and acceptance by stakeholders)
- Exclusions (out-of-scope items for the project and product)

Is an out-of-scope section important? You may think that once you have established an in-scope description, everything not mentioned is out-of-scope. Therefore, developing an out-of-scope section is unnecessary and redundant. That makes sense if you have a small group of stakeholders who agree to the scope. But if you are managing a large project, for example with 20 stakeholders around the country or world, they may misinterpret the in-scope description. This could lead to discussions on everyone's understanding of the scope description! Hence to remove the gray area and vagueness, it is important that you specify the out-of-scope work as well.

Process 4: Create WBS (Work Breakdown Structure)

PMBOK®: Page 156
Process Group: Planning

Do you develop WBS for your projects at your workplace? If you do not, spend more time to learn WBS because you will have questions in the PMP Exam. To correctly answer those, you need to understand WBS, control accounts and planning and work packages and their characteristics and relationships.

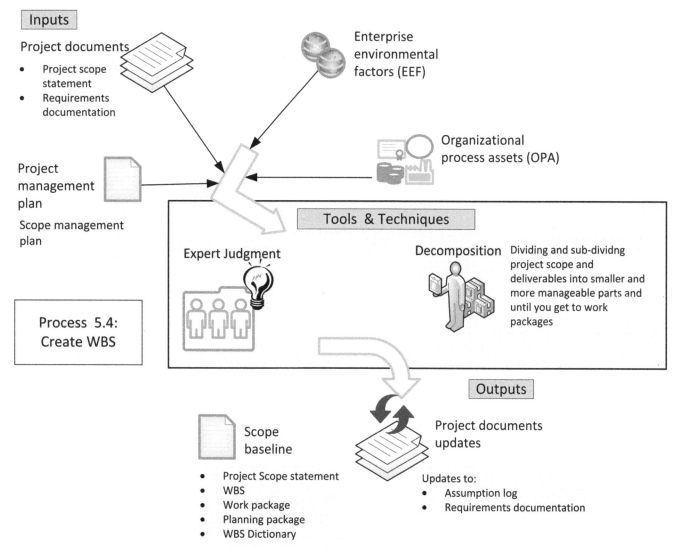

Inputs

Project documents
- Project scope statement
- Requirements documentation

Project management plan

Scope management plan

Enterprise environmental factors (EEF)

Organizational process assets (OPA)

Process 5.4: Create WBS

Tools & Techniques

Expert Judgment

Decomposition — Dividing and sub-dividng project scope and deliverables into smaller and more manageable parts and until you get to work packages

Outputs

Scope baseline
- Project Scope statement
- WBS
- Work package
- Planning package
- WBS Dictionary

Project documents updates

Updates to:
- Assumption log
- Requirements documentation

Figure 5-8: ITTO for Create WBS process

What is WBS? It is a project document that shows the hierarchical decomposition of work scope that must be done to create the required deliverables and meet the project objectives.

What do you need to develop a WBS? Key inputs are:

- the scope management plan, which describes how the project scope statement will be used to create the WBS,
- the project scope statement, which has the details about the deliverables, in-scope work and excluded work, and
- the requirements documentation, which lists the business needs and requirements that form the basis of the in-scope work.

How do you create the WBS? You use decomposition and expert judgment. Decomposition is a technique to divide and sub-divide the scope and deliverables into smaller components.

Figure 5-9 shows an example WBS with four levels.

For simple deliverables, two levels of decomposition could be enough. For complex deliverables, you may need three or more levels of decomposition. The components in the final level are called **work packages**, highlighted in yellow in Figure 5-9.

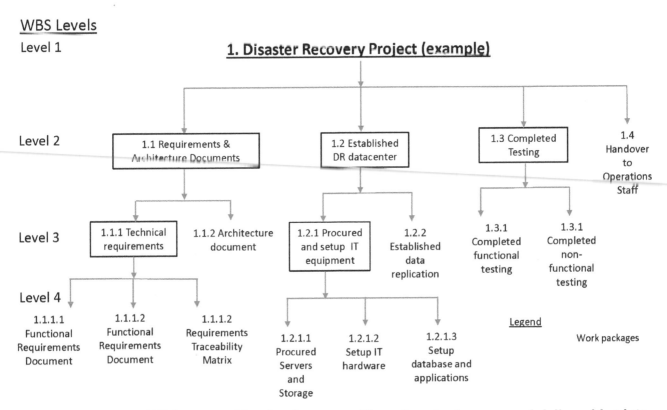

Figure 5-9: Sample WBS, created by the decomposition of project scope and deliverables into work packages

Remember there is a risk that may end up with an excessive decomposition. That leads to problems such as difficulty in aggregating data over too many layers and a high overhead to maintaining a large number of small work packages. A work package is the lowest level of the WBS. You need to stop decomposing as soon as you reach a level, that has deliverables with features of a work package, which are:

- The time required to complete a work package can be estimated,
- The work can be completed by an individual with assistance from others if needed,
- The work can be outsourced, if needed, and
- The work should be completed within two weeks (rule of the thumb).

What are some guidelines for developing a WBS? Those are:

- Identify and analyze the project deliverables,
- Decompose (or split) the upper-level deliverables into lower-level detailed components,
- Stop as soon as you reach components, that have features of a work package,
- Assign identification codes to components at all levels.

Each level in the WBS hierarchy consists of components or smaller pieces of the previous level. Different deliverables will have different levels to which they will be decomposed to get to the work packages.

Does the project manager, alone create the WBS? No! The project team members must contribute and help in developing the WBS.

Control Accounts and Planning Packages

Each work package is assigned to a single control account. But a control account may include one or more work packages.

For the Exam
Note that a work package (WP) can be assigned to only one control account (CA).
A control account can have multiple work packages and/or planning packages.
For example:
- WP A belongs to CA1
- WP B, WP C, and Planning Package Y belong to CA2
- WP E belongs to CA3

How does a control account help? At the control account, the scope, actual cost incurred and schedule are combined and compared with the earned value of the completed work. Managing and controlling costs, scope and schedule can be done at a control account level, which has a group of work packages.

A control account may also have planning packages, where each planning package has a certain amount of work but without details such as work schedule.

The key output of the **Create WBS** process is the scope baseline. Figure 5-10 shows the components of a scope baseline. Note that a control account is made up of work package(s) and may also include planning package(s).

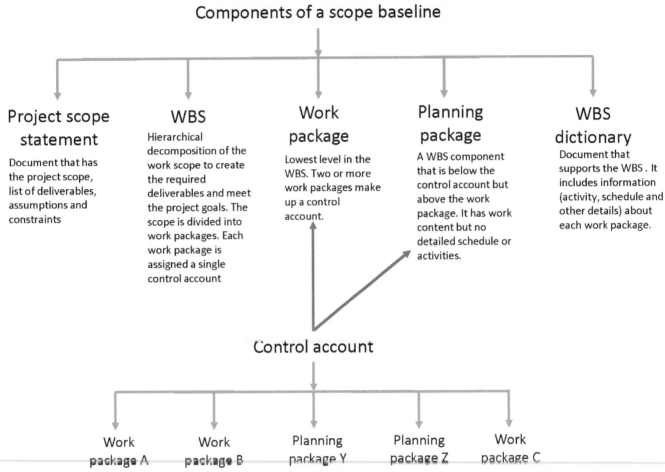

Figure 5-10: Components of a scope baseline. Note that a control account consists of one or more work packages and may contain one or more planning packages.

Process 5: Validate Scope

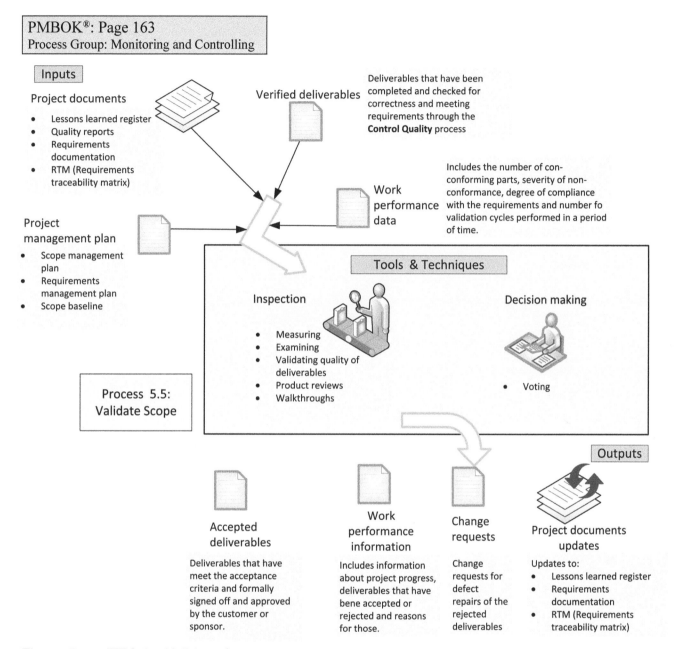

Figure 5-11: ITTO for Validate Scope process

Validate Scope may sound like the **Define Scope** process and you may think that the **Validate Scope** process provides one more opportunity to revise the scope. But that's wrong! The **Validate Scope** process happens after project execution. By now, you have the completed deliverables. The deliverables have also been inspected as part of **Control Quality** process, which is usually done by the project team.

In **Validate Scope** process, you meet with the customers or sponsor to gain acceptance of the deliverables. If they do not accept, you develop a list of required changes.

This process may also sound like **Close Project or Phase**. But think of what could be the differences between **Validate Scope** and **Close Project or Phase**?

Validate Scope process is about getting signoff for one or more deliverables and can be in the middle or at the end of a project. The sponsor or customer may accept the deliverables, or your meeting may end with change requests to modify certain features. On the other hand, **Close Project or Phase** process is for you to get acceptance and signoff for the entire project. By this time, you must have already gained acceptance for the individual deliverables.

What are the outputs of the **Validate Scope** process? Remember that whenever, you look for outputs of a process, think of what you expect to get. In this case, you are looking to get sign off from the sponsor or customers and add the deliverable to your list of **accepted deliverables.** In case, there are deficiencies, you would create **change request**(s), get approvals and go back to planning and executing to correct the deliverables. All these would lead to more **work performance information** and **updates to project documents**, including quality checklists, requirement documentation, lesson learned, requirements traceability matrices, etc.

Process 6: Control Scope

PMBOK®: Page 167
Process Group: Monitoring and Controlling

In an ideal world, once you have a signed scope baseline, you would not have to modify that. But situations change! Here are two reasons why scope changes happen:

- The scope was relevant and good at the time it was established, but since then the requirements and conditions may have changed. You will have to therefore, revise the scope, to meet the new requirements.
- Also, new stakeholders or users may have joined the project. They have new requirements which could be in conflict with the existing requirements and want to get their requirements included in the project.

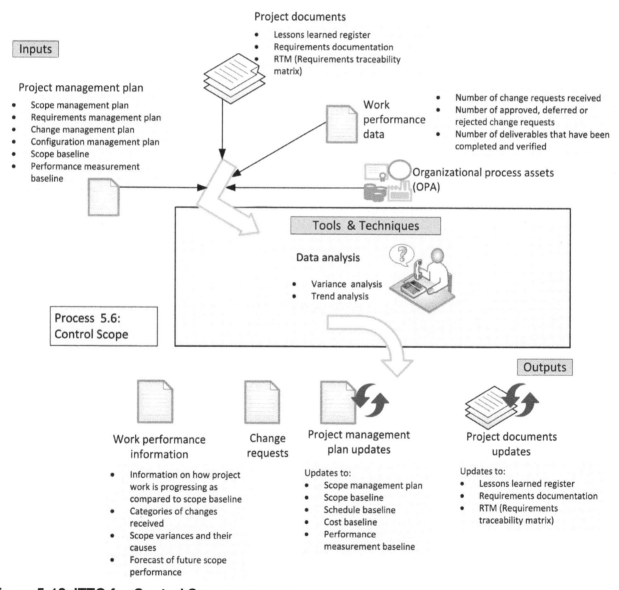

Figure 5-12: ITTO for Control Scope process

What can you do? You do not have to include everything that is requested! On one hand, you must avoid scope creep and gold plating. You need to control additions or changes to the scope baseline. On the other hand, if you, in consultation with the project team and sponsor, feel sure that the requested changes are valid, the project team must:

1. assess the impact of the requested changes
2. submit the change requests through the **Perform Integrated Change Control** process
3. follow the change management process to gain approvals and
4. in case, the changes are approved, update the baselines and project plans.

What are the inputs to controlling project scope? First, you need to know the scope baseline (from the project management plans). You also need the requirements documentation and what has been completed so far (work performance data).

You then compare the work completed so far with the baselines. That will show if there is any variance of the completed work with the baselines and need for changes to the baselines.

All these analyses will lead to various outputs, such as:

- work performance information for the completed portion of the project,
- change requests, and
- updates to project documents such as baselines (scope, cost, and schedule), scope management plan, lessons learned register, requirements documents, etc.

More points for the exam:

- A WBS must be developed and used for each project.
- Scope changes must be first evaluated for its impact on cost, quality, customer satisfaction, schedule, risks, available resources, etc.
- Scope changes must follow the change control procedures, where you
    - o identify options to mitigate the impact on cost, schedule, etc.
    - o develop a change request and gain approvals, and
    - o update the impacted baselines, change log and other project documents.
- The highest level of the WBS is the entire project. The lowest level consists of work packages.
- Each lower level of the WBS consists of smaller tasks or deliverables.
- A work package is a deliverable for which you can estimate the required cost, time and resources, complete the work without the need for further information and can outsource the work if so want.
- A WBS does not show the dependencies between deliverables or work packages.
- You must avoid scope creep (adding scope without an approved change request) and gold plating (adding functionality that is not asked for).

Practice Questions for Chapter 5

1. Which one of the following, is a key input for the Collect Requirements and Define Scope processes?
   A. Scope management plan
   B. Stakeholder register
   C. Scope baseline
   D. Project charter

2. Max Mueller is a project manager for a large consumer product firm. He has prepared work packages and is now developing control accounts. Which of the following is not true for control accounts?
   A. A control account contains work packages and/or planning packages.
   B. A control account can be used to conduct an earned value analysis (EVA) for the work completed so far.
   C. A work package can be associated with only one control account.
   D. Completion of work in a control account serves as a milestone for procurement administrator to collect payments from the customer.

3. Which of the following is an output of the Create WBS process?
   A. Work performance data
   B. Change requests
   C. Scope statement
   D. Scope baseline

4. Joel Jackson is using the stakeholder register to collect functional and non-functional requirements from the stakeholders. He needs to connect the requirements to the architecture and design of the finished product. Which of the following should he use to record the relationship grid?
   A. Requirements document
   B. Requirements management plan
   C. Product quality metrics
   D. Requirements traceability matrix

5. Carlos Gomez has completed the project scope. He schedules a meeting with the project sponsor and stakeholders to conduct the Validate Scope process. Which of the following best describes the benefit of this meeting?
   A. The meeting will establish criteria for the acceptance or rejection of the final product, service or result.
   B. It will provide one more opportunity for Carlos and the stakeholders to review and update the project scope and avoid scope creep.
   C. It will help Carlos either gain formal acceptance or get reasons for rejection of the completed deliverables. This will help improve the probability of acceptance of the final product later by the stakeholders.
   D. It will help verify or validate the functional and non-functional scope of the final product.

6. Which of the following is true for components of a work breakdown structure (WBS)?
   A. A control account is the first level of decomposition for a work breakdown structure (WBS).
   B. A planning package is similar to a control account.
   C. A planning package consists of one or more control accounts.
   D. A control account can have multiple work packages but a work package can belong to only one control account.

7. Tim Thompson is managing a project, but due to delay in equipment delivery from his vendor, the schedule and cost need to be increased. He has created two change requests and now needs to get approval. Which process must he follow?
   A. Validate Scope
   B. Perform Integrated Change Control
   C. Monitor and Control Project Work
   D. Control Scope

8. You have collected requirements for a product. You now need to document the requirements so that they can be used to design the final product. Which of the following product analysis techniques are not relevant for this task?
   A. Value engineering
   B. Requirements analysis
   C. Systems analysis
   D. Context diagrams

9. Steve Simpson is a project manager for a global pharmaceutical firm. He is developing work packages for a large project to rollout a new ERP application for his offices around the world. Which of the following is not a characteristic of the work packages, that he needs to develop?
   A. Steve must be able to reliably determine the duration for each work package and schedule those.
   B. He must be able to estimate the cost for each work package.
   C. He must be able to monitor and control each work package.
   D. He must be able to get signoff on every work package from the end-client.

10. David Disney has prepared a work breakdown structure (WBS) for a project to deploy a new physical security system for his international offices. He is now preparing planning packages and control accounts to report to-date performance for the completed work. Which of the following is not true for control accounts, planning packages and work packages?
    A. A control account consists of planning packages and/or work packages
    B. A work package can belong to multiple control accounts. This helps to validate the accuracy of performance parameters, computed using earned value analysis.
    C. A control account is a management control point where performance is measured by comparing the planned scope, budget and schedule to actual work completed, expenses and time taken.
    D. A planning package is a WBS structure below the control account and consists of known work content but without detailed schedule or activities.

11. The lowest level of a work breakdown structure (WBS) is a work package, which has a unique identifier. These identifiers are used to develop a hierarchical structure and estimate the required costs, time, resources, and skills. Such a hierarchical structure is called a:
    A. Control account
    B. WBS dictionary
    C. Code of accounts
    D. Planning package

12. A software application development project team has prepared a mock-up to show how the user interface will guide the user through the various screens. The goal is to get input from stakeholders to improve user experience. A key requirement is ease-of-use and user-friendliness. Such as mock-up of screens is called:
    A. Context diagrams
    B. Storyboarding
    C. Mind mapping technique
    D. Facilitated workshop

13. Jill Jackson is a project manager at a real estate development firm that specializes in constructing and maintaining commercial complexes. The firm is bidding for several new projects. Jill creates a matrix to rank the projects based on factors such as uncertainty, risk levels, valuation, etc. This technique is called:
    A. Alternative analysis
    B. Monte Carlo simulation
    C. Mind-mapping
    D. Multicriteria decision analysis

14. Which one of the following processes, has change requests, as an output?
    A. Validate Scope
    B. Control Scope
    C. Define Activities
    D. All of the above processes

15. Jill Johnson is managing a project. Several engineers in the team want to implement an extra functionality that will help users with their future requirements. Jill needs to prevent scope creep. How should Jill explain scope creep to the engineers?
    A. Scope creep is adding features to a product without getting approval from users.
    B. Scope creep is an uncontrolled addition to a product or project without an approved change request for revising impacted constraints, resources or baselines.
    C. Scope creep is adding features without getting approval from the project sponsor.
    D. Scope creep is adding characteristics that are not essential but improves non-functional aspects such as usability and reliability of the product.

ANSWERS

Question Number	Correct Answer	Explanation
1	D	Project charter contains the high-level project description, names of stakeholders and product objectives. All these are needed to gather requirements and prepare a detail scope statement.
2	D	A work package is not associated with the collection of payments from customers. Page 161 of the PMBOK® has details on work packages, control accounts and planning packages.
3	D	The output of the **Create WBS** process is the scope baseline. The three baselines (scope, cost and schedule) are important project documents and you need to know the process names that have the baselines as an output.
4	D	Requirements traceability matrix (RTM) is a grid that links the product requirements to the product features that satisfy the requirements. See Page 148 of the PMBOK®.
5	C	The key benefit of **Validate Scope** process is that it brings objectivity and increases the probability of acceptance of the final product.
6	D	A control account can have multiple work packages. Also, a work package can belong to only one control account.
7	B	The **Perform Integrated Change Control** process is used to get approvals for change requests.
8	D	Context diagrams are not used for this purpose but are used to show how people (or systems) use a service or product. Page 153 of the PMBOK® has a list of product analysis techniques for defining scope and requirements.
9	D	Getting client signoff on completion of each work package is not a requirement. A work package is the lowest level of the WBS for which cost and duration can be estimated and managed.
10	B	A work package can belong to only one control account. Control accounts consist of planning packages and work packages. Control Account 1 → Planning package P1 → Work package W3 → Work package W4 Planning package P1 → Work content A, Deliverable Z Later, when there is more clarity of the content in a planning package, it can be decomposed into work packages.

11	C	The hierarchical structure and the identification system are called a code of accounts. It consists of work packages, planning packages, control accounts, etc. where each component has an identifier. See Page 161 of PMBOK®.
12	B	The answer is storyboarding, which is a prototyping technique. In software development, mock-ups can be used to show how a user interface will guide users through a series of screens or web pages. See Page 147 of the PMBOK®.
13	D	Multi-criteria decision analysis is a technique where a decision matrix is used to evaluate and rank various criteria (such as risks, uncertainties, and impact).
14	D	Change requests are an output of all the listed processes.
15	B	Scope creep is adding features or scope without an approved change request.

CHAPTER 6

Schedule Management

Schedule management is about planning and managing the timely completion of a project. It includes developing a detailed plan to show how and when the products and deliverables will be completed as specified in the project scope.

Activities and their attributes (such as activity duration, start and finish dates, needed resources, activity dependencies, etc.) are entered into a scheduling application to create a project schedule. It is important that you develop the plan and milestone completion dates are realistic. If those are not possible, you need to work with the sponsor or customer to set realistic dates. In almost all projects, there are unforeseen delays and milestone dates are missed. You may have buffers and contingencies for delays! But it is a bad idea to start a project with a schedule that you know, is unrealistic.

Later in this chapter, you will learn about ways to speed up project execution, such as fast-tracking and crashing. Should you use these techniques when planning a project schedule? No! These are optionally used, for projects that are behind schedule, to reduce the total duration and try to complete the project on time.

In this chapter, we will discuss schedule network diagrams, which can be created using project scheduling applications such as Microsoft Project. For the exam, you must know how to manually develop a schedule network diagram for a small set of activities.

There are 6 processes in the **Schedule Management** Knowledge Area.

Planning Process Group	Monitoring and Controlling Process Group
6.1) Plan Schedule Management 6.2) Define Activities 6.3) Sequence Activities 6.4) Estimate Activity Durations 6.5) Develop Schedule	6.6) Control Schedule

Trends and Emerging Practices

Various applications (such as Microsoft Project, Oracle Primavera, etc.) are used to develop schedules. There is a growing trend to using cloud-based applications such as FastTrack Schedule (from AEC Software Inc.) and Zoho Projects (from Zoho Corp.) Some of the cloud-based applications can be internally-hosted to meet regulatory compliance or privacy requirements.

Adaptive scheduling is becoming more and more prevalent. In adaptive scheduling, a high-level schedule is initially developed. Once the work starts and progresses, new knowledge is acquired and that helps to add further details to the schedule. Two emerging practices in schedule development are:

- **Iterative scheduling**: In this type of scheduling, the requirements (for product and project) are documented as user stories. Each user story has a brief description of what the user wants to see in the deliverables or products. It is an informal description of requirements. It states the type of user, what he or she wants and why. The user stories are then fine-tuned and prioritized based on its urgency and importance. Time-boxed periods of work are scheduled to fulfill the requirements described in the user stories.

  A **timebox** is a pre-determined period of time during which a team or person works steadily to complete an agreed-upon objective. As soon as the time expires, the work is stopped regardless of whether the objective was met or not. The work is evaluated to see what was accomplished.

  The benefit of this approach is that it provides the opportunity to include changes in the product and project throughout the project lifecycle.

- **On-demand scheduling**: In this type of scheduling, details of the schedule and what will be done next are developed from a backlog (or existing queue) of work. A **backlog** is a set of requirements (short description of features and functionality) that are needed in the product or deliverable. A backlog is not supposed to be a complete or upfront description of all required features. It is updated as more clarity emerges about the product scope. A certain number of requirements are pulled from the backlog and completed as resources become available.

  On-demand scheduling has been prevalent in environments where concepts related to lean manufacturing and Kanban systems are in use. Kanban (billboard or signboard in Japanese) is a scheduling system that tracks production within a factory and limits buildup of excess inventory at each production points.

Tailoring Considerations

There are 5 processes from the **Schedule** Knowledge Area in the **Planning** Process Group. Out of these, the last four processes are about defining and sequencing activities, estimating activity durations and developing the project schedule. These four processes can be done together for small projects.

Tailoring or customizing the processes in the **Schedule Management** Knowledge Area depends on:

- project complexity,
- lifecycle approach adopted for the project,

- methods used to evaluate project progress and product novelty,
- methods used to assess technological uncertainty,
- availability of equipment, talent, and other resources, and
- applications used to develop and maintain the project schedule.

Considerations for Agile/Adaptive Environments

Agile and adaptive environments use short periods of time to do work, review results, take feedback and adapt the process for the next iteration.

For large projects, the approach could be a predictive, adaptive or a hybrid of the two. The high-level schedule is usually predictive (waterfall) and based on the known scope and estimated durations. Once work is in progress and there is more clarity on requirements and scope, detailed activities can then be added to the schedule. Development and refining the schedule, therefore, must follow an adaptive or agile methodology.

Irrespective of the scheduling methodology, a project manager must know and apply the relevant tools and techniques effectively, to develop and maintain the project schedule.

Process 1: Plan Schedule Management

PMBOK®: Page 179
Process Group: Planning

In this process, you decide and document the policies and procedures to develop, execute, and control the project schedule. The output is a schedule management plan. It helps develop, monitor and control the project schedule throughout its life cycle.

Figure 6-1 shows the inputs, tools and techniques and outputs for this process. Here you evaluate the various alternatives (options) and develop a plan that will be later used to create and maintain the project schedule.

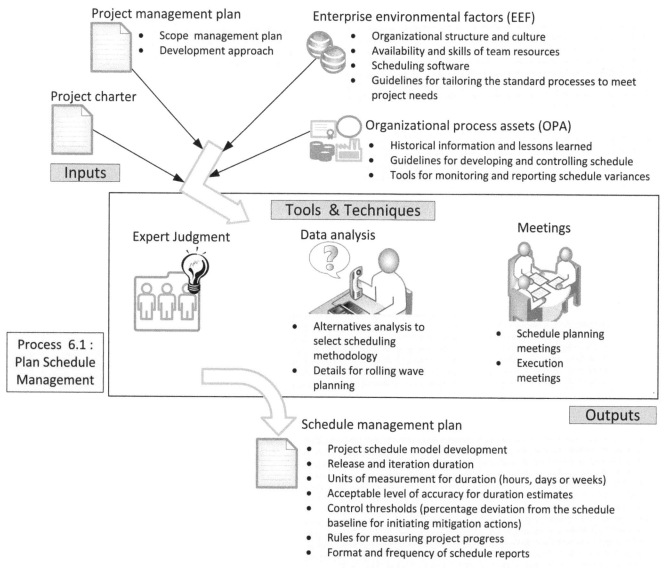

Figure 6-1: ITTO for Plan Schedule Management process

Meetings with industry experts and stakeholders, and various data analysis techniques (such as alternatives analysis) are used to develop the schedule management plan.

> *** For the Exam ***
> Note that the schedule management plan is not the project schedule (or timeline). The project schedule as we will see later in this chapter is an output of **Develop Schedule** process.

The schedule management plan consists of:

- procedures for scheduling activities during project execution,
- procedures to update the project schedule,
- the proposed method to develop the activity list and it attributes,
- the units of measure (for example the units for activity durations are in days or weeks),
- levels of accuracy, that must be maintained for estimating activity durations,
- the process to calculate and report schedule variances,
- the format for reporting project schedule and schedule variances,
- threshold variances, that should prompt change requests to bring the schedule back on track, and
- the planned frequency for reporting status about project schedule.

Small projects may not require a formal plan for schedule management. Nonetheless, you need a plan to develop and implement the project schedule.

Process 2: Define Activities

> PMBOK®: Page 183
> Process Group: Planning

In this process, you identify and document all the activities that must be done to meet the project deliverables and objectives. The key output of this process is the **activity list**. It provides a basis for estimating, scheduling and executing the project work.

The inputs, tools and techniques and outputs are shown in Figure 6-2.

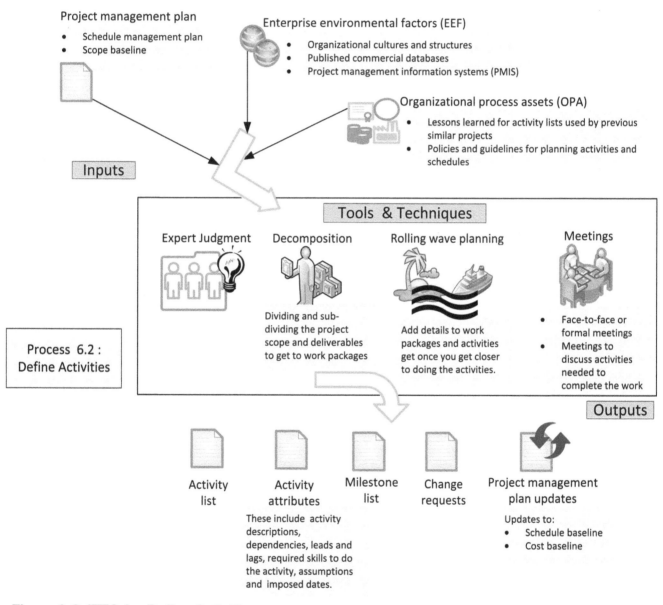

Figure 6-2: ITTO for Define Activities process

As seen in the previous chapter, WBS has work packages at its lowest level. How do you start with work packages and develop a list of activities?

You must **decompose** (divide and sub-divide) each work package into smaller chunks to form activities. These activities need to be completed to produce the deliverables in the corresponding work package.

The project team must be involved in decomposing the work packages into activities. For certain work packages, the team may not be able to foresee activities (due to lack of information or experience). Decompose those work packages, to whatever level of detail is available during the planning phase.

As and when the project team gets more information and clarity, the work packages are then decomposed into activities. This is called **Rolling Wave Technique**. It is an iterative planning tool (similar to progressive elaboration).

Once you have the activities, the next step is to define their attributes, such as:

- unique identifier (ID) for the activity,
- equipment and skills required to do the activity,
- assumptions and constraints,
- relationship with other activities,
- predecessors (activities that must be completed prior to starting this activity),
- successors (activities that can be started only after this activity is complete),
- leads and lags with other activities, and
- imposed dates for scheduling the activity.

Another output for the **Define Activities** process is the milestone list. Milestones have **zero duration** and are not activities. They are events that signify completion of important tasks in the schedule.

There will be questions in the exam that require you to know the distinction between milestones and activities.

---

* For the Exam *
- Activities have a finite time duration (for example, 4 days) in the project schedule.
- Milestones are significant events in the schedule but have zero time duration.

Process 3: Sequence Activities

PMBOK®: Page 187
Process Group: Planning

This process helps you identify the relationships between activities and develop a logical sequence to maximize efficiency given the various constraints and assumptions. These would help develop a schedule diagram.

Figure 6-3 has the inputs, tools and techniques and outputs for the **Sequence Activities** process.

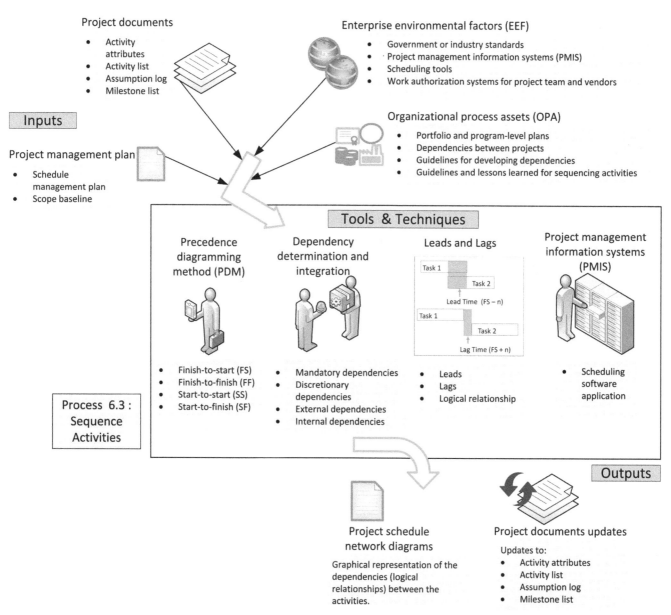

Figure 6-3: ITTO for the Sequence Activities process

Activity attributes lead to dependencies between activities. For example, the activities below must be done in the listed sequence:

(a) develop server and storage architecture
(b) develop build of material or BoM, and
(c) place order to purchase the items in the BoM.

Once you have a list of the activities and their attributes (from the **Define Activities** process), the next step is to sequence the activities in the order that those can be started. This is done using activity relationships and dependencies, to get a project schedule network diagram. It is a visual representation of the schedule.

The common techniques for creating schedule network diagrams are:

- Precedence Diagramming Method (**PDM**) or Activity on Node (**AON**),
- Arrow Diagramming Method (**ADM**) or Activity on Arrow (**AOA**),
- Gantt chart,
- Graphical Evaluation and Review Technique (**GERT**) chart, and
- Program Evaluation and Review Technique (**PERT**) chart

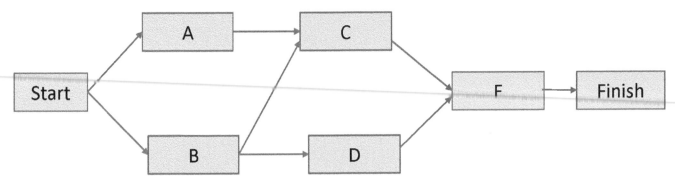

Figure 6-4: Precedence Diagramming Method (PDM) or Activity on Nodes (AON)

Precedence Diagramming Method (**PDM**) is widely used for network diagrams. It uses boxes (or nodes) to represent activities. The boxes are connected by arrows that represent dependencies (Fig. 6-4).

Arrow Diagramming Method (**ADM**) or Activity on Arrows (**AOA**) is another network diagramming technique where arrows represent activities.

Gantt chart is a graphical representation of a schedule. It represents activities as horizontal bars with the length of the bar indicating the duration of the activity. The relationships between activities are shown by curved arrows. This technique was developed as a production control tool in 1917 by Henry Gantt, an American engineer and social scientist.

A Graphical Evaluation and Review Technique (**GERT**) chart is like PDM, and uses nodes to represent activities. But there is one important difference between a GERT chart and PDM. A GERT chart uses loops and branches to represent activities that need to be repeated several times. GERT techniques have special use cases but are not widely used.

A Program Evaluation and Review Technique (**PERT**) chart has numbered nodes that represent events or milestones. It has directional lines or vectors that connect the nodes and represent activities. It was used in the 1950s to manage submarine missile programs.

Activities have dependencies on each other. Fig. 6-5 shows the four common dependencies between activities.

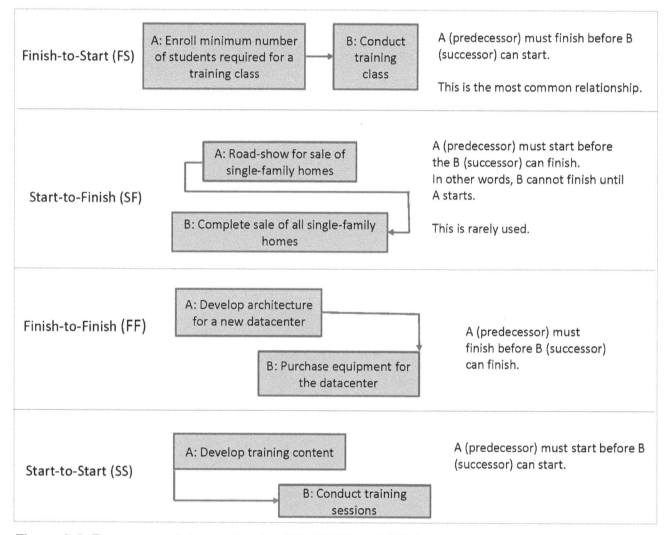

Figure 6-5: Four types of dependencies (FS, SF, FF and SS) between activities shown as a Precedence Diagramming Method (PDM)

Dependencies can be classified according to their source and nature into:

- external or internal dependencies, and
- mandatory or discretionary dependencies.

Table 6-1 has a description of these dependencies.

	Definition	Examples
External dependencies	These dependencies are outside the control of the project members.	For drug manufacturers, the FDA (Food and Drug Administration) must schedule and complete the audit, before the manufacturer can claim certification for its facility or processes.
Internal dependencies	These dependencies are within the control of the project members.	You need to do setup network switches and storage in the data center. You have the engineers in the project team. You can control and schedule these activities.
Mandatory dependencies	These are hard or required dependencies. For example, Activity A must complete before B can start.	A software program must be tested before it is deployed for production use.
Discretionary dependencies	These are soft or preferred dependencies. It is not a hard requirement and is based on best practices or knowledge. When you need to fast-track a project, this is where you first look to reduce timelines.	Installing a fence and painting the fence does not have a finish-to-start relationship. You can wait to finish installation first. But if you want to reduce the project schedule, you can start painting immediately after you start the installation.

Table 6-1: Types of Activity Dependencies

For each activity dependency, you need to document whether it is internal or external and mandatory or discretionary. This categorization will help you identify risks and constraints, associated with the activities.

---

* For the Exam *

You need to distinguish between discretionary activity and discretionary dependency:

- A discretionary activity is optional. For example, it is not necessary to apply a layer of primer, before painting. You can avoid this activity of "applying primer" entirely and hence it is a discretionary or optional activity.
- A discretionary dependency is not a hard requirement. For example, user training sessions can start before or after starting application deployment. Alternatively, it can start after completing deployment. This dependency is discretionary because training can be done in parallel with or after deployment of the application.

When an activity is dependent on another, the successor does not need to start immediately after the predecessor is completed. The successor can start in advance (lead) of completion of the predecessor. Or the successor can wait for some time (lag) after a predecessor completes (Figure 6-6).

	Definition	How it is represented
Leads	The amount of time that a successor activity can be advanced relative to a predecessor activity.	Leads reduce time needed to complete a project. Hence they are denoted by "-" sign. For example, FS-10, SF-10, SS-10 or FF-10.
Lags	The amount of time that a successor activity can be delayed, after a predecessor activity is completed.	Lags increase the time needed to complete a project and are therefore denoted by "+" sign. For example, FS+4, SF+4, SS+4 or FF+4.

Table 6-2: Leads and lags for an activity

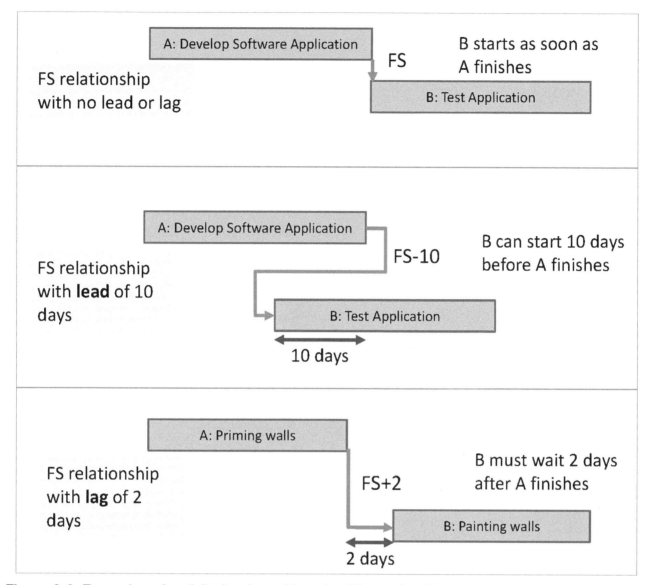

Figure 6-6: Examples of activity leads and lags for FS relationship

Leads are used for fast-tracking. Fast-tracking is a technique used to compress project duration. Tasks which were earlier planned to be in sequence (with no overlap) are forced to overlap. For example, 'test code' activity with a finish-start (FS) relationship on 'develop code' activity before fast-tracking, is changed to, for example, 'FS-10d' relationship. This implies that testing will start 10 days prior to completion of 'develop code' activity.

Process 4: Estimate Activity Durations

PMBOK®: Page 195
Process Group: Planning

After you have defined the activities, decided their sequence, estimated the required resources, it is time to decide how long (in hours, days or months) each activity will take.

Figure 6-7 shows the inputs, tools and techniques and outputs for the Estimate Activity Durations process.

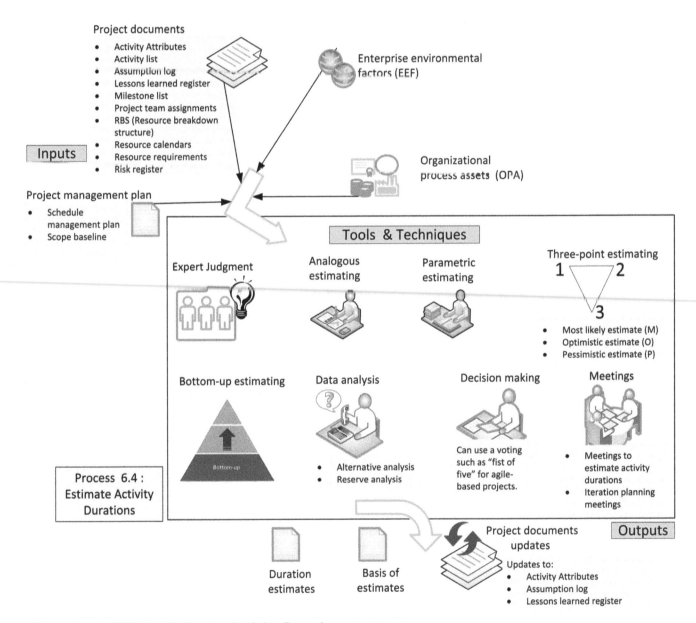

Figure 6-7: ITTO for Estimate Activity Durations process

As a project manager, would you know how long each activity will take? Yes for some activities! Certainly not for all the activities! Also you cannot say, "I guess it should take 2 weeks and I will double that to 4 weeks to cover for unknowns". Your estimate and adding time for unknowns could be wrong! You need to get estimates from project team members, experts and stakeholders, who may have more information and experience with similar activities.

You cannot mitigate for unknowns by adding an arbitrary percentage to the duration. Neither should you hide the uncertainties! Uncertainties should be discussed with the project team and listed in the risk register.

---

* For the Exam *

There will be questions in the exam that will try to assess if you are okay and accepting of padded estimates for duration and cost estimates.

Remember, padding is unacceptable for developing schedules. Your projects will have uncertainties, for which you must identify threats or opportunities, document them in the risk register and add reserves to the estimates to cover for identified risks! You should never resort to padding your estimates!

Table 6-3 describes the techniques used to estimate activity durations.

#	Technique	Description
1	Analogous estimating	In this technique, you use actual data from a previously-completed but similar project, to develop an estimate. You can then adjust and fine-tune the estimate using differences between the two projects. This technique is an example of top-down estimation. It provides a quick estimate, but it is less accurate.
2	Parametric estimating	This is more accurate than analogous estimating. Here you select a parameter (from previous similar activities or expert judgment) and use that to estimate activity duration. For example, if your web developer can develop 4 pages per day and if your new project needs a website with 60 pages, the 'site creation activity' will have a duration of 15 days (60 pages/4).
3	Single-Point estimating	Using this technique, you get one estimate for each activity and use that to develop the project schedule. It is quick, but the estimates are often unrealistic. This technique can force the estimator to pad the initial estimates, since he or she must provide one value for the activity duration. Project schedules based on these estimates can be unrealistic and difficult to justify.
4	Three-Point Estimating	In this technique, you ask the estimator to provide three estimates for duration: • Optimistic (O) • Most likely (M) • Pessimistic (P) Then you use one of the formulas (triangular or beta) to estimate the **expected duration**: • **Triangular** distribution average = $(O + M + P)/3$. This is also called mean, 3-point distribution or simple average. • **Beta** distribution average = $(O + 4M + P)/6$. This is also called weighted or PERT (Program Evaluation and Review Technique) average. Remember, these formulas can be used to estimate activity cost also, as we will see in the chapter on **Cost** Knowledge Area. Here are formulas for standard deviation (SD) and range: • $SD = (P - O)/6$ • Variance = Square of SD (or SD*SD) • Range = Expected duration +/- SD • Upper value of the range = 'Expected duration + Standard Deviation' • Lower value of the range = 'Expected duration - Standard Deviation'.

5	Bottom-up estimating	In this technique, each activity is broken (decomposed) into sub-tasks or sub-activities. You get a duration estimate for each sub-activity. These estimates are added (aggregated) to arrive at an estimate for the activity.
6	Alternatives Analysis	In this technique, you identify various plausible options (alternatives) to accomplish a particular task or objective. Each option has its requirements related to cost, skills, duration, equipment, decisions, etc. For example, a software product or tool can be developed internally, purchased, or outsourced to a vendor. The project team must analyze the pros and cons of these options and select the most optimal alternative.
7	Reserve Analysis	There are two types of reserves for activity or project durations: 1. **Contingency reserves**: These are time reserves or buffers that are used to cover for known risks, for which you have mitigation responses. Contingency reserves are included within the schedule baseline. They are used to cover for **known-unknowns**. 2. **Management reserves**: These are a specified amount of time reserved for unforeseen situations that could impact project duration. This time however is not included in the schedule baseline, but it is included in the overall project duration requirements. This time is used to cover for **unknown-unknowns**.
8	Group Decision-Making Techniques	In this technique, you engage a group to brainstorm and provide duration estimates for each activity. Later you review the initial estimates and finalize the numbers. One group decision-making technique that is commonly used is voting. One variation of voting is fist-of-five voting. Here the project manager asks the team to vote on a decision, where: ▪ A closed fist shows no support. ▪ One or two fingers show weak or very low support. ▪ Three or four fingers show medium support. ▪ Five fingers show full support. Those who show weak support or hesitation in voting are asked to state their objections. This continues till there is a consensus (everyone holds up three or more fingers).

Table 6-3: Techniques used to estimate activity durations

---

* For the Exam *

In the exam, you will see single-point estimates for activity durations, especially for questions related to computing durations for critical paths. Single-point estimates provide a quick way to calculate critical path duration.

Other questions could be for weighted (beta or PERT) averages and ranges for durations.

Various techniques are described in the Table 6-3. The technique you choose to use will be based on the information you have for that activity and the source of that information.

---

* For the Exam *

When asked in the exam to calculate the expected activity duration, which formula would you use? The formula for triangular or for beta estimates? Watch for indicative words in the question.
- If it says simple, triangular, mean or average, use $(O + M + P)/3$.
- If it says weighted or beta or PERT (**Program Evaluation and Review Technique**), use $(O + 4M + P)/6$.

Here is one exercise for expected activity durations.

EXERCISE TIME 1:

Estimate the expected duration for activities

Question: Compute the expected activity duration in the table below, using simple average or triangular distribution.

Also, estimate the standard deviation and range for each activity.

The pessimistic (P), most likely (M) and optimistic (O) values are in days.

Activity	P	M	O	Expected duration for the activity using simple average	Standard Deviation (SD)	Upper value of the Range	Lower value of the range
Purchase fence	15	12	8				
Install fence	10	7	5				
Paint fence	20	16	14				

Solution:
Remember that the expected duration in this case is a simple average. It is also known as mean or triangular distribution. Formulas to be used are:
- Expected duration using simple average = (O + M + P)/3
- SD = (P – O)/6
- The upper value of the range is expected duration + SD.
- The lower value of the range is expected duration - SD.

Calculated values for averages, standard deviations and ranges:

Activity	P	M	O	Expected duration using simple average	Standard Deviation (SD)	Upper value of the Range	Lower value of the range
Purchase fence	15	12	8	11.66	1.17	12.83	10.5
Install fence	10	7	5	7.3	0.83	8.17	6.5
Paint fence	20	16	14	16.66	1.00	17.67	15.67

Here is another question on the expected duration for activities using weighted averages.

EXERCISE TIME 2:

Question:
Compute the expected activity duration in the table below using weighted average or Beta Distribution. Also, estimate the standard deviation and range for each activity.

The pessimistic (P), most likely (M) and optimistic (O) values are in days.

Activity	P	M	O	Expected duration for the activity using weighted (PERT or Beta) average	Standard Deviation (SD)	Upper value of the range	Lower value of the range
Purchase fence	15	12	8				
Install fence	10	7	5				
Paint fence	20	16	14				

Solution:
The expected duration, in this case, is a weighted average, also known as PERT or beta distribution. The formulas are same as for the above problem except for the weighted average to estimate the expected duration, which is $(O + 4*M + P)/6$.

Activity	P	M	O	Expected duration for the activity using weighted (PERT or Beta) average	Standard Deviation (SD)	Upper value of the range	Lower value of the range
Purchase fence	15	12	8	11.83	1.17	13	10.67
Install fence	10	7	5	7.17	0.83	8	6.33
Paint fence	20	16	14	16.33	1	17.33	15.33

As you can see from the above examples for simple and weighted averages, the values for the averages are close to each other, regardless of the formula used.

So far, we have estimated the expected durations, standard deviations and ranges for individual activities. What would be those values for an entire project? Here is a technique to estimate those for a project:

- Expected duration for the project = Sum of expected durations for individual activities. You need to add the durations for each activity. The assumption is that the activities have finish-to-start (FS) relationships with no leads or lags.
- Standard deviation (SD) for the project = Square root of (sum of variance of activities). Note that variance of an activity is square of its standard deviation. The steps are:
  1. Calculate the SD for each activity using (P-O)/6 formula.
  2. Square the activity SD (the square is called variance for that activity).
  3. Sum up the variances of all activities.
  4. Compute the square root of the sum. This is the SD for the entire project.
- Range for a project = (Expected duration for the project) +/- (SD for the project)

Let us compute the expected duration, SD and range at the project level for the earlier question with weighted averages.

- Expected duration for the project = 11.83 + 7.16 + 16.33 = 35.33 days
- To compute the SD for the project:
  1. Get the activity SDs which as we can see from the table above are 1.17, 0.83 and 1.
  2. Get the variance of each activity by squaring its SD. Variances, therefore, are 1.36, 0.69 and 1.
  3. Add the variances to get 3.06.
  4. Get the square root of 3.06, which is 1.75 days and is the SD for the entire project.
- Range for the project = (Expected duration for the project) +/- (SD for the project) = 35.33 +/- 1.75 days = 37.08 to 33.59 days

What is the significance of the range computed by adding or subtracting one SD from the mean? Why not add or subtract two times SD or three times SD, which would give you a wider range? But by default, ranges are computed using one SD. However, you can compute ranges using 2 or 3 SD and those ranges would be wider. For wider ranges, the probability will be higher, that your measured values would happen to be within the range. Table 6-4 shows ranges computed with 1, 2 and 3 SDs and probability that the measured value will be within the ranges.

Range for an activity or project	Probability (confidence) that your measured results will be in this range (assuming normal distribution)	Range for the above project with expected duration=35.33 and SD =1.75 days
Expected duration +/- 1*SD	68.27%	37.08 to 33.59 days (as computed above)
Expected duration +/- 2*SD	95.45%	35.33 +/- 2* 1.75 days = 38.83 to 31.84 days
Expected duration +/- 3*SD	99.73%	35.33 +/- 3* 1.75 days = 40.58 to 30.09 days

Table 6-4: Percentage confidence for each range, assuming a normal distribution

If the range is computed with one SD, the confidence or probability that actual results will be in the range is only 68.27%.

For the exam, you could have a question with an expected duration and SD for an activity or project with normal distribution and you are asked to compute the range, which will have 99.73% confidence that your actual outcome will be within the range. The upper limit of the range would then be expected duration plus three times the SD and the lower limit would be expected duration minus three times the SD.

Process 5: Develop Schedule

PMBOK®: Page 205
Process Group: Planning

Now that you have the activity relationships (FS, FF, etc.) and durations, you can develop a project timeline with dates, identify the critical path(s) and prepare a schedule baseline for the project.

The inputs, tools and techniques and outputs are shown in Figure 6-8.

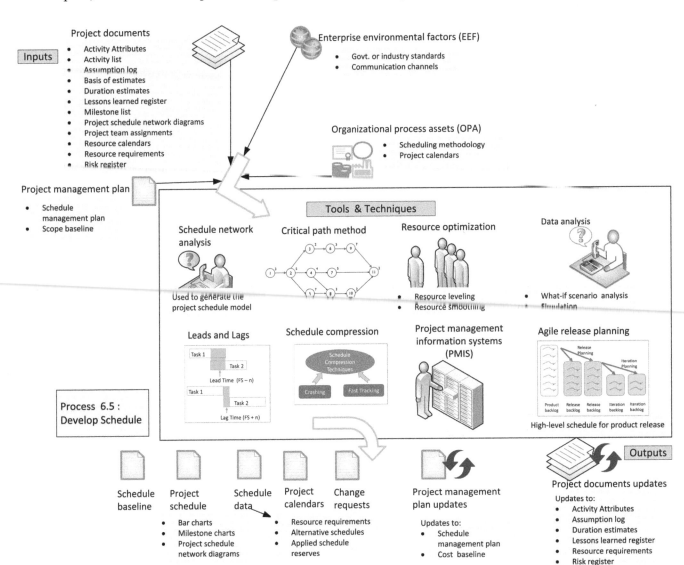

Figure 6-8: ITTO for Develop Schedule process

But first, what do you need to create a schedule (input)? You would need:

- Activity list,
- Activity attributes,
- Activation durations estimates, so you know long many days to allocate for each activity,
- Milestone list with target dates,
- Relationships (FS, FF, SS, or SF) between the activities,
- Project schedule network diagram, so you know the dependencies and activities that must be done earlier,
- Resource calendar, which tells you the availability of resources and their location, and
- Schedule management plan, which tells you about the tools and processes to use to develop the schedule.

An important technique for developing project schedule is the Critical Path Method (CPM). It is a method that provides you with:

1. Minimum duration required for the project
2. Amount of scheduling flexibility on the logical network paths
3. Early start (ES) and early finish (EF) using a forward pass and late start (LS) and late finish (LF) backward pass for all activities
4. Amount of flexibility (float or slack) that you have for each activity or each path as described in the table below.

What is a float? It is the amount of time that an activity can be delayed without delaying its successor activities (free float) or the completion date for the project (project float).

	Type of float or slack	Applies to	Description
1	Free float	Activity	This is the number of days that an activity can be delayed without delaying the early start dates for its successor activities.
2	Total float (Most common type)	Activity or path	This is the number of days that the early start date for that activity can be delayed without hurting (or delaying) the project completion date. But it can delay the start date for its successor activities.
3	Project float	Project	This is the number of days that a project can be delayed without delaying a completion date imposed by the sponsor or client or committed by the project team.

Table 6-5: Types of float (or slack)

---

* For the Exam *
What is the total float (or slack) for activities on the critical path? Zero.
But what about non-critical paths? Each of the non-critical paths will have a total float. If your project has three non-critical paths, you will have total floats for each.

The critical path is one where the sequence of activities takes the longest time to complete and therefore that is the duration required for the project. The other paths will take a shorter time than the critical path. A project will usually have one critical path. But can a project have two or more critical paths? Yes. That is rare but possible. A project can have multiple critical paths and the duration of all those will be the same. That critical path duration is the project duration.

A project will have near-critical paths. The durations of the near-critical paths are slightly less than the critical path duration. If you have changes in activity durations or dependencies, a near-critical path can become a critical path and vice-versa.

> *** For the Exam ***
> Can a critical path change while the project is in-progress? Yes. If you change activity durations or dependencies or if you crash or fast-track certain activities, the critical path(s) can change and you will have a revised schedule.

Resource optimization

Do you have enough resources for your projects? Probably not! Are your project team members working on other projects as well? Probably yes! In the real world, availability of resources is a constraint. Table 6-6 describes two techniques you can use to adjust your project schedule to accommodate the availability of resources.

Technique	Description
Resource leveling	In this technique, you **adjust the start and finish dates** of the activity, to work around the non-availability of one or more resources. This can end up increasing the durations of activities and of the critical path.
Resource smoothing	In this technique, you **adjust the activities** such that you do not take up too much time from a resource (who is in high demand). You can move the dates for an activity but only within their free and total float. The completion dates of the activities are not delayed and the critical path does not change. Because of all these limitations, resource smoothing is not able to optimize all resources.

Table 6-6: Techniques to accommodate resource availability and conflicts

Schedule compression

Have you been asked to finish a project sooner than planned? And without any reduction in scope! What would be your answer? As a project manager, you should first say "It should be possible, but I need to evaluate how to make it happen and its impact on cost, resources and risks". Later once you have analyzed, you can say "We can reduce the schedule, but it will cost $12,000 more and I will need three more resources!"

Table 6-7 describes two techniques you can use to reduce your project timelines.

Technique	Description
Crashing	You try to reduce the activity time by adding more resources, expedited shipping and travel, working overtime, etc. This increases cost and risks and reduces quality. Why would crashing increase cost, when you are completing the activity in fewer days? Crashing costs higher because the man-hours used are not reduced. Now, instead of paying at standard wage rates for those man-hours, you could be paying overtime rates. If you need equipment, you could be paying extra to expedite delivery of the equipment. How do you select an activity to crash? First, you identify activities in the critical path. Reducing their time would help reduce the project duration. Out of those you select the activity where the 'extra spent per day' ratio (as denoted below) is the least. $$ExtraSpentPerDay = \frac{\text{Delta Dollars (additional spending for the activity)}}{\text{Delta Days (number of days reduced for the activity)}}$$ You should select activities where the additional expense per day is the least.
Fast tracking	Fast tracking is executing activities in parallel even if the activities were earlier planned to be done in sequence. If you fast track activities that are on the critical path, it will help you reduce the project duration. What are the effects of forcing those activities in parallel? ▪ You increase risks ▪ You may have poor quality ▪ You may be forced to do rework ▪ You need to communicate about why you have changed the project schedule to fast track mode. This technique works only if you can find activities, within your schedule, which can be fully or partially overlapped (done in parallel). An example would be that the software architecture is only half-completed but you start coding anyway. Later while the code is only half-developed, you start testing the code. This helps you complete the work quicker but reduces quality and may later require rework to fix bugs.

Table 6-7: Techniques to compress schedule

Does it help you to crash or fast track activities that are outside the critical path? Usually no! The longest path is the critical path. Reducing that will help reduce project duration! But if you reduce the critical path too much, another non-critical path may turn into a critical path and you, therefore, need to start shortening the new critical path.

An example of crashing is shown in Figure 6-9. Activity A can be crashed from 8 days to 5 days, but the 3 days of savings costs an extra $400 ($1,200 - $800). Thus, the additional expense is $133.33 per day ($400/3 days).

Alternatively, you can crash activity B from 20 days to 8 days. This savings of 12 days comes at an additional expense of $800 ($2,000 -$1,200) which makes the additional per day expense to be $66.66 ($800/12 days). The additional expense per day is less when crashing Activity B. Therefore crashing Activity B is a better choice than crashing Activity A.

Before crashing activity A: 8 days

Activity A: 8 days

Cost for 8 days = $800

Additional cost per reduced day=(Delta $)/(Delta days) = $400 /3 days =$133.33/day

After crashing activity A: 5 days

➡️ | Activity A: 5 days | ⬅️

Cost for 5 days = $1,200

Before crashing activity B: 20 days

Activity B: 20 days

Cost for 20 days = $1,200

Additional cost per reduced day=(Delta $)/(Delta days) = $800 /12 days =$66.66/day

After crashing activity B: 8 days

➡️ | Activity B: 8 days | ⬅️

Cost for 8 days = $2,000

Question: Which activity (A or B) is less expensive when crashed?
Answer: Activity B.
Why? Because the extra dollars spent, for each day of reduced duration, is lower for activity B ($66.66) than for A ($133.33).

Figure 6-9: Example of crashing an activity

EXERCISE TIME 3:

The table below has the normal and crash durations for activities A to F and associated costs.
Identify the activity that you should crash given the normal cost and number of days in the table.

Activity	Duration for Normal work	Duration if crashed	Days saved	Total cost for normal work	Total cost if crashed	Total extra expense if crashed	(Extra expense) / (days saved)
A	12 days	10 days	2	$10,000	$15,000	$5,000	$2,500
B	10 days	6 days	4	$12,000	$20,500	$8,500	$2,125
C	8 days	6 days	2	$10,000	$14,000	$4,000	$2,000
D	12 days	10 days	2	$20,000	$25,000	$5,000	$2,500
E	14 days	11 days	3	$10,000	$ 16,000	$6,000	$2,000
F	8 days	7 days	1	$10,000	$12,000	$2,000	$2,000

Question 1: You need to reduce the schedule by 4 days. Which activities should you select to crash? Assume that the all the 6 activities must be done in sequence.
A. Crash Activity B
B. Crash Activity A and C
C. Crash Activity A and D
D. Crash Activity E and F

Question 2: You need to reduce the project duration by 2 days. What is the least additional expense that you will need to pay?
A. $4,500
B. $5,000
C. $3,000
D. $4,000

Solution 1: You need to crash the activities where you will incur the least additional expense.
Note that each of the choices provides a savings of 4 day. You need to estimate the additional expenses:
A. Crash Activity B -- additional expense is $8,500
B. Crash Activity A and C -- additional expense is $5,000 + $4,000 = $9,000
C. Crash Activity A and D -- additional expense is $5,000 + $5,000 = $10,000
D. Crash Activity E and F -- additional expense is $6,000 + $2,000 = $8,000

The least additional expense is $8,000 for choice D. Hence the correct answer is choice D (crash activities E and F).

Solution 2: Out of all the listed activities, you can crash any by 2 days except for activity F (which you can crash by 1 day only). For Activities A to E, the least additional expense per day of crashing is for Activity C as well as for Activity E, which is $2,000 per day of crashing. It adds to $4,000 for 2 days of crashing. The correct answer is therefore, $4,000 or choice D.

When you have the option of crashing two or more activities, it is a good practice to select the activity that occurs earlier, because in case you encounter unexpected issues you still have the opportunity to crash the later activities.

Figure 6-10 is an example of fast tracking. A series of activities that would normally take 20 days is rescheduled to run in parallel. This reduces the total work duration to 12 days and is possible if the activities have discretionary dependencies.

Before fast tracking, project duration =20 days

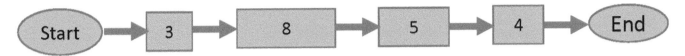

After fast tracking, project duration =12 days

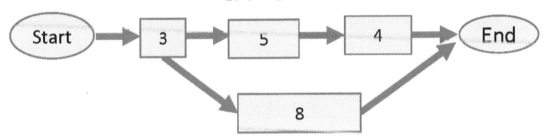

Figure 6-10: Example of fast tracking a schedule

Here is another question on fast tracking, illustrated in Figure 6-10.

EXERCISE TIME 4:

Question:
If all the 4 activities in Figure 6-10 are fast tracked, what will be the project duration?
- A. 3 days
- B. 7 days
- C. 8 days
- D. 9 days

Solution:
Fast tracking all activities means that all are done in parallel. The project duration will then be the duration of the longest activity, which is 8 days. Hence the correct answer is C.

Now that we know how to fast track a schedule and crash an activity, let us see how you can develop a schedule. We will talk about the Critical Path Method (CPM). There are other methods described in the PMBOK, that you should also know. You will certainly have a few questions related to CPM in the exam.

Figure 6-11 shows the keys required to develop a schedule using critical path method (CPM).

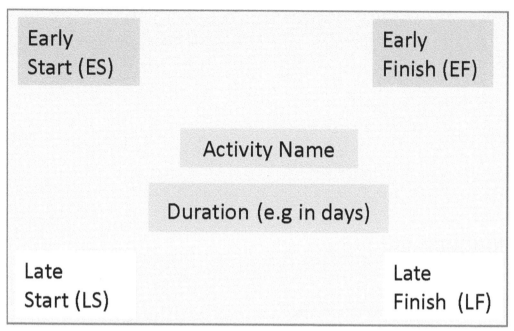

Figure 6-11: Keys for an activity node

Table 6-8 has the steps to develop a schedule using critical path method (CPM).

Step	What you do
Step 1	Note the dependencies and draw the network diagram with activity names and durations.

Step 2	Do the forward pass and write the ES and EF for all activities. Write ES=0 for the first activity and EF=duration. In the PMBOK you will see the ES=1 for the 1st activity. That procedure is also correct as well and you can do so if you want, but the calculations will be different. However, the end results such as the critical path, project duration, floats, etc. will be the same.
	
	For all subsequent activities:
	  ▪ ES is the highest of EF values amongst all its preceding activities
	  ▪ EF = ES + duration

Step 3	Now try and identify the critical (longest) path. For simple network diagrams and most problems for the PMP exam, you should be able to (But if you cannot, that is ok! Go to Step 4.). For all activities on the critical path, write LS and LF, where LS=ES and LF=EF.
Step 4	Now do a backward pass, and write the LF and LS for all remaining paths

Step 5	Calculate the **total and free float** for each activity:
	  ▪ For activities on the critical path, both are zero
	  ▪ For activities on the non-critical path:
	    o Total float = LS – ES (which is same as LF - EF)
	    o Free Float = ES of its successor – EF of current activity.
	If there are multiple successor activities and hence multiple free floats, take the least value.

Table 6-8: Steps to develop a schedule using the Critical Path Method (CPM)

* For the Exam *
If the question says just 'float' assume total float.

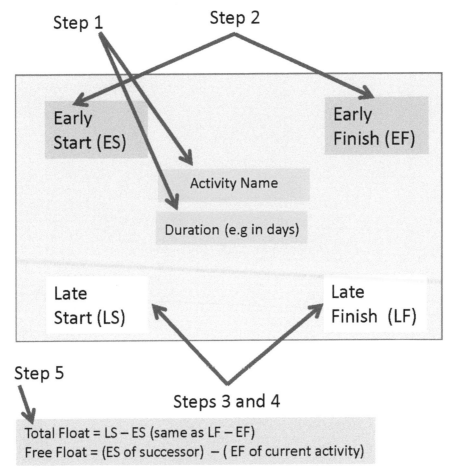

Figure 6-12: What to fill in each step to develop a project schedule using CPM?

Table 6-8 is an illustration of the five steps to develop a schedule. The work in step 3 can be done in step 4 for complex schedules.

Step	What you do	Example
Step 1	You could be given a precedence table in the exam and asked to develop a network diagram and estimate the floats. Review the activity description in the table to the right and construct the activity sequence. Write the activity names and durations (days, weeks, etc.).	<table><tr><td>**Activity**</td><td>**Predecessor**</td><td>**Duration (days)**</td></tr><tr><td>A</td><td>--</td><td>10</td></tr><tr><td>B</td><td>A</td><td>20</td></tr><tr><td>C</td><td>B</td><td>15</td></tr><tr><td>D</td><td>A</td><td>80</td></tr><tr><td>E</td><td>C,D</td><td>10</td></tr></table>

Step 2	Do the 'forward pass'. For the first activity, A: ▪ ES=0 ▪ EF=Duration= 10 days But for all subsequent activities: ▪ ES is the highest of EF values amongst all its preceding activities ▪ EF = ES + duration It is called forward pass because you start with the first activity and move to the last. You calculate the ES and add the duration to get EF. For B, ES is the EF of A, which is10. The EF of AB = 10 + duration of 20 = 30. But for activity E, you have two predecessors namely C and D. Their EF are 45 and 90 days. Before you can start E, you need to wait for both C and D to complete. Hence the ES for E=90 and EF=90+10=100.	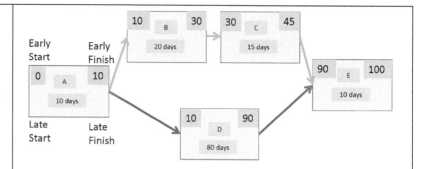 **Note:** • Early Start (ES) = Highest EF value of all its preceding activities • Early Finish (EF) = ES + its duration **Process for 'forward pass':** 1. Start with the first activity, ES=0 and EF = duration 2. Work forward to the last activity 3. For each activity, first calculate the ES, which is the highest of the EF values for all its predecessors 4. Then compute the EF, which is ES + duration
Step 3	Identify the critical path (path with the longest duration). In this case, it is path A –D- E. The LF and LS for the activities in the critical path will be the same as its EF and ES values, respectively.	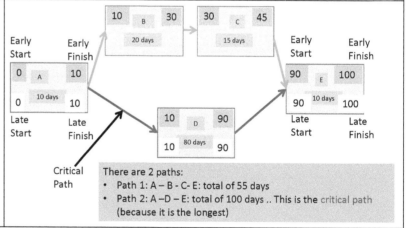 There are 2 paths: • Path 1: A – B - C- E: total of 55 days • Path 2: A –D – E: total of 100 days .. This is the critical path (because it is the longest)

Step 4	Do a 'backward pass', and write the LF and LS for all remaining paths. It is called 'backward pass' because you start from the LF of the last activity and work back. You first calculate the LF and then subtract duration to get LS. For the last activity, E: • LF = EF = 100 • LS=100- duration =90 For all other activities: • LF = least LS value for all its successors • LS–LF- duration For example, for activity C, LF=LS of E =90 and LS =90-15 = 75 For activity A, there are 2 predecessors namely B and D and the LS values are 55 and 10. The least is 10 and that is the LF for A. LS for A=10 – 10=0.	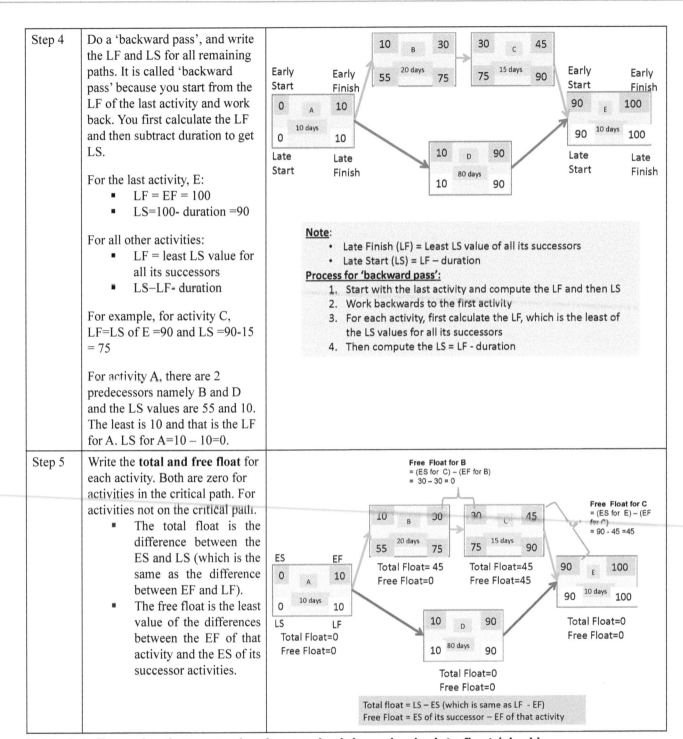
Step 5	Write the **total and free float** for each activity. Both are zero for activities in the critical path. For activities not on the critical path. • The total float is the difference between the ES and LS (which is the same as the difference between EF and LF). • The free float is the least value of the differences between the EF of that activity and the ES of its successor activities.	

Table 6-8: Example of steps to develop a schedule and calculate float (slack)

EXERCISE TIME 5:

Question:

The table below has a sequence of activities. Compute the duration of the critical path and free and total float for all the activities.

Activity	Predecessors	Duration (days)
A	- -	15
B	A	15
C	A	30
D	B, C	45

Solution:

First develop a schedule diagram and do a forward pass

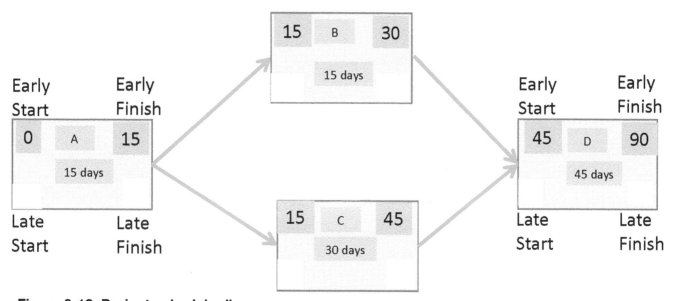

Figure 6-13: Project schedule diagram

Identify the critical path. The **critical path is A – C- D** which adds to 15 + 30 + 45 = 90 days. For the critical path, LS = ES and LF=EF. Also, free float (FF) and total float (TF) are both zero.

Then start with the last activity, D.

Do a backward pass for the non-critical path, which is A –B –D.

For Activity B, the LF is the same as "LS of its successor activity D", which is 45 days.

The LS for Activity B = 45 days minus its duration = 45 – 15 = 30 days.

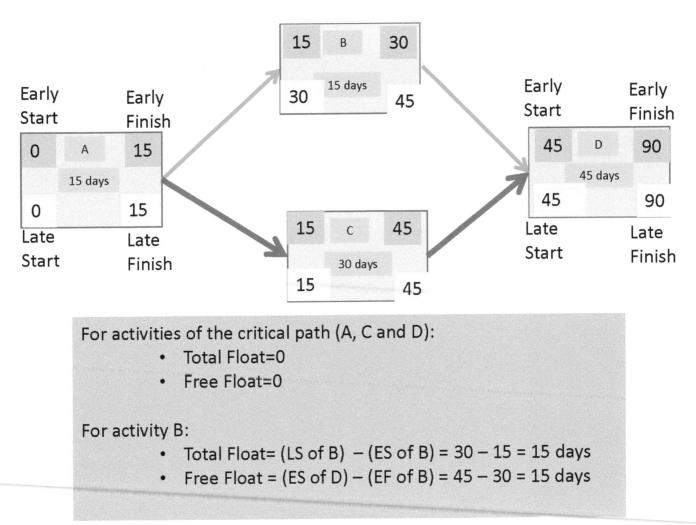

For activities of the critical path (A, C and D):
- Total Float=0
- Free Float=0

For activity B:
- Total Float= (LS of B) − (ES of B) = 30 − 15 = 15 days
- Free Float = (ES of D) − (EF of B) = 45 − 30 = 15 days

Figure 6-14: Project schedule diagram with critical path A-C-D and activity floats

Here is another question on selecting an activity to crash.

EXERCISE TIME 6:

Question:
You tell the sponsor that the project will take 90 working days. They think it is too long! They want you to crash the activities to 80 days, while keeping the additional expenses as low as possible! Assuming the cost in the table below, which activity would you crash?

Activity	Normal Cost ($)	Normal Duration (days)	Cost if crashed ($)	Duration if crashed (days)
A	$15,000	15	$25,000	10
B	$15,000	15	$25,000	10
C	$20,000	30	$40,000	20
D	$40,000	45	$80,000	35

Solution:
You know that the critical path is A-C-D. You need to compress one of these three activities by 10 days. You need to estimate the additional expense incurred per reduced day for A, C and D. Then select the activity that has the least additional expense.

The calculations are highlighted in the table below.

Activity	Normal Cost ($)	Normal Duration (days)	Cost if crashed ($)	Duration if crashed (days)	Total additional expense	Total reduced days	Additional expense per reduced day
A	$15,000	15	$25,000	10	$10,000	5	$2,000
B	$15,000	15	$25,000	10	There is no need to crash Activity B because it is not in the critical path.		
C	$20,000	30	$40,000	20	$20,000	10	$2,000
D	$40,000	45	$80,000	35	$40,000	10	$4,000

As you can see, the additional expense will be $2,000 for each day that you compress activities A or C. They are both on the critical path and the additional expenses are least for both. But now, which should you select? Activity A or C?

As you can see, there are two ways to get a reduction of 10 days:

Option 1: You can crash Activity A for 5 days (which costs $10,000) and then crash Activity B by 5 days (which also costs $10,000). Hence it costs $20,000 to crash by 10 days.

Option 2: You can crash only Activity C by 10 days which would cost the same ($20,000).

The best answer is Option 1. As a rule of thumb, you should crash activities that are earlier in the schedule, if the cost is not higher. This provides you the opportunity to crash downstream activities, in case, you encounter problems.

Process 6: Control Schedule

PMBOK®: Page 222
Process Group: Monitoring and Controlling

In this process, you monitor the status of various activities and manage changes that are needed for the schedule baseline (if any). It also helps you identify deviations from the schedule baseline and take up preventive and corrective actions to bring the schedule back on track.

The inputs, tools and techniques and outputs are shown in Figure 6-15.

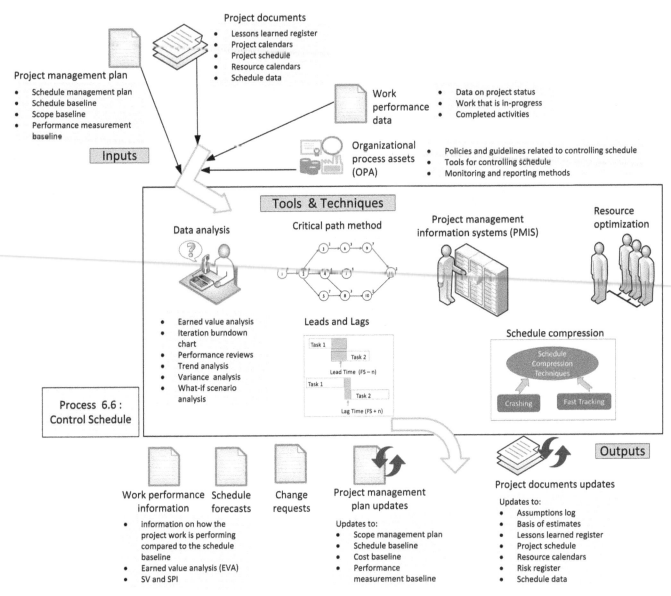

Figure 6-15: ITTO for Control Schedule process

But how do you control the schedule for your projects? There are two steps:

1. First, you measure the progress made so far and compare that to the plan. Are you on track to complete the project by its end-date? If not, you need to take up corrective actions, which is the second step. For this, you can use:
   - Trend Analysis helps you analyze the past performance and see if the performance has been improving or deteriorating. It also helps compare actual to-date performance to performance that is needed in the future to meet completion dates.
   - You need to pay attention to the critical path. Any slippage or delay in the critical path will impact the project end-date. Before it is too late, you need to identify risks and existing issues and develop a plan to mitigate the issues.
   - You can use earned value management (EVM) formulas to estimate schedule variance (SV) and schedule performance index (SPI). This will show whether the actual work completed so far is as ahead or below what was planned to complete by now. This will help you decide if you need corrective or preventive actions.

2. The second step, as mentioned earlier, is to take up corrective actions to bring the schedule back on track.
   - You adjust activities based on resource availability for different activities.
   - You can hasten the progress by fast-tracking and crashing the schedule
   - You can also change the schedule baseline. At the beginning of the project, you have created the most realistic schedule, obtained approvals and created a baseline. But as the project progresses the assumptions and conditions change. The realities are now different than they were at the beginning of the project. Is it okay to change the baseline? Yes. But this needs a change request and approvals as described in the **Perform Integrated Change Control** process. This is an important process for changes to any baseline (cost, scope or schedule).

What are the key outputs of the **Control Schedule** process? Those are:

- Work performance information, for example by using variance analysis (to estimate PV and EV) or earned value analysis (to estimate SV and SPI) for the work completed so far,
- New forecasts for the schedule using trend analysis,
- Change requests, and
- Updates to various project documents such as the baselines (for cost, schedule and scope), schedule management plan, project schedule, resource calendars, etc.

More points for the exam:

- Having a realistic schedule and milestone dates are responsibilities of a project manager.
- If there are delays, the ideal mitigation is to adjust future activities (by crashing or fast tracking) rather than creating a change request to ask for additional time.
- The duration for a milestone is zero.
- A critical path is the path with the longest duration. It is also the project duration.
- A project can have multiple critical paths.
- To reduce project duration, you need to reduce durations of activities on the critical path.

Practice Questions for Chapter 6

1. Which one of the following processes, has activity list and attributes as outputs?
   A. Define Activities
   B. Define Scope
   C. Develop Schedule
   D. Create WBS

2. Donald Dylan is determining relationships between activities using the precedence diagramming method (PDM) for his project to relocate employees to a new office building. Which of the following dependencies or relationships is usually uncommon between activities?
   A. Finish-to-start (FS)
   B. Finish-to-finish (FF)
   C. Start-to-start (SS)
   D. Start-to-finish (SF)

3. Brian Bistro is a project manager for an oil and gas exploration and production (E&P) firm. He is preparing a project schedule using critical path method (CPM) to determine the flexibility. He has an activity with an early start (ES) of 15 days and a late start (LS) of 28 days. What is the total float for that activity?
   A. 28 days
   B. 13 days
   C. 43 days
   D. There is not enough information to compute total float

4. Which of the following processes has milestone list as an output?
   A. Plan Schedule Management
   B. Define Activities
   C. Sequence Activities
   D. Develop Schedule

5. Rosy Rosales is a project manager for a pharmaceutical research and manufacturing firm. She has developed a list of activities and a schedule network diagram. She also has the duration of each of the activities from her project team. What should she do next?
   A. Sequence the activities using the precedence diagramming method (PDM)
   B. Compute leads and lags for the activities
   C. Use a technique such as critical path method (CPM) to develop a project schedule and schedule baseline.
   D. Develop a list of activity attributes

6. Jerry Johnson is a project manager and has completed a schedule network diagram using precedence diagramming method (PDM), Which process has Jerry just completed?
   A. Define Activities
   B. Sequence Activities

C. Plan Schedule Management

D. Develop Schedule

7. You are working on an urgent project which must be completed within four weeks. There are several short tasks, which can be done in parallel. You develop a project schedule and find that you have three critical paths. What does that signify and what should you do?

A. You may have to use management reserves for additional resources to cover schedules slippages, if any, in the critical paths.

B. You should pad more time in the schedule, especially along the three critical paths.

C. You should consult with the project sponsor and client and let them know that you need more resources to add float into the critical paths.

D. The risk to the project schedule is higher due to the three critical paths.

8. William Dixson is developing a project schedule. The work environment is fast-paced and the product requirements are not completely firmed up. The project sponsor tells William that once the work starts there would be more changes to product requirements and scope. William needs to use an adaptive approach to develop the project plans. Which of the following should William not do?

A. Use short time-windows to schedule and undertake work

B. Frequently review the results and adapt the product requirements and scope as needed.

C. Pull work from a backlog or intermediate queue of work for immediate execution as resources become available

D. He can assume that the overall project duration that was initially determined, will not change, despite minor variations in the schedule.

9. You are sequencing the project activities and determining activity dependencies, leads and lags. What is the key output of this process?

A. Project schedule network diagrams

B. Schedule baseline

C. Project schedule

D. Activity list

10. You are developing a list of activities and activity attributes. Which of the following is not an activity attribute?

A. Skills and equipment required to do the work.

B. Successors and predecessors for each activity.

C. Date and time when each activity will start and end.

D. Activity constraints and assumptions.

11. Tim Dickenson is a new project manager. He is being asked, by the operations team, to add features to an existing product. He starts preparing an activity list and activity attributes for adding the new features. Who can he work with for this?

A. Project sponsor.

B. Operations team members who will later support the product.

C. Project team members who had earlier helped develop the WBS.

D. Project management office (PMO).

12. Alex Andersen is developing a sequence of activities for his new project to repair sections of the interstate highway between Kansas City and Denver. Ordering materials must start 3 weeks before selecting service vendors is completed. Which of the following represent this scenario?
    A. Finish-Start + 3 weeks
    B. Finish-Start – 3 weeks
    C. Start-Finish + 3 weeks
    D. Start-Finish – 3 weeks

13. You are constructing a schedule network diagram in which activities are represented by nodes and are graphically linked by one or more relationships to show the sequence in which they must be performed. What is this technique called?
    A. Arrow diagramming method (ADM)
    B. Activity-on-arrow (AOA)
    C. Critical path method (CPM)
    D. Precedence diagramming method (PDM)

14. Which of the following is not true for resource leveling?
    A. It adjusts the start and finish dates of activities to align with the availability of resources.
    B. It is used when there is a need to keep resource utilization within a certain limit.
    C. It is used when the availability of certain resources is limited.
    D. It does not lead to changes in the critical path.

15. Peter Perkins has prepared a network diagram (shown below) for the activities in his project to rollout a new ERP application for all the international offices within his company. What is the total project duration?

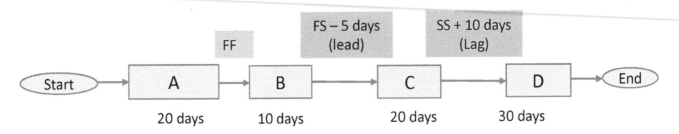

    A. 80 days
    B. 85 days
    C. 45 days
    D. 55 days

16. Which of the following is true about negative float analysis?
    A. It can be used to find possible ways to bring a delayed schedule back on track.
    B. It can be used to improve quality as well as reduce expenses.
    C. It is more applicable for agile methodology rather than predictive or waterfall methodology.
    D. It can be used in conjunction with resource smoothing to make sure that the project resources are evenly distributed.

17. You have installed a new 30-feet fence. You have estimated from a previous, similar activity that it takes a team of two painters about 2 hours to paint 5 linear feet of a fence. How many hours will it take the team to paint the new fence?
    A. 30 hours
    B. 15 hours
    C. 10 hours
    D. 12 hours

18. You are managing a software application development project with a new test team in Hungary while the software development team is in Canada. The testing of the modules can start only after some of the modules are developed and integrated but there is no need for all modules to be developed. What is the dependency between module development and testing?
    A. Mandatory dependency
    B. External dependency
    C. Internal dependency
    D. Development dependency

ANSWERS

Question Number	Correct Answer	Explanation
1	A	A list of activities and their attributes (such as skill required to do the work, dependencies, leads, lags, constraints, etc.) are developed and recorded during the **Define Activities** process.
2	D	SF (start-to-finish) relationship is rarely used. An example of SF is that Activity A (functioning and operations in the new office) must start before activity B (demolition of old office) finishes. See Page 190 of the PMBOK® Guide. Note that FS (finish-to-start) is the most common relationship.
3	B	Total (or activity) float is LS − ES (which is the same as LF − EF). In this case total float = LS − ES = 28 − 15 = 13 days.
4	B	The answer is **Define Activities** process, where you identify activities which are used to prepare a milestone list. The milestone list consists of significant events such as completion of key deliverables.
5	C	Rosy Rosales has already made a schedule network diagram. That tells us that she has completed the **Sequence Activities** process. She also has activity durations. The next process is the **Develop Schedule** process, whose output is a project schedule and a schedule baseline.
6	B	Schedule network diagram is an output of the **Sequence Activities** process. Another hint is that PDM is a tool or technique in the **Sequence Activities** process.
7	D	The risk of schedule slippage is high. A delay in any of the three critical paths will increase the overall project duration! You need to record the schedule-related risks and develop mitigation plans.
8	D	He cannot assume that the project duration will not change. In an adaptive life cycle, the project duration is difficult to determine at the beginning of the project. Once work starts, changes in scope and requirements, will impact the duration of activities, schedule and the overall project.
9	A	You are in the **Sequence Activities** process, where you identify and document relationships (dependencies) among the activities. The key output is a project schedule network diagram, which is a graphical representation of the activity relationships, as shown on Page 193 of the PMBOK®.
10	C	The time when each activity will be done is not an activity attribute. Determining activity start and end dates is part of developing a project schedule, which is done during the **Develop Schedule** process.
11	C	Tim needs to work with the project team. They know what needs to be done to meet the new requirements.
12	B	This is a finish-to-start relationship with a lead of three weeks. Leads are represented by a negative value. Selecting service vendors is the predecessor activity. The successor activity (ordering materials) must start 3 weeks before completion of predecessor. The relationship is finish-start − 3 weeks.

13	D	The correct answer is PDM. - Precedence diagramming method (PDM) is a technique where you use nodes to show activities and arrows to represent dependencies. It is also called activity on nodes (AON). - Arrow diagramming method (ADM) is the reverse, where arrows are used to represent activities and nodes are used to show dependencies. Therefore, this technique is also called activity-on-arrow method (AOA). - CPM is a method to estimate the minimum project duration, critical path and the float (schedule flexibility) on the network paths.
14	D	Resource leveling can lead to changes in the critical path since the activity dates are modified to accommodate the availability of resources. Example: Suppose Activity A on the critical path needs Tom for 16 hours. You would think Activity A can be done in 2 days (at 8 hours per day). But if Tom is available for only 2 hours per day, Activity A will now take 8 days to complete. You now need to change the start and finish dates to accommodate a 8-day duration for Activity A.
15	D	If all activities would have FS relationship, the project duration would then be 20 + 10 + 20 + 30 = 80 days. But we need to subtract time because of overlaps caused by the leads and lags (or add the days if the activities are distanced away). - For FF relationship, between A and B, note that both activities finish at the same time. That means B starts 10 days after A starts. We need to subtract 10 days from the total of 80 days since A and B overlap. - For FS-5 between B and C, C starts 5 days before B finishes. There is an overlap of 5 days. We need to subtract 5 days from 80 days - For SS+10 between C and D, D starts 10 days after C starts. The duration of C is 20 days and hence there is a 10-day overlap. We need to subtract 10 days from 80. The total duration, therefore, is 80 − 10 − 5 −10 = 55 days.
16	A	Negative float analysis is a technique to find efficient ways to bring a delayed schedule back on track. See Page 210 of the PMBOK®.
17	D	It takes 2 hours to paint 5 feet. Hence it will take 12 hours to paint 30 feet. That is an example of parametric estimation technique.
18	A	Notice the keywords 'only after', which implies that this is the only option. Hence it is a mandatory dependency.

CHAPTER 7
Cost Management

Are you involved in making initial budgets for your projects? Are you involved in getting fund approvals? Do you have experience in tracking planned versus incurred expenses? Are you required to do an earned value analysis (EVA) for your projects?

Some prior experience in cost management will help you understand the concepts in this chapter.

Even if you do cost analysis for your projects, you may not be using all the parameters to track the cost health of a project. You may not be conversant with the various EVA formulas that you need for the PMP exam. Expect to see about 10% of the exam questions on cost management. You must understand the concepts in this chapter and its use in projects.

There are 4 processes in the **Cost Management** Knowledge Area:

Planning Process Group	Monitoring and Controlling Process Group
7.1) Plan Cost Management 7.2) Estimate Costs 7.3) Determine Budget	7.4) Control Costs

Here are a few terms that you will see in the exam.

	Terms	Definition	Examples
1	Opportunity cost	When you have two or more (mutually exclusive) alternatives and you can choose only one, there is a loss from not having taken up the next best alternative. That loss is the opportunity cost.	▪ Those with a fulltime job who take up evening or weekend classes, do so because they cannot afford the loss (or opportunity cost) of a salary. ▪ On the other hand, for those who move from a full-time job to being a full-time student, the opportunity cost (loss) = tuition fees to be paid + missed salary.

2	Lifecycle costing	Sum of all expected one-time and recurring expenses over the lifetime of a particular service or product.	You are the project manager responsible for the setup and go-live of a new factory to assemble cars. There are 3 components to the lifecycle cost: 1. The one-time cost for buying machinery and setting up the factory. 2. The recurring expenses of **operations** and maintenance (O&M) of the factory 3. Later if you must close the factory, you will have to start another project to shut down and remove all the equipment.
3	Depreciation	Accounting method used to allocate the cost of a tangible asset over its useful life. It is done to show the reduction in the value of an asset with the passage of time.	You have set up a new IT server farm and storage with a capital purchase of $30,000. Accounting department depreciates the asset over three years using straight-line depreciation. They will take $10,000 each year for 3 years. At the end of 3 years, the hardware is 'fully depreciated'.
4	Benefit-Cost ratio (BCR)	This is the ratio of the benefits of a project (or product or proposal) relative to the costs required for its setup and maintenance.	▪ A project has a cost of $1.5M and benefits add up to $2.5M. The benefit cost-ratio is 2.5/1.5=1.67. ▪ Projects with BCR>1.0 are profitable and with BCR<1 are bad investments. ▪ For the exam, if you need to select between projects with stated BCR, select the project with the highest BCR.
5	Present Value (PV)	It is also known as present discounted value. It is the value of a future amount (income or expense) that has been discounted to today's value.	Let us say that you are supposed to receive $1,000 one year from now. But what is that worth today? In other words, what is the PV of that $1,000? Assume an interest rate of 10%. PV== $1000/(1 +0.1) = $909.09.
6	Net Present Value (NPV)	NPV for a project is the PV of all benefits (incoming cash flow) minus the PV of all expenses (cash outflows) over a period. Projects that have a positive NPV are suitable for investment. Projects that have zero or negative NPV should be avoided.	Step 1: you identify the amount of all cash inflows (income) and cash outflows (expenses) and when they occur Step 2: You compute the PV of all the inflows and outflows using a standard interest rate (for example 5%) Step 3: NPV = (sum of PV of all cash inflows or income) – (sum of PV of all cash outflows or expenses)
7	Internal rate of rerun (IRR)	It is the interest rate at which the net present value (PV of incoming cash flow or profits minus PV of all outgoing cash flows or expenses) is zero over a period of time. The higher the IRR, the more profitable is the project.	You must select between three projects, A, B and C which have an IRR of 15%, minus 30% and 20% respectively. Which is the best selection for execution? Answer: Project C, since the IRR is highest for Project C.

| 8 | Discounted Cash Flow (DCF) | It is a cash flow summary (of income or expenses) where the amount has been changed to reflect the time value of money.

DCF is a process to calculate the PV of a project or investments future cash flows (income and expenses) in order to arrive at today's fair value for the project or investment.

The adjustment is done using a standard or preset interest rate. | NPV is part of and used to estimate DCF.

$DCF = CF_1/(1+r)^1 + CF_2/(1+r)^2 + CF_3/(1+r)^3 ...+ CF_n/(1+r)^n$

Where:
CF_1 = cash flow in period 1
CF_2 = cash flow in period 2
CF_3 = cash flow in period 3
CF_n = cash flow in period n
and
r = discount rate (or required rate of return) |
| 9 | Law of Diminishing returns | If you continue to add more resources, after a certain point, the benefit per resource will start reducing. | If you have an optimal team size working to develop code for an application, but you nevertheless go ahead and triple the number of people, the amount of work done per person will reduce. |

Table 7-1: Terms for Cost Management Knowledge Area

Trends and Emerging Practices

Traditionally earned value analysis (EVA) was used to estimate variances for cost and schedule. In EVA, schedule variance (SV) and schedule performance index (SPI) uses earned value (EV) and planned value (PV).

The new trend is to use earned schedule theory. In this theory, schedule variance (SV) and schedule performance index (SPI) does not use EV and PV. Instead, SV and SPI use earned schedule (ES) and actual time (AT). Table 7-2 has formulas for SV and SPI for both EVA and schedule theory.

	Variance parameter	Earned value analysis (EVA)	Earned schedule (ES) theory	Explanation
1	Schedule variance (SV)	Earned value – Planned value (EV – PV)	Earned schedule – actual time (ES – AT)	This indicates whether the project is behind or ahead of the planned schedule. If ES – AT is: • 0: indicates that the schedule is on track • Positive: indicates that the project is ahead of schedule • Negative: indicates that the project is behind what was previously planned or scheduled
2	Schedule performance index (SPI)	EV/PV	ES / AT	This indicates the efficiency with which the project is being executed. If ES/AT is: • 1: indicates that the actual efficiency has been the same as earlier planned (or baselined). • More than 1: indicates that the actual efficiency of the work is better than planned • Less than 1: indicates the actual efficiency is less than what was planned

Table 7-2: Formulas for SV and SPI for EVA and Earned Schedule Theory

Tailoring Considerations

There are four processes in the **Cost Management** Knowledge Area. The project manager needs to decide the relevance of the four processes for the project.

Tailoring and customization depend on policies related to cost, use of EVA to monitor the project progress, governance policies required by the organization, use of agile or waterfall methodologies and its impact on cost management processes.

Considerations for Agile/Adaptive Environments

Certain projects undergo a lot of changes in their requirements and scope. Such variations complicate the estimation of cost variances and performance indices. Projects with changing requirements and scope are ideally managed by agile or adaptive methodologies.

In such cases, detailed cost estimations or variance analysis is not beneficial due to changing requirements. It is best to do a high-level calculation of variances, actual and expected expenses (operating and capital), estimate at completion (EAC), etc. with the available data. Later the calculations are refined as more information and clarity emerges.

Process 1: Plan Cost Management

> PMBOK®: Page 235
> Process Group: Planning

In this process, you will develop and document the methods to establish the budget and monitor project expenditures. It also contains procedures to control the project costs and bring the expenses back on track, in case there are cost over-runs.

The decisions made in this process support the cost-related activities throughout the project life.

A key input is the project charter because it has the project scope, budget estimates, timelines, etc. It helps with identifying stakeholders for approvals of the initial budget and its revisions.

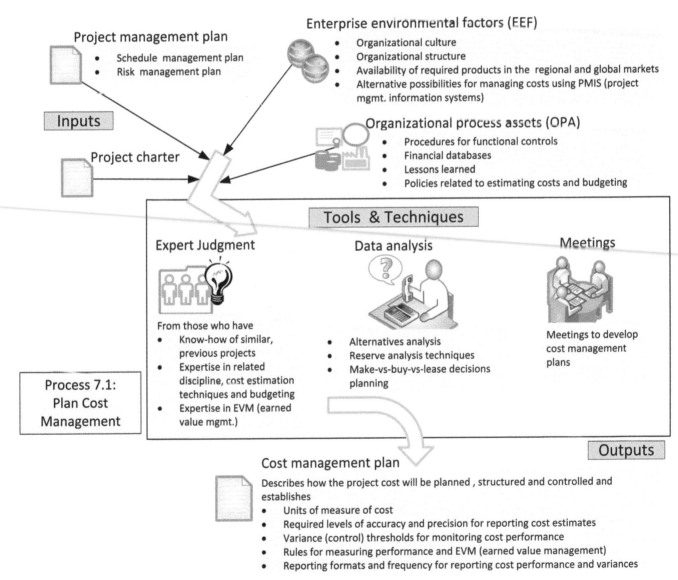

Figure 7-1: ITTO for Plan Cost Management process

The key output of this process is the cost management plan (also called budget plan). It has the policies and procedures related to:

- cost estimation,
- expenses reporting mechanisms such as report format, frequency, target audience, rounding expense figures, number of decimal places, etc.,
- range of accuracy (for example 10% or 5%) for the cost estimates,
- indirect (overhead) costs that are shared by various projects,
- direct (fixed and variable) costs,
- parameters of earned value analysis (EVA) to be included in the project reports, and
- thresholds (for cost variances, cost performance indices, etc.) required to initiate change requests and corrective actions.

Process 2: Estimate Costs

PMBOK®: Page 240
Process Group: Planning

In this process, you estimate the cost of each activity, which is in the next process, **Determine Budget**.

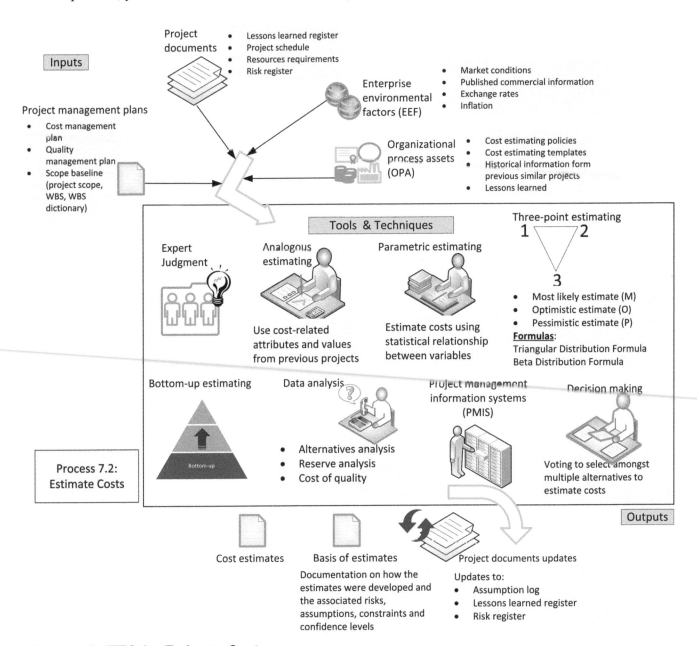

Figure 7-2: ITTO for Estimate Costs process

Table 7-3 shows the tools and techniques used to estimate costs for various activities.

	Name of the tool or technique to estimate costs	Description
1	Expert Judgment	Identify internal or external experts, who have experience in similar activities and get them to provide an estimate.
2	Analogous estimation (also called top-down estimate)	This is quick and cheap, but not very accurate. Here you or your project team uses (a) historical information from previous projects, (b) data from expert judgment and (c) values such as scope and activity duration, complexity etc. to come up with the cost of each activity. This is called top-down because you look at the activity, work package or the entire project as a whole and estimate its cost.
3	Parametric estimation	In this case, you first, identify a parameter such as square footage to be painted, or number of software modules, to be developed. Then, you get the unit cost data from previous projects or expert judgment and use the unit cost as a parameter to compute the activity or project cost.
4	Bottom-up estimation	You first break up the tasks or activities into pieces and then estimate the cost of each of the individual pieces. You then roll (or add) the individual costs to come up with the cost for each activity or work package
5	3-point Estimation	Here you come up with 3 estimates: • cO: optimistic estimate • cM: most-likely estimate • cP: pessimistic estimate You then use these three estimates to compute the average.
	You can use one of the following two formulas to estimate the average cost for the activity.	
	Triangular Distribution average	• Activity Cost = (cP + cM + cO)/3 • Also called simple, straight, 3-point or triangular average.
	Beta Distribution or PERT (Project Evaluation and Review Techniques) average	• Activity Cost = (cP + 4*cM + cO)/6 • Also called beta, PERT or weighted average.
	The formulas below compute the SD, variance and range for the estimates.	
	Standard Deviation (SD)	SD = (cP - cO)/6
	Variance	Variance = {(cP - cO)/6}^2 or square of SD
	Range	• Lower limit of the range = Average + SD • Upper limit of the range = Average - SD
6	Alternatives analysis	You identify various options and then select the most optimum option for execution.
7	Reserve analysis	You estimate the reserves (or allowances) need for risks and uncertainties that may come up later. • **Contingency reserves:** Used for known-unknowns and are part of the cost baseline. An example is risks to global projects that arise due to fluctuations in currency exchanges rates. It is known that fluctuations will happen, but the amount of fluctuation is unknown. • **Management reserves:** Used for unknown-unknowns and are not part of the cost baseline but are part of the project budget. An example is unanticipated market entry by an international retail giant that wiped out the businesses of the local store owners. Another example is an unanticipated and unseasonal rain that damaged the fresh, exterior paint of a new building.

| 8 | Cost of quality analysis | You analyze the cost for activities that would help you conform to quality requirements versus cost for not conforming and later incurring rework, warranty and product recall expenses. As far as cost is concerned, spending too much on tests and quality improvement may sometimes be unnecessary and result in low benefit-cost ratio. |

Table 7-3: Formulae related to activity costs

---

* For the Exam *

For problems on estimating averages, you must identify if you need to use triangular or BETA distribution formulas. Look for clues/guidance in the question.
- If it says simple, straight or 3-point use the triangular formula.
- If it says weighted or beta use the PERT formula.

Estimating variance and range for an activity

If you know the cP, cM and cO estimates for an activity, you can use either the triangular or BETA distribution to get the average.

There are other parameters such as variance, standard deviation and range for the estimates. These can be computed using the following formula:

- Standard Deviation (SD) for the estimates = (cP – cO)/6
- Range for the estimates = (average using Triangular or PERT formula) +/- (SD)

Standard deviation is a measure of uncertainty in the estimates or how spread-out the numbers are.

If you have 6 time estimates for Activity A, and these estimates are 10 days, 12 days, 14 days, 15 days, 16 days and 18 days. What is the variance and SD for this set of estimates?

First, compute the variance. The SD will be the square root of the variance. Use the following steps to compute the variance and SD:

1. Find the arithmetic mean or simple average of the 6 estimates (which in this case is 14.17 days)
2. For each of the 6 estimates, get the difference between the estimates and 14.33 and square the difference. You now have six squared numbers.
3. Variance = simple average of the six squared numbers.
4. Standard Deviation = square root of the variance.

EXERCISE TIME 1:

Question:

You are estimating the time needed for an architect to prepare blueprint architecture for a building. You speak with several experts and architects and ask them for an optimistic, most likely and pessimistic estimate (in man-hours). You then average those to come up with the following:

- cO = optimistic estimate = 180 man-hours
- cM = most-likely estimate = 200 man-hours
- cP = pessimistic estimate = 230 man-hours

What are the PERT average, standard deviation and range of the estimates?

Solution:

	Need to get	Formula	Calculation	Answer
1	PERT (beta or weighted) average	(cO + 4*cM + cP)/6	(180 + 4*200 +230)/6 = 1210/6 = 201.66 man-hours	201.66 man-hours
2	Standard Deviation (SD)	(cP – cO)/6	= (230-180)/6 = 8.33 man-hours	8.33 man-hours
3	Range	Estimate +/- SD	The upper bound of the range = Average + SD = 201.66 + 8.33 = 210 man-hours The lower bound of the range = Average –SD = 201.66 – 8.33 = 193.33 man-hours	Range is from 210 to 193.33 man-hours

You can also compute the variance for the estimates, which is square of the standard deviation. In this case the **variance** for the time estimates = 8.33 * 8.33 = 69.4 (man-hours)^2.

The following question has descriptions of 5 techniques used for estimating activity cost. Map the technique name to the description.

EXERCISE TIME 2:

Question (Five scenarios):

The 5 techniques for estimating activity cost are:

- Parametric estimation
- Bottom-up estimation
- PERT analysis
- Analogous estimation
- Expert judgment

Map the technique name to the description in the table below.

#	Description	Technique used to estimate activity cost
1	You work with experts and get the optimistic, pessimistic and most-likely duration (in man-days) to develop an application module for a global enterprise project. You use beta distribution to compute the average man-days and then you compute the variance and standard deviation for the development. You multiply the average man-days by $500 to get a cost estimate.	?
2	You are visiting your friend. He shows his garden and yard where he has installed a play area, swings and a slider for his children. You have a garden of similar size. You would also like to install a similar play area for your son. You ask your friend what it cost him for labor and material. You use that to estimate your expected expenses.	?
3	You are asked to estimate the labor cost to deploy a new set of VPN firewalls for your company. The project will involve buying hardware and engineering time to install and configure the equipment. You know that your friend at another company has successfully completed a similar project. You meet with him to get an estimate of the project cost.	?
4	You need to estimate the cost to install and operate a private cloud of servers and storage. The list of activities are: ▪ Develop architecture ▪ Develop build of material and get quotes ▪ Get approval for budget ▪ Process purchase order for procurement ▪ Install and configure the hardware and applications, and ▪ Provide training to the support staff You multiply the time for each activity by the labor rate (dollars per hour) and add the cost of the hardware and applications to develop a forecast.	?
5	You need to develop a datacenter (DC) with power, cooling, perforated floor tiles and overhead tiles. The area above the overhead tiles will have the network and power cables. The space below the floor tiles will be used for circulating cold air to the racks. From prior similar projects, you find that: ▪ The cost to build and setup a DC is $1,200 per square feet (SFT), and ▪ The maintenance cost to operate a DC is $800 per rack per month.. You know that your new datacenter is 500 SFT and you plan for 6 racks. You use these numbers to estimate the build and operating expenses for the first year.	?

Solution:

	Answers: Techniques used to estimate activities cost in the above table
1	PERT analysis
2	Analogous estimation
3	Expert judgment
4	Bottom-up estimation
5	Parametric estimation

Process 3: Determine Budget

PMBOK®: Page 248
Process Group: Planning

In this process, you will prepare a cost baseline, which is one of the most important project documents (like the project charter and schedule baseline).

The project work is divided into control accounts, which is decomposed into work packages, which contain activities. The hierarchy is: project work → control accounts → work packages → activities. Activities have duration and cost estimates, which are used to develop a cast baseline and budget.

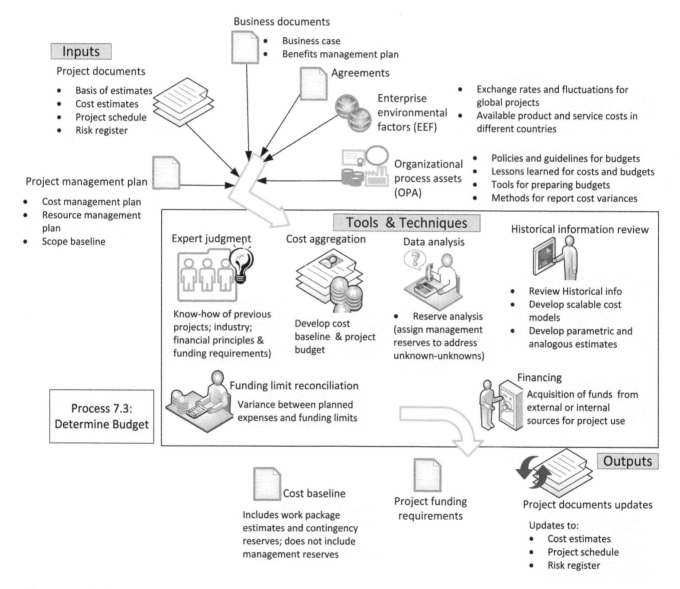

Figure 7-3: ITTO for Determine Budget process

You can use the following steps to develop a project budget:

a. For each work package, calculate work package estimate = sum of cost estimates for all activities + contingency reserves at activity level (optional)
b. For each control account, you calculate a cost estimate = sum of estimates for all work packages in the control account.
c. Project cost estimate = Sum of all control account estimates.
d. Cost baseline (budget at completion or BAC) = project cost estimate + contingency reserves at the project level to address known-unknowns.
e. Project budget = cost baseline + management reserves to address unknown-unknowns.

The cost baseline is also called the budget at completion (BAC) and is the approved amount for your project. See Figure 7-4.

If you need more money for the project, you need an approved change request to transfer funds from management reserves to the cost baseline, which increases the BAC (or baseline).

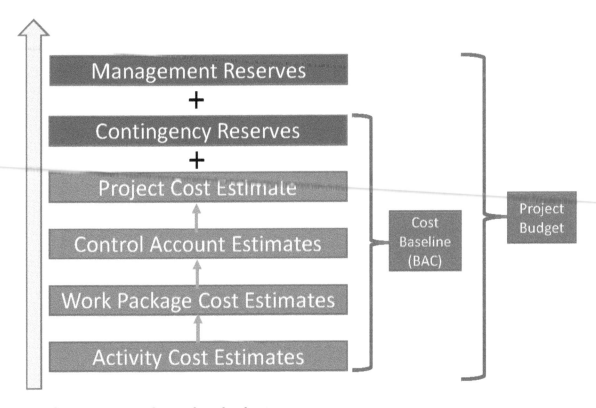

Figure 7-4: Components of a project budget

> *** For the Exam ***
> - Cost baseline (or BAC) includes contingency reserves but not management reserves.
> - Project budget = cost baseline (or BAC) + management reserves.

The cost baseline is used for the next process, **Control Costs**, to track cost health and make adjustments.

The other key output of the **Determine Budget** process is the project funding requirements. This document specifies how and when money will be given to the project team for expenditures. It could be given at the completion of certain project milestones, such as for capital purchases. Part of the money could be evenly distributed across the project life, for example, to pay for labor expenses.

Process 4: Control Costs

PMBOK®: Page 257
Process Group: Monitoring and Controlling

In this process you will monitor the incurred expenses, deviations (if any) between the planned and incurred expenses, update the cost baselines as needed. Figure 7-5 has the inputs, tools and techniques and outputs of the **Control Costs** process.

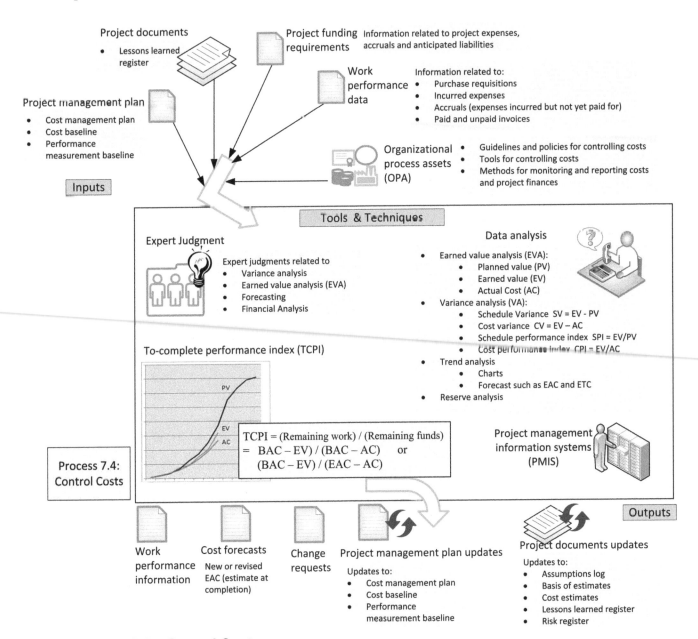

Figure 7-5: ITTO for Control Costs process

The key inputs for the **Control Costs** process are the cost baseline and cost management plan. The key outputs are cost forecasts are work performance information.

The data analysis techniques used to control costs are:

- Earned Value Analysis (EVA)
- Variance analysis
- Trend analysis
- Reserve analysis

Earned Value Analysis (EVA)

It is a technique to measure how the project is progressing, as related to scope, schedule and cost baselines. You can use the metrics in EVA to answer various exam questions such as:

- Is the work completed so far (earned value or EV) behind or ahead of the planned schedule (schedule baseline)?
- Is the money spent so far (actual cost or AC) less than what was planned or has the actual cost exceeded the planned amount?

Note that the project progress is measured against three baselines:

- Scope baseline
- Schedule baseline
- Cost baseline

Let us first review the cost-related terms and formulas (see Table 7-4), needed for the exam.

#	Terms	Acronym	Formula	Explanation	Unit
1	Budget at Completion	BAC	NA	Initial authorized or approved amount. It does not include management reserves.	$
2	Actual Cost	AC	NA	Amount actually spent so far.	$
3	Planned Value	PV	Expected amount of work to have been completed by now. Note that the total PV for the project is BAC. $$\frac{\text{Time Spent}}{\text{Total Scheduled Time}} * BAC$$		$ or unit of work
4	Earned Value	EV	Actual amount of work that has been completed so far (it is planned value of completed work) $$\frac{\text{Completed Work}}{\text{Total Work}} * BAC$$		$ or unit of work

5	Schedule Variance	SV	EV – PV	At a given point in time, it shows whether the completed work is ahead or behind plan. If it is: ▪ Zero: project is on time! ▪ (+)ve value: ahead of schedule. That is good! ▪ (-)ve value: behind schedule. Bad!	$ or unit of work
6	Cost Variance	CV	EV – AC	Shows whether the value of the completed work is more or less than actual incurred cost. If it is: ▪ Zero: Spending is on track! ▪ (+)ve: project has achieved more than it has spent. Good! ▪ (-)ve: indicates over-spending. Bad!	$
7	Cost Performance Index	CPI	EV/AC	We are getting $\$CPI$ of work out of every $1 spent. Value: ▪ 1= spending is on track ▪ Greater than 1 = work completed is more than expected. Good! ▪ Less than 1 = work completed is less than expected. Bad!	Ratio
8	Schedule Performance Index	SPI	EV/PV	Measures project progress as compared to expectation (schedule baseline) Value: ▪ 1= project is progressing as expected! ▪ Greater than 1 = ahead of schedule. Good! ▪ Less than 1 = behind schedule. Bad!	Ratio
9	Estimate at Completion	EAC	▪ BAC/CPI ▪ AC + BAC – EV ▪ AC + Bottom-up ETC ▪ AC + (BAC-EV)/(CPI*SPI)	The expected amount to complete all project work. It includes the actual cost (AC) incurred so far.	$
10	Estimate to Complete	ETC	▪ EAC – AC ▪ Re-estimate for remaining work (can use bottom-up approach)	Expected amount to finish all the remaining work.	$
11	To Complete Performance Index	TCPI	$$\frac{\text{Remaining Work}}{\text{Remaining Funds}}$$ $$\frac{BAC - EV}{BAC - AC}$$ $$\frac{BAC - EV}{EAC - AC}$$	This is ratio of the remaining work to the amount of remaining money in the project (CPI for the remainder of the project). • Use the 1st formula if the budget remains at BAC. • Use the 2nd formula if the budget is revised to EAC. If TCPI is: ▪ 1= just continue working with the same efficiency! ▪ Greater than 1 = need to be more efficient in future. This is harder! ▪ Less than 1: future efficiency can be lower!	Ratio

| 12 | Variance at completion | VAC | BAC - EAC | The additional amount needed (beyond the initially approved budget or BAC) to complete the work
Value:
▪ Zero= working as planned
▪ (+)ve: Actual expenses to complete the project will be below the budget. Good!
▪ (-)ve: project expenses will be more than planned! Bad! | $ or unit of work |

Table 7-4: Earned Value Analysis (EVA) terms and formulas

Figure 7-6 has a graphical illustration of the EVA concepts.

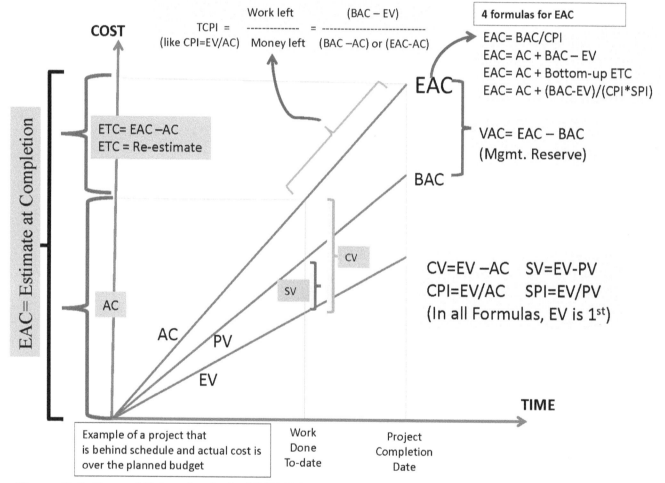

Figure 7-6: Earned Value Analysis (EVA) Terms and Concepts

Estimate at Completion (EAC)

When a project starts, a BAC is established. However, once the project has started, it may seem like the initial BAC is not viable anymore. Based on the performance for the completed work, there may be a need to revise the BAC. The new estimated amount for the project is EAC. There are 4 ways to estimate the EAC:

1. **BAC/CPI**: In this method, you first estimate the CPI for the completed portion of the project and assume that the future work will have the same CPI. The formula BAC/CPI will give you the revised budget or EAC.

2. **AC + BAC – EV**: This method ignores the CPI and performance for the work completed so far. It assumes that the remaining work will be completed by using all of the remaining funds. There is no need to add or subtract from the budget. Such an assumption needs to be validated and confirmed by risk analysis.

3. **AC + Bottom-up ETC**: In this method, you review the remaining work; decompose that into smaller units and estimate the cost of each unit. You then sum up the costs of the units and add that to the AC. Your experience with the work completed so far in this project will help in the cost estimation for the units.

4. **AC + {(BAC-EV)/(CPI*SPI)}**: You first estimate the CPI and SPI of the work completed so far and then use the formula for this method. This formula assumes that the efficiency (for doing the work and maintaining the budget) that we have seen in the project, will continue to be upheld for the remainder of the project.

To Complete Performance Index (TCPI)

CPI is related to the work completed in the past. On the other hand, TCPI is an index for the work to be done in the future. It is a ratio of the work remaining (BAC –EV) and the funds remaining. There can be 2 situations about the funds remaining:

a. Where the management decides that there will be no change to the allocated budget. In this case, you have no choice but to complete the project with whatever funds are left which is BAC –AC. TCPI is therefore equal to (BAC –EV)/(BAC-AC)

b. You are allowed to change the budget and therefore have a revised amount called EAC (estimate at completion). The remaining funds are therefore EAC –AC. This is the new denominator for TCPI. TCPI is equal to (BAC –EV)/(EAC-AC).

EXERCISE TIME 3:

Question:

For a project to setup a new video conferencing services between two offices, it is estimated that the work will take 1 month and $2,000. The planned value (PV) for week 1 was $600. However, at the end of Week 1, EVA estimates show that the earned value (EV) is $600 and the actual spend has been $500.

What are the CV, SV, CPI and SPI? If the project will continue to spend money at the same rate, what is the revised budget and TCPI?

Solution:

The provided values are:
- BAC = $2,000
- AC = $500
- PV = $600
- EV = $600

The computation and answers are shown below:

#	Compute values for?	Computation	Answer
1	CV	EV – AC = $600 - $500 = $100. This is good as it shows that you have achieved more than the actual spend!	$100
2	SV	SV = EV – PV = $600 - $600 = $0. We are on schedule!	$0
3	SPI	EV/PV = 600/600 = 1 Work is progressing on time and as per the plan.	1
4	CPI	EV/AC = 600/500 = 1.2. This is good because we are getting 20% more work than we planned to get.	1.2
5	EAC	New revised budget or EAC = BAC/CPI = 2000 /1.2 = $1,667 The entire project will require $1,667, although we had initially assigned $2,000.	$1,667
6	TCPI	TCPI = work remaining / funds remaining = (BAC –EV) / (EAC – AC) = (2000 – 600)/(1667 – 500) = 1400/1167 = 1.2. Note that TCPI is same as CPI. Why? Because, we shrank the budget to a new value of $1,667 and used that to estimate the TCPI.	1.2

In the PMP Exam, there will be questions that require you to use formulas in this exercise.

Here is another exercise on EVA.

EXERCISE TIME 4:

Question:
You need to paint all the 4 sides of your garden fence. Each side is supposed to take 2 days and have a finish-to-start relationship. Each side is budgeted for $1,000. At the end of day 6, you have completed only Side 1 and Side 2 and spent $4,000. Compute the values in the table below.

#	What are the values for each of these?	Computation	Your answer
1	BAC for the project		
2	PV		
3	EV		
4	CV		
5	SV		
6	SPI		
7	CPI		
8	EAC, assuming the same efficiency will persist for the remaining work		
9	VAC		
10	ETC		

Solution:

Initial baseline:
- Number of days = 8
- Planned work = 4 sides
- BAC = $1,000 x 4 sides= $4,000

Side 1: completed
Side 4: Not started
Side 2: completed
Side 3: Not started

Status at end of Day 6:
- AC = $4,000
- EV = completed 2 sides = $2,000
- PV = supposed to have completed 3 sides in 6 days = $3,000

	What are the values for each of these?	Computation	Answer	Explanation
1	BAC for the project	This is the total budget = $1,000 per side x 4 sides	$4,000	Allocated budget at the start of the project, for 8 days of work and to complete all 4 sides.
2	PV	In 6 days, we should have completed 3 sides or $3,000 worth of work	$3,000	As per the plan, we should have done $3,000 worth of work
3	EV	We have completed 2 sides, which is $2,000 worth	$2,000	In reality, we have done $2,000 worth of work.
4	CV	EV – AC = $2,000 - $4,000 = - $2,000	- $2,000	We have over-spent by $2,000.
5	SV	EV – PV = $2,000 - $3,000 = - $1,000	- $1,000	At the end of day 6, we should have completed 3 sides as per the plan. But we have completed only 2 sides. We are behind schedule by 1 side or 2 days, equivalent of $1,000.
6	SPI	EV/PV = $2,000/$3,000 = 0.66	0.66	We are progressing at 66% of the rate that was planned.
7	CPI	EV/AC = $2,000/$4,000 = 0.5	0.5	The completed work (EV) is worth only 50% of the money we spent (AC).
8	EAC, assuming the same efficiency will persist for the remaining work	The CPI is 0.66. For the remaining work, we will assume the same CPI. Hence the new revised budget or EAC = BAC/CPI = $4,000/0.5 = $8,000	$8,000	The entire project will cost us $8,000 (not $4,000 which was planned earlier).
9	VAC	Since the new budget is EAC or $8,000, VAC = BAC - EAC = $4,000 - $8,000 = - $4,000	- $4,000	We will be $4,000 over the budget.
10	ETC	EAC – AC = $8,000 - $4,000 = $4,000	$4,000	From this point onwards, we will need to spend $4,000 to complete the painting.

Remember the formulas in this exercise.

EXERCISE TIME 5:

Question:
The graph below represents the costs for a project work.

(a) Which of the following statements is true for this project?
  A. Behind schedule and over budget.
  B. Behind schedule and under budget.
  C. Ahead of schedule and over budget.
  D. Ahead of schedule and under budget.

(b) Also what are the CV, SV, CPI and SPI for the completed portion of the project?

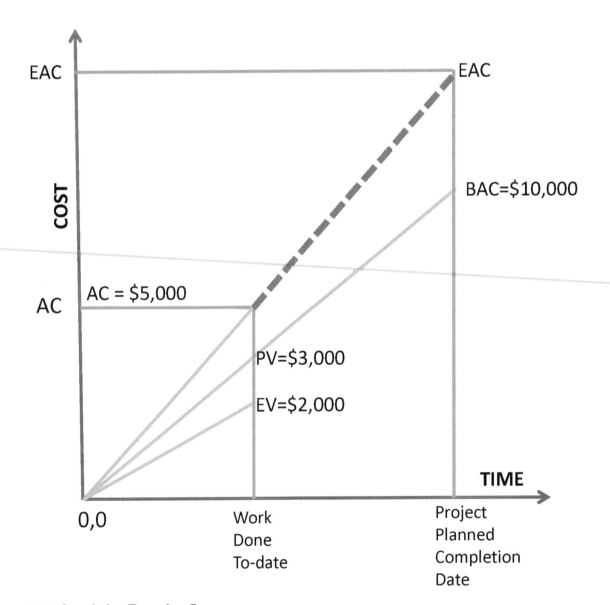

Figure 7-7: Graph for Exercise 5

Solution:

(a) The correct answer is A (behind schedule and over budget).

Why? For the completed work, EV < PV which implies that the project is behind schedule.

Also EV<AC, therefore the project is over budget.

(b) The calculations are in the table below.

#	What are the values for these?	Computation
1	CV	EV – AC = $2000 - $5000 = - $3,000 The spending is over budget.
2	SV	EV – PV = $2000 - $3000 = - $1,000 The project is behind schedule.
3	SPI	EV/PV = 2000/3000 = 0.67 The work completed is only 67% of what was planned.
4	CPI	EV/AC = 2000/5000 = 0.4 We have 40 cents worth of completed work from every dollar spent. Not good!

You will see graphs in the exam, where you will be asked to interpret whether the project is over or under budget and whether it is behind or ahead of schedule. Scenarios A, B and C shown below, are representations of three different combinations of schedule and cost variances.

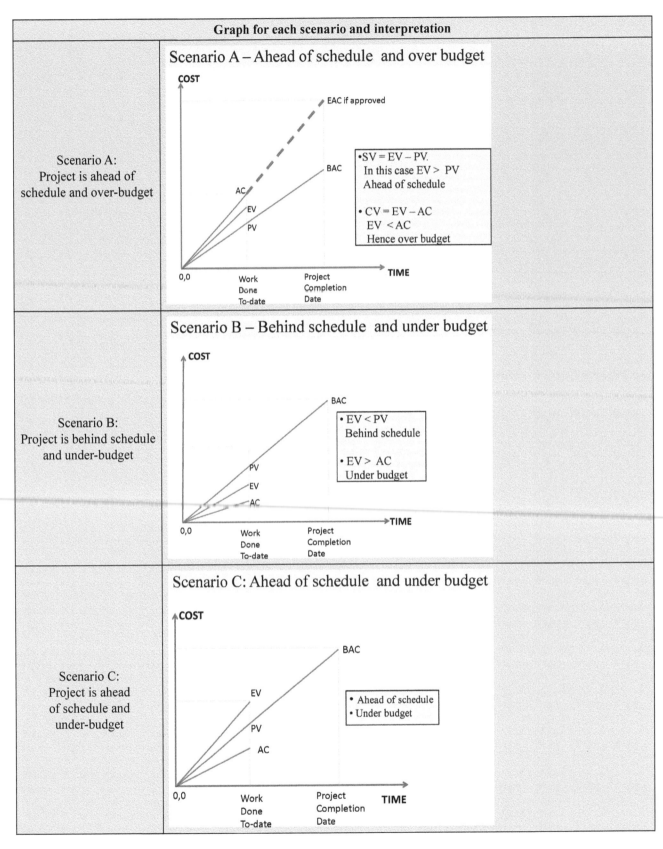

In these situations, use EV and compare that to PV and AC. If EV is higher that is good.

EXERCISE TIME 6:

Question:
The initially-assigned budget is $3,000 for one of your projects. You conduct an EVA and see the following results:

- AC = $1200
- EV = $ 800
- PV = $1600

A. What are the values for CPI and VAC?

B. You prepare a Change Request (CR) to ask for more funds, which assumes that the project is expected to continue to perform at the same efficiency and rate until the completion. However, the CR was not approved by the Change Control Board (CCB). The management has made it clear that there will be no more additional funding for the project.

You will need to increase your team performance and efficiency to make sure that the project completes within the allocated budget. What TCPI do you need to maintain for the remainder of the project?

Solution:
A. CPI = EV/AC = $800/$1,200 = 0.67

VAC= BAC – EAC and we know that BAC=$3,000. But we now need to estimate EAC, which is BAC/CPI.

- EAC = BAC/CPI = $3,000/0.67 = $4,500
- VAC = BAC – EAC = $3,000 - $4,500 = - $1,500

B. TCPI = remaining work / remaining funds
The remaining work = BAC – EV
The remaining funds = BAC – AC since the EAC is not approved.

TCPI = (BAC – EV) / (BAC – AC)
    = (3000-800) / (3000-1200)
    = 2200/1800
    = 1.22
This means that you will need to get $1.22 worth of work for every dollar spent for the remainder of the project.

Here is another exercise related to EVA.

EXERCISE TIME 7:

Question:

For a project with an assigned budget of $2,000 you have conducted an EVA at a time, when half the money had been spent. EVA shows that:

- AC = $1,000
- EV = $500
- PV = $800

a) What is the EAC for the project? Assume that the remaining project work will maintain the cost and schedule performance indices for the work that has completed so far.

b) What is the TCPI assuming that the EAC is approved by the Change Control Board (CCB)?

c) What is the TCPI assuming that the calculated EAC was not approved by the CCB and you need to complete the project with whatever funds are left from the initially-assigned amount?

Solution:

a) $EAC = AC + (BAC - EV)/(SPI*CPI)$
$SPI = EV/PV = \$500/\$800 = 0.625$
$CPI = EV/AC = \$500/\$1,000 = 0.5$
$EAC = \$1,000 + (\$2,000 - \$500)/(0.625 * 0.5)$
$\quad = \$1,000 + \$1,500/0.3125$
$\quad = \$1,000 + \$4,800$
$\quad = \$5,800$

b) $TCPI = \text{remaining work} / \text{remaining funds}$
$\quad = (BAC - EV)/(EAC - AC)$
$\quad = (\$2,000 - \$500)/(\$5,800 - \$1,000)$
$\quad = \$1,500/\$4,800$
$\quad = 0.3125$ (note that this is CPI * SPI which was used to estimate the EAC.)

c) In the next scenario, $TCPI = (BAC - EV)/(BAC - AC)$
$\quad = (\$2,000 - \$500)/(\$2,000 - \$1,000)$
$\quad = \$1,500/\$1,000$
$\quad = 1.5$

Besides computing the variances, trends and forecasts, it is also important to know their interpretation. You will have questions to test your understanding of the significance of different variances, performance indices and trends and their combinations.

More points for the exam:

- Life-cycle costing = cost to develop the product + cost to maintain the product over its lifetime.
- All project resources and vendors must be compensated for their role and contribution to the project.
- The formula for cost or schedule variance is earned value (EV) minus AC or PV.
- The formula for cost or schedule performance index is earned value (EV) divided by AC or PV.
- Cost baselines include contingency reserves.
- Project budget = cost baseline (budget at completion) + management reserves.
- The project manager can authorize the use of contingency reserves and cannot authorize the use of management reserves.

Practice Questions for Chapter 7

1. Which of the following is an output of the Determine Budget process?
   A. Project budget
   B. Contingency and management reserves
   C. Cost forecasts
   D. Cost baseline

2. Which of the following is not true for a cost baseline?
   A. Any changes to the cost baseline must be approved through formal change control procedures.
   B. The baseline is used by earned value analysis (EVA) technique to estimate variances.
   C. It includes contingency reserves for activities and work packages.
   D. It includes management reserves.

3. Which of the following is the most relevant formula to compute estimate at completion (EAC) given that the efficiency of the work completed so far in the project will not be maintained in the future?
   A. Re-estimate the cost of the individual activities for remaining work and add those.
   B. Use the formula EAC = BAC/CPI
   C. Use the formula EAC = AC + BAC - EV
   D. Use the formula EAC = AC + [(BAC -EV)/(CPI * SPI)]

4. Which of the following is not something you would do when trying to control costs?
   A. Make sure that the cost remains under what has been authorized at the work package, control account and project levels.
   B. Bring cost overruns within accceptable limits
   C. Estimate variances and include those in the work performance reports
   D. Establish management reserves for unforeseen work as you get more clarity about the scope and as the project activities are being done.

5. Your project has a budget of $50,000. Halfway down the project duration, you see that you have completed only 20% of the work and spent $20,000 so far. What is the schedule performance index (SPI)?
   A. 0.25
   B. 0.30
   C. 0.50
   D. 0.40

6. You have a project budget of $560,000 including a management reserve of $60,000. Quarter-way down the project duration, you see that you have completed only 10% of the work and spent $200,000 so far. What is the TCPI (to-complete performance index) that must be maintained to complete the project at the initially-approved amount?
   A. 1.00
   B. 0.25
   C. 0.40
   D. 1.50

7. Roberts Richardson is planning the budget for a new project. He comes across documents of another project that was completed 6 months ago. He uses the previous project to make an analogous estimate for the budget for his new project. What can he assume for the analogous technique that he used for the new budget?
   A. Analogous estimation is usually less accurate
   B. Analogous estimation uses parametric techniques to estimate cost or duration
   C. Analogous estimation can use bottom-up estimation techniques for certain parts of the activity or project.
   D. Analogous estimation uses three-point estimation such as PERT or triangular distribution

8. Your project has a budget at completion of $50,000. Halfway down the project duration, you see that you have completed only 20% of the work and spent $20,000 so far. What is the cost variance (CV)?
   A. -$20,000
   B. -$5,000
   C. -$15,000
   D. -$10,000

9. Susan Zanders is preparing a budget for a new project. She has a detailed project schedule, activity list and a WBS. Which of the following would not be a suitable technique for her to include while preparing a budget?
   A. Reserve analysis
   B. Cost aggregation
   C. Expert judgment
   D. All the above are suitable techniques for preparing a project budget

10. While doing an earned value analysis, you see that the earned value (EV) is less than the planned value (PV). What does this mean for schedule variance (SV) and schedule performance index (SPI)?
   A. SV is positive, and SPI is less than 1.
   B. SV is positive, and SPI is more than 1.
   C. SV is negative, and SPI is more than 1.
   D. SV is negative, and SPI is less than 1.

11. Which of the following is not true for management reserves?
   A. It is kept for unforeseen work that could be later deemed to be within the project scope.
   B. It is kept for unknown unknowns.
   C. It is part of the overall project budget but it is not part of the cost baseline.
   D. It is spent only if the project manager agrees and approves the expense request.

12. During which process do you review if the amount allocated for contingency and management reserves are still needed for the project or not, and if any amount should be added to or subtracted from the reserves?
   A. Plan Cost Management
   B. Estimate Costs
   C. Determine Budget
   D. Control Costs

13. You see that the earned value (EV) is less than the planned value (PV). What can you conclude about the project status?
    A. Project is ahead of schedule.
    B. Project is on schedule.
    C. Project is behind schedule.
    D. There is not enough information to make a conclusion about project status.

14. You have an 8-month project and a budget of two million dollars. You are 6 months into the project but you have spent all two million dollars so far and only half the work is completed. You have asked for one million more to complete the rest of the project. What is the planned value of the project?
    A. One million dollars
    B. One and half million dollars
    C. Two million dollars
    D. Three million dollars

ANSWERS

Question Number	Correct Answer	Explanation
1	D	The key output of the **Determine Budget** process is the cost baseline. It is an approved budget at completion (BAC) for the project.
2	D	A cost baseline does not include management reserves. See Figure 7-8 and 7-9 on Page 255 of the PMBOK®.
3	A	When the efficiency of the past work is not relevant or maintained for the future work, you must get a bottom-up estimate for the future work. See Page 267 of the PMBOK®.
4	D	Establishing management reserves must be done during project planning and not when you are trying to control cost based on cost variances. While controlling costs, you can, however, make updates to the management reserves.
5	D	In these problems, you need to first write whatever has been provided in the question. ▪ BAC (budget at completion) = $50,000 ▪ PV (planned value) so far is 50% (halfway) of $50,000 = $25,000 ▪ EV (earned value) is only 20% of $50,000 = $10,000 ▪ AC (actual cost) so far = $20,000 The question asks for SPI = EV/PV = $10,000/ $25,000 = 0.40 See Appendix C in this book for a list of formulas.
6	D	The TCPI that must be maintained to complete the remaining work using the remaining funds, is the first formula for TCPI on Page 267 in the PMBOK® and in Appendix C in this book. ▪ TCPI = (remaining work) / (remaining funds) = (BAC – EV) / (BAC – AC) ▪ BAC (budget at completion)= $560,000 - $60,000 = $500,000 ▪ Work completed = earned value (EV) = 10% of $500,000 = $50,000 ▪ AC (actual cost) = $200,000 ▪ TCPI = (BAC – EV) / (BAC – AC) = ($500,000 - $50,000) / ($500,000 - $200,000) = $450,000/$300,000 = 1.5 The future work must be done at performance index of 1.5 We now have the answer but let us look at a few issues with the project. ▪ In the past the CPI (cost performance index) has been EV/AC = $50,000/$200,000 = 0.25 ▪ Also in the past the SPI (schedule performance index) has been EV/PV = $50,000/ (0.25 * $500,000) = $50,000/$125,000 = 0.40 Note that the past CPI and SPI have been 0.25 and 0.40. Those are lot less than the TCPI of 1.5 required in the future to complete the remaining project work assuming no change in approved budget. That is going to be a lot harder to accomplish.
7	A	Analogous estimation is a technique where you use historical data, from a completed project or activity with a similar scope, to estimate cost or duration for a future project or activity. An analogous estimate is usually less accurate than a bottom-up or parametric estimate.
8	D	In these problems, you need to first write whatever has been provided. ▪ The BAC (budget at completion) is $50,000 ▪ PV (planned value) so far is 50% (halfway) of $50,000 = $25,000 ▪ EV (earned value) is however only 20% of $50,000 = $10,000 ▪ AC (actual cost) so far = $20,000 The question asks for CV= EV – AC = $10,000 - $20,000= -$10,000

9	D	All the choices are techniques for the budget preparation. See Page 252 in the PMBOK®.
10	D	Schedule variance (SV) is negative and schedule performance index (SPI) is less than 1. ▪ SV = EV – PV. Since EV < PV, SV is negative. ▪ SPI = EV/PV. Since EV < PV, SPI is less than 1.
11	D	The project manager is not authorized to approve the expenditure of the management reserves. The project manager needs to create a change request, get approval from CCB (change control board), update the cost baseline to include the approved amount and then spend the funds. See Page 252 in the PMBOK®.
12	D	During the **Control Costs** process, you monitor the status of the reserves (contingency and management reserves) funds. These reviews happen during the **Monitoring and Controlling** Process Group, where the only cost-related process is the **Control Costs** process.
13	C	The project is behind schedule since the earned value or completed work is less than what was planned.
14	B	The planned value is $1.5 million. PV is how much work should have been completed, based on the time spent so far in the project. The planned spending for 6 out of 8 months is 75% of $2 million, which is $1.5 million. Now you have asked for $1 million more and if that is approved, then: ▪ Estimate at completion (EAC) = $3 million ▪ Estimate to complete (ETC) = $1 million ▪ To complete performance index (TCPI) = 1.0 ▪ Variance at completion (VAC) = negative $1 million Make sure you understand the application of formulas in Appendix C (in this book) for the Exam.

CHAPTER 8
Quality Management

Quality is the degree to which the products, deliverables or processes meet the pre-defined requirements. One the other hand, quality management is about developing and implementing policies to meet pre-determined requirements and success criteria (for a product and/or project).

The project team is responsible for both project and product qualities:

- **Project quality** is about developing thorough project artifacts and plans, and methodical execution concerning the established plans and baselines. It also ensures that project planning and execution are effective and efficient.
- **Product quality** is about the features, functionality and fitness for use of the end-products (or deliverables) of the project.

For some projects, there may not be adequate attention to quality. This could be due to an urgency to complete the project, unavailability of resources or lack of experience. It could also be due to a view that spending on quality in the short-term will not necessarily yield long-term savings. Such a view could be mistaken and based on wrong assumptions.

Spending time early on in the project, on quality planning will save you from lots of efforts and expenses later in the project. This is because:

- Lack of quality will invariably lead to change requests and rework, requiring more time and resources.
- A change introduced during execution or later, makes it difficult to stay within the cost and schedule baselines.
- If products with flaws or poor quality are delivered to consumers, the defects will be discovered during use. Fixing those will be expensive, time-consuming and result in lost trust with the consumers.

It is, therefore, better to develop quality plans and activities during project planning and implement those during execution. There are 3 processes in the **Quality Management** Knowledge Area:

Planning Process Group	Executing Process Group	Monitoring and Controlling Process Group
8.1) Plan Quality Management	8.2) Manage Quality	8.3) Control Quality

Here are more quality-related points, which would be helpful for exam questions:

- As a project manager, you should develop quality requirements for processes (metrics, checklists, etc.) as well as for products (deliverables).
- Understand and document the quality requirements and strive for:
  - **Conformance to requirements**: project deliverables meet the customer or user requirements. The project delivers what it was created to produce.
  - **Fitness for use**: the service or product meets the real needs for usability of the product.
- Prevention is usually better and less expensive than inspection or rework.
- It is cheaper and more convenient to build quality into the product, rather than deliver products with defects, which would lead to rework, liabilities, warranty expenses and loss of business and trust.
- The project management team should not be the only one responsible for quality.
- Management must be responsible for quality. They must lead the efforts to develop and implement quality plans.
- The project team must implement a continuous improvement plan (CIP) for quality of the product and project processes.
- Each project activity and deliverable should be compared to and meet the quality objectives before it is marked as complete.

Continuous Improvement (Or Kaizen)

Continuous improvement is about making a continuous series of small improvements in quality. It is also called Kaizen, which is made of two Japanese words: *kai* which means to change and *zen* which means to improve.

The leading continuous-improvement initiatives are:

1. Plan-do-check-act (PDCA) cycle
2. Total Quality Management (TQM)
3. Six Sigma
4. Lean Six Sigma
5. Just-in-Time (JIT)
6. OPM3 (Organizational Project Management Maturity Model)
7. CMMI (Capability Maturity Model Integrated)

Plan-Do-Check-Act (PDCA) Cycle

PDCA (Figure 8-1) was first advocated by Shewhart. The concept was later modified by Dr. Edwards Deming. PDCA is also known as Shewhart cycle, Deming cycle or Control Circle. It consists of the following actions:

- Plan: Establish objectives and activities that are required to achieve those objectives.
- Do: Execute the planned activities and collect results for further analysis.
- Check: Compare the results against expected results to identify deviations, if any. Charting data can make it easier to see trends over multiple PDCA cycles. The charts will provide trends and help you develop a revised set of activities.
- Act: If the Check shows that the new Plan and Do is an improvement compared to the prior standard (baseline), the new Plan becomes the standard (baseline). But if the Plan is not an improvement, there are no changes to the baseline.

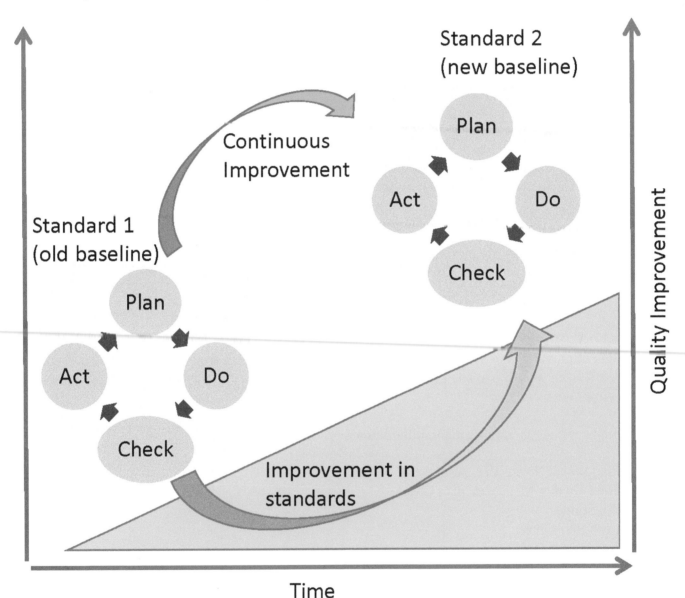

Figure 8-1: PDCA cycles with continuous improvement in quality

Total Quality Management (TQM)

TQM represents an organizational culture and a broad approach to managing organizational quality. In TQM, the focus is on achieving long-term success through customer satisfaction.

In TQM, quality improvement is not a one-time activity. It is a continuous process, where each team member strives to help in continual improvement of services, processes, and products. This results in improved quality of the project processes and deliverables.

TQM has been around since the 1950s and was initially derived from the Japanese industry. The 8 fundamental principles of TQM are:

1. Total employee involvement
2. Customer-focused attitude
3. Process-centric approach (processes are defined and continuously monitored for variations)
4. Continual improvement,
5. Interconnected functions and systems,
6. A systematic approach to integrating quality to achieve organizational goals,
7. Fact-based decision making
8. Communications to improve employee morale and motivation at all levels.

Like other quality control methodologies, TQM is end-user-focused. It looks at customers to provide quality requirements and judge the product or service quality.

Six Sigma

Six Sigma is a statistical methodology to eliminate defects in a product or process. It advocates:

- Making decisions based on verifiable data and statistical methods, and not on guesswork and assumptions,
- Making continuous efforts to achieve stability, reduce variations in product characteristics and decrease the number of defects,
- Obtaining a strong commitment from senior management to achieve and sustain quality improvement plans,
- Focusing on the characteristics of manufacturing and business processes, that can be defined, measured, analyzed, improved and controlled (DMAIC).

The name 'Six Sigma' comes from statistical quality control used in manufacturing processes. It is the ability of those processes to produce components within the specification limits.

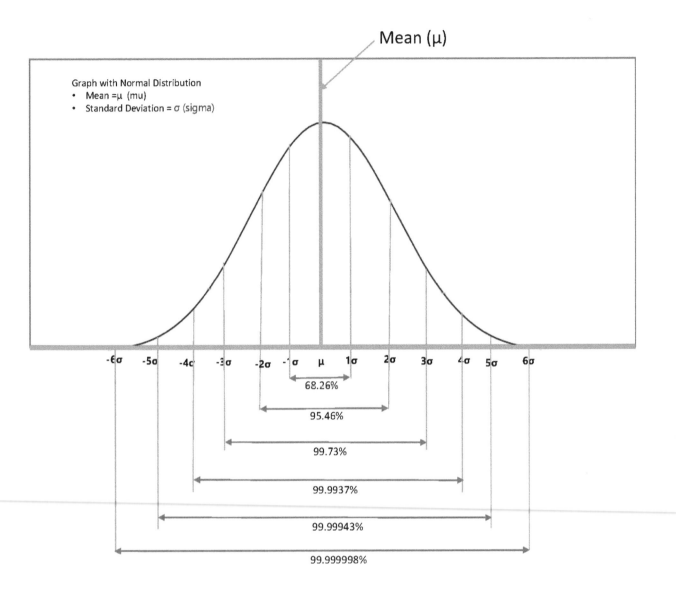

Figure 8-2: Normal Distribution with a percentage of data sets within 1σ (std. deviation) to 6σ of the mean.

Figure 8-2 shows a normal distribution. Early statisticians noticed the same shape coming up repeatedly in disparate quality control data sets. The shape was bell-curved, symmetric and the median and mean values were identical and at the center of the data set. This graph was called a normal distribution.

Note the following about normal distributions:

- Mu (μ) is mean or average
- Sigma (σ) is the standard deviation.
- For a quality requirement of 6σ, the spread between upper and lower control limits is 12σ (6σ on the left + 6σ on the right)
- For a 1σ quality requirement, there is 2σ spread between the upper and lower control limits. 68.26% of the measurements (occurrences) must be within these control limits.
- For a 2σ requirement, 95.46% of the measurements must be within these control limits.

- For a 3σ requirement, 99.73% of the measurements must be within these control limits.
- For a 6σ requirement, 99.999998% of the measurements must be within these control limits (a spread of 12σ).

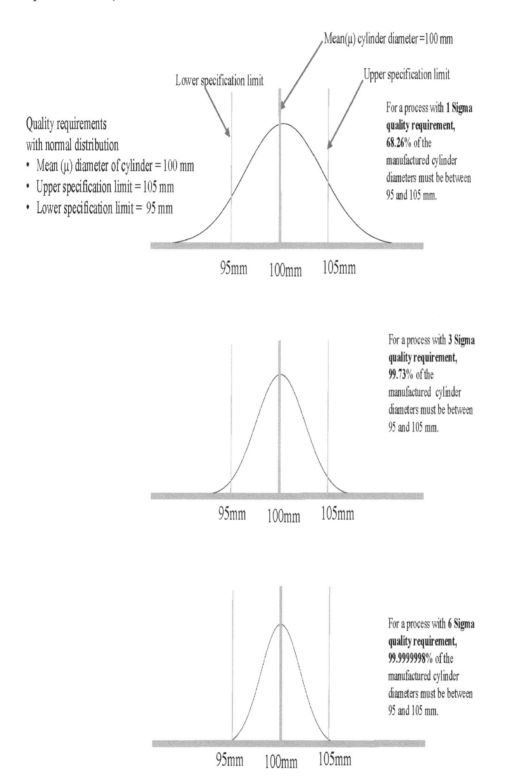

Figure 8-3: Three example processes with normal distribution and quality requirements of 1σ, 3σ and 6σ.

Figure 8-3 shows three processes with quality requirements of 1σ, 3σ and 6σ. For 1σ requirement and given a normal distribution, 68.26% or more of the manufactured cylinder diameters must be within the specification limits.

For 6σ quality requirement, 99.9999998% or more of the manufactured cylinder diameters must be within the specification limits, which is a more stringent requirement.

The maturity of a manufacturing process can be rated by a sigma designation. The designation0 indicates its percentage of defect-free products. For real-world industry processes, a Six Sigma quality requirement is one in which, 99.99966% of all opportunities to produce some feature of a product, are free of defects.

Lean Six Sigma

While Six Sigma focusses on reducing variation and defects, Lean focusses on reducing waste. Lean advocates techniques to fine-tune manufacturing processes to:

1. Reduce transportation time and cost,
2. Reduce Inventory,
3. Reduce movement of raw materials and end-products,
4. Reduce waiting time,
5. Reduce over-processing,
6. Reduce over-production at any time, and
7. Reduce under-utilization of employee talent.

Lean Six Sigma projects combine:

- Lean's focus on reducing waste, and
- The Six Sigma's focus on reducing variations and defects.

This is illustrated in Figure 8-4.

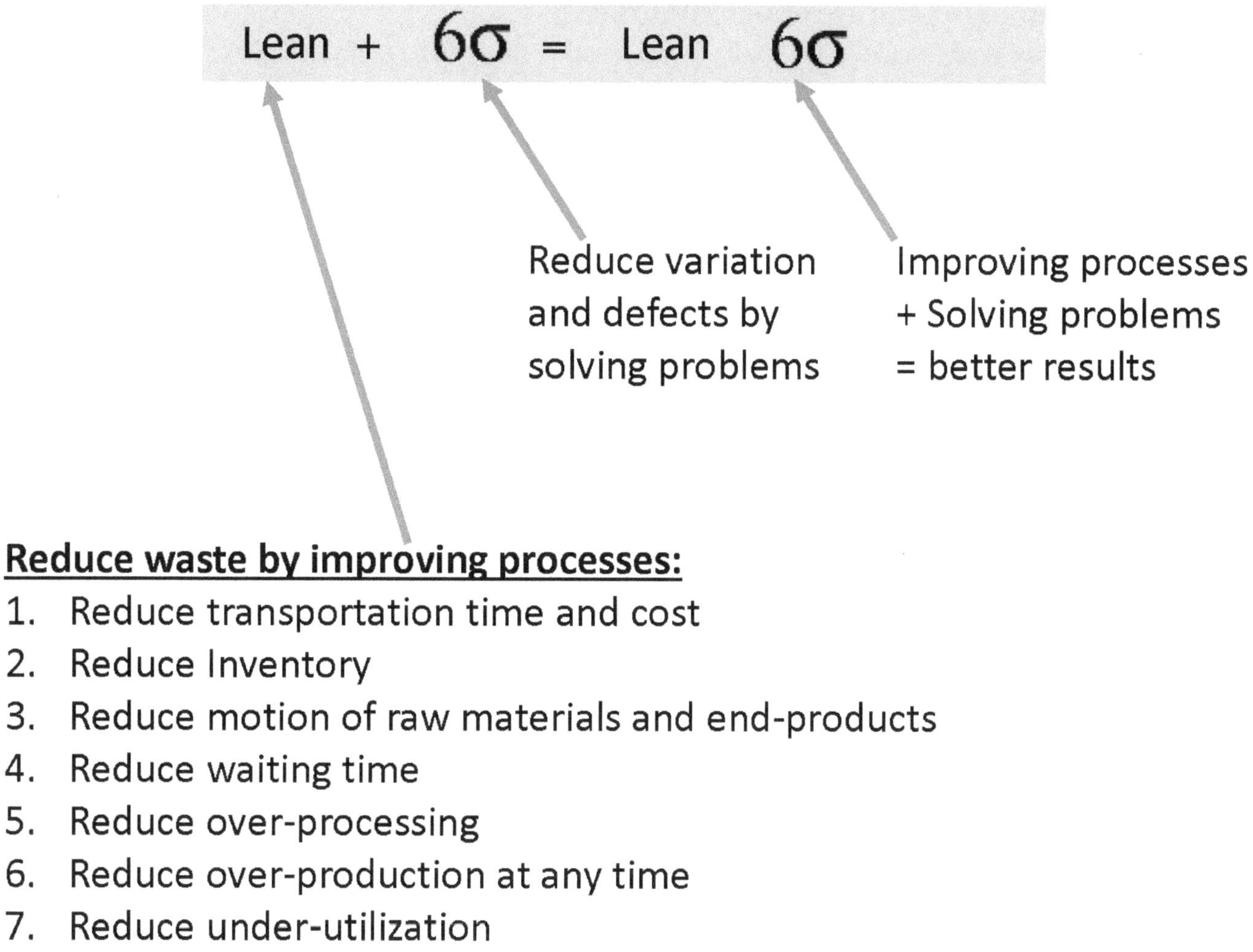

$$\text{Lean} + 6\sigma = \text{Lean } 6\sigma$$

Reduce variation and defects by solving problems

Improving processes + Solving problems = better results

Reduce waste by improving processes:

1. Reduce transportation time and cost
2. Reduce Inventory
3. Reduce motion of raw materials and end-products
4. Reduce waiting time
5. Reduce over-processing
6. Reduce over-production at any time
7. Reduce under-utilization

Figure 8-4: Lean Six Sigma

Just in Time (JIT)

JIT is a methodology to help reduce flow times with production systems and response times with clients and suppliers. It started as an inventory strategy to increase efficiency and decrease waste by receiving goods only when required on the production lines. Raw materials must arrive just in time to be used by the manufacturing operations. This reduces material movement and storage expenses.

Like several quality improvement initiatives, this was initially established by Toyota in Japan. An example of JIT implementation would be a manufacturer, who depends on a supply chain system to receive parts and raw materials not in advance, or after, but just in time when required by the factory or assembly lines.

OPM3 (Organizational Project Management Maturity Model)

OPM3 is a maturity model that examines the project management process capabilities within an enterprise. It has various guidelines that can be used to direct how project management processes can be improved within an enterprise.

CMMI® (Capability Maturity Model Integrated)

CMMI is a process model that defines what an organization must do to promote behavior and practices that can lead to improved efficiency. It was developed by Carnegie Mellon University (CMU) and is now administered by the CMMI Institute, which is part of ISACA (Information Systems Audit and Control Association).

Distinction between Grade and Quality

What is the difference between grade and quality? A grade is a design intent. It consists of features or capabilities of a product. The categorization of a product into different grades is based on its features and functionality.

For example, there are datacenter-grade air conditioning units (similar in size to a large refrigerator). There are also room-cooling grade air-conditioners (portable and about the size of a microwave oven). These are not meant for small network rooms or telecom closets. The cooling capacity, size, etc. of these two grades of air-conditioners are different. You need to identify and purchase a grade of equipment that meets your requirements.

Good quality, on the other hand, is about being defect-free and easy to operate and manage and one that provides a good user experience. Quality aspects are not about features or functionalities. Problems related to quality create inconvenience and difficulty for users.

Products in a higher grade could be of low quality. Products in a lower grade could be of high quality.

Distinction between Accuracy and Precision

We are not done with lexicons, yet! What is the difference between accuracy and precision? These terms are often used in measurements. Accuracy is the difference between the actual values and the desired target value. It is a measure of correctness. If the actual values are close to the target, it is said to be accurate (Figure 8-5).

Precision is the variation amongst the actual values. If the actual values are close together, they are said to be precise. In certain cases, the actual values can be far from the desired target value and still be precise (bunched together) but not accurate.

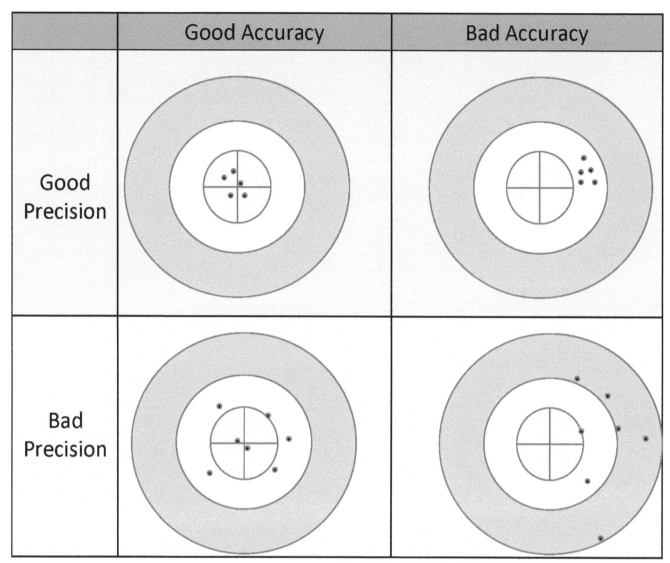

	Good Accuracy	Bad Accuracy
Good Precision		
Bad Precision		

Figure 8-5: Precision versus accuracy illustrated using darts on a board

Distinction between the Three Processes in Quality Management

Table 8-1 shows the differences between the three processes in the **Quality Management** Knowledge Area.

Plan Quality Management process	Manage Quality process	Control Quality process

This process is about making decisions on quality objectives and criteria for:
   ■ deliverables
   ■ end-products of the project, and
   ■ project management
You decide on a plan on how you will go about project execution to attain those objectives. These decisions are documented in the quality management plan.
	This process is part of **Executing** process group. Here you make sure the project team follows the plans and procedures to attain the quality objectives.	This process is part of **Monitoring and Controlling** process group. Here you make sure that the procedures are yielding the desired results.
		
		You check the deliverables (completed or in-progress) using the quality metrics and checklist. If there are quality problems, you get to the root cause, identify resolutions and implement those.

Table 8-1: Differences between the three processes in Quality Management

Trends and Emerging Practices

The new trend in quality management is to seek ways to improve accuracy and precision to meet the product requirements.

There is a growing keenness to meet the customers' needs. This is done by making products that meet:

- previously-specified requirements, and
- real needs of the customers.

Various quality initiatives are becoming popular. These include:

- Plan-do-check-act (PDCA) cycle
- Total quality management (TQM)
- Six Sigma
- Lean Six Sigma

There is a growing realization that quality can be improved only if senior management in the organization takes ownership and responsibility for quality planning and implementation.

An honest and committed partnership between management and external vendors and partners is also critical for success. There is also a growing acceptance that commitment from all involved parties will exist only if all parties see a long-term value and win-win scenario in the relationship.

Tailoring Considerations

The quality requirements for each product are unique. You will have to, therefore, customize the three processes in **Quality Management** to meet the quality requirements. The key factors for tailoring are:

- quality-related policies and procedures in the organization
- required government regulations for the project deliverables
- stakeholder requirements and
- need for continuous quality improvements for the project deliverables.

Considerations for Agile/Adaptive Environments

Agile environments require frequent quality reviews, which must be spread throughout the project life cycle. These reviews result in feedbacks and suggestions on techniques to improve quality in the subsequent batches.

It is best to produce small batch sizes, while the quality metrics are being finalized. Small batch sizes help to reduce the cost of non-conformance. It also helps accommodate changes in product requirements and scope.

Process 1: Plan Quality Management

PMBOK®: Page 277
Process Group: Planning

The **Plan Quality Management** process is about developing and documenting policies to enforce quality in the product and project management processes. Quality can be for the end-product, the project documents, deliverables and project processes.

In this process, you identify the quality requirements and standards that must be followed. The quality requirements can be necessary for compliance with government regulations or to meet internal mandates.

Once you have the quality requirements, you also develop and document a plan to enforce and validate quality throughout the project lifecycle.

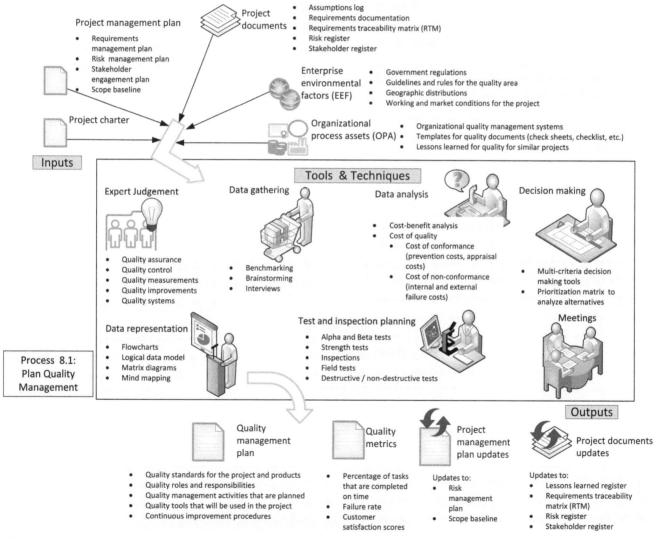

Figure 8-6: ITTO for Plan Quality Management process

Key inputs for the **Plan Quality Management** process are:

- Project charter, which has the product characteristics, approval requirements and success criteria that will influence the quality activities for the product and project,
- Requirements management plan, which has the approach for identifying and managing requirements that are used to develop quality management plan and quality metrics.
- Scope baseline, which has the WBS, list of deliverables and acceptance criteria for the deliverables,
- Requirements (functional and non-functional) documentation, which has the quality requirements for the product or service. For example, for IT services, the requirements would be for related to availability, security and ease-of-use,
- Risk register, which has the threats or opportunities that might affect the project or product quality,
- Stakeholder register, which has the quality requirements, needed by each stakeholder.

Cost of Quality

Cost of quality (COQ) is an important tool and technique for this process. It helps you compare the expenses for quality implementation and benefits.

The comparison will help decide if it is worth spending on quality or not! If the COQ is $40,000 and hard benefits are $50,000 plus the soft benefits of improved goodwill and branding, spending on COQ is worth it. But if the hard benefits are only $20,000, you could decide to not invest in quality.

COQ consists of two components (see Figure 8-7):

1. Costs of Conformance: expenses incurred to build quality into and for inspection of the products and project management processes, and
2. Costs of Non-conformance: expenses incurred due to defects found in the products or processes.

Which of the two is lower? In most cases, the cost of conformance would be lower. It is usually cheaper and easier to build deliverables right the first time, rather than having to later identify and fix defects.

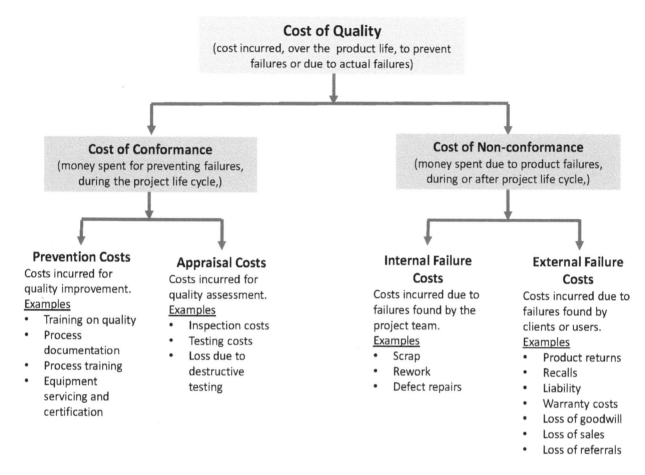

Figure 8-7: Cost of Quality for conformance and non-conformance with examples

> *** For the Exam ***
> - Throughout the process of quality management, you need to be aware of the difference between *prevention* and *inspection*.
> - If you need to select between the two in the PMP Exam, prevention is usually the better answer.
> - As a proactive project manager, you need to focus on prevention, which is often less expensive and quicker than having to inspect and correct the defective parts.

Design of Experiments

Design of Experiments is a technique used for planning and implementing quality in a product. This method was developed by Sir Ronald Fisher (1890 – 1962) in the 1920s. It is a statistical method to determine factors (independent or X variables) that impact certain outcomes or features (dependent or Y variables). It also determines the extent of impact or sensitivity of the Y variable to the X variable. Design of Experiments is used to conduct sensitivity analysis. It is also used for risk analysis.

For example, you can conduct a survey to determine the impact of advertisement expenses on sales volume. The more the money spent on advertisement (X variable), the greater the sales (Y or dependent variable). The sensitivity (increase in sales divided by the increase in expense) will be higher in the beginning but will decline after a certain threshold amount has been spent on advertisements.

Another example of Design of Experiments, although complex, would be to determine the behavior of a jet engine (Y variable) which is dependent on thousands of X variables (such as quality of jet fuel, compressor power, turbine strength, nozzle area, etc.).

Force Field Analysis (FFA)

Force Field Analysis diagrams (Fig. 8-8) is another quality planning tool that shows forces in favor of and against implementing organizational changes for quality improvements. The forces can be numerically rated to show the prevailing sentiments that are either against or in favor of the proposed changes.

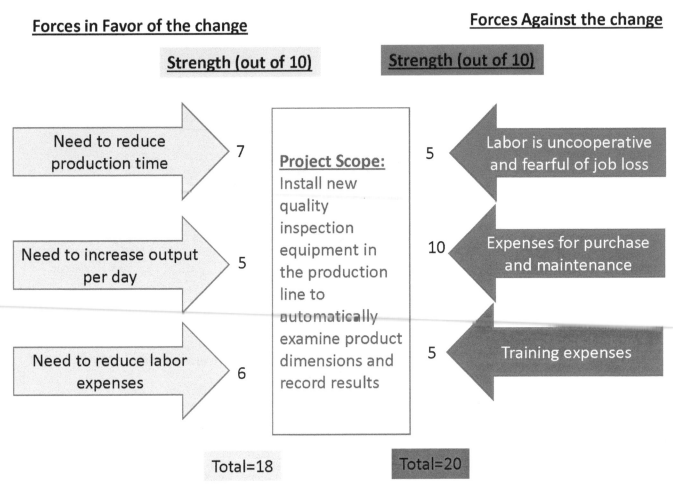

Figure 8-8: Force field analysis

Flowcharts (Process Maps)

Flowcharts are maps that show the sequence of activities that lead to a defect. It also shows the various branching possibilities ending up to final deliverables. Flowcharts start with input(s) and end with the output(s). In the middle, they have loops, decision points and logic and parallel paths.

Flowcharts help in understanding the effort, time and cost required to build quality in a process. As a project manager, you can then decide if the output is worth the needed effort and cost.

The SIPOC (Supplier, Input, Process, Output and Customers) Model is an example of a flowchart that takes suppliers and other inputs, and then processes those to create outputs for customers.

Matrix Diagrams

A matrix diagram is a table that shows the relationship or bonding strength between multiple factors (project objectives, root cause of problems, etc.). These factors are placed on the column and row headings. The value in each cell represents the strength of the relationship between the factors in the particular column and row. This tool is used to analyze the influences and significance of each factor.

Quality Audits

Another important tool for quality management is quality audits. It is usually performed by an independent internal group or by an external vendor.

Quality audits can also be conducted by an audit or PMO team to asses the project deliverables. It is called project success check (PSC) or gate review. If a project successfully passes the PSC or gate review, the project goes ahead to the next set of activities or milestone. If it fails, the audit (or PMO) team develops a list of corrective actions for the project team.

The goal of quality audits is to ensure that the project processes are in-line with the organizational requirements and government regulatory compliances (if applicable). The objective should be to find the gaps and areas of improvement and later develop a list of action items to bring the project on track or comply with the requirements.

Outputs of Plan Quality Management Process

The most important output of this process is a quality management plan document. It contains the quality requirements and policies and how the project will implement those.

Another output is the quality metrics, which specifies required product attributes and process to test compliance to those attributes. It also describes the acceptable limits. For example, the thickness of the produced iron bars should be 15 mm with a tolerance of +/- 0.5 mm. The acceptable thickness limits are, therefore, from 14.5 mm to 15.5 mm.

Quality metrics can be for project attributes as well. A project could have a set of quality metrics, such as a maximum of 10 scope change requests, a maximum of 10 delayed activities and a minimum allowed SPI (schedule performance index) of 0.8.

Another output is the process improvement plan (Fig. 8-9). It contains the steps to identify and correct quality-related problems and improve various processes.

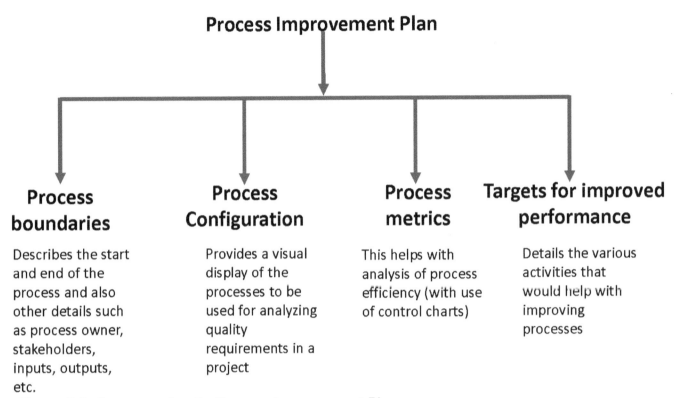

Figure 8-9: Components of a Process Improvement Plan

Process Improvement Plan

Process boundaries

Describes the start and end of the process and also other details such as process owner, stakeholders, inputs, outputs, etc.

Process Configuration

Provides a visual display of the processes to be used for analyzing quality requirements in a project

Process metrics

This helps with analysis of process efficiency (with use of control charts)

Targets for improved performance

Details the various activities that would help with improving processes

Process 2: Manage Quality

PMBOK®: Page 288
Process Group: Executing

This process is concerned with incorporating the quality requirements of the product and project. The objective is to make sure that the needed quality requirements are built into the product development activities. This process includes tasks to identify the causes of poor quality (if any) and facilitate the improvement of quality.

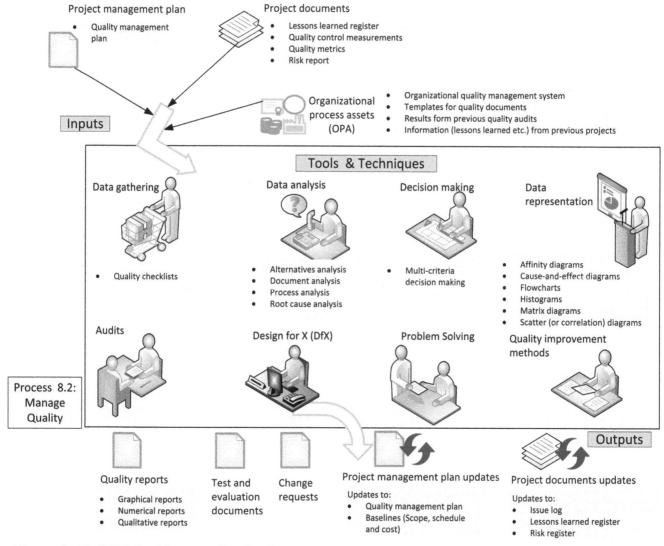

Figure 8-10: ITTO for Manage Quality Process

Documents such are quality management plan, process improvement plan and quality metrics (output of **Plan Quality Management** process) are input to **Manage Quality**. Another input is measurements data (output of **Control Quality** process). These measurements are compared with quality metrics. You can use control charts to make sure that the measurements are within specification and control limits.

Affinity diagrams

Affinity diagrams (Fig. 8-11) are used to categorize causes of defects into groups. This makes it easier to understand the significance of each group. If a particular group is identified as causing the most quality-related issues, you must develop action items to resolve issues in that group.

The concept and use of affinity diagrams were developed by Jiro Kawakita in the 1960s. It was called the K-J Method. It helps improve group decision-making and prioritize actions. In the 1970s affinity diagrams were commonly used for Total Quality Control (TQC) initiatives in Japan.

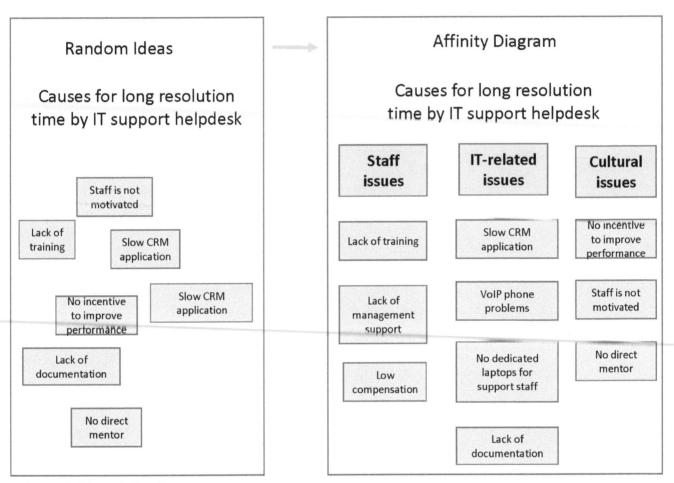

Figure 8-11: Affinity diagrams

Cause-and-effect diagrams (fishbone, why-why or Ishikawa diagrams)

The cause-and-effect diagrams (Fig. 8-12) help connect effects (consequences) to the causes (factors). For example, if there are problems with producing engine cylinders with a particular target diameter, a cause-and-effect diagram can help identify the assignable cause(s) of the problem. The project team can then identify corrective actions to eliminate the causes or reduce their impact.

How do you construct the cause-and-effect or fishbone diagram? The effect or problem is written at the head of the fishbone. The primary causes are written at the tail of the main arrows in the cause section. Secondary causes are written on smaller arrows that lead to the main arrow. This is done until all reasonable possibilities are exhausted.

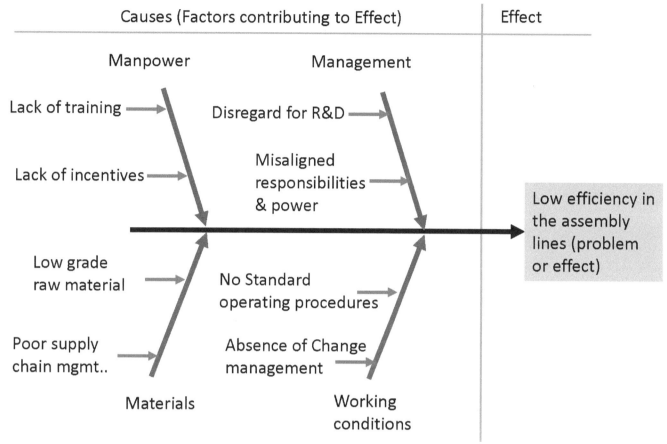

Figure 8-12: Cause-and-effect (also called fishbone, Ishikawa or why-why) diagrams

Histograms

A histogram (Fig. 8-13) is a bar chart that shows the number of occurrences of each category (problems or root causes). It provides a visual way to identify a category that has the most number of occurrences. Like the Pareto diagram, it identifies the category or problem that has the most occurrences. Histograms can be ordered to show a central tendency or can be unordered.

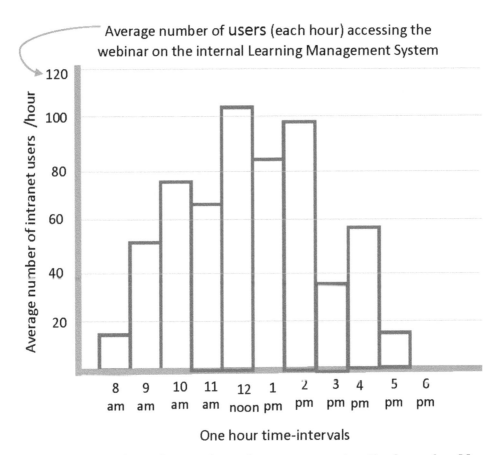

Figure 8-13: Histogram to show the number of users accessing the Learning Management System each hour

Scatter diagrams (Correlation charts)

A scatter diagram is a graphical representation that shows the relationship (if any) or correlation between two variables or factors. The X axis has the independent variable. The Y axis has the dependent variable. The plots on a scatter diagram help identify a correlation between the two variables. The relationship or correlation (see Fig. 8-14) between X and Y can be:

- Positive correlation: When X increases, Y also increases.
- Negative correlation: When X increases, Y decreases.
- Zero or No correlation: When X increases, Y can increase or decrease.
- Curvilinear correlation: When X increases, Y increases (or decreases) and then moves in the opposite direction.

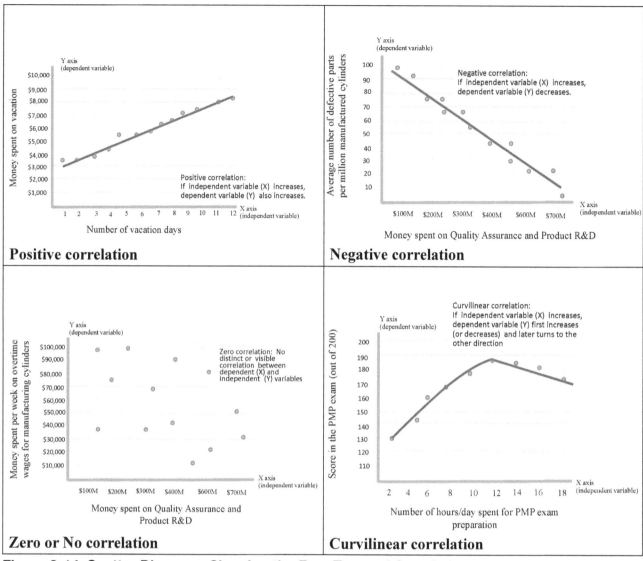

Figure 8-14: Scatter Diagrams Showing the Four Types of Correlations

Interrelationship digraphs

An interrelationship digraph (Figures 8-15 and 8-16) is a type of relationship diagram that shows the cause-and-effect relationship between the factors. For a simple process, with 3 or 4 factors, it is easy to comprehend how the causes and effects are related. But for a complex system, for example with 50 or 100 components or factors, the interrelationship diagram is needed to identify relationships between factors.

Certain aircrafts are made up of 300,000+ components, provided by 1,000+ vendors from more than 30 countries. The interrelationship diagrams, that show the causes (due to defects in the components) and effect on the overall system, are complex.

Main Problem: Low efficiency in the factory

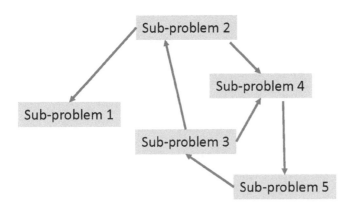

Interrelationship digraphs:

1. Use input data form Fishbone diagram, tree diagram, affinity diagram, etc.

2. Are used when multiple factors are influencing each other.

3. Are used to arrive at creative solutions for complex scenarios or problems.

Sub-problem	Box shows a cause or effect of the main problem
⟶	Arrow show a direct relationship from cause to effect

Figure 8-15: A generic interrelationship digraph

Fig 8-16 shows an interrelationship digraph to identify the relationship between factors and root causes of poor service quality in a hospital.

Main Problem: Poor service quality for patients in a hospital

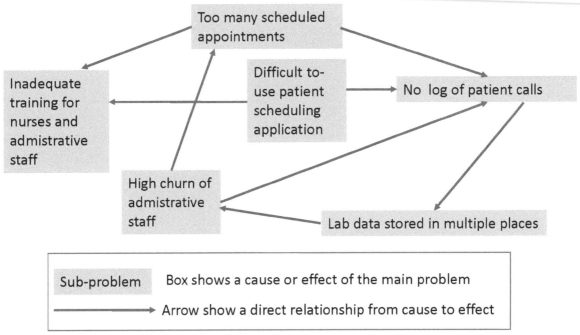

Sub-problem	Box shows a cause or effect of the main problem
⟶	Arrow show a direct relationship from cause to effect

Figure 8-16: Another interrelationship digraph showing causes of poor service quality in a hospital

Process decision program charts (PDPC)

There are various risks that could derail a quality management process. You need to identify the risks that have a high likelihood and develop a contingency (mitigation) plan. PDPC is used to understand the:

- quality-related objectives,
- possible problems and risks and
- steps (action plan) to mitigate those problems.

Fig 8-17 shows five 'possible problems' that could disrupt the implementation plan for a high-quality cloud-based procurement system. Out of the five possible problems, four are less likely to happen and, therefore, temporarily ruled out. These are marked with 'X' in Figure 8-17. For the problem with the highest likelihood of occurrence and impact, you develop a counter-measure or contingency plan.

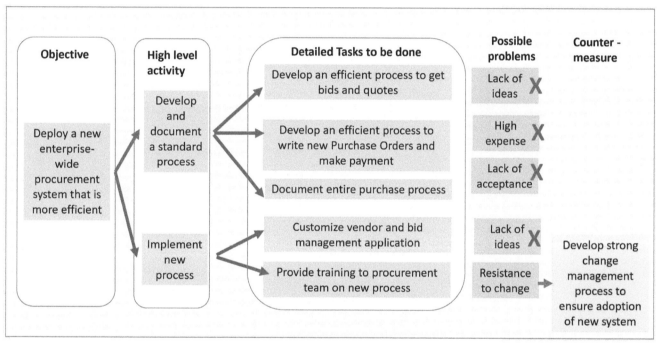

Figure 8-17: Process decision program charts (PDPC) to identify the most likely issues and develop mitigation plans

Tree diagrams (systematic diagrams)

A tree diagram (Figure 8-18) is used to show hierarchical decomposition. It can be shown:

- Horizontally, as in Figure 8-18, and often used for RBS (risk breakdown structure) and decision trees, or
- Vertically, often used to document reporting hierarchy, OBS (organization breakdown structure) or WBS (work breakdown structure).

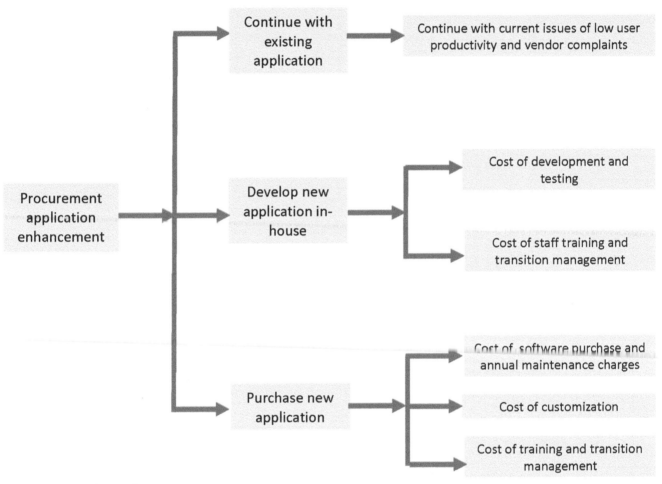

Figure 8-18: Tree diagram

Besides showing hierarchical or parent-to-child relations, tree diagrams are also useful for building a decision tree, where each branch represents a likely outcome. Each outcome has a probability of occurrence (expressed as a percentage) and impact (often expressed as a monetary value).

Prioritization matrices

A prioritization matrix is a simple table to rank or prioritize various items by documenting the items, factors for ranking and using a weighted criterion (based on relative significance). The weighted scores are used for ranking or prioritization.

Project ID	Project Description	RoI and savings benefit (weight = 3 out of 10)		Regulatory and compliance benefit (weight = 2 out of 10)		Improved productivity benefit (weight = 5 out of 10)		Sum of Weighted scores	Project Rank
		Raw Score	Weighted score	Raw Score	Weighted score	Raw Score	Weighted score		
Project 1	ERP upgrade	3	9	8	16	5	25	50	3
Project 2	Procurement application upgrade	4	12	3	6	5	25	43	4
Project 3	Disaster Recovery Setup	5	15	6	12	6	30	57	2
Project 4	Cloud authentication project	7	21	9	18	7	35	74	1

Table 8-2: Prioritization matrix to rank projects based on its benefits to the organization

Prioritization matrices can be used to rank projects, issues, solutions or activities using certain predetermined criteria. A numerical value (weight) is assigned to each criterion. Table 8-2 shows an example prioritization matrix with 3 criteria with weights of 3, 2 and 5.

The raw score for each project or issue is multiplied by the weight to provide a weighted score. The sum of the weighted scores is used to rank the project or issue. In the exam, you may be given a partially-filled prioritization matrix and asked to identify the most or least important project or issue.

The key outputs of this process are quality reports and test and evaluation documents. The quality reports are used to plan corrective actions to fulfill the required quality objectives. Another output is change requests, which result in updates to the project baselines and plans.

Process 3: Control Quality

PMBOK®: Page 298
Process Group: Monitoring and Controlling

In this process, you review the quality data (product measurements, control charts, computed variances, etc.), identify problems and their root causes and develop an action plan to eliminate the root causes.

This process helps you produce results (products and deliverables) that will be accepted by the key stakeholders when it is time for them to review and sign-off.

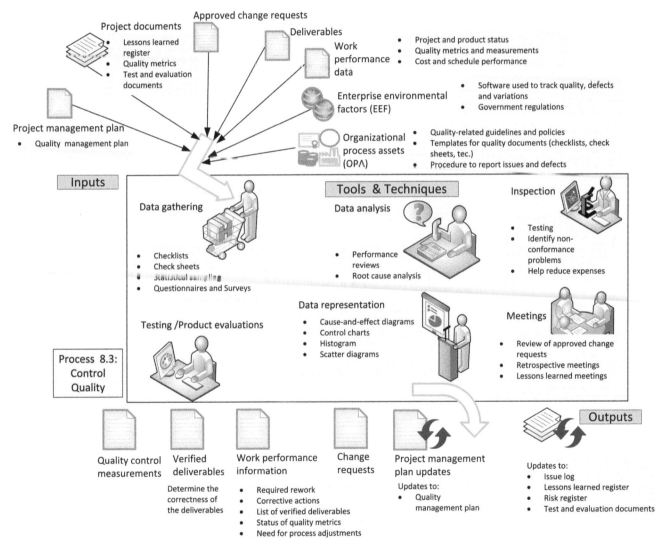

Figure 8-19: ITTO for Control Quality process

Key inputs for the **Control Quality** process are quality management plan, quality metrics, test and evaluation documents, and the list of project deliverables.

How do you control quality? To control quality, you first get a sample from the produced batch or from the previously-identified defective pieces which have since been rectified. You then inspect the sample to see if the pieces meet the planned quality standards. This is done using check sheets, checklists, quality metrics, etc.

---

* For the Exam *
Control Quality is the only process, which has verified deliverables as an output.

Check sheets (Tally sheets)

A check sheet (Fig. 8-20) is a form or document, used to record data about features of a product in real-time (as the produced is being produced). For example, if small iron cylinders are being ground in the factory, the machinist inspects the ground cylinders and records the number of defective cylinders on a check sheet. The information recorded in a check sheet can be represented using Pareto diagrams.

Cylinder Acceptance CheckSheet (Tally sheet)
Name of Quality Control Data recorder: Alberto Garcia

Location: Peoria, Illinois

Defect Description	Number of defect occurrences							Total Number of occurrences
	Week 1	Week 2	Week 3	Week 4	Week 5	Week 6	Week 7	
Misaligned press fit	⊬⊬⊤ ⊬⊬⊤	⊬⊬⊤ ⊬⊬⊤	⊬⊬⊤ ⊬⊬⊤ IIII	⊬⊬⊤ ⊬⊬⊤ ⊬⊬⊤	⊬⊬⊤ ⊬⊬⊤ III	⊬⊬⊤ ⊬⊬⊤ II	⊬⊬⊤ ⊬⊬⊤ IIII	88
Cylinder diameter outside specification limit	III	III	I	II	II	IIII	II	17
Visible crack lines on cylinder surface	I	I	II	II	I	II	II	11
Imperfect grinding of cylinder base	I	I	I	I	I	II	I	8
Defective pieces per week	15	15	18	20	17	20	19	124

Figure 8-20: Check sheet used to collect data on the number of defective cylinders produced each week

Another tool is the quality checklist. It is a document with a set of steps or tasks that need to be performed for a component or product. It helps as a reminder and builds consistency for all products. Table 8-3 shows the differences between a check sheet and a checklist.

Quality check sheet (Tally sheet)	Quality checklist
Document to record data about a product feature or attribute in real time as they are measured or generated.	Document with a list of steps (tasks) that need to be performed on a product.

Table 8-3: Difference between a quality check sheet and checklist

Statistical Sampling

Statistical sampling is a technique where you randomly select a subset of the population (batch) for inspection. The sample selected must represent the entire population. If there are various lots (batches) of products, a subset must be taken from each lot to ensure representation from all lots.

Why would you take a subset for testing and not test the entire set (100% testing)? Because testing all the pieces would be too time-consuming and expensive. Also, some of the testing procedures could be destructive to help determine the tensile or compressive strength of the pieces. In such procedures, the selected pieces are subjected to forces until it snaps, and you record the breaking force.

If your test procedures are non-destructive, would you test the entire lot? Yes! It would certainly be more time-consuming and expensive. In some cases, the customer or used could demand that 100% of the pieces in the batch must be tested before they can accept those.

As shown in Table 8-4, most of the quality-related information is either in the form of

- an attribute data (for example red or green, good or bad), or
- a variable data, which is a number within a pre-defined range.

	Attribute sampling	Variable sampling
Definition	The characteristics are defined as having or not having a feature or attribute. Each item is inspected and classified as either possessing or not possessing a feature.	The characteristic is measured numerically and could be anywhere but within a range. The data points are measurements on a numerical scale such as for density, the coefficient of friction, tensile strength, etc.
Examples	▪ The surface of the iron bar is either smooth or rough. ▪ A liquid is either alkaline or acidic.	▪ The cross-sectional area (e.g. 12 square mm.) of iron bar ▪ The pH value (e.g. 11) of a liquid

Table 8-4: Two Types of Statistical Sampling: Attribute Sampling and Variable Sampling

Control charts

A control chart (Fig. 8-21) is a visual representation that shows whether a process is stable and has predictable performance. It has two limits:

- Upper and lower specification limits: These are the maximum and minimum allowed values. They are based on prior agreements with the user or customer. There are penalties imposed if a product is outside these limits.
- Upper and lower control limits: These limits are based on the organizational policies and project requirements. They are specified by the process owner or project team. The spread between the

control limits is smaller than the spread between the specification limits. A process is considered out of control if we have any one of the following 3 scenarios:

o A data point is outside the control limits
o Seven consecutive plots are above the mean line
o Seven consecutive plots are below the mean line

In case the process is out of control, corrective action must be taken.

Control charts were initially used for manufacturing processes. But they are also now widely used to monitor cost variance, schedule variances, the frequency of scope changes, etc.

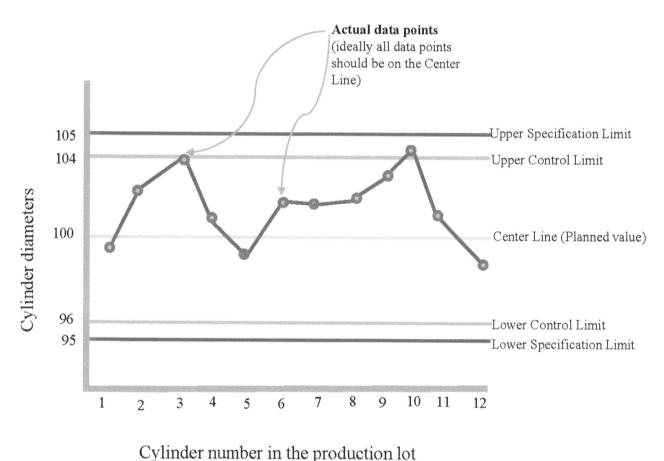

Cylinder number in the production lot

Figure 8-21: Control Charts

The inspection results are represented using control charts, histograms, scatter diagrams, etc. If defects are found, the root cause is identified using techniques such as fishbone diagrams. The root cause is used to develop corrective and preventive actions. This leads to change requests, which are an output of the **Control Quality** process.

Pareto diagrams

A Pareto diagram (Figures 8-22 and 8-23) is another technique for representing quality test data. It consists of vertical bar charts, where each bar represents the percentage of occurrences for each problem. The Y-axis is the percentage of the occurrence, accounting for 100% of the observations. The X-axis has the problem categories.

It helps to identify the causes or defects that lead to most of the observed problems. Pareto advocated an 80/20 principle (Pareto's Principle) which states that 80% of the problems are due to 20% of the causes. Fixing those 20% of the causes will yield the most improvements for product quality. Once those causes are resolved, then you can go ahead and identify the top root causes once again, from amongst the remaining ones, and focus on resolving those.

Pareto Diagram based on CheckSheet (Tally sheet)
Name of Quality Control Data recorder: Alberto Garcia
Location: Peoria, Illinois

Defect #	Defect Description	Total Number of defective occurrences (n) over 7 weeks	Percentage (n*100/124)
1	Misaligned press fit	88	70.97%
2	Cylinder diameter outside specification limit	17	13.71%
3	Visible crack lines on cylinder surface	11	8.87%
4	Imperfect grinding of cylinder base	8	6.45%
	Defective pieces over 7 weeks	124	100.00%

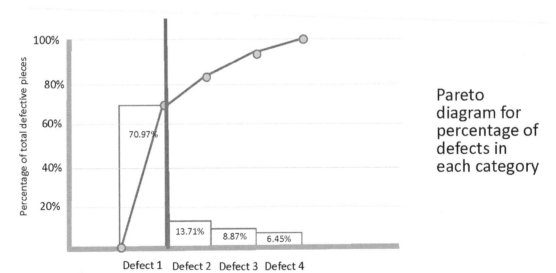

Pareto diagram for percentage of defects in each category

Figure 8-22 Example of a Pareto Diagram showing percentages of defects in produced cylinders

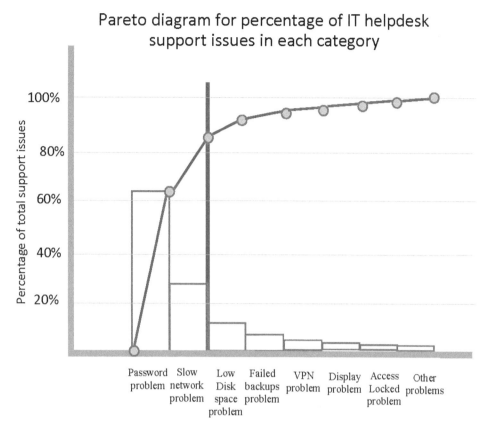

Figure 8-23: Example of Pareto Diagram showing percentages of IT helpdesk support problems

The key outputs of the **Control Quality** process are quality control measurements and work performance information. The in-progress or completed deliverables are inspected and this leads to verified (tested) deliverables and change requests to correct defects, if any.

More points for the exam:

- For quality-related questions, think of yourself a project manager in a factory or assembly line.
- Quality is sometimes binary (pass or fail).
- Usually, quality is about the degree to which the produced deliverables meet the pre-defined requirements.
- Preventing problems is generally easier and cheaper than resolving problems.
- The project team decides which quality metrics will be used during the project.
- Before signoff on any deliverable or work package, the **Control Quality** process must be used for validation.

Practice Questions for Chapter 8

1. Which of these would be considered as an appraisal cost?
   A. Cost for replacing the machinery after it was appraised and judged to be defective.
   B. Cost for testing a subset of the parts in a new lot.
   C. Cost for reviewing the quality of the factory equipment used for mass-production.
   D. Cost for revising the check sheets and checklists used for quality inspections.

2. Which of the following is not a suitable comparison between the grade and the quality of a product?
   A. Grade and quality can be used interchangeably provided the context is understood and conveyed in advance.
   B. A poor grade of a product will hinder its use just like poor quality will.
   C. Grade, just like product quality, should be kept at a high level for the product to be of benefit to most users.
   D. Grade is due to the intended design and planned functionality of a product. Quality is how well the product meets the requirements.

3. Which of the following is not an example of internal failure cost?
   A. Cost for rework to fix issues in parts identified by the quality control team before the parts are assembled.
   B. Cost for disposal of defective parts.
   C. Cost for testing to identify defective parts.
   D. Cost for regrinding of the parts that were identified as being too rough for use.

4. You are planning the quality budget for the products. You can invest in preventing problems or fixing the problems after the quality control team or customers have identified issues (if any). Which of the following would be the right thing to do?
   A. Spend money on prevention rather than trying to later fix defects.
   B. The cost of lost goodwill can be huge. Hence it is necessary to spend money to identify and prevent problems before the product goes to the customers.
   C. Defects found by customers can lead to bad publicity and potential for steep loss in sales and profits. Therefore, it is best to spend as much as possible, on building the right quality into the products.
   D. Look for a balance in spending money on preventing issues versus fixing defects. After a particular point, there is almost no return on the money spent on preventing problems.

5. Which of the following is not a suitable comparison between the specification limits and control limits of a product or process?
   A. Specification limits specify the range of acceptable outcomes. Control limits, on the other hand, identify the allowable boundaries of statistical variation for the product or process.
   B. Specification limits are usually defined by the client or user. But the control limits are defined by the required precision and accuracy for the process.
   C. Specification limit helps separate acceptable and unacceptable products. Control limits help guide the process and actions.
   D. A product that is outside the control limits is usually not acceptable since it is outside the specifications limits provided by the client or users.

6. Responsibility for quality policies lies with the:
   A. Project manager
   B. Project team members
   C. Senior management
   D. Project sponsor

7. Peter Perkins is a project manager at an engineering firm, which designs and manufactures cylinders and crankshafts for automobile manufacturers. He is explaining the distinction between accuracy and precision in a training session for the new quality inspectors. Which of the following would be true for him to state?
   A. Precision and accuracy refer to how close you are to the target dimensions.
   B. Accuracy is about how close the actual dimensions are to the target (or required) value. Precision is about how closely the actual measurements are grouped or clustered together. If the actual dimensions are closely clustered, the manufacturing is precise and if wide apart, they are not precise.
   C. If the manufacturing is precise, the dimensions will be close together and accuracy will be guaranteed to be acceptable.
   D. All the above statements are true.

8. The technique for continuous quality improvement, that was defined by Shewhart and later revised by Dr. Edwards Deming is:
   A. Plan-do-check-act (PDCA)
   B. Lean Six Sigma
   C. Total Quality Management (TQM)
   D. Delphi technique

9. Given a normal distribution, what percentage of the values, would lie within a band of six standard deviations around the mean?
   A. 68.27%
   B. 95.45%
   C. 99.74%
   D. 99.99%

10. Alan Simpson is a project manager in a jungle resort. He is trying to identify relationships (if any) between the predicted rainfall and the number of booked rooms in the resort. Which of the following diagrams could he use to illustrate the relationship?
    A. Scatter diagram
    B. Fishbone diagram
    C. Pareto diagram
    D. Cause-and-effect diagrams

11. Boyce Berry has joined a manufacturing firm in Japan as a project manager. She finds that the management system at the firm aims to involve all employees in continual improvement with a goal to achieve long-term success through customer satisfaction. Such a management approach is known as:
    A. Total Quality Management (TQM)
    B. Six Sigma
    C. Continual Improvement
    D. SIPOC (suppliers, inputs, process, outputs and customers) model

12. Detailed schedule estimates for the short-term horizon aimed at reducing flow times within production systems and response times when working with suppliers, internal teams and customers is referred to as:
    A. Plan-do-check-act (PDCA) methodology
    B. Supply chain management (SCM)
    C. Just-in-time (JIT) methodology
    D. SIPOC (suppliers, inputs, process, outputs and customers) model

13. Jessica Lee has joined a car manufacturer in Nagoya City, Japan. She sees that the company uses visualization tools in various departments. She enquires and comes to know that the boards enable improvement of the work flow by making work quantities and bottlenecks visible. There are tasks in various columns titled "need to do", "in-progress", "waiting", "done", etc. Such boards are referred to as:
    A. Kanban boards
    B. Information radiators or boards
    C. Work display boards
    D. Status report boards

14. Which of the following is true about Quality Management?
    A. Prevention is preferred over inspection.
    B. Prevention is about making sure that the processes are error-free. Inspection is about making sure that the errors or defective deliverables do not get to the users or customers.
    C. The hard and soft costs of correcting errors, once it is found during the inspection or during use by the customers, are usually higher than the cost of preventing mistakes.
    D. All the above statements are true

15. Which of the following would make a product hassle-free and easy-to-use for the users?
    A. High grade and low quality
    B. Low grade and high quality
    C. Low grade and low quality
    D. None of the above combinations is good enough for the product to be useful to the users.

ANSWERS

Question Number	Correct Answer	Explanation
1	B	Appraisal cost is cost related to inspecting the project deliverables or products. It is not about inspecting or upgrading machinery, equipment or documentation. These expenses are part of prevention cost.
2	A	Grade is due to the planned design and intention of the product's use. Quality is how well the product meets the planned design and intention. See Page 274 of the PMBOK®.
3	C	The cost of testing is appraisal cost (part of cost of conformance). The other choices are related to fixing defects and are failure costs (part of cost of non-conformance). Note the difference between appraisal and failure costs: ▪ Appraisal costs are for testing or inspections. It is possible that the tests may show that there are no defects. Hence there would be no failure costs. ▪ Failure costs, on the other hand, are due to defects, which must be fixed.
4	D	Sometimes, excess spending in trying to build quality or prevent defects may not be cost-effective.
5	D	A product can be outside the control limit, but it can still be within the specification limits and hence acceptable to the client or users.
6	C	The ownership of the quality (for policies, strategy and goals) at the organizational level is with the senior management. But the ownership of the quality of the project deliverables is with the project manager.
7	B	Accuracy is about being close to the required (target value. Precision is about measurements being close together and not widely spread around, regardless of how far those measurements are from the target value. It is possible that measurements are precise (closely clustered together) but far from the required value and hence not accurate.
8	A	PDCA was initially developed by Shewhart and later made popular by Dr. Edwards Deming, who is considered as the father of modern quality control. PDCA is used for continuous improvement of products and processes. Another version of PDCA is OPDCA were O stands for observation of current conditions.
9	C	For a normal distribution, you have ▪ 68.27% of the values within a band of 2 standard deviations around the mean, ▪ 95.45% of the values within a band of 4 standard deviations around the mean and ▪ 99.74% of the values within a band of 6 standard deviations This is referred to as 68-95-99.7 rule in statistics.
10	A	A scatter diagram is used to identify the relationship or correlation (positive, negative or none) between two variables. In this case the two variables are predicted rainfall and number of reserved rooms. ▪ Fishbone (also called cause-and-effect or Ishikawa) diagram is a wrong answer because it is used to identify the root cause of a problem. ▪ Pareto diagram is also a wrong answer because it is used to identify causes that lead to most of the issues.

11	A	TQM is a management approach where the effort for all the employees is to establish a customer-focused organization.. The 8 principles of TQM are: 1. Customer-focused efforts 2. Total employee involvement 3. Process-centered approach 4. Integrated systems 5. Systematic and strategic approach to achieving the organization vision and mission 6. Continual process improvement 7. Fact-based decision making 8. Effective communications These principles cannot be implemented in one step. Instead, it is implemented through a series of small improvements.
12	C	Just-in-time (JIT) methodology is aimed at reducing supply times for material, in-house inventory and production cycle time. In the 1990s the term *JIT* was replaced by *lean manufacturing*. Either of these could be in the exam.
13	A	Kanban boards are physical boards. They have cards with task names. Each card is placed in one column. The simplest boards have three columns titled, "things to do", "in-progress" and "done". This allows everyone to see the work status, identify bottlenecks and work on removing those.
14	D	Prevention is better and usually less expensive than fixing problems, found during the inspection or actual use.
15	B	Quality is about being defect-free. A high quality is required for a product to be easy to use and hassle-free. Grade of a product is about the features and functionalities of a product. Use of a low-grade product will be hassle-free, if the quality is high. A low-grade product would have limited functionalities but would also be less expensive than a high-grade product with more features.

CHAPTER 9
Resource Management

When we talk about resources, we usually think of people and the project team. However, in a project, in addition to human resources, you have material resources as well. Human resources include the project team, vendors, partners, testers, clients, business analysts, finance analysts, communication leads, deployment leads, etc. Material resources include equipment, office space, machinery, raw materials, etc. Most of these resources are shared amongst various ongoing projects.

The human and material resources are usually assigned part-time to various ongoing projects. Some resources may be assigned full-time to a project. However, it is your job, as a project manager, to request and get commitment for the required resources from the resource owner or functional manager. At the close of the project the resources must be released for other efforts within the organization.

There are 6 processes in the **Resource Management** Knowledge Area:

Planning Process Group	Executing Process Group	Monitoring and Controlling Process Group
9.1) Plan Resource Management 9.2) Estimate Resource Activities	9.3) Acquire Resources 9.4) Develop Team 9.5) Manage Team	9.6) Control Resources

Trends and Emerging Practices

There is an increasing trend of moving from a command-and-control structure to a collaborative and supportive approach. This approach is especially relevant for projects in an agile environment, where decision-making powers are usually delegated to the project team members.

Another trend is the reduction in the availability of project resources. Resources are pulled to help with operational run-the-business activities and help with multiple projects. They are under increased pressure to deliver more in less time. Therefore, project managers must get a commitment for resources and block resource time well in advance.

Table 9-1 lists a few techniques that can be used to manage scarce resources (raw material, semi-finished goods, project team, etc.).

#	Techniques to manage scarce resources	Definition
1	Lean management	Lean project management is about achieving improvements in productivity and quality by modifying processes (or even removing processes) that cause any resource wastage. It aims to streamline processes with a goal to reduce costs, eliminate waste, increase productivity and improve quality, thus leading to increased profits.
2	Just-in-time (JIT) management	It is an inventory strategy that increases efficiency and decreases waste by receiving goods just when they are required for production. This helps reduce inventory handling and storage costs. However, it requires that the buyers forecast demand accurately and order all raw materials in time. JIT was first developed and perfected within Toyota by Taiichi Ohno.
3	Total productive maintenance (TPM)	TPM is a maintenance program that focusses on keeping all equipment in top working conditions, with a modest investment in maintenance. The goal is to avoid any breakdowns or delays in the manufacturing processes and enhance production and employee morale. It was first advocated by Seiichi Nakajima, when he worked at Nippondenso, a company that manufactured parts for Toyota.
4	Theory of constraints (TOC)	TOC is a suite of management concepts, developed by Dr. Eliyahu M. Goldratt in his landmark book, "The Goal" published in 1984. He later adapted the concept to project management in another book, "Critical Chain", published in 1997. TOC helps identify the most important limiting factor (bottleneck or constraint) that is obstructing the achievement of a goal and then works to reduce the impact of that factor until it is no longer a limiting factor. Then it identifies the next most limiting factor and so on until there are no significant limiting factors.
5	Kaizen concept	Kaizen is a Japanese word that means "continual improvement" or "a change for the better". In business, it refers to activities that aim to *continuously improve* processes with a goal to reduce waste, improve efficiency and increase profits.

Table 9-1: Tools for managing resources (material or human) that are in short supply

Usually the work pressure within each organization is high and there is an implicit need to be effective and efficient. Nevertheless, the project manager must maintain a high degree of emotional intelligence (EI). EI is an ability to understand one's own as well as other people's emotions and then use that understanding to appropriately guide thoughts and actions. Figure 9-1 has the definitions and examples of inbound and outbound components of EI.

The study by Daniel Goleman in 1995 showed that EI makes up 67% of the abilities that are needed for superior performance in leaders and mattered twice as much as IQ (intelligence quotient) or technical expertise. He explained that EI consists of four key capabilities namely:

- Self-awareness,
- Self-management,
- Social awareness and
- Social skills.

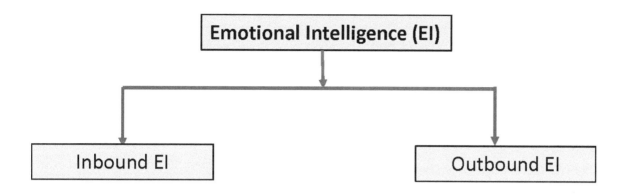

Inbound EI

Definition:
Ability to understand one's own feelings and reasons for those.

Example:
- Self-awareness
- Self-management
- Self-confidence
- Self-Control
- Trustworthiness
- Initiative-taking propensity
- Conscientiousness
- Adaptability

Outbound EI

Definition:
Ability to understand others feelings and relate to their feelings.

Example:
- Social awareness
- Organizational awareness
- Social skills
- Relationship management
- Communication skills
- Conflict management
- Teamwork and collaboration
- Influencing skills

Figure 9-1: Two Categories of Emotional Intelligence (EI)

Emotional quotient (EQ) is about understanding that there is a chain reaction that causes emotions. Those with high EQ are honest about their own emotions, and not hesitant to express their feelings. However, they must do so in a manner, that does not show others down or cast blame on anyone. A project manager with a high EQ brings openness and trust to the project and team members feel safe about expressing and discussing their emotional states. This in turn, brings about an improved level of communication and mutual understanding, leading to higher productivity and efficiency.

Another emerging trend is for more and more project resources (including project managers) to be freelancing or contracting. If the current trend of moving towards freelancing continues, the number of freelancers in the US workforce is expected to exceed the traditional fulltime job-holders.

Another evolving trend is towards self-organizing teams, where there is no centralized control. There is an expectation that the team will:

(1) accept and incorporate feedback into their activities,
(2) adapt themselves to the changing requirements,
(3) manage themselves without active monitoring, and
(4) get the work completed within the pre-determined time duration.

Another trend is towards geographically-distributed and virtual teams, where the project resources are spread across the world. This has been necessitated by the need to tap into expertise, regardless of where the resource is located. But on the other hand, it brings in handicaps such as language differences, lower trust, lack of transparency in sharing information, lack of appreciation of mutual efforts and accomplishments, etc. As a project manager, you need to mitigate the distributed team-related issues by:

- Storing all project documents on a shared folder or cloud-based application,
- Responding to emails, messages and phone calls immediately to reduce the feeling of remoteness, and
- Using video-conferencing.

There is also a trend of hiring project resources as consultants, who prefer to work remotely from their own home-office although they may be too far from the employer location. This trend of using remote resources for projects is expected to become more dominant and common in the future.

Tailoring Considerations

All the processes in **Resource Management** Knowledge Area and their techniques need not apply to all projects. The process details need to be customized or tailored based on the location of the resources, the diversity amongst the resources, the skills required for the project and their extent of involvement (part-time or full-time) in the project.

Considerations for Agile/Adaptive Environments

Projects that have frequent changes in requirements and scope need a highly collaborative environment. This can be done with self-organizing teams, which provides:

- more innovative ideas for solving problems,
- easier integration of activities that initially appear quite incongruent and different,
- a higher amount of on-the-job training and knowledge-sharing, and
- more flexibility for scheduling tasks.

Table 9-2 describes the three types of teams, based on the authority and scope of the team members. Out of these three, self-organizing teams are usually the most suitable for agile projects.

	Types of teams	Definition
1	Manager-led teams	In these teams, the project resources report to the project manager, who functions as the boss of the team and project lead. The project manager, in turn, reports to the project sponsor or another person external to the project. This is an example of a linear hierarchy.
2	Self-organizing teams	These teams are somewhere in between manager-led and self-governing teams. The overall work scope and direction comes from outside. However, the team decides on how the work will be scheduled, executed and monitored to complete the deliverables. These teams are usually found to most effective and efficient in an agile environment, where the requirements and work scope are not fixed.
3	Self-governing teams	These teams are self-formed and self-directed. The team is self-formed because the team consists of members who have been selected by each other to be in the team. The team is self-directed because they do not have a nominated or appointed manager or leader. The governance of the team comes from within the team. The near-term work scope is also something that the team has decided to do.

Table 9 -2: Types of project teams

Process 1: Plan Resource Management

> PMBOK®: Page 312
> Process Group: Planning

In this process, you define how you will estimate and acquire what you need (physical and human resources) for the project and how you will utilize those resources.

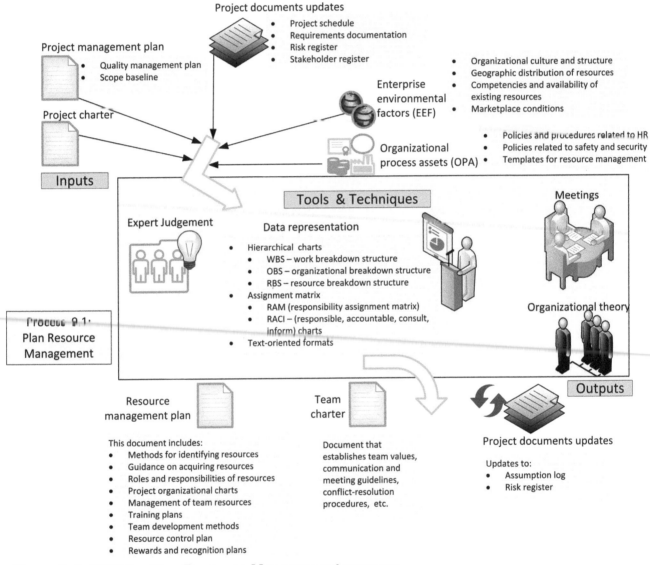

Figure 9-2: ITTO for Plan Resource Management process

The key inputs are:

- Project charter: It has the approved work scope, budget and time estimates, although without any details. However, those can help in determining the amount and type of resources required to complete the work within the allocated time frame.

- Quality management plan: the required quality determines the skill level and characteristics of the resources.
- Scope baseline: the scope and deliverables determine the resources necessary for the project.

The output is a resource management plan that helps establish:

- responsibilities and roles of each of the assigned staff members
- an organizational hierarchy for the project
- reporting relationships
- schedule for acquisition and release of resources
- team-building strategies and activities
- training requirements
- plans for performance-based recognition and rewards
- safety and compliance requirements for the work executed by the project team

The resource management plan contains the roles and responsibilities for the team members. This can be documented in one of the following three formats:

1. Hierarchical format,
2. Matrix-based format, and
3. Text-oriented format.

1. **Hierarchical format for role and responsibilities**: This is suitable for representing high-level roles. One example, which we have seen earlier, is the work breakdown structure (WBS). For resource management, we can use a similar graphical, top-down format to show positions and relationships.

Examples of hierarchical formats are:

(a) Work breakdown structure (WBS): WBS is used to show the deliverables, work packages, and areas of responsibilities.
(b) Organizational breakdown structure (OBS, Figure 9-3): This shows the organization's departments, teams or units. The project activities or work packages are listed under each unit. Each team or unit can look at its portion in the OBS to see all the activities that they own, instead of having to scan the entire project plan or WBS.

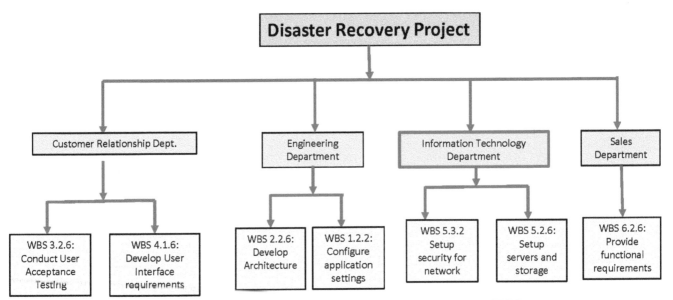

Figure 9-3: Hierarchical chart for Organizational Breakdown Structure (OBS)

(c) Resource breakdown structure (RBS, Figure 9-4): It is a hierarchical chart for all resources (staff members, equipment, and facilities) assigned to a project. Each lower or descending level has a more detailed description of the resource, until it is specific or small enough, to be used in conjunction with the WBS. RBS is also used to track project costs, as incurred, be each resource type.

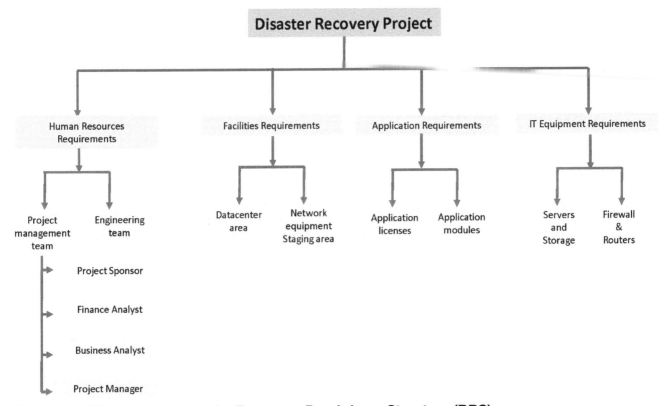

Figure 9-4: Hierarchical chart for Resource Breakdown Structure (RBS)

2. **Matrix-based format for role and responsibilities**: This is a grid or table that shows the project resources assigned for each work package or activity. It is called a responsibility assignment matrix (RAM), and created for various assignments of ownership, as in Fig. 9-5. For example, there could be a primary or secondary owner for each work package. Another example of an assignment matrix is a RACI (responsible, accountable, consult and inform) matrix, which shows a clear delineation of ownership and assigned work.

3. **Text-oriented format for role and responsibilities**: These are used when you need a detailed description of the responsibilities, skills and authority of the resources. The text-based document is also known as positions description document or role-responsibility-authority document.

Two examples of a Responsibility Assignment Matrix (RAM)

Primary and Secondary Contact for each work package for Project A				
Work package /Team member	Ben L.	Kerner W.	Williams A.	Stephen G.
Architecture and Design	P			B
User acceptance Testing	B	P		
Requirements documentation			B	P
Business case development			B	P

Legend: P=Primary Contact   B=Backup Contact

RACI Matrix for Project A				
Work package \Team member	Ben L.	Kerner W.	Williams A.	Stephen G.
Architecture and Design	R	C	C	A
User acceptance Testing	A	R	C	I
Requirements documentation	I	I	A	R
Business case development	C	A	R	C

Legend: RACI (Responsibility, Accountable, Consult and Inform) Matrix

Figure 9-5: Two matrix-based formats for Responsibility Assignment Matrix (RAM)

Regardless of the format used, each team member must have a clear understanding of their roles and responsibilities in the project. Figure 9-6 shows the various components of a resource management plan:

- Role and responsibilities plan: describes the function, granted authority, assigned duties and required competency for the resources needed for the project.
- Staffing management plan: specifies how the resource requirements will be met. A key component of the staffing management plan is the resource histogram (Figure 9-7). It is a graphic representation of how many hours a particular resource, person or team is needed during each month or week for a project.
- Project organization chart: has a graphic depiction of the team members and their reporting relationships.

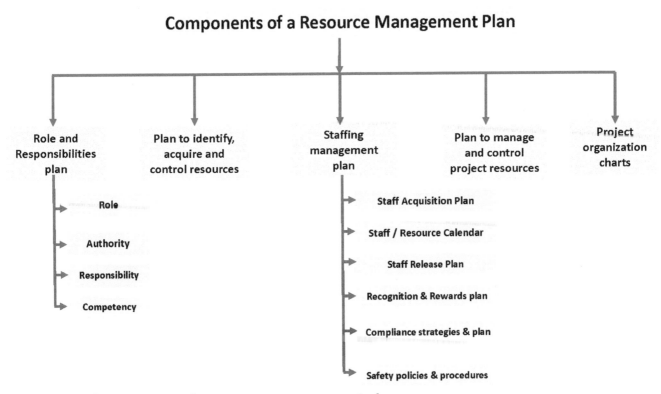

Figure 9-6: Components of a resource management plan

Figure 9-7 shows a resource histogram where the planned (forecasted) and utilized (actuals) man-months for a project team are shown for each month.

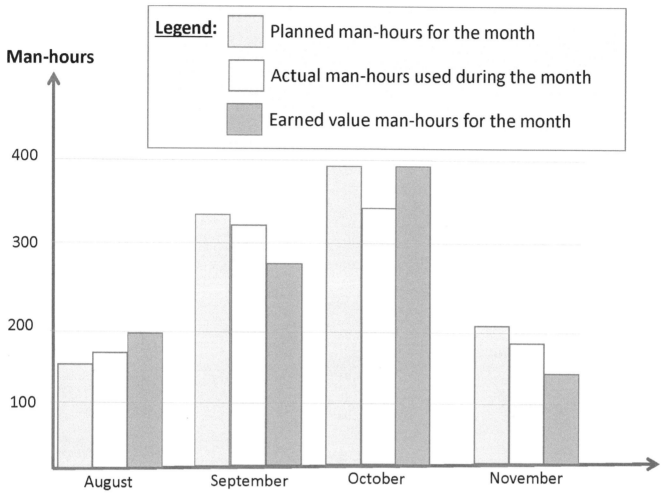

Figure 9-7: Resource histogram showing planned, actual and earned value man-hours for a 4-month project

Besides the resource management plan, another output is the team charter, which is a document containing the team values, operating guidelines, meeting guidelines, communication guidelines, a process to resolve conflicts if any, and agreements between the functional teams.

Process 2: Estimate Activity Resources

PMBOK®: Page 320
Process Group: Planning

In this process, we estimate the resources required for each activity, such as:

- Raw or processed material
- Equipment or machinery
- Consumables
- Manpower
- Skills and know-how

The inputs, tools and techniques and outputs are shown in Figure 9-8.

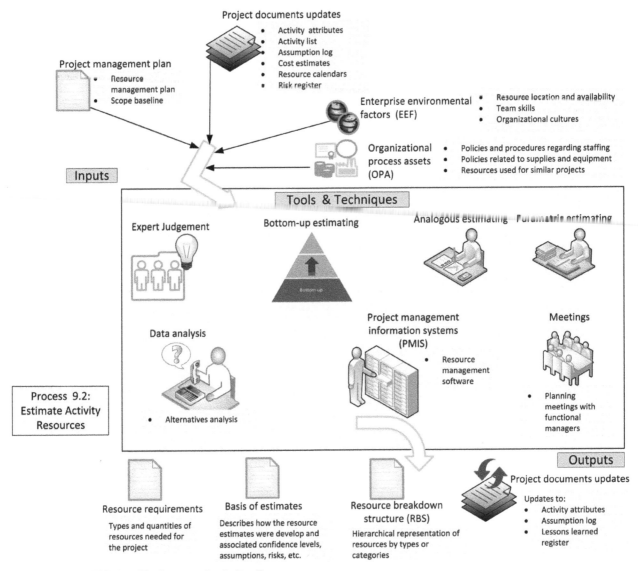

Figure 9-8: ITTO for Estimate Activity Resources process

You also determine the quantity and characteristics for the required resources. Think about why you must know what is required to complete each work package or activity? You would need this to estimate the time needed (duration) for each activity and to develop the project schedule.

How would you estimate the resources needed for each activity? You can use data published for each activity by different organizations. A common technique is **bottom-up estimating**, which involves the following two steps:

1. You estimate the required resources for the lowest-level components of the WBS. But if these activities are too complex to estimate, you can decompose these into smaller tasks and estimate the resources needed.
2. You then aggregate or add the required resources to get an estimate at the activity level.

Besides bottom-up estimation, the other two techniques are:

-   **Analogous estimation,** where the estimate is based on actual numbers from a previous similar project
-   **Parametric estimation**, where you identify a parameter and use that to estimate the resources needed. For example, if painting 5 linear feet of fence uses a two-liter can of paint, 100 linear feet of fence would need 20 cans.

The key outputs are the resource requirements (required skills and experience levels, the quantity of resources needed, when they will be needed, etc.) and the resource breakdown structure (Figure 9-4).

Process 3: Acquire Resources

PMBOK®: Page 328
Process Group: Executing

This process is concerned with acquiring resources needed for a project. The resources could be equipment, facilities, machinery, hardware, application licenses, etc. These resources may belong to certain departments, functional managers, partners, vendors, users, etc. Do you think that it is necessary to let them know, well in advance, that you will temporarily need their resources? Usually, yes! You must first, decide what you require and when. Then you can ask the resource owner for a commitment to provide the needed resources.

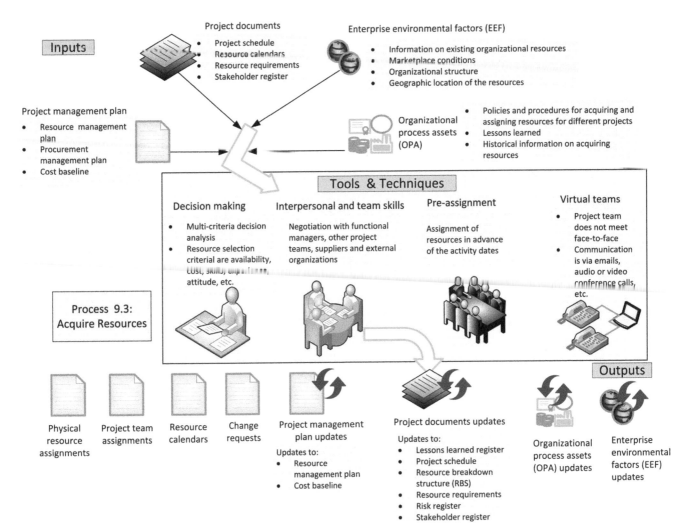

Figure 9-9: ITTO for Acquire Resources process

In a project-based organization, acquiring resources may be easy because the project team reports to the project manager. But, in a matrix or functional organization, the project staff does not report to the project manager. The project manager, therefore, must negotiate with the functional manager and get a commitment for resource time.

How do you decide on what is needed for the project? Before you negotiate with the functional managers or external parties for staff hours, you need to decide on a list of members you require for the project. But how do you select members for the project team? You need to develop a set of criteria to select your project team such as:

- Skills, knowledge and ability of the team members
- Experience in similar roles
- Availability of the team members
- Cost per hour of the member
- Attitude to see if the team member can work cohesively with others in the project team.

The next step would be to work and negotiate with the resource owners. You can be sure that there are other projects and operational tasks competing for the same resources. Organizational objectives, project priority and interpersonal skills play a strong role to decide if resources are allocated to your project or not! The project management team needs to negotiate with division heads, vendors, partners, suppliers and contractors for resources needed for the project. Negotiation and inter-personal skills are important tools for this process. A project management team's ability to influence is a critical factor in getting resources for the project.

The key outputs are:

- Physical resource assignments: a document containing the physical resources needed, when they are needed, the geographical location of those resources, etc.
- Project team assignments: a document containing the names of assigned resources and their roles and responsibilities.
- Resource calendars: contains the availability of resources, a list of holidays, etc.
- Change requests: In case, a resource is not available when needed for an activity on the critical path, and there are no workarounds, you will need to create a change request to extend the schedule baseline. If you can find a workaround but it is more expensive, you again may need a change request to increase the project budget.

Process 4: Develop Team

PMBOK®: Page 336
Process Group: Executing

The objective of this process is to improve capabilities, know-how, skills and motivation of the project team members. Another objective is to improve the interaction amongst the members for smoother project progress and higher performance.

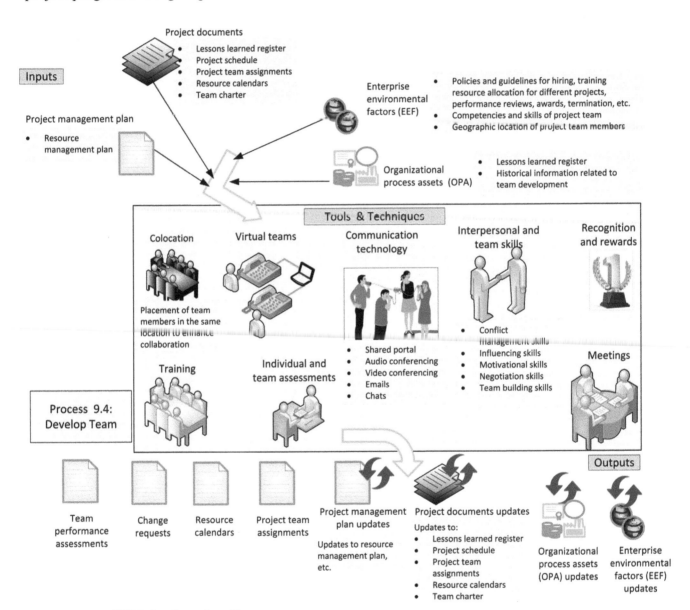

Figure 9-10: ITTO for Develop Team process

There are two key areas of development for the project team:

1. Development of abilities, competencies and knowledge: This can be done by formal training, on-the-job training and by cross-training and mentoring between the team members. The project managers need to arrange for these to happen.
2. Development of trust, cooperation and teamwork: This is done by creating a cohesive and collaborative team culture, where each member works for the progress of the project.

Table 9-3 shows the five stages of team development, which is known as the Tuckman-Ladder model.

	Phases	Bruce Tuckman and Jensen 1977: 5 phases of Team Formation
1	Forming	• Team meets and learns about the project and their roles. • There is anxiety but politeness and reliance on the project management team for information. • Team members tend to be independent and not open.
2	Storming	• Team begins to question the project work, decisions & approach. • There is a sense of conflict, disagreements and "I do not want to do this" thoughts. • Team members are neither collaborative nor open to proposed ideas. • The environment is not productive.
3	Norming	• Team members begin to work together and adjust their views and actions to support each other. • There is a new sense of unity, trust and willingness to work together towards the common good of the project.
4	Performing	• There is a sense of inter-dependence and "we are in this together". • There is interest in getting the work completed by helping each other. • Members collaborate and work through issues, efficiently and successfully.
5	Adjourning	• Deliverables are completed (as part of the **Close Project or Phase** process). • Staff members are released from the project. • Team moves on to another project or group.

Table 9-3: Five stages of team development in the Tuckman-Ladder model

Process 5: Manage Team

PMBOK®: Page 345
Process Group: Executing

The goal of the **Manage Team** process is to boost the performance of the resources and make sure that the project progresses as planned.

How is this done? This is done by tracking the performance of the resources and by identifying and removing roadblocks, conflicts and behavioral issues. You need to make sure that the resources are performing and that the project progresses as expected.

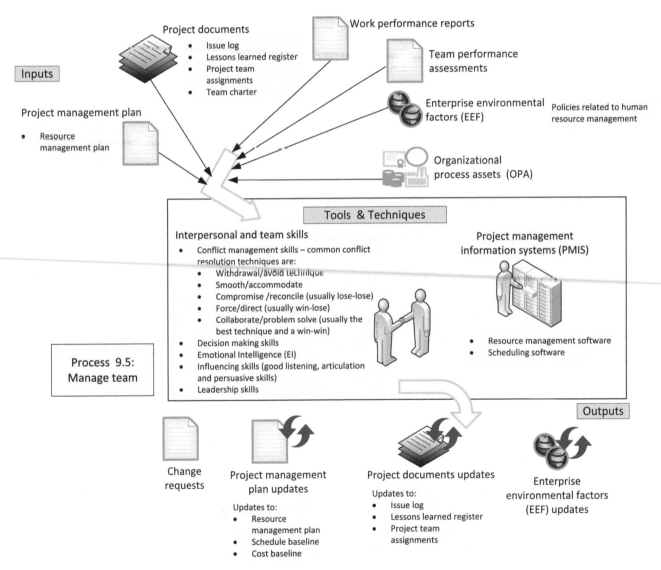

Figure 9-11: ITTO for Manage Team process

For the exam, you need to remember the key management styles. Which is the best style? It depends on the situation and circumstances.

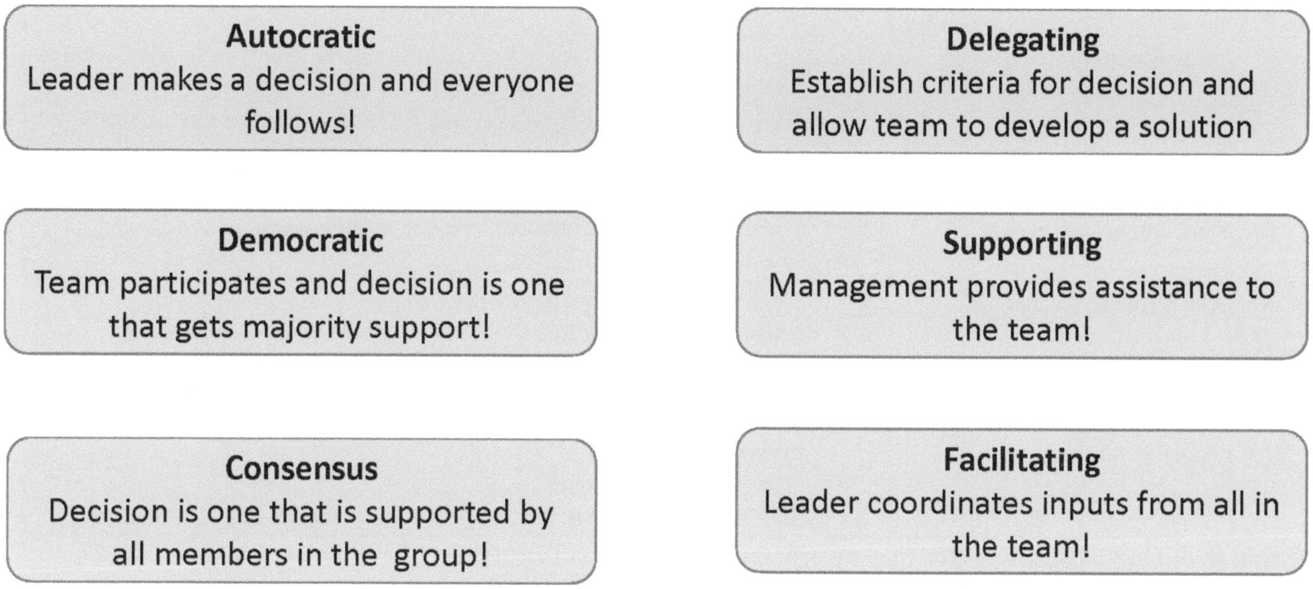

Autocratic Leader makes a decision and everyone follows!	**Delegating** Establish criteria for decision and allow team to develop a solution
Democratic Team participates and decision is one that gets majority support!	**Supporting** Management provides assistance to the team!
Consensus Decision is one that is supported by all members in the group!	**Facilitating** Leader coordinates inputs from all in the team!

Figure 9-12: Management styles, adopted for managing resources in a project

For the exam, you will need to also know the various theories or techniques related to resource management.

Conflict resolution techniques

Do conflicts happen? Yes! The reasons for conflict are disagreements between stakeholders or resources on the project schedule, priorities, resource availability, expenses to be incurred, technical preferences, administrative procedures, etc. Note that, contrary to what you may think, personality is not a root cause for conflict. Usually, in the workplace, the other factors mentioned above are root causes of conflict. However, personality differences may pose a hindrance in resolving conflicts.

Resolving conflicts is also an important tool for managing resources. How do you resolve conflicts? There are 5 general techniques (Table 9-4 and Figure 9-13), also known as Thomas/Kilmann model. These techniques are not all common sense and you need to know the names and definitions for the exam!

#	Conflict resolution techniques	Description
1	Withdraw/Avoid	▪ Ignore the conflict since it is uncomfortable to deal with it. Also, there is no time for it, now! ▪ Wish that someone else will resolve it or you will get around to that later! Or, the conflict will go away on its own! ▪ This is the worst approach
2	Smooth/Accommodate	▪ Focus on points of agreement, and not on differences ▪ lose-lose resolution!
3	Compromise/Reconcile	▪ None of the parties get their way! ▪ Lose-lose for both sides
4	Force/Direct	▪ Enforce one viewpoint and discard everything else
5	Collaborate/Problem Solve (also called confront)	▪ Include everyone, take the problem head-on and arrive at a resolution that everyone buys into! ▪ This is the best approach! ▪ Win-win for all parties!

Table 9-4: Description of the five conflict-resolution techniques

In the exam, you will be given a description and you will be asked to identify which of the five techniques is being described. Which do you think is usually the most effective for resolving conflicts? Think for a minute before you go ahead and read the answer. The answer is collaboration and problem solving, because this technique results in buy-in and commitment from the involved members.

Now that you know the five conflict-resolution techniques, the one you choose to use depends on factors such as:

- the degree of cooperation provided by those involved in the conflict,
- time pressure to get to the resolution,
- stand (position) taken by those involved,
- intensity or importance of the conflict,
- the degree of assertiveness of those involved, and
- need for a quick, short-term resolution versus the need for a stable, long-term resolution.

The Thomas/Kilmann model shows the preferred technique to be used, when faced with factors listed in the horizontal and vertical axes in Figure 9-13.

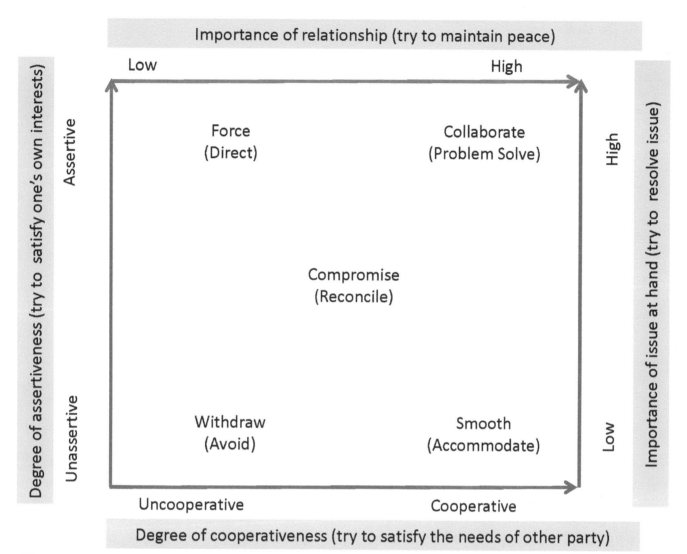

Figure 9-13: Thomas/Kilmann Model: recommendation for the use of a conflict-resolution technique

EXERCISE TIME:

Question:
The table below describes a few situations where the objective is to resolve conflicts. Which of the 5 techniques (Collaborate, Compromise, Smooth, Withdraw, Force) in the Thomas/Kilmann model is being deployed in each of the cases described below?

- Case 1: "Okay! Let us hear everyone's view and we will then try to get to a resolution that we can all agree upon!"
- Case 2: "Okay! Let us get this completed! Each of you do what is best for your part of the project"
- Case 3: "Okay! I need to go! Let us take this up later!"
- Case 4: "Okay! You both want the progress of the project in mind! But your decisions are not aligned. Please discuss amongst yourselves and come to a middle path."
- Case 5: "Okay. I have heard your viewpoints and solutions. I have a different solution. Let us resolve this my way!"
- Case 6: "Okay! Harry thinks we need to purchase a faster storage array, but Tim thinks the existing ones are fast enough! Let us test what we have before we make a decision!"
- Case 7: Okay! I understand that you both want to purchase a new server! But I do not have funds and there is no way I am going to buy that server now!"

Please identify the technique used for the above cases before reading ahead to the answers.

Solution:
- Case 1: Collaborate/ Problem Solve
- Case 2: Smooth / Accommodate
- Case 3: Withdraw / Avoid
- Case 4: Smooth / Accommodate
- Case 5: Force/Direct
- Case 6: Collaborate/ Problem Solve
- Case 7: Force/Direct

We will now look at theories for motivating project members. These will appear in the exam. You need to know which of the motivational theories presented here apply best to a given situation.

McGregor's Theory of X and Y

This was suggested by Douglas McGregor (1906 – 1964). He was a management professor at the MIT Sloan School of Management and president of Antioch College from 1948 to 1954. He also taught at the Indian Institute of Management at Kolkata, India.

He proposed 'Theory X and Theory Y', describing that some workers want to avoid work, do as little as possible to get by and they need a great deal of direction. Theory Y states that the other group of workers is sincerely interested in doing their best and given the freedom, will do well.

#	Theory X workers	Theory Y workers
1	Dislike work and wish to avoid it.	Want to take an interest in work and enjoy work.
2	Must be forced to work hard enough and comply.	Direct themselves towards a common goal.
3	Want to avoid responsibility and must be directed.	Thrive on taking up more responsibility.
4	Have almost no creativity or ambition.	Are highly creative when given the opportunity or recognition.
5	Are motivated by fear and possible loss of job and salary.	Are motivated by a desire of self-development and wish to contribute to the world.

Table 9-5: Theory X and Theory Y, as proposed by Douglas McGregor

Herzberg's two-factor Theory (Motivation-Hygiene Theory)

Frederick Herzberg (1923 – 2000) was an American psychologist, who became one of the most renowned management professionals in the USA. He advocated that there are two sets of factors at a workplace: hygiene and motivational factors. He also theorized that job satisfaction and job dissatisfaction act independently of each other.

Hygiene (maintenance) factors include company policies, benefits, relationship with the boss, workplace conditions, sense of job security, etc. These factors do not provide motivation for improved performance. However, if these are not implemented or if they are improperly deployed, there will be wide-spread dissatisfaction and apathy, which will lead to reduced performance. Hygiene factors must, therefore, be correctly implemented.

On the other hand, motivational factors lead to improved performance by each worker. These include freedom, increased responsibility, recognition and opportunity for advancement and self-growth. These factors must also be implemented.

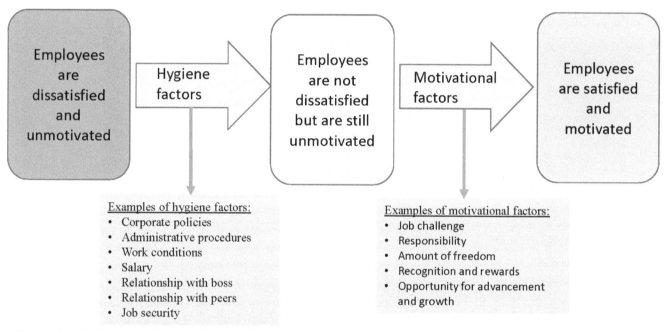

Figure 9-14: Herzberg's two-factor theory on hygiene and motivational factors at the workplace

Maslow's Hierarchy of Needs

One of the most popular motivational theories is Maslow's Hierarchy of Needs as shown in Figure 9-15. It states that human beings have lower-level fundamental needs such as physiological and safety-related needs. These must be met first before they can move on to the next level of needs such as social and self-esteem and then later move to self-actualization needs. The final level of self-actualization includes acceptance of facts, attaining contentment and reaching one's full potential for creativity.

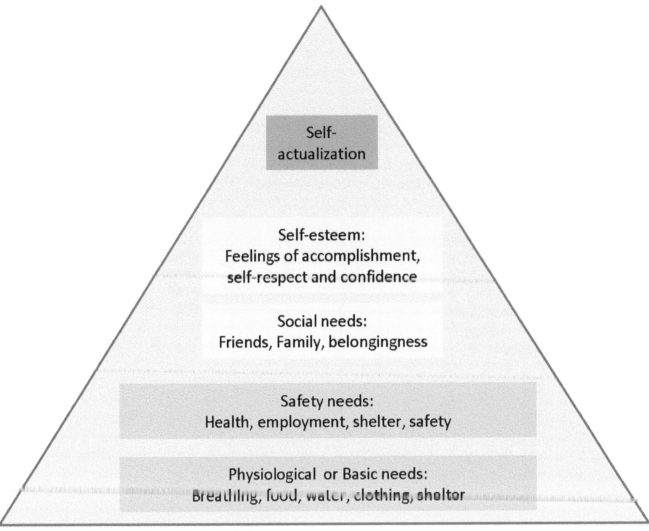

Figure 9-15: Maslow's Hierarchy of Needs

ERG (Existence, Relatedness and Growth) Theory

ERG Theory (Fig. 9-16) focuses on three key levels namely **E**xistence, **R**elatedness and **G**rowth. It is like Maslow's Hierarchy of Needs.

- Existence includes basic needs such as food, water, safety and shelter.
- Relatedness includes the need to feel connected to others and the need to establish and maintain relationships.
- Growth includes the need for personal achievement and self-actualization.

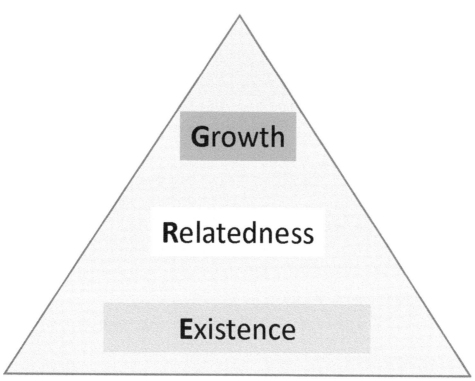

Figure 9-16: ERG Needs

David McClelland's Theory of Needs

David McClelland's (1917 – 1998) was an American Psychologist. He developed his Theory of Motivation which advocates that people are motivated by power, achievements and/or affiliation. This is also called "Three Needs Theory".

- Those motived by **power**: They like to organize, motivate and lead others. They are motivated if they get more and more responsibility.
- Those motived by **achievement**: They like challenges (reasonable and attainable ones) and they are motivated by the vision of attaining seemingly difficult goals and gaining recognition for their achievement and results.
- Those motived by **affiliation**: They like to be a part of a team and are motivated by a sense of acceptance by a group.

Vroom's Expectancy Theory

Professor Victor Vroom (b. 1932) is a professor at the Yale School of Management in New Haven, CT, in the US. He is an authority on the psychological analysis of behavior, particularly on decision-making and leadership.

He developed an Expectancy Theory (Fig. 9-17) which explains that the amount of effort or work from a staff member depends on the perception or expectation that his or her efforts will result in the desired outcome. Staff members and employees are motivated when they believe and expect the followed:

- Their efforts will lead to better job performance.
- Improved job performance will lead to rewards, such as an increase in benefits and salary.
- These rewards will help the member or employee achieve personal goals.

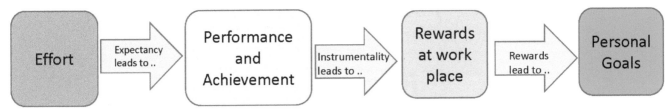

Figure 9-17: Victor Vroom's Expectancy Theory

Vroom's Expectancy Theory (Fig. 9-17) establishes the link between employee's efforts, achievements and meeting organizational goals, rewards and fulfillment of personal goals.

Process 6: Control Resources

PMBOK®: Page 352
Process Group: Monitoring and Controlling

Control Resources is a process of making sure that the previously-committed resources are available, deployed effectively and working as efficiently, as planned. It compares the actual utilization of the resources versus what was planned.

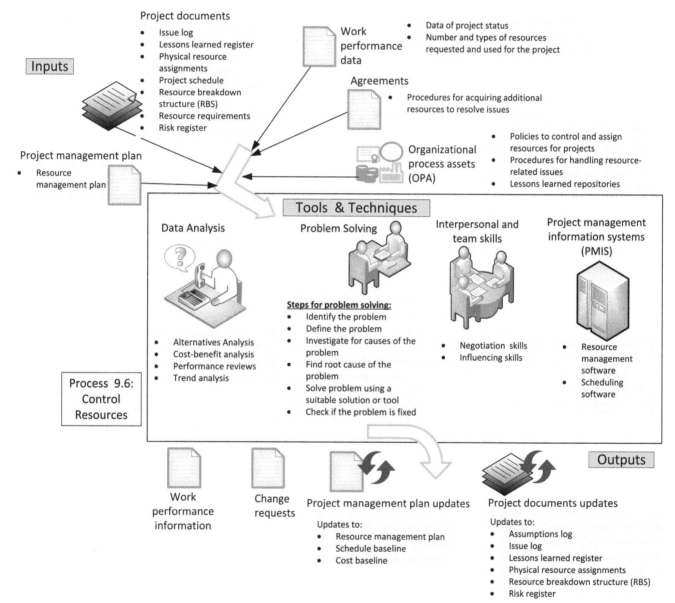

Figure 9-18: ITTO for Control Resources process

The key inputs are the resource management plan and project documents such as the issue log, physical resource assignments, resource breakdown structure (RBS), project schedule, resource requirements, risk register, etc.

- The project schedule can be used to show what, where and when resources will be required for each project activity.
- The resource requirement specifies the details of what (material, manpower, equipment, supplies, etc.) are needed for the project.
- The risk register specifies the risks that can impact the availability of the previously-committed resources for the project.

Do you get into a situation when some resources (equipment, manpower, etc.) were promised but could not be delivered or provided when actually needed! There could be several problems that can lead to unavailability of the committed resources. The problems could be from within the organization. Other projects may need the same resources. These conflicts are taken up at a higher level for resolution and the decision is not in the project manager's control. The problems could also be due to external sources. A vendor may have gone out of business.

How do you make sure that you get and control resources? Getting resources does not mean you must push or shoulder away other projects to make space for your own. It is about solving problems in an open, collaborative and honest manner. You need to keep "what is good for the organization" as the central criteria. You, first, need to accurately identify the problem, then investigate alternate solutions and select the most optimum solution for implementation. All this requires collaboration and good negotiation and interpersonal skills.

Controlling resources also requires that you make good use of the resources allocated to your projects. You must analyze the actual utilization of the resources and compare that to the planned utilization. If there are variations, then you need to again identify the various alternate solutions to resolve the variances. You can use cost-benefit analysis to rank the solutions. This will help you select the most optimum solution to resolve the variances.

The outputs of the process are work performance information, change requests to implement the selected solutions and updates to the various project documents and plans. The work performance information shows gaps in *planned* versus *actual* resource availability and work completed using the resources.

More points for the exam:

- You are working in a strong matrixed organization which adds complexity to team-building and conflict resolutions.
- The responsibilities of the project manager are to:
    - o Get commitment from functional managers for required resources
    - o Confirm the availability of resources
    - o Ensure team-building
    - o Ensure high performance by the project team
    - o Resolve conflicts, preferably by collaboration and
    - o Establish a rewards and recognition system.
- The project team helps develop project plans, but coordination and ensuring progress are the project manager's responsibility.
- The project manager is in-charge of the project, but not the resources and is also not an authority (or subject matter expert) on technical matters.
- Conflicts are unavoidable and can be beneficial for the project because it can, in turn, lead to discussions and identification of problems with the project plans and execution.

Practice Questions for Chapter 9

1. Which of the following powers can help motivate project resources to be more effective and efficient?
   A. Referent power
   B. Formal power
   C. Reward power
   D. Penalty power

2. You are managing a virtual team of 20 members located in Europe, Asia and South America. You need to document their location, availability, national holidays, expertise, etc. Such a document is known as:
   A. Resource attributes
   B. Resource breakdown structure
   C. Resource assignments
   D. Resource calendar

3. You are working with a project team with members in different time zones. Which of the following techniques cannot be used for team-building?
   A. Co-location
   B. Use of recognition and rewards to motivate the team
   C. Use of your conflict management skills
   D. Use of your negotiation and influencing skills

4. Which of these is not an example of a hierarchical chart?
   A. Resource breakdown structure
   B. Work breakdown structure
   C. Organizational breakdown structure
   D. Responsibility assignment matrix

5. Which of the following is not one of the trends or emerging practices in resource management?
   A. Command-and-control structures for managing projects
   B. Delegating more and more decision-making down to project team members
   C. Developing a collaborative and supportive approach or managing projects
   D. Encouraging a trend towards self-organizing teams

6. Sue Simpson is working for a global natural gas driller with its headquarters in Perth, Australia, that is structured as a matrix organization. She has almost no legitimate power and little control over them. Why?
   A. Because of the geographical separation and the fact that the team members are not in Perth.
   B. Because she does not know the technologies for natural gas drilling.
   C. Because of the absence of an incentive-reward program.
   D. Because the team members do not report to her.

7. A methodology to identify the most critical limiting factor or bottleneck and then work to remove those, until it is no longer a limiting factor, is known as:
   A. Total productive maintenance (TPM)
   B. Total quality management (TQM)
   C. Continual improvement
   D. Theory of constraints (TOC)

8. Harold Powers is a project manager for a software development firm. He is estimating the types and quantity of computer equipment and resource skills that he will require for a new project to customize and deploy an ERP application. The team also needs to support the network infrastructure at client offices in New Zealand, South Africa and Peru. Which of the following techniques can Harold use?
   A. Bottom-up estimating
   B. Alternatives analysis
   C. Parametric estimating
   D. All of the above

9. Which of the following is the best practice for when creating a RACI (responsible, accountable, consult and inform) matrix?
   A. Make sure that the accountability for each activity is with only one person.
   B. For resource leveling, it is best to make sure each person is accountable for one activity only, especially if the activity is on the critical path. This helps the person dedicate his time to that activity.
   C. A project team member should be accountable for only one activity, regardless of whether the activity is on the critical path or not. Also, accountability for an activity should be on only one person.
   D. Multiple persons can be consulted and informed for an activity. But only one person should be held responsible and accountable for an activity. This helps avoid confusion on who is in charge of the activity.

10. Bob Belkin is working to obtain team members and equipment for his project to relocate employees to a new office in another part of the city. Which of the following project documents does he require to do the work?
    A. Project schedule
    B. Resource requirements
    C. Resource calendars
    D. All of the above

11. Which of the following is not a technique for development of project resources?
    A. Try to place all active team members in the same office.
    B. Maintain an online team calendar.
    C. Use work performance information to optimize utilization of resources.
    D. Promote the use of online chats or instant messaging amongst team members.

12. Alexa Ashton is managing an oil and natural gas exploration project in a remote area in northern Australia. She has a team of 30 field engineers but they are exhausted and see no end to the project. They have also been working with little breaks and are tired of working overtime. What should she do?
    A. Ask the customer to temporarily halt the project
    B. Speak with the customer to reduce the project scope or allow more time for the project
    C. Hire contingent and temporary workers from the local area
    D. Continue to make the existing engineers work overtime

13. A manager who trusts that the employees are internally motivated and that they aspire to improve their work performance and quality is:
    A. Theory X manager
    B. Theory Y manager
    C. Theory Z manager
    D. A manager who follows McGregor principals

14. Tom Timbers is a project manager for a softwood lumber exporter in the British Columbia, Canada. He senses a lot of conflicts between fellow project managers over assignment of loggers, lumberjacks and equipment. Which of the following is possibly not a key cause for conflicts between the project managers?
    A. A scarcity of resources, that must be distributed between the projects
    B. Differences in salaries
    C. Scheduling priorities
    D. Personal work styles

15. Which of the following is a technique for controlling resources?
    A. Alternatives analysis
    B. Cost-benefit analysis
    C. Trend analysis
    D. All the above

ANSWERS

Question Number	Correct Answer	Explanation
1	C	All choices are correct, but you need to pick the best answer. Reward power is the best choice. Referent (respect that others hold for your experience and credibility) and formal (positional) power can help in the near term, but may not help in the long-term. Penalty power (ability to provide negative consequences) will not motivate today's well-informed and hyper-connected teams.
2	D	A resource calendar is a document that has the availability of the project resources (people, equipment, machinery, etc.), skills levels, geographical location, holidays, etc. See Page 323 in the PMBOK®.
3	A	Colocation is placing team members in the same physical location to enhance their ability to work together as a team.
4	D	Responsibility assignment matrix is not a hierarchical chart. A hierarchical chart is a way to represent the organizational hierarchy and is used commonly for WBS, OBS and RBS charts.
5	A	An emerging trend is to move away from command-and-control structures and move towards use of agile, self-organizing teams, where project team members have more decision-making authority.
6	D	In a matrix organization, the team members do not report to the project manager. The project manager has almost no legitimate power over the team members.
7	D	Theory of constraints (TOC) is a method to identify and remove the most critical or limiting factor. Once that is removed, the next most critical factor is identified and removed. This methodology was introduced by Dr. Eliyahu Goldratt in his book "The Goal" in 1984.
8	D	Harold is estimating the resources required by the project. He is now in **Estimate Activity Resources** process. All the stated choices are tools and techniques for this process.
9	A	In the RACI matrix, it is best to have the accountability (A) for an work package or deliverable assigned to only one person. This helps avoid misperception on who has authority and is-charge for each deliverable. However, multiple people could be responsible, consulted or informed for those. See Page 317 of the PMBOK®.
10	D	He needs all the stated inputs to acquire the needed resources for the project, namely: • the project schedule • the resource requirements, which describe the needed skills or equipment features, and • the resource calendars, which have the availability of the resources.
11	C	Optimizing the utilization of resources is not the applicable technique. The activity, "development of project resources", that is being discussed is part of **Develop Team** process. A, B and D are techniques used to develop the project team. Optimizing the utilization of resources (Choice C) is part of the **Control Resources** process. It is done after you have developed the team, completed part of the project and have work performance information that can help prepare a variance report of the actual versus the planned resource utilization.
12	C	The correct answer is to get additional manpower for the project. Trying to change the scope or schedule is not preferable.

13	B	Managers, who accept Theory Y, believe that workers are internally motivated to do a good job even without supervision Theory Y and Theory Z are incorrect for this scenario. ▪ Managers, who accept Theory X, believe that people need to be micro-managed and coerced to work hard. ▪ Theory Z, advocated by management professor William Ochi in Japan, states that workers who are given opportunities for advancement develop a sense of commitment, do their job to their utmost ability and work for the well-being of the organization and fellow co-workers.
14	B	Salary offered to the project team is usually not a cause of conflicts. The key causes of conflict are resource scarcity, differences in personal work styles, scheduling priorities, etc.
15	D	All the stated choices are techniques for the **Control Resources** process.

CHAPTER 10

Communications Management

Which is one task that you think takes up most of a project manager's time during a typical work day? The answer is communications, and could be either spoken or written. The realm of communications covers various activities. A project manager could be busy with developing a project artifact, report or presentation for stakeholders, conducting a meeting, writing meeting minutes, writing follow-up emails, socializing about projects, managing expectations, coaching team members, etc. All these are forms of verbal or written communications, which takes up the bulk (70% to 90%) of the working hours. Like it or not, a project managers job is primarily about communications and then about managing stakeholders.

There are 3 processes in the **Communications Management** Knowledge Area:

Planning Process Group	Executing Process Group	Monitoring and Controlling Process Group
10.1) Plan Communications Management	10.2) Manage Communications	10.3) Monitor Communications

There are two key tasks for effective project communications:

- Developing a communications plan and strategy, and
- Conducting communications (which involves creating the content and disseminating it verbally or in writing) and then collecting feedback and using that to improve subsequent communications.

What you send in an email or say in a meeting can be misinterpreted. It is likely that the reader can misconstrue an email message. It is essential to review and revise before clicking 'send' on an email. The content in emails or project documents and what you say in meetings need to follow these 5C's:

1) Correct – there should be no spelling, sentence structure or grammatical errors.
2) Concise – the message should be brief and relevant to the audience.
3) Clear – the message must be unambiguous.
4) Coherent - the flow of ideas should be logical.
5) Controlled – the flow of word and graphics should make sense.

Trends and Emerging Practices

There is a trend of involving more and more stakeholders in project reviews and meetings. Earlier stakeholders were primarily involved during project initiation and planning.

But the new trend is to:

- involve stakeholders for development and approvals of significant changes,
- monitor stakeholder engagement and support throughout the project life,
- periodically (weekly or daily) send generic updates to stakeholders,
- customize and send specific project information that is required by each stakeholder.

Another growing trend is to use social media tools (WhatsApp, SMS, instant messaging, etc.) for informal or 1:1 communication. These were initially used by younger generations, but they are now becoming popular across the workforce. Widespread use of these tools has led to more information exchange. On one hand, it helps create a deeper level of trust and openness but on the other hand, it could sometimes lead to disagreements and conflicts regarding minor details.

Tailoring Considerations

What and how you communicate project information is unique for each project. This depends on the

- stakeholder preferences and what they require,
- the location of the project resources, and
- communication techniques, used to develop, send and store the messages and information.

Another factor is the language used for communications. Nowadays, given the globalization, project resources are in different countries. Many countries use English for business communications. But certain countries use their national language for business, in which case messages, meant for residents within that country, need to be in their local language. This makes it easier for residents to understand and respond.

Considerations for Agile/Adaptive Environments

For projects that have changing requirements and scope, it is essential the evolving details are quickly and frequently communicated amongst all stakeholders who need to know the changes.

Why is this important? If they know the changes in advance and justification for the changes, they will be more willing to offer their support.

How do you make sure that the communications are adequate? This is done by

- holding review sessions with the stakeholders,
- noting their changes in the communication preferences,
- making timely and relevant updates to project documents,
- storing those in a shared folder that can be easily accessed by the stakeholders, and
- letting everyone know of changes.

All these appear like endless work, but it will help you gain and maintain support from stakeholders, which in turn will lead to project success.

Process 1: Plan Communications Management

PMBOK® Page 366
Process Group: Planning

This process deals with developing an approach and plan for project-related communications to meet the needs of the stakeholders.

The project charter, resource and stakeholder management plans, requirements documents and stakeholder register are all key inputs for this process.

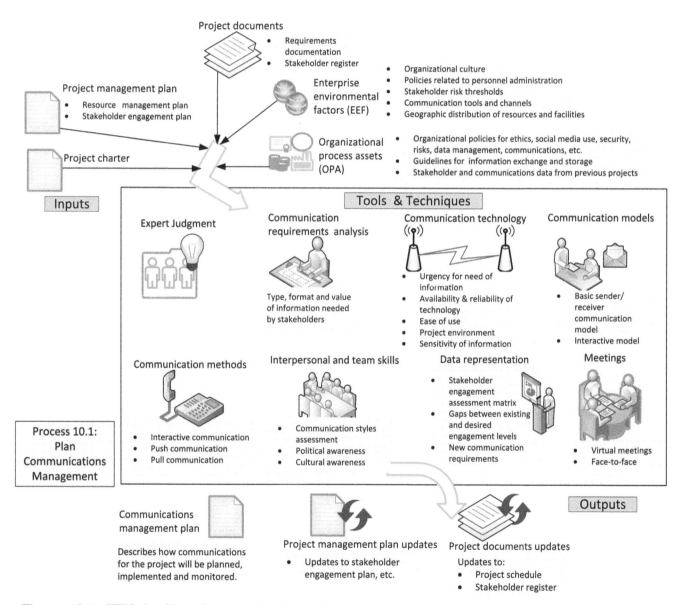

Figure 10-1: ITTO for Plan Communications Management process

Before we discuss tools and techniques, let us identify the outcomes of this process. The key outputs are the communications management plan and updates to existing project plans and documents.

The communications management plan is a document that describes how the communications for a project will be planned, conducted and monitored. It contains:

- Communication requirements by the stakeholders (email, weekly reports, presentation, face-to-face meetings)
- Level of details in each communication along with format and content
- The frequency of distribution of each communication
- The process to develop and get approval for the communication content
- Target recipient for each communication
- Mode of delivery of the communications (via email, presentation or meetings)
- Glossary of terms that will be used in the communications
- Process for updating the communications plan
- Escalation process for issues related to the communications
- The flow of information within the project

Table 10-1 shows a typical communications plan for a project.

#	Communications	Delivery and Format	Frequency of distribution	Content developer	Communication Sender	Recipients
1	Meeting minutes	Email (see template)	After each meeting	Project manager (Joseph Garcia)	Project manager (Joseph Garcia)	All meeting attendees
2	Executive presentation on project status	Face-to-face presentation of a PPT deck (30-minute meetings)	End of each calendar month	Project manager (Joseph Garcia)	Project sponsor (Jim Handers)	CIO, project sponsor, PMO
3	Advance information about application outages	Email	24 hours in advance of planned outage	Application lead (Bob Mason)	Application manager (Brad Jose)	Application users, IT managers
4	Notice of an application availability after a planned outage (change request window)	Email	Immediately after application is available (after the change window)	Application lead (Bob Mason)	Application manager (Brad Jose)	Application users, IT managers
5	Weekly status report	Email	Friday before 5 pm	Project coordinator (Karl Grover)	Project sponsor (Jim Handers)	CIO, project team, IT managers, PMO

Table 10-1: Sample Communications Plan for a Project

Figure 10-1 shows a proposed template (filled example) to be used for meeting minutes as mentioned in the communications plan.

PROJECT	Disaster Recovery (DR) Setup for ERP Applications		
MEETING TIME	Friday, Sept 14 at 10:00 am PST		
ATTENDEES	☒ Jim Handers ☒ Wahid Kari	☒ Alexander Gill ☒ Gary Garcia	☒ Henry Hooks
URL FOR PROJECT DOCUMENTS	https://www.box.com/files/6/r/722091762581/DR-Setup-for-ERP		

Meeting Agenda

#	Topic
1	Review DR architecture
2	Review Build of material (BoM)
3	Procurement Lead time

Discussion

#	Topic	Activity / Decision / Risk
1	Firewall compatibility with new servers in the DR datacenter and needed changes to the existing architecture and BoM	Risk
2	Use of Mobile Device Management (MDM) application for ERP users on mobile devices	Activity
3	Backup at the DR datacenter	Activity
4	Discuss and finalize data replication plan	Decision

Action Items

#	Action Items	Responsible	Due Date	Comment
1	Resolve the firewall compatibility issues with the servers	Andy Ashton	11/7	
2	Analyze existing MDM solutions and propose one for internal DR use	Jim Handers	11/14	
3	Develop replication procedures and failover test	Mike Mason	11/14	
4	Develop DNS failover procedures	Gary Garcia	11/21	
5	Finalize BoM for purchase	Henrique Hanes	11/31	

Next Meeting: Wednesday, Oct/26 at 10:00 am PST / 1:00 pm EST

Thanks,

Jim Handers, Project Manager

Figure 10-1: Example meeting minutes

There are various models for communication and exchange of information. Figure 10-2 shows the sequence of steps in a basic communication model:

1. The sender has a message (meetings minutes, project status, etc.) that he or she needs to send.
2. The sender then records (encodes) the message into an email, document or a presentation.
3. The message or information is then transmitted to the recipient.
4. The recipient receives the message.
5. The receiver translates (decodes) the message into ideas or thoughts.

6. The receiver then acknowledges that he or she has received the message. This does not mean that the receiver agrees to the message or has been able to understand the content.

7. The receiver understands the message and sends his response to the sender.

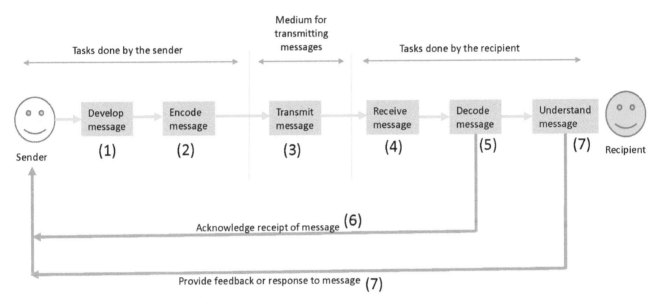

Figure 10-2: Steps Involved in a Basic Communication Model

Figure 10-3 shows three communication methods:

▪ interactive,
▪ push, and
▪ pull

In the exam, you will be described a method or situation and asked to identify if that is an example of pull, push, or interactive communications. For example, if a document is placed on a shared network drive or intranet portal and the project team is expected to edit the document, is that a push, pull or interactive? Please pause and think before you read ahead to the answer. The document requires that the project staff member proactively go to the site, download and review the document. That is a form of pull communications.

For interactive communications, an increase in the number of participants increases the number of potential communication paths between individuals, which in turn, causes a rapid increase in the complexity of communications. If there are **n** participants in a communication, the number of potential communication paths are **n*(n - 1)/2**. Note that **n** must include the project manager, if he/she is involved in the communications.

Communication Methods

Interactive Communication

Multi-directional exchange of information between 2 or more participants. Most efficient way to ensure understanding and buy-in.

Examples:
• Phone Conference calls
• Meetings
• Video Conferencing

Push Communication

One-directional information sent to certain stakeholders (audience). Does not guarantee that the communication has reached or was understood by the target audience.

Examples:
• Emails
• Letters
• Voice messages

Pull Communication

One-directional information that requires the target audience to download (retrieve) the content. This also does not guarantee that the communication did reach the audience or was understood by them.

Examples:
• Documents placed on the network drive or portal
• On-demand e-learning
• Knowledge repositories
• Webinars

Formula for potential channels for interactive communication:
• Number of participants = n
• Potential communication channels = n * (n -1) /2

Examples of interactive communication:
Question: If the number of people in a communications = 15 (include project manager, if he or she is part of the communications), what is the potential number of communication channels?
Answer: Number of communication channels
$$= n * (n-1)/2$$
$$= 15*(15-1)/2$$
$$= 15*7$$
$$= 105 \text{ communication channels}$$

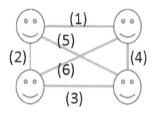

Another example with n=4 persons in a communication

If n=4, the number of communication channels = 4*(4-1)/2 = 6

Figure 10-3: Communication Methods

Process 2: Manage Communications

PMBOK®: Page 379
Process Group: Executing

Manage Communications process is about how project information is created, collected, distributed, stored and finally disposed. All these are done as per the guidance in the communications management plan. If correctly planned and executed, this results in an effective communications flow and continued support from stakeholders.

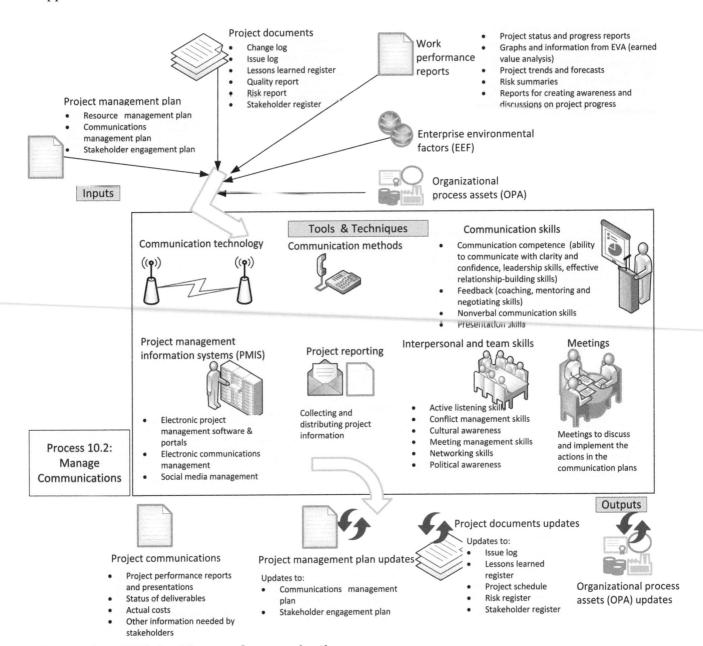

Figure 10-4: ITTO for Manage Communications process

This process is not about merely generating and distributing information. Successful communications is about making sure that the information is relevant to and understood by the target audience. There must be a way for the recipients to ask for clarifications and more information.

It is also essential that you understand how each stakeholder wants the delivery of the project information. There are four communication ways, as shown in Figure 10-5:

- Formal verbal
- Formal written
- Informal verbal
- Informal written

The project communications plan must address which delivery technique is best suited for each stakeholder and mechanism to distribute project status or information.

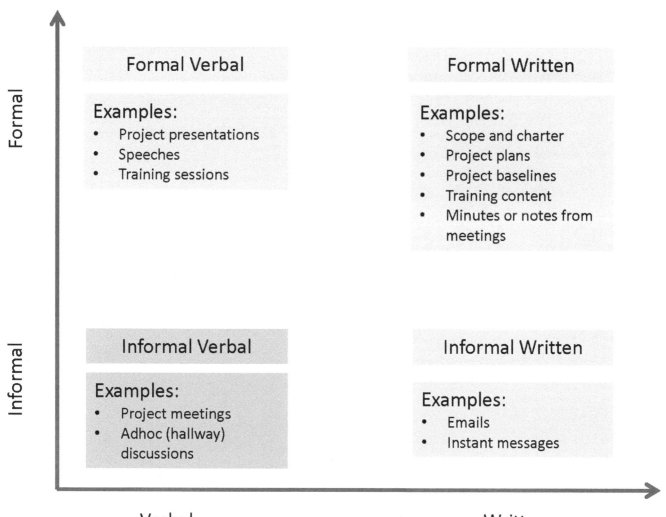

Figure 10-5: Types of communications: Formal or Informal, Written or Verbal

What makes communication and reporting time-consuming, is that each stakeholder has his or her preferences. Some like brief reports while others want details. Some like an in-person meeting. Some prefer a group discussion, while others just want an email or prefer that you upload the report on a shared project portal.

You may think that it is impossible to keep everyone happy! But you neither need to despair over nor under-estimate stakeholder requirements. If you follow the communication guidelines listed below, you will get it usually right with your project stakeholders. It will also help you select the correct choices during the PMP exam! Here they are:

- Remove barriers to interactive communications.
- Select a communication media that is suitable for the context. Know when to use written, oral, formal, informal communications; when to schedule face-to-face meetings and when to just send an email!
- Within the message, provide opportunities for the recipients to ask for clarifications.
- Use an active voice as much as possible.
- Correct all sentence structure and spelling errors.
- Prepare an agenda for each meeting.
- Listen actively. Ask for clarifications and summarize to make sure that you and everyone else have the same understanding.
- Conflicts happen. Be open to dealing with conflicts.
- Whenever possible, build consensus by collaborating and arriving a decision that everyone buys into (instead of forcing, smoothing or ignoring).
- During in-person or video meetings, observe the body language and the implicit under-currents.
- Be aware and acknowledge that the participants sometimes try to convey messages implicitly through non-verbal behavior.

Process 3: Monitor Communications

PMBOK®: Page 388
Process Group: Monitoring and Controlling

In this process, you monitor and control communications across the entire project life cycle. This ensures an optimal information flow between the project team and stakeholders and the stakeholders receive what they require.

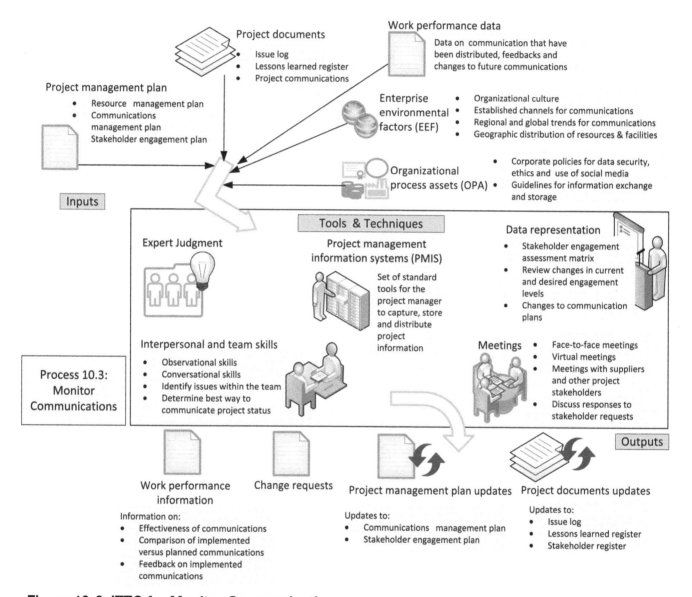

Figure 10-6: ITTO for Monitor Communications process

The inputs for this process are:

- The project management plan, especially the
  o Resource management plan
  o Communications management plan
  o Stakeholder engagement plan

  These above plans provide the requirements for the stakeholders, frequency for distribution of information to the stakeholders, project resources who will develop and distribute the information, and the target recipients for each communication.
- The project documents (such as communications draft, project status, work completed, costs incurred, etc.) provide the material and content to develop the work performance information (output of this process).
- The issue log provides the status, resolution plan for issues, who is responsible for resolution and target dates. Do you keep an issue log for all your projects? You must. Each project needs an issue log. Stakeholders will ask for that. It has stakeholder needs and problems that must be addressed in the communications. It also contains a history of issues that have been resolved or in-progress.
- The work performance data related to previous communications consists of feedback and questions about previous communications sent to stakeholders. Do you survey stakeholders to see if your communications have been effective and if they meet what stakeholders expect? Again, you should be doing that! The survey results will help you improve future communications.

The tools and techniques are:

- the information management systems,
- expert judgments from PMO, stakeholders and consultants, and
- meetings where you can review project performance data.

Meetings will help you get information to prepare project reports and respond to stakeholder queries.

Information systems are applications and software tools that you can use to collect project data and develop summary and reports. You can also use software packages to automate consolidation of data in a format suitable for your presentations.

The output is work performance information, change requests and updates to various project documents and plans. Remember that a key activity in this process is that work performance data (input) is summarized and categorized to develop work performance information (output) which is then used to create project reports and presentations.

More points for the exam:

- Stakeholders have different understandings about the project status and plans.
- However, project information is required by stakeholders.
- You need to prepare and provide adequate and relevant information to let them know what they need.
- Project team meetings are not meant to collect status from team members. That is better done via status reports on a shared portal or folder. Meetings are meant to identify risks and dependencies, improve collaboration between teams and develop solutions to issues.
- Body language and non-verbal communications are important means to understand the relationships and team dynamics.

Practice Questions for Chapter 10

1. You are managing a virtual team. Which of these can you do to enhance the ability of the team to work together?
   A. Use video conferencing for meetings
   B. Store all project artifacts in a shared portal
   C. Maintain an online team calendar
   D. All the above

2. Communication is an exchange of information, such as ideas, instructions or emotions. Which of the following are mechanisms by which information can be exchanged?
   A. Formal or informal mechanisms
   B. Spoken or written forms
   C. Using gestures or words
   D. All of the above

3. As a project manager, you can expect that the bulk of your time will be spent on:
   A. Managing stakeholder expectation
   B. Planning and monitoring the execution of project activities
   C. Communications
   D. Providing project updates

4. You are executing a project, but you are short of resources since a few resources have been taken away for another project that is more critical. You discuss this with your program manager, who advises you to make a formal request to the functional managers for additional resources. Which of these would not be a formal communication to request a new commitment for resources?
   A. Make a request in the project and portfolio management application.
   B. Setup a meeting with the functional manager and record the request in the meeting notes.
   C. Send an email to the functional manager asking for resources.
   D. Create a project change request to update the resources assigned for activities in the project schedule baseline.

5. As a project manager, you keep all project artifacts on the intranet portal that the project team and stakeholders can access. Which of the following communication methods are you using to share the artifacts?
   A. Social media
   B. Push communication
   C. Pull communication
   D. Network communication

6. You have taken over a project and find a lot of existing conflicts and disagreements amongst the team members. You are unable to get focused discussions and decisions in the meetings. Which is the best communication technique for you to use to resolve the conflicts and reach decisions?
   A. Push communication to enable transparency.
   B. Informal communication within the project team.
   C. Face-to-face communication in small group settings.
   D. Formal escalation to project sponsor.

7. A communication type where the audience needs to download and view the content when they are free to do so, is known as:
   A. Pull communication
   B. Interactive communication
   C. Network communication
   D. Discretionary communication

8. Jason Johnson has joined a global retail conglomerate as a project manager. He is in-charge of a new project to establish a new supply chain management (SCM) process to enable just-in-time (JIT) order fulfillment. However, several stakeholders in different countries are resistant to the project objectives. The progress is stalled due to lack of support. Which of the following is most likely to help Jason develop consensus among the stakeholders?
   A. Use of video-conference during meetings so everyone can see non-verbal communication and interpret those
   B. Use of verbal communications
   C. Use of written and formal communications
   D. Use of written and informal communications

9. Robert Greenberg is a program manager for a global oil and gas exploration and production (E&P) firm in Brazil. He needs to hire new project managers to work with suppliers and customers around the world. Which of these skills should he look for when interviewing candidates?
   A. Documentation skills to develop accurate and easy-to-understand content for international stakeholders
   B. Technical skills and prior experience in the energy E&P sector
   C. Ability to communicate effectively with stakeholders, project team and vendors
   D. Ability to influence senior management, vendors and customers

10. Samuel Johnson is managing a staff relocation project that is about 90% complete but the stakeholders are unhappy due to issues with the new office setup, lack of conference rooms and inconsistent Wi-Fi connectivity within the office. The project sponsor asks Sam for a report that compares the plan with the results. What report should Sam provide?
    A. Notes and minutes of the weekly project meetings
    B. Variance report
    C. Project schedule and how the work got completed in time
    D. Project scope and how the amenities and features in the new office were in line with plans

11. Which of the following contains the timeframe and frequency of communications required by the stakeholders and why they require the information?
    A. Stakeholder management plan
    B. Communications management plan
    C. Requirements management plan
    D. Information management plan

12. Posting project artifacts on the intranet portal is a method of:
    A. Social computing communication
    B. Push communication
    C. Mass communication
    D. Pull communication

13. Which of these signifies a minimal connection between the sender and recipients?
    A. Mass communication
    B. Public communication
    C. Push communication
    D. Social computing communication

14. Which of the following processes helps you ensure that the stakeholders have the information that they need?
    A. Plan Communications Management
    B. Plan Stakeholder Engagement
    C. Monitor Communications
    D. Monitor Stakeholder Engagement

15. Andrew Ashton has taken over a project to upgrade the network bandwidth for all 200 offices around the world. However, the team members have internal conflicts as well as conflicts with the service provider. What approach and actions should Andrew adopt to resolve the conflicts?
    A. Andrew must work on reconciling or smoothing the differences, to improve team collaboration and effectiveness.
    B. Andrew must resolve the conflict immediately, in order to prevent work slowdown and inefficiency.
    C. Andrew must intervene and find a way to accommodate the needs or demands of the members to keep the schedule from slipping.
    D. Andrew must assess the level of conflict. If that is too high, he must try a collaborative approach to resolve the conflicts. But if it is low, he need not do anything as a low level of conflict leads to improved creativity and performance.

ANSWERS

Question Number	Correct Answer	Explanation
1	D	All the stated choices are good. Besides, you can use email, chat, discussion threads, etc. to improve interaction and team-building.
2	D	All the choices are valid mechanisms for exchanging information. The exchange can be written such as status reports or meeting notes or oral such as an in-person project update. During in-person meetings and video conferences, the use of gestures and non-verbal communications are as important as the choice of words.
3	C	The correct answer is communications. All the four choices appear like correct answers but communications is a general term that includes the other choices. Research shows that about more than 80% of a project manager's time is spent on communications.
4	C	Sending an email is usually not a formal communication.
5	C	Pull communication is one that requires the audience to access the content at their own discretion.
6	C	To resolve issues, a face-to-face discussion in small group settings is ideal. Small groups establish a non-threatening environment where it is easier to have honest and open discussions.
7	A	Pull communication is one where the audience needs to reach out and view the content whenever they wish.
8	C	Written and formal communications is the best answer because the stakeholders are in various countries and there is a strategic need to change stakeholder support for the project objectives. Written and formal communication establishes authenticity and mutual respect.
9	C	Good communication skills are required to successfully manage a global project team and stakeholders. This includes written, non-verbal and oral communications as well as interpersonal skills.
10	B	The sponsor asks for a comparison of the plan with actuals. This is a variance report.
11	B	Communications management plan contains: ▪ information that must be distributed to stakeholders, ▪ frequency of distribution, and ▪ reasons why stakeholders require the information.
12	D	The answer is pull communications because the audience must go to the portal to view the project artifacts.
13	A	Mass communication is the correct answer because the recipient is an anonymous and large group.
14	C	The **Monitor Communications** process ensures that the stakeholders get the information that they require.
15	D	If there is a high degree of conflict, it will reduce the effectiveness of the team and must be resolved using a collaborative (problem-solving) approach. However, if the conflict level is low, no action is required. A low conflict level is preferred because it leads to better decision-making, creativity, and progress.

CHAPTER 11

Risk Management

This chapter discusses project risks, their probability of occurrence, their effects on the project and techniques to enhance or mitigate the effects.

---

* For the Exam *
- A risk is an event that can happen in the future but has not yet occurred.
- An issue is a negative risk that has already happened and must now be mitigated.

Remember that risks can either be:
- a threat (having a negative impact on the project) or
- an opportunity (having a positive effect on the project)

There are 7 processes in the **Risk Management** Knowledge Area.

Planning Process Group	Executing Process Group	Monitoring and Controlling Process Group
11.1) Plan Risk Management 11.2) Identify Risks 11.3) Perform Qualitative Risk Analysis 11.4) Perform Quantitative Risk Analysis 11.5) Plan Risk Reserves	11.6) Implement Risk Responses	11.7) Monitor Risks

A risk is defined as an uncertain condition and if it occurs, it can have a negative or positive effect on the project. A risk is usually perceived as having a negative consequence and such risks are called threats. You can have risks that have positive consequences and such risks are called opportunities.

Figure 11-1 describes known and unknown risks. Known risks are those that can be identified and defined during the initiating or planning phases and documented in the risk register. Unknown risks, on the other hand, are those that cannot be initially identified but become identifiable later, as the project progresses.

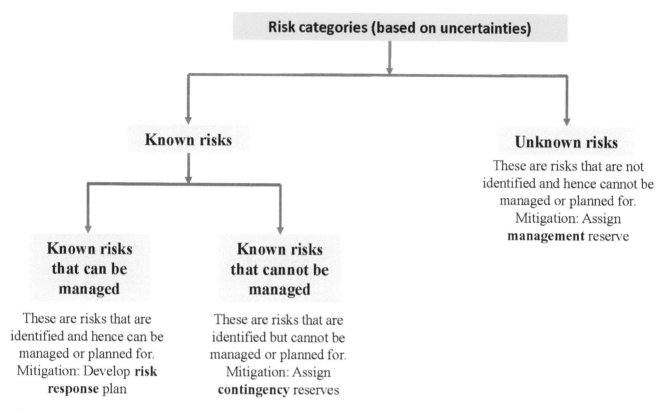

Figure 11-1: Known and unknown risks and their mitigation plans (note the difference between contingency and management reserves)

Risks can also be classified, based on their source and impact, into the following two types:

a. **Individual project risks**: These are risks that affect one or more project objectives.
b. **Overall project risk**: This risk arises from a combination of individual project risks or from the uncertainty of overall project. It affects the overall project objectives.

Figure 11-2 shows the factors that affect the stakeholder's or organization's attitude towards risk.

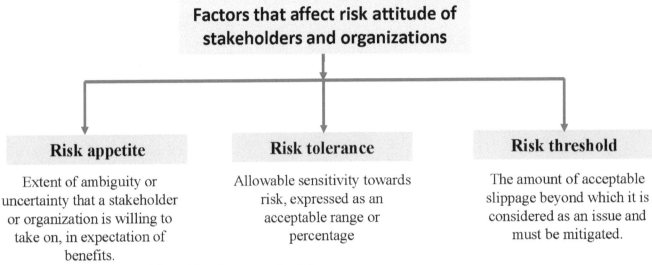

Figure 11-2: Stakeholder attitude towards risks

You must be able to differentiate between risk appetite, tolerance and threshold:

- Risk **appetite** is the amount of risk that an organization or stakeholder is willing to accept in hopes of a benefit. It is a qualitative (high, medium or low) assessment. Stakeholders may have a high-risk appetite for a critical project where the expected benefits are high. But they may not be willing to accept risks for another project with low expected benefits.
- Risk **tolerance** is the acceptable limits towards a risk. It is usually expressed as a percentage or range. For example, if you are managing a 20-month project, it could have an assigned tolerance of +/- one month or +/- 5%.
- Risk **threshold** is the maximum exposure or amount of allowed slippage. For example, a time-and-material contract of 20 weeks with allocated funds of $30,000 can have an allowable threshold of 23 weeks and $55,000. If the duration or spending exceeds these values, it is an issue and must be mitigated.

Trends and Emerging Practices

The objective of risk management is to make sure risks are understood and planned for. For risks that are not known or planned, there must be a management reserve.

There could be risks related to certain events such as a key resource leaving the organization, a vendor going out of business, etc. On the other hand, some risks are not associated with any event (see Figure 11-3). These could be due to ambiguity in the requirements or procedures. It is also due to a high degree of variation in the quality of the end-deliverables.

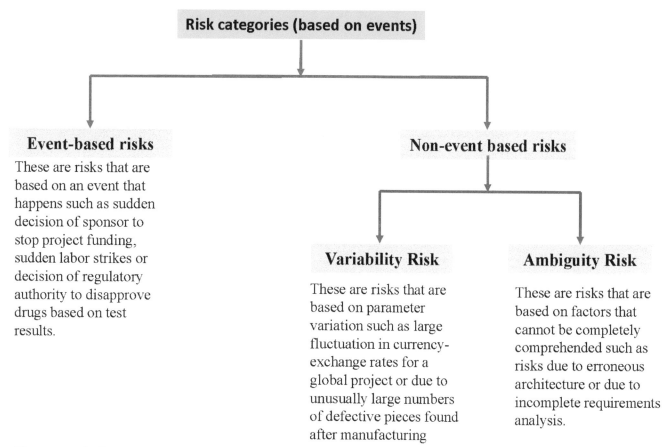

Figure 11-3: Event and non-event risks

Also, there are risks due to unknown-unknowns, which cannot be comprehended or documented during project planning. They become evident only during project execution or closing. The mitigation plan would be to:

- provide for schedule and budget contingencies,
- conduct frequent risk assessments and
- update project plans and baselines in case the risks become issues.

Tailoring Considerations

Risk management needs to be tailored based on factors such as project size, project complexity, the significance of the project for the organization and the methodology (waterfall, agile, iterative, tec.) used to manage the project lifecycle.

Considerations for Agile/Adaptive Environments

Environments that have high variations in project requirements and operating conditions are subject to a higher degree of risks. When using an agile or adaptive approach, risks must be evaluated and managed during each iteration or wave. Project requirements must be updated in each iteration, and the tasks must be re-prioritized to reflect any new understating of the project scope, requirements or risks.

Process 1: Plan Risk Management

> PMBOK®: Page 401
> Process Group: Planning

The **Plan Risk Management** process is about developing a plan that would provide guidance for identifying risks, evaluating their impact, creating a mitigation plan and implementing the actions in the mitigation plan.

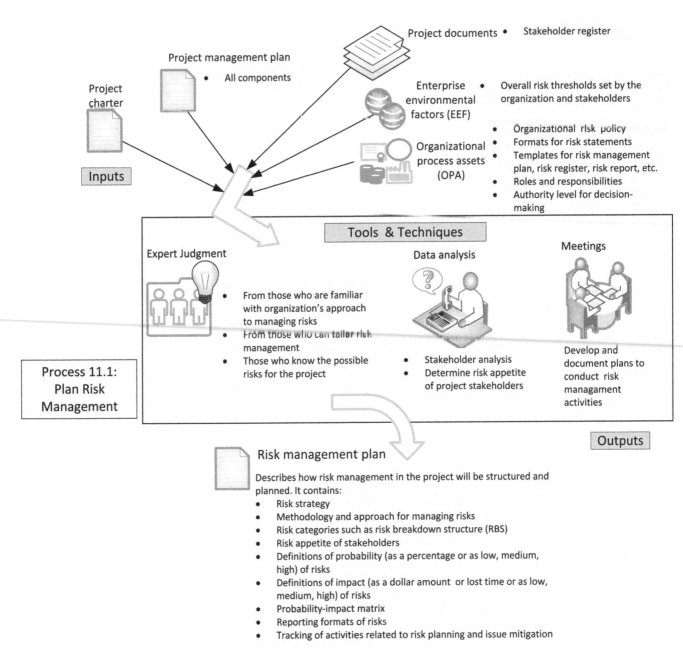

Figure 11-4: ITTO for Plan Risk Management process

The two key input documents for developing a risk management plan are:

- The project charter document (output of the **Develop Project Charter** process)
- The stakeholder registers (output of the **Identify Stakeholders** process)

The only output of this process is the risk management plan. It consists of the following:

- Strategies for managing the risks
- The methodology used to develop and implement risk mitigation steps
- Role and responsibilities of different members on who will develop, implement, lead, support or monitor risk-related activities
- Risk categories, based on the source of risks, impacted objectives and factors that are documented in the risk breakdown structure (Figure 11-5).
- Risk appetite of the stakeholders
- Definition of the probability (low, medium or high) of occurrence
- Definition of the impact (low, medium or high) of the risk

---

* For the Exam *

Note that for all knowledge areas, the 'Plan Management' process has a 'management plan' document as an output.

In reality, the risk management plan need not include all the above and must be tailored to include content, relevant to the project.

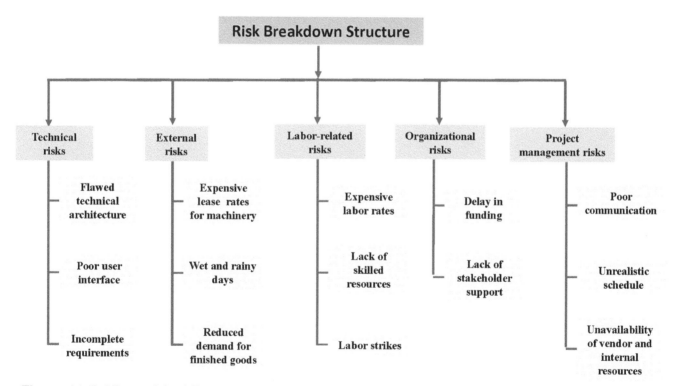

Figure 11-5: Hierarchical Representation of Risks in a Risk Breakdown Structure (RBS)

Process 2: Identify Risks

PMBOK®: Page 409
Process Group: Planning

In this process, you identify the risks and their details, such as the source of risk, project objectives that are affected by the risk, etc.

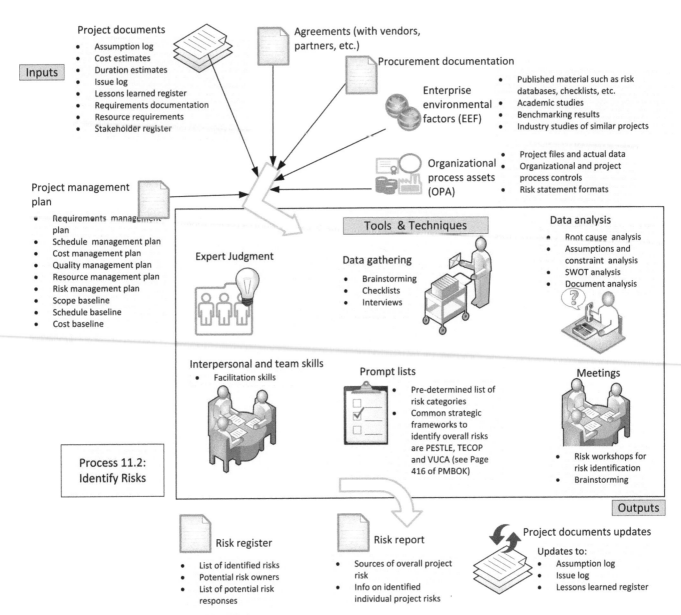

Figure 11-6: ITTO for Identify Risks process

Figure 11-7 shows the key techniques used to identify risks.

Risk Register

An important output of the **Identify Risks** process is the risk register. It includes information such as:

- list of identified risks,
- the time that the risk was identified
- the source of the risks,
- probability of occurrence (expressed quantitatively as a number or percentage or qualitatively as high, medium or low),
- effect of the risk on project baselines (scope, cost and schedule),
- whether the risk is a threat or an opportunity,
- possible risk responses, which will be further developed during the **Plan Risks Responses** process,
- risk triggers (conditions that can lead to the risk becoming an issue) and
- WBS reference numbers of the affected deliverables, tasks or scope.

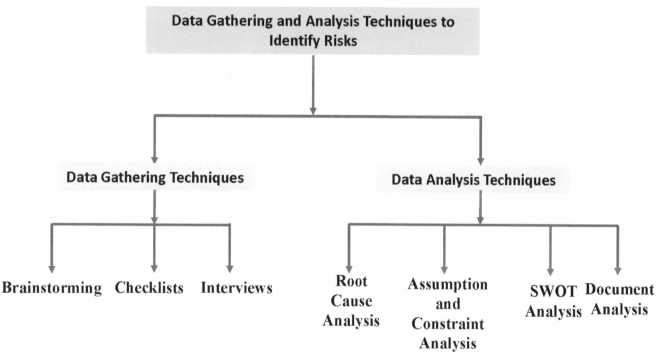

Figure 11-7: Key techniques used to identify project risks

Table 11-1 shows a sample risk register.

▪ **Project Title: Disaster Recovery Datacenter Setup Project ID PPM 004151** ▪ **Date of Initial Draft: March 20th Date of last revision: March 30th**									
Risk ID	Risk Statement	Probability of risk occurrence	Impact on				Risk Score	Responsible Party (Owner)	Risk Response
			Scope	Schedule	Budget	Quality			
Unique ID Number	Description of expected circumstance or event related to risk	Likelihood of happening, expressed as a percentage or a number in an assigned range	Effect on each project objective if the risk occurs				Probability x Impact	Who will follow through if the risk occurs	What will be done in advance to prepare for the risk and what will be done in case the risk occurs?
R1	Test resource is not available	70%	--	Completion delayed	Increased lease duration	--	--	Project manager	Use contract vendor resource for testing
R2	Delay in leasing machinery	50%	--	Missed completion deadline		--	--	Procurement administrator	Identify alternate lease vendor

Table 11-1: Example of a Risk Register

When should risks be documented? Many project managers wait till execution begins to see if problems or issues arise. Should any issues come up, they document the problem in the risk register and in the issue log. But this is not acceptable. Details of known risks are evident and must be documented at the start of the project.

Another important output of the **Identify Risks** process is a risk report. Table 11-2 has details of the risk register and risk report.

Types of risk documents	Risk Register	Risk Report
Which risks are documented?	▪ Individual project risks	▪ Overall project risks ▪ Individual project risks
Which processes in the **Risk Management** Knowledge Area update this?	The risk register is updated by: ▪ Perform Qualitative Risk Analysis ▪ Plan Risk Responses ▪ Implement Risk Responses ▪ Monitor Risks	The risk report is updated by: ▪ Perform Qualitative Risk Analysis ▪ Perform Quantitative Risk Analysis ▪ Plan Risk Responses ▪ Implement Risk Responses ▪ Monitor Risks
What is contained in this document?	The risk register contains: ▪ List of identified risks ▪ Risk owners ▪ Risk responses ▪ Risk sources	The risk report contains: ▪ Sources of overall project risks ▪ Summary of individual project risks

Table 11-2: Difference between a Risk Register and a Risk Report

Process 3: Perform Qualitative Risk Analysis

PMBOK®: Page 419
Process Group: Planning

In this process, you rank (or prioritize) the individual project risks. That is done by assessing:

- the probability of occurrence and
- impact value of the risk

This helps to identify the critical risks. You can then develop detailed mitigation plans for and also monitor the critical risks.

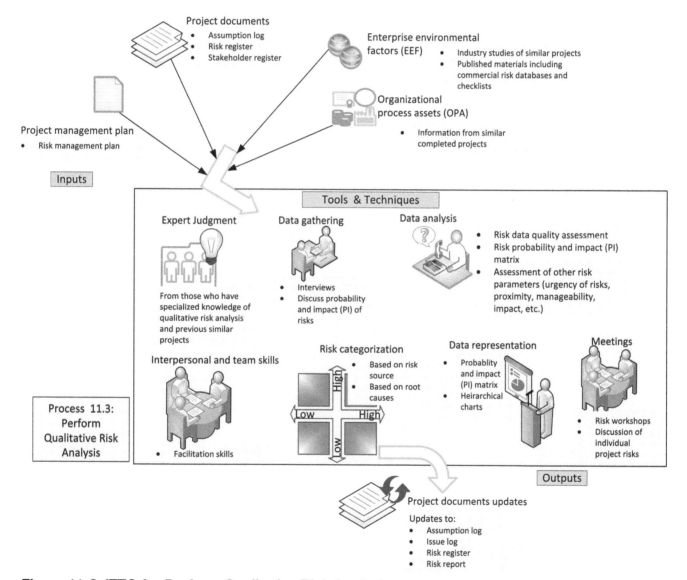

Figure 11-8: ITTO for Perform Qualitative Risk Analysis process

The key input to this process are the project management plan and project documents such as assumptions log, risk register, stakeholder register, etc.

There are various tools and techniques for the qualitative analysis of risk data (see Figure 11-9).

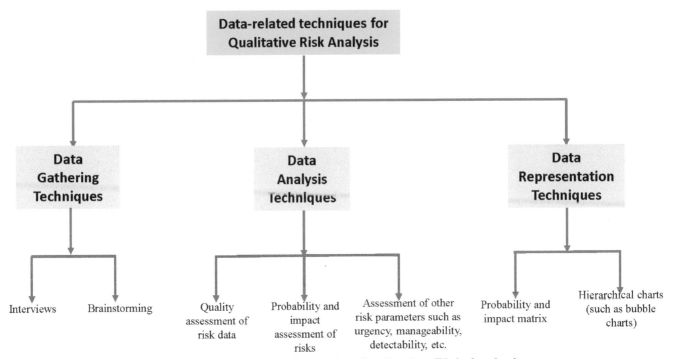

Figure 11-9: Data-related tools and techniques for Qualitative Risk Analysis

Data-gathering techniques: These include interviews, meetings and brainstorming sessions. For these sessions to be successful, there must be an environment of confidentiality and trust during the meetings. This sets up a background for free sharing of thoughts and discussion of risks, impact and possibility of occurrence. Facilitating these sessions requires good inter-personal and team-building skills. Honest discussion, even about disagreements, will help the team to reach a consensus. The key output is risk characteristics such as risk impact, probability, urgency, sources, etc.

Data-analysis techniques:

(a) **Quality assessment of risk data**: Here you look at the quality of the data. Does the data make sense? Is the data reliable and true? Does it seem rational? You can use a questionnaire to assess the quality and then use a weighted score for each data. What if you find that all the collected data seem poor and get low weighted scores? Then you need to start gathering data once again.

(b) **Probability and impact assessment of risks**: If the quality of gathered data is acceptable, you can assess the probability that the risk will occur. The probability can be specified qualitatively as low, medium or high or as a percentage.

Impact assessment is the effect of the risk on the project in case the risk becomes an issue. It can be expressed qualitatively (low, medium or high) or quantitatively (for example by a number between 1 and 10, where 1=least effect and 10=highest effect).

(c) **Assessment of other risk features:** In addition to probability and impact, there are various other risk features such as risk urgency, proximity, manageability, detectability, propinquity, etc. Risk proximity is about how quickly the risk will begin to impact the project, once it becomes an issue. Risk urgency is about how quickly the risk responses must be implemented, after the risk becomes an issue.

Data-representation techniques: Now that you have gathered and analyzed the data, it is time to visually represent the data. Data-representation technique is about showing the data in an easy-to-understand manner. These include making matrixes and charts to present details of the risks.

(a) **Probability and impact (PI) matrix for the risks**: This is a matrix (see Table 11-3) that has the probability of occurrence on one axis and impact on the other axis. It is a grid to map the probability of occurrence and impact in case it occurs.

(b) **Hierarchical charts about the risks**: The PI matrix is relevant when you want to show two parameters. But, if you want to show three parameters, you need to use a hierarchical chart such as a bubble chart, where two parameters are represented by the two axes (X-axis and Y-axis) and the third parameter is represented by the size of the bubble.

Table 11-3 shows the threats listed in a probability and impact (PI) matrix. Once we have an outline of the matrix, you fill each cell with the Risk ID numbers (taken from the risk register) and the risk score (which is probability x impact) highlighted in yellow.

Probability of occurrence (scale of 0.01 to 0.99)		Impact on the project if the risk were to occur (scale of 1 to 10)				
		Insignificant impact	Minor impact	Moderate impact	Major impact	Catastrophic impact
		2	4	6	8	10
Almost certain to happen	0.9	1.8 Risk ID R12 Risk ID R14	3.6 Risk ID R16	5.4 Risk ID R18	7.2 Risk ID R19	9.0 Risk ID R20
Likely to happen	0.7	1.4 Risk ID R21	2.8 Risk ID R28	4.2 Risk ID R29	5.6 Risk ID R22	7.0 Risk ID R26
About 50% possibility of happening	0.5	1.0 Risk ID R39	2.0 Risk ID R31	3.0	4.0 Risk ID R33	5.0 Risk ID R37 Risk ID R30
Unlikely to happen	0.3	0.6	1.2 Risk ID R41	1.8 Risk ID R44	2.4	3.0 Risk ID R46
Very unlikely to happen	0.1	0.2 Risk ID R81	0.4 Risk ID R91	0.6 Risk ID R88	0.8	1.0 Risk ID R84 Risk ID R87

Table 11-3: Risk Probability and Impact (PI) Matrix where red cells indicate critical risks

The outputs from this process are updates to the project documents:

- assumption log: where you update the assumptions after doing a qualitative analysis of the risks,
- issue log: where you add new issues or change details for existing issues,
- risk register: where you update the risk category, the probability of occurrence, the impact on the project, risk owner, risk score (product of probability and impact), risk priority, etc.,
- risk report: where you update the most important individual project risk.

Process 4: Perform Quantitative Risk Analysis

PMBOK®: Page 428
Process Group: Planning

In this process, you establish a numerical score that shows the combined effect of various risk characteristics on the project.

The inputs are the project documents and plans as shown in Figure 11-10. The key outputs are updates to the risk report.

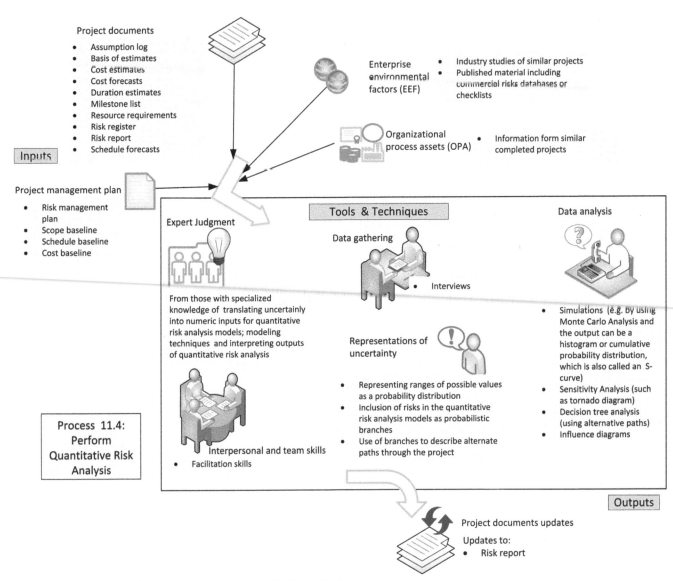

Figure 11-10: ITTO for Perform Quantitative Risk Analysis process

How do you do a quantitative analysis of the risks? First, you gather data using interviews, meetings and brainstorming sessions with stakeholders and experts. The perception of the risks can vary wildly between individuals. It takes the team and interpersonal skills to overcome bias and disagreements and eventually arrive at a consensus.

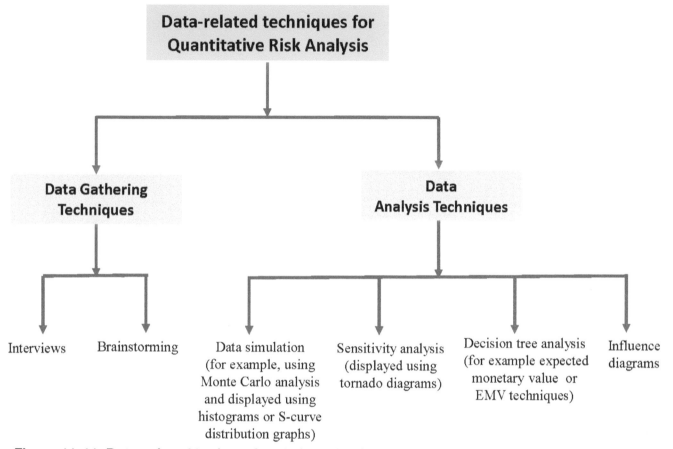

Figure 11-11: Data-related tools and technique for Quantitative Risk Analysis

Secondly, you use various quantitative techniques listed in Figure 11-11 and described below to analyze risk data:

(a) Data simulation: This is a technique that simulates the effect of multiple risks and uncertainties on project objectives. An example is the Monte Carlo analysis, where input values are chosen at random and used to generate corresponding output values. The output values are shown as a histogram or as an S-curve (Cumulative probability distribution).

(b) Sensitivity analysis of risk data: This is used to rank risks based on their magnitude of impact on project outcomes. An example is a tornado diagram, where risks having the highest impact are placed on top and the risks with the least impact are placed at the bottom of the diagram.

(c) Decision tree analysis: These are used to map possible scenarios with their probability of occurrence and impact value. The products of the probabilities and their corresponding impact values are added to arrive at a statistical or weighted average, called expected monetary value (EMV) for the entire scenario.

(d) Influence diagrams: These are diagrams that represent project situations as a set of elements (uncertainties, risks, influences, decisions) along with the relationship between them and effect caused by them.

Here are some questions related to decision tree analysis and EMV.

Numerical 1 of 3 on expected monetary value (EMV)

Question:

The following figure represents choices of either upgrading an existing software application or developing a replacement application from scratch. The cost at each node and probability are mentioned. Which of the two paths can potentially lead to a higher profit?

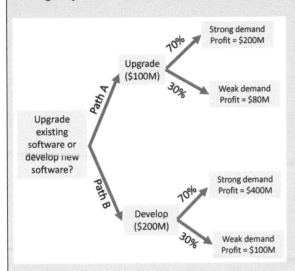

Solution:

You can solve this in two steps:

- Step 1: Compute the EMV for each path, by adding the products of percentage (possibility) of occurrence and impact value.
- Step 2: Select the higher EMV as your answer.

Step 1:

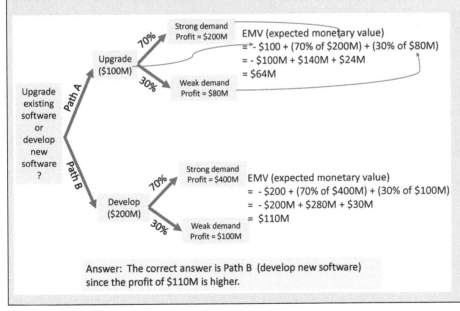

For Path A, the EMV is the sum of the cost of upgrades ($100M) and profit from strong and weak demands. Since the cost is an expense, it is subtracted. The EMV is therefore $64M.

For Path B, the cost is $200M. It is subtracted from the profit for strong and weak demands. The EMV is therefore $110M.

Step 2: EMV for Path A and B are $64M and $110M respectively. The answer is Path B since it has a higher EMV.

Here is another numerical on EMV. Do the computations before you read ahead to the solution.

<u>**Numerical 2 of 3 on expected monetary value (EMV)**</u>
Question:
An environment conservation program team needs to decide whether to build a dam or not. The cost of building a dam is $100M. The chances for a flood are 70%. The loss from a flood would be $400M if there is no dam but building a dam would reduce the damage to $150M. Is it cost-effective to build a dam?

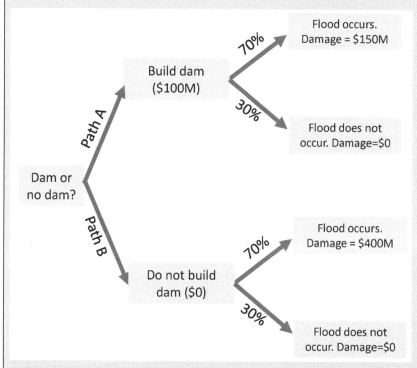

Solution:
The EMV for building a dam (Path A) has two components: (a) the cost of building and (b) the product of the probability of flood and damage due to flood. These add to an EMV of $205M. Both are negative since they are both expenses or outgoing money.

If a dam is not built (Path B), the EMV or total loss is $280M.

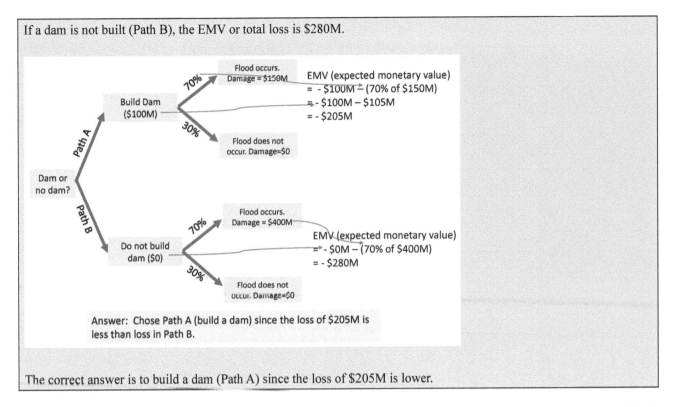

Answer: Chose Path A (build a dam) since the loss of $205M is less than loss in Path B.

The correct answer is to build a dam (Path A) since the loss of $205M is lower.

In the PMP Exam, you may be asked to calculate the net path value (NPV) for a path or choice. This is the gain or loss for a path without considering (or weighing) the percentage or possibility of occurrence. Let us compute the net path value (NPV) for the plausible paths in the previous scenario.

Computing net path value (NPV)

Question: What is the net path value for Path A1, A2, B1 and B2?

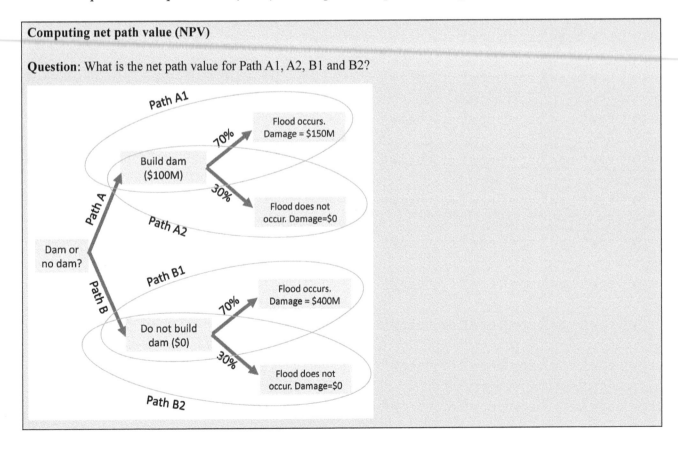

Solution: NPV is the sum of the impacts for each path, with no consideration for the possibility. Expenses are negative and gains are positive.

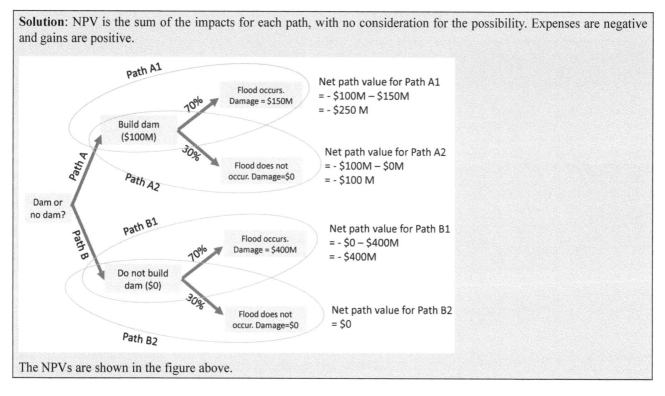

The NPVs are shown in the figure above.

Here is another example of EMV.

<u>**Numerical 3 of 3 on expected monetary value (EMV)**</u>
Question:
You have a choice of establishing either a factory for electric cars or one for gasoline-operated cars. The expenses are $200M and $400M respectively.

The market scenario is that the chances for strong vehicle demand are only 60%. If you produce electric cars, strong demand would give you a profit of $800M and weak demand of $200M. On the other hand, if you produce gasoline-operated cars, strong demand would give you a profit of $1,200M and weak demand of $400M. What is the right path to adopt?

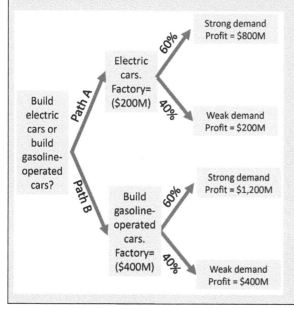

Solution:
In these problems, it is best to quickly draw a flowchart on paper and compute the EMV for each scenario. Trying to do this mentally during the exam, could be difficult, given the time pressure.

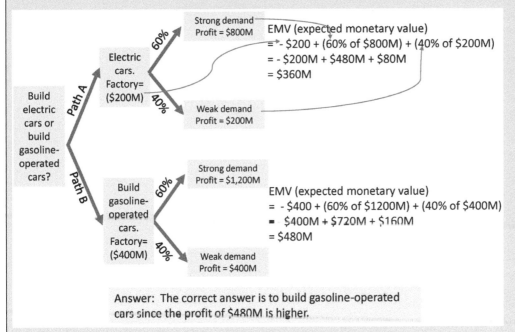

- For Path A, the factory expense of $200M is subtracted from the weighted gains of strong and weak demands, which are $480M and $80M respectively
- For Path B, the factory expense of $400M is subtracted from the weighted gains of strong and weak demands, which are $720M and $160M respectively.

The correct answer is to build gasoline-operated cars (Path B) since the expected net profit of $480M is higher than for the case for electric cars, where the net profit is only $360M.

Here is another problem on net path value (NPV) for the previous scenario.

Question: What are the net path values for Path A1 and Path B1?

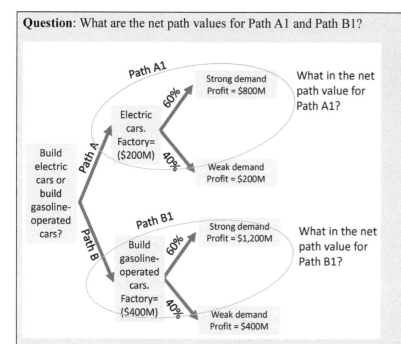

Solution: The NPV estimations are shown below. Note, that the cost for establishing a factory is negative and the profit from sales is positive as it is incoming money.

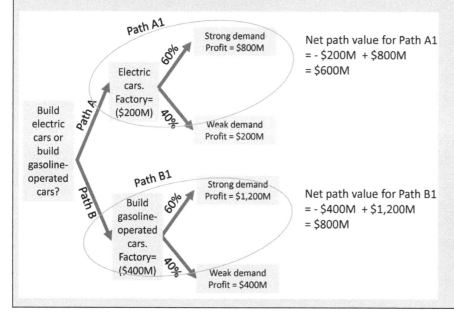

Process 5: Plan Risk Responses

PMBOK®: Page 437
Process Group: Planning

Now that you have identified the risks and done a qualitative and quantitative analysis of the risks, the next step is to decide what you would do in case the risk (threat or opportunity) were to occur. These actions are documented in the risk register and risk report.

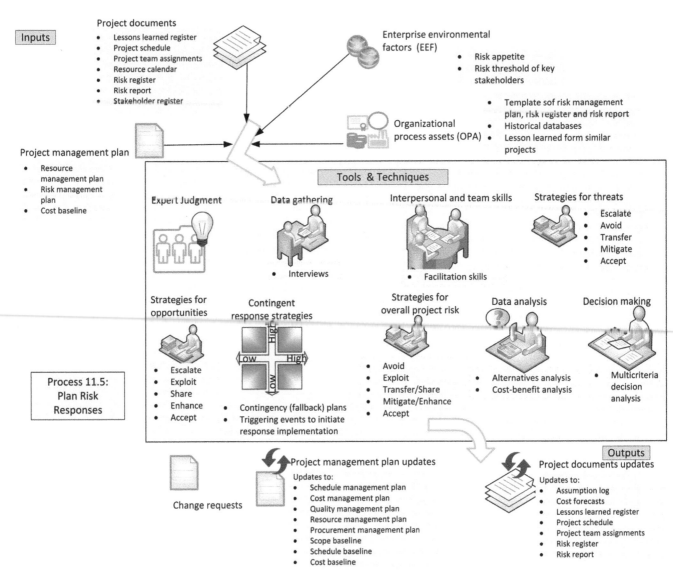

Figure 11-12: ITTO for Plan Risk Responses process

What do you need (as inputs) to plan your risk responses? You need project management plans and documents such as the risk report, risk register, stakeholder register, and lessons learned document.

You need to also know the resources that are pre-assigned for the project. Despite the pre-assignment and commitment of resources, your project may require more time or resources than committed. This could be due to risks that have turned into issues and resources are now needed to implement the risk responses. For this, you need to know the availability or non-availability of resources, which you can get from resource calendars.

How do you get information to develop risk responses? You need to get those from experts, stakeholders and risk owners (listed in the risk register). You need to get their time and attention. You need to facilitate a discussion, provide risk-related information, schedule interviews to generate and compare various risk response strategies and select the most appropriate ones. All this requires facilitation, interpersonal and soft skills.

Based on your discussions with stakeholders and experts, you can develop a list of mitigation steps to deal with threats, opportunities and overall project risk (Figures 11-13 and 11-14).

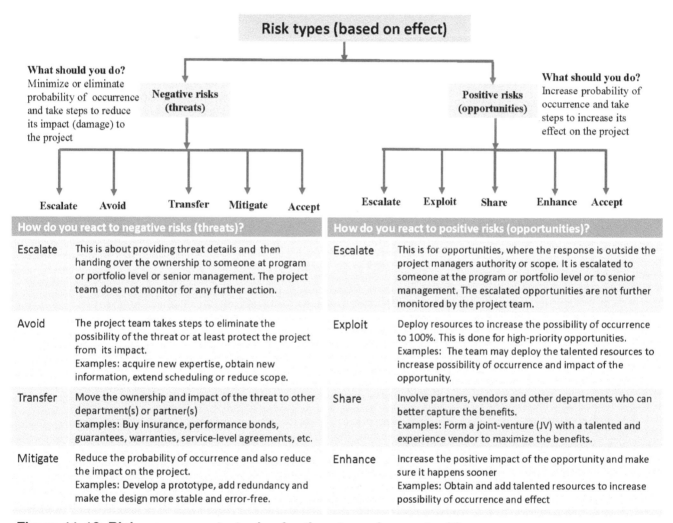

How do you react to negative risks (threats)?		How do you react to positive risks (opportunities)?	
Escalate	This is about providing threat details and then handing over the ownership to someone at program or portfolio level or senior management. The project team does not monitor for any further action.	Escalate	This is for opportunities, where the response is outside the project managers authority or scope. It is escalated to someone at the program or portfolio level or to senior management. The escalated opportunities are not further monitored by the project team.
Avoid	The project team takes steps to eliminate the possibility of the threat or at least protect the project from its impact. Examples: acquire new expertise, obtain new information, extend scheduling or reduce scope.	Exploit	Deploy resources to increase the possibility of occurrence to 100%. This is done for high-priority opportunities. Examples: The team may deploy the talented resources to increase possibility of occurrence and impact of the opportunity.
Transfer	Move the ownership and impact of the threat to other department(s) or partner(s) Examples: Buy insurance, performance bonds, guarantees, warranties, service-level agreements, etc.	Share	Involve partners, vendors and other departments who can better capture the benefits. Examples: Form a joint-venture (JV) with a talented and experience vendor to maximize the benefits.
Mitigate	Reduce the probability of occurrence and also reduce the impact on the project. Examples: Develop a prototype, add redundancy and make the design more stable and error-free.	Enhance	Increase the positive impact of the opportunity and make sure it happens sooner Examples: Obtain and add talented resources to increase possibility of occurrence and effect

Figure 11-13: Risk response strategies for threats and opportunities

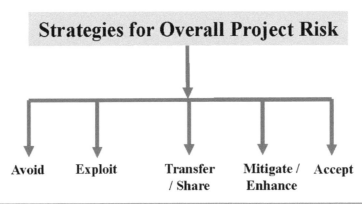

		How do you react to overall project risk (threat or opportunity) ?
1	Avoid	Here you take action to minimize the possibility of occurrence and effect of threat Examples: reduce project scope to remove risky elements; in the extreme case cancel the project
2	Exploit	If the risk is positive, take steps to improve the effect and possibility of occurrence. Example: add certain tasks to the scope, talented resources and budget to maximize the chances of occurrence and effect of the opportunity.
3	Transfer / Share	In case of negative overall risk, transfer the risk by paying for insurance premium; or collaborate with a vendor to share the risk. In case of positive overall risk, involve an experienced vendor or partner to improve the possibility of occurrence and effect; form a joint venture(JV) or special purpose vehicle (SPV).
4	Mitigate / Enhance	In case of negative overall risk, mitigate the risk by lowering chances of occurrence and effect. In case of positive overall risk, enhance the effect and possibility of occurrence. Example: add talented resources; change project scope , schedule or budget; change priority; extend delivery timelines, etc.
5	Accept	No proactive steps are taken except for periodically monitoring and reviewing risks for expected effect and possibility of occurrence. This is done for cases where any action is either impossible, too expensive or outside the project scope. Make sure you have enough contingency reserves (in terms of time, money and resources) to deploy in case the risk were to occur.

Figure 11-14: Risk response strategies for overall project risk

Once you have the risk responses, you need to prioritize the list and select the effective responses. The data analysis techniques used for the selection are:

- Alternative analysis: You use this technique to compare the features and requirements of the various responses to select the preferred ones.
- Cost-benefit analysis (CBA): For each risk response, you need to quantify the benefit and cost of implementing that response. The cost-effectiveness of a risk response is the ratio of the change in benefit level due to its implementation and the cost of implementation. A higher cost-effectiveness value is better.

$$Cost-effectiveness = \frac{Change\ in\ Impact\ level}{Implementation\ cost}$$

- Multicriteria-decision analysis: This analysis uses a decision matrix to rank (prioritize) the risk response strategies based on cost-effectiveness, resource availability to implement the response, probability of occurrence, level of impact if the risk occurs, possibility of secondary risks due to the implementation of the responses, etc.

The key outputs from this process are:

- change requests
- updates to various project plans, and
- updates to project documents such as risk register, risk report, resource assignments, forecasts (for cost, milestone completion dates, etc.), assumptions log, lessons learned register, etc.

Process 6: Implement Risk Responses

PMBOK®: Page 449
Process Group: Executing

You have a set of action items (response plan) developed in the previous process (**Develop Risk Responses**) and documented in the risk register and risk report. The next step is to implement the mitigation action items and monitor their effectiveness (using **Monitor Risks** process).

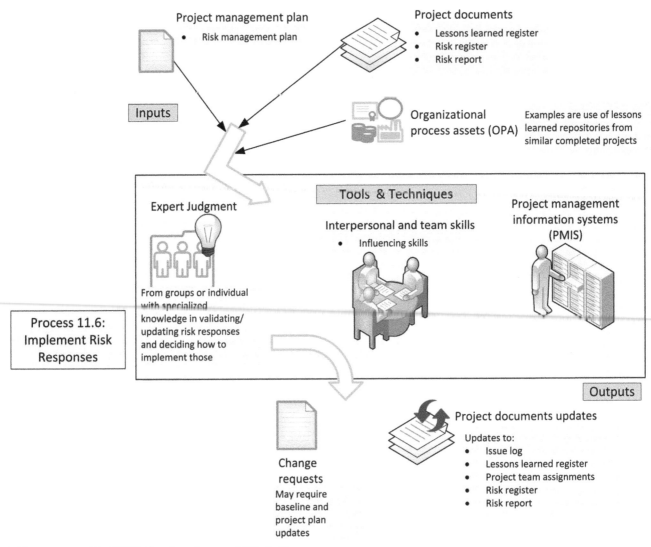

Figure 11-15: ITTO for Implement Risk Responses process

What do you need to implement risk responses? You need the risk register and risk report. You also need any lessons learned from work done related to risk implementation, earlier in the project.

How do you implement risk responses? First, you need to decide on what to do. You need to review the risk responses in the risk register and evaluate which of these need to be done. This requires that you now consult with a few experts who have the domain know-how and experience to help you decide on what to do.

Secondly, you need to work with the internal project team members, risk owners (as documented in the risk register) and those outside the project team to take action. They need to drop what they are doing and help you implement the risk responses. Will they do that? Project managers who have 'political capital', good influencing and interpersonal skills can get the people lined up to implement the risk responses.

Now, what are the outputs of this process? Note that by now, you have implemented what was written in the risk-related documents. You also know what worked, what did not work and what should have been the optimal responses. Implementation of some or all the risk responses would lead to changes to the baselines and project plans.

You, therefore, need to create change requests, get approvals and revise the project documents and plans such as baselines, risk register, lessons learned register, etc.

Process 7: Monitor Risks

PMBOK®: Page 453
Process Group: Monitoring and Controlling

This process is about:

- watching the project progress to identify new risks (if any)
- tracking identified risks
- implementing risk responses if a risk becomes an issue
- monitoring and evaluating the effectiveness of the implemented risk responses
- making sure that risk management policies are being followed
- making sure that the previously-decided approach and strategy are still appropriate, and
- monitoring project assumptions to ensure they are valid and making changes, as needed.

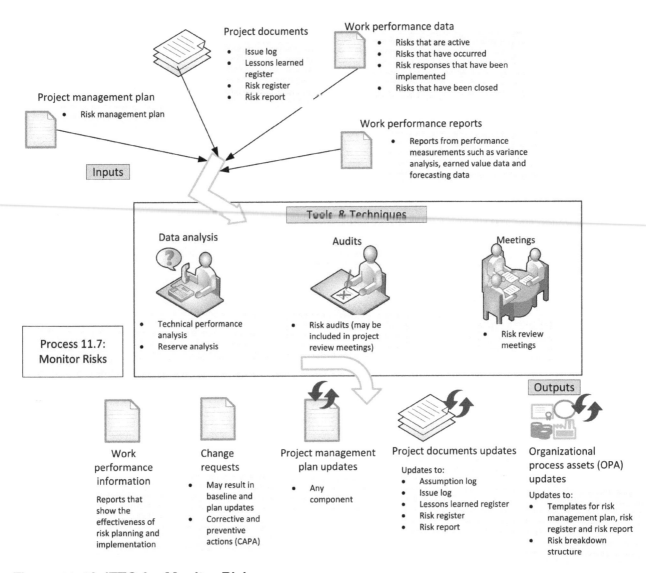

Figure 11-16: ITTO for Monitor Risks process

Figure 11-17 shows the various techniques used to monitor risks.

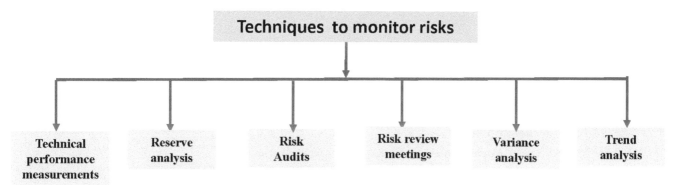

Figure 11-17: Common techniques to monitor project risks

The techniques to monitor risks are:

- **Technical performance analysis**: At the beginning of the project you develop project plans and baselines. This analysis is comparing actual results and progress against the d plans and baselines. If there is a difference, it may lead to new risks (threat or opportunity) or require you to update the plans and baselines.
- **Reserve analysis**: You have a reserve (contingency or management) in the project budget and schedule. You need to analyze how much of that has been used (or burnt) so far and if the remaining is enough for the rest of the project.
- **Risk audits**: Here you assess whether the risk management process is being effective or not. It is conducted usually by an external group and the report is presented to the project management team.
- **Risk review meetings**: These meetings are conducted by the project team to:
    - o Identify any new individual or overall project risks,
    - o Assess the status of current risks,
    - o See if any of the risks have become an issue,
    - o Assess the effectiveness of risk responses that have been implemented to resolve issues, and
    - o Close risks that are no longer relevant.

  Risk review meetings can be a dedicated session or included as part of regular project meetings.
- **Variance analysis**: This is used to compare actual results to the project plan or baselines. Earned value analysis (EVA) is a form of variance analysis. It helps identify deviations, possibility of risks becoming an issue and updates to the plans or baselines.
- **Trend analysis**: This helps determine the direction that a project is moving. It is helpful to foresee a pattern building up and forecasting possibilities in the future. This helps to implement a risk response in advance to reduce the impact of threats.

The techniques explained above will lead to:

- project information on whether the risk response planning and implementation have been effective or not,
- change requests,
- corrective or preventive actions to address the risks that have occurred,

- updates to baselines (especially schedule and cost),
- updates to issue log and assumption log, and
- updates to the risk register and risk report.

More points for the exam:

- A risk management plan is a prerequisite to developing scope, cost and schedule baselines.
- The project team must pay attention to identifying risks and developing mitigation plans, throughout the project life.
- Risks and issues must be discussed during all project meetings.
- The risk register and risk report must be updated throughout the project life.
- Issues must already have a mitigation plan in the risk register.

Practice Questions for Chapter 11

1. Jose Juwan is developing a risk response plan for opportunities in his new project. Which of the following is not a valid response for him to include in his response plans?
   A. Accept
   B. Escalate
   C. Avoid
   D. Exploit

2. Which of the following is a true and suitable comparison between individual project risks and overall project risk?
   A. An individual project risk impacts one or more objectives of the project. But an overall project
   A. risk impacts the project as a whole.
   B. Individual and overall project risks have similar overall effects on the project.
   C. An individual project risk impacts one objective of the project. But an overall project risk impacts multiple objectives.
   D. An individual project risk impacts one or two of the three project baselines (cost, scope or schedule). But an overall project risk is one that impacts all the three baselines.

3. Which of the following is not true for ambiguity risks?
   A. An ambiguity risk is a type of non-event based risk.
   B. An ambiguity risk is due to uncertainties (or ambiguities) about the future.
   C. An ambiguity risk can be mitigated by identifying areas where there is a lack of understanding and filling those areas by external inputs, benchmarking and best practices from the industry.
   D. An ambiguity risk impacts the cost baselines especially for international projects where the currency exchange variations are ambiguous and uncertain.

4. Which of the following is true about event-based risks and non-event risks?
   A. Event-based risks are due to uncertain events that may or may not happen in the future. But non-event risks are due to unknowns about the degree or variations that may occur and due to ambiguities about the accuracy of various project decisions, solutions, assumptions, etc.
   B. Event-based risks are related to future events that are known to occur. Non-event risks are not about events but about the variations that will happen about what is assumed or planned.
   C. Event-based risks are related to future events. Non-event risks are related to what has happened already but their impact on the project is unknown.
   D. Event-based risks are related to factors that can be controlled by the project team. Non-event risks are related to factors that are controlled by the industry, partners or vendors and are not in the control of the project team.

5. Richard Reskins is a project manager at a mining company in Angola. He is developing a risk management plan for a project to develop a new mine near Luanda, the capital of Angola. Which of the following could he exclude from the risk management plan?
   A. Risk categories, where risks are grouped using a risk breakdown structure (RBS)
   B. Risk strategy for the project
   C. Methodology for managing risks in the project
   D. Project assumptions and constraints

6. Risk register is an output of:
   A. Plan Risk Management
   B. Identify Risks
   C. Perform Qualitative Risk Analysis
   D. Plan Risk Responses

7. You are prioritizing the individual project risks based on their probability of occurrence and their potential impact on the project. What process are you in now?
   A. Plan Risk Management
   B. Identify Risks
   C. Perform Qualitative Risk Analysis
   D. Plan Risk Responses

8. Which one of the following is an example of a hierarchical chart that can be used to show three dimensions of data?
   A. Bubble chart
   B. Gantt Chart
   C. RACI chart
   D. Burndown chart

9. You are numerically analyzing the individual project risks along with your project team. You have developed a detailed probabilistic analysis of the risks represented by S-curve and tornado diagrams. Which process have you just completed?
   A. Plan Risk Management
   B. Identify Risks
   C. Perform Qualitative Risk Analysis
   D. Perform Quantitative Risk Analysis

10. You have a choice to either purchase or internally develop a software product. The software purchase price is $2 million.

    If you develop it internally, the added advantage is that you can sell subscriptions in the open market which can be profitable given strong demand. A strong market (25% possibility) will get you a net profit of $20 million after subtracting for development expenses. But a weak demand (75% possibility) will result in a net loss of $10 million. What should you do?
    A. Purchase the software
    B. Build (internally develop) the software
    C. There is not enough information to make a decision
    D. You can either build or buy because the expected monetary value is the same in both scenarios.

11. Amy Aniston is a program manager at a cloud services provider. Due to upcoming demand and lack of internal infrastructure for clients, she needs to either build a new datacenter (DC) at $50 million or upgrade the existing DC at $20M.
    ▪ For a new DC, the profits would be $200M in case of strong demand (60% possibility) and $50M for weak demand (40% possibility).
    ▪ For an upgraded DC, the profits would be $100M in case of strong demand and $40M for weak demand.

The decision tree with EMV calculations is shown below.

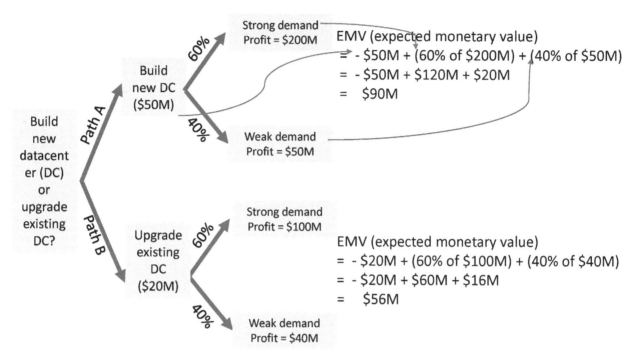

What should Amy Ashton do?

A. Build a new DC.
B. Upgrade the existing DC.
C. Postpone the decision for now and wait for the possibility of strong demand to improve.
D. There is not enough information to make a decision.

Note: The next 3 questions refer to the decision tree in Question 11.

12. In **the example decision tree in Question 11**, what is the net path value (NPV) for a strong demand for a new DC?
    A. $50M
    B. $200M
    C. $250M
    D. $150M

13. In **the example decision tree in Question 11**, what is the net path value (NPV) for a weak demand for an upgraded DC?
    A. $20M
    B. $40M
    C. $60M
    D. - $20M

14. In the **example decision tree in Question 11**, what is the revised EMV value for a new datacenter in case the possibility for strong and weak demand for cloud services is 50-50?
    A. - $75M
    B. $200M
    C. $75M
    D. - $50M

15. Your project team has come up with a special type of bar chart, where the data categories are listed vertically, and the largest bar appears at the top of the chart. The team finds that the chart is useful for comparing the relative impact of various variables. What is such as bar chart called?
    A. Histogram
    B. Tornado diagram
    C. Gantt chart
    D. Inverted bar chart

16. You have a set of risks and you need to do simulation and prototyping to understand how you can manage and effectively respond to those risks. Such risks are classified as:
    A. Non-event risks
    B. Event-based risks
    C. Variability risks
    D. Ambiguity risks

17. Which of the following processes have change requests as an output?
    A. Plan Risk Management
    B. Identify Risks
    C. Plan Qualitative Risk Analysis
    D. Implement Risk Responses

ANSWERS

<table>
<tr><th>Question Number</th><th>Correct Answer</th><th>Explanation</th></tr>
<tr><td>1</td><td>C</td><td>'Avoid' is not one of the strategies for opportunities (or positive) risks. It is a strategy for threats (or negative) risks.</td></tr>
<tr><td>2</td><td>A</td><td>Based on their impact on the project, there are two types of risks:<ul><li>Individual project risks are those that impact one or more objectives of the project.</li><li>Overall project risk is one that arises from all sources of uncertainty and affects the project as a whole.</li></ul></td></tr>
<tr><td>3</td><td>D</td><td>The example provided in Choice D is for variability risks (and not for ambiguity risks). The amount of variation in currency exchange rates will determine the degree of impact on the cost baseline.

See Page 398 of the PMBOK®.</td></tr>
<tr><td>4</td><td>A</td><td>Event-based risks are due to events that we are uncertain whether they will occur or not.

But non-event risks are due to unknowns about the variations and ambiguities in the project planning and solutions.</td></tr>
<tr><td>5</td><td>D</td><td>Project assumptions and constraints are not in the risk management plan but are included in the project charter.</td></tr>
<tr><td>6</td><td>B</td><td>Risk register is an output of the Identify Risks process. It contains details of identified individual risks, risk owners and risk responses.

On the other hand, a risk report contains sources of overall project risk and a summary of identified individual project risks.</td></tr>
<tr><td>7</td><td>C</td><td>Perform Qualitative Risk Analysis is a process where you use the probability of occurrence and impact to prioritize the risks. In this process, you also identify new risk owners and responses. This information is used to update the risk register.</td></tr>
<tr><td>8</td><td>A</td><td>A bubble chart is used to display three dimensions of data, represented by the X-axis, the Y-axis and the bubble size.

See the figure on Page 426 of the PMBOK®.</td></tr>
<tr><td>9</td><td>D</td><td>In Perform Quantitative Risk Analysis, you numerically analyze the probability and impact of project risks using S-curve charts and tornado diagrams.</td></tr>
</table>

10	A	Buying the software has a loss of $2M. Building (internally developing) the software has a loss of $2.5M. The correct answer therefore is to buy the software. 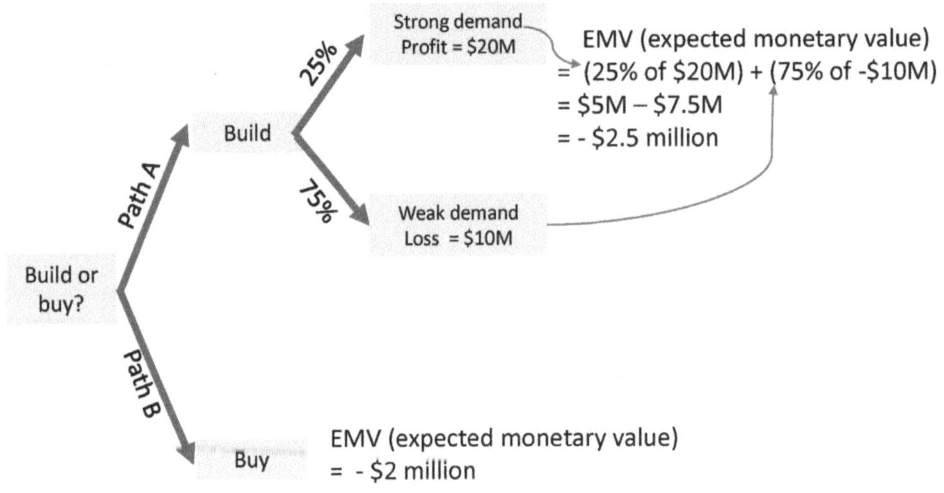 In such questions in the exam, you need to: (a) Draw a decision tree, as shown here, (b) write the numbers and compute the EMV (expected monetary) for each path, and (c) Select the path that has a higher profit (if any path is profitable) or least loss (if both paths have losses). There may be one or two questions on EMV in the exam. Decision tree and EMV estimations are explained on Page 435 of the PMBOK®. You may have questions that just ask for NPV (net path value) or EMV for a path. In some cases, the question may have the completed decision tree and you will be asked to identify the EMV or NPV for a path.
11	A	The correct answer is to build a new datacenter because the EMV for a new DC ($90M) and is higher than the EMV for an upgraded DC ($56M).
12	D	For NPV questions, the path is assumed to occur, and you do not need to consider possibility or percentage. The NPV is -$50M + $200M = $150M. The cost of building a new DC is $50M and it is subtracted from the profit of $200M to get the NPV.
13	A	The NPV is -$20M + $40M = $20M. In this case, the upgrade cost of $20M is subtracted from the profit of $40M.
14	C	The revised EMV is (-$50M + 50% * $200M + 50%* $50M) $$= (-\$50M + \$100M + \$25M) = \$75M.$$

15	B	A Tornado chart or diagram is a special type of bar chart, where the data categories are vertical, instead of being horizontal. The longest bar appears on top of the chart. The second longest appears just below that and so on. The completed bar chart appears like a tornado. It is used to identify the most impacting variable on a particular outcome.
16	D	The answer is ambiguity risks which are a type of non-event risks, addressed by prototyping or simulation. These risks are also managed by identifying the gap areas (where skills and capabilities are lacking) and then getting industry experts to fill the gaps. See Page 399 of the PMBOK®.
17	D	The **Implement Risk Responses** process has change requests as an output. Usually processes in the **Executing** and the **Monitoring and Controlling** process groups have change requests as an output. However, there are exceptions such as the **Plan Risk Responses** process.

CHAPTER 12

Procurement Management

Many project managers may not have extensive experience in procurement and contracts. However, you will have questions in the exam related to various types of agreements, contracts, procurements and associated terms.

You need to know that some contract types can be unfavorable to the buyers and others are unfavorable to the sellers. For successful project outcomes, you need to maintain a middle ground, where the terms present a win-win scenario for both the parties.

* For the Exam*
Assume you are the buyer, unless otherwise specified in the question.

The PMBOK refers to vendors as sellers. However, in the exam, you could have other terms for a seller such as service provider, partner, contractor, supplier, bidder, etc. A buyer could be referred to a purchaser, service requestor, client, customer or acquiring organization.

At first glance, contracts and agreements appear similar. But there are differences between them, as listed in Table 12-1. Agreements are usually neither binding nor enforceable. Contracts, on the other hand, are enforceable in a court of law and have financial penalties, if terms are not met. Some agreements such as service level agreement (SLA) and non-disclosure agreement (NDA) are similar to contracts. They are enforceable in a court of law and have penalty clauses.

There are three processes in the **Procurement Management** Knowledge Area:

Planning Process Group	Executing Process Group	Monitoring and Controlling Process Group
12.1) Plan Procurement Management	12.2) Conduct Procurements	12.3) Control Procurements

#	Agreement	Contract
1	An arrangement (usually informal) between two or more parties, but it is not enforceable in a court of law.	A formal and legal arrangement between two or more parties signifying the terms and conditions of the relationship and commitment from each party, including penalties that are enforceable in a court of law.
2	Can be written or verbal, but has no legal binding.	In a written form and has legal enforcement.
3	Usually with an internal group or division.	Usually with an external person or organization.
4	Benefits: • Less burdensome to draft and get sign-offs • Flexible in the fulfillment of agreed obligations.	Benefits: • All terms are clearly documented • Provides an assurance that the agreed obligations will be fulfilled • If a party cannot fulfill obligations, the contract has clauses for a court to provide a remedy for the injured or impacted party and enforce penalties.
5	Suitable for less stringent situations, where adherence to constraints (such as time, cost, quality, etc.) is expected but not legally enforceable.	Required for conducting business, when adherence to constraints (such as time, cost, quality, customer satisfaction) are mandatory and enforceable in a court of law.
6	Examples: • Project charters • Project management plans • Project baselines • Internal emails • Verbal agreements	Examples: • Purchase orders • Sales contracts • Time and Material (T&M) contracts • Fixed-price (FP) contracts • Cost-reimbursable (CR) contracts • Employment contracts • End-user license agreements • Non-disclosure agreements (NDA) • Service-level agreement (SLA) • Statement of work (SOW)

Table 12-1: Differences between an agreement and a contract

Figure 12-1 shows the steps in a procurement process for good or services. If you have not planned or conducted procurements at work, you must get familiar with all the terms and concepts in this chapter.

Sequence of steps in a typical procurement process

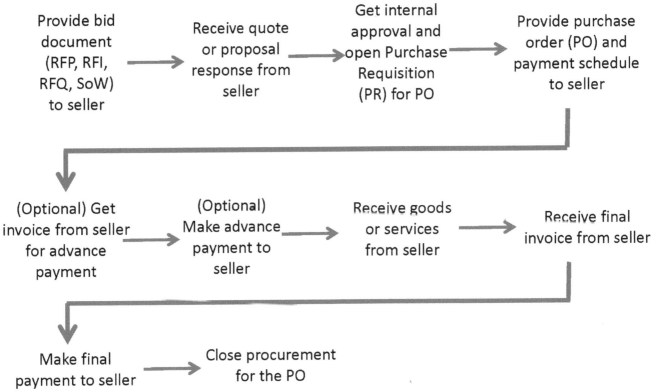

Figure 12-1: Sequence of Steps in a Typical Procurement Cycle

Trends and Emerging Practices

There are several new applications and practices in supply chain management that are influencing procurement processes.

One emerging trend, that is made possible by new tools and cloud-based applications, is the use of a single online platform by sellers to advertise, find buyers and conduct all supply chain management processes for their services or products.

Certain industries, such as construction and infrastructure development follow the predictive approach for managing their projects. For them, use of building information management (BIM) is becoming popular as it saves time and money. BIM is a digital or online representation of the functional and physical features of infrastructure such as a bridge, commercial complex, airport, etc. The virtual model is used by architects and engineers to visualize, fine-tune and present the design. It is also used by contractors and procurement administrators to view the required products and place orders.

Another emerging trend is risk-sharing between the buyers and sellers, based on their ability to own and manage each risk. For example, increases in the cost of raw material, labor and manufacturing could be owned by the sellers. However, risks related to changes in work scope, features and quality are best managed by the buyers.

Another trend is the globalization of the procurement process. This is necessary for large projects with work sites, suppliers, stakeholders and labor in different countries. Contract forms and agreements must be written to comply with regulatory requirements in different countries. Buyers and sellers must work within the laws or each country and collaborate to take advantage of bulk purchases, discounts, currency exchange rates, etc. Government regulations may require procurement administrators to purchase a certain portion of the goods and services from local vendors.

Another growing trend is to conduct a proof of concept (PoC) or trial engagement with multiple suppliers, before committing to one or more suppliers. The trail can be a formally-paid contract for a small portion of the project. This helps in continued (although minor) progress, while the buyer gets an opportunity to evaluate multiple sellers and select one for the remaining (and major) portion of the project.

Tailoring Considerations

There are several processes and steps in a procurement cycle. These must be tailored to suit the project requirements. Tailoring of procurement processes is based on factors such as:

- amount of goods or services to be purchased,
- availability of the sellers who can qualify to undertake the contract,
- the physical location of the buyers and sellers and
- government regulations and relevant laws.

Considerations for Agile/Adaptive Environments

For projects in an agile environment, the seller often must collaborate with the buyer. Contract clauses, where the seller shares in the risks and rewards, necessitate that both parties collaborate as partners for a successful outcome.

Large projects usually benefit if they use an agile and collaborative approach to procure certain services and goods. Procurement of certain services could be better suited for a stable, well-defined contract, while procurement of other services, especially where the scope cannot be completely defined due of lack of visibility and information, are better suited for an open time-and-material contract that allows for the scope, functionality, quality, etc. to be revised during execution.

However, an over-arching master services agreement (MSA) between the buyers and sellers is required to establish a foundation for sound working relationships and to avoid ambiguity and conflicts.

Process 1: Plan Procurement Management

> PMBOK®: Page 466
> Process Group: Planning

This process is concerned with developing and documenting decisions such as:

- approach for procuring good or services,
- criteria to decide whether to build internally, outsource or purchase,
- eligibility criteria to shortlist suppliers,
- right time in the project cycle to engage with suppliers,
- factors to help decide if you should conduct bid conferences for shortlisted suppliers.

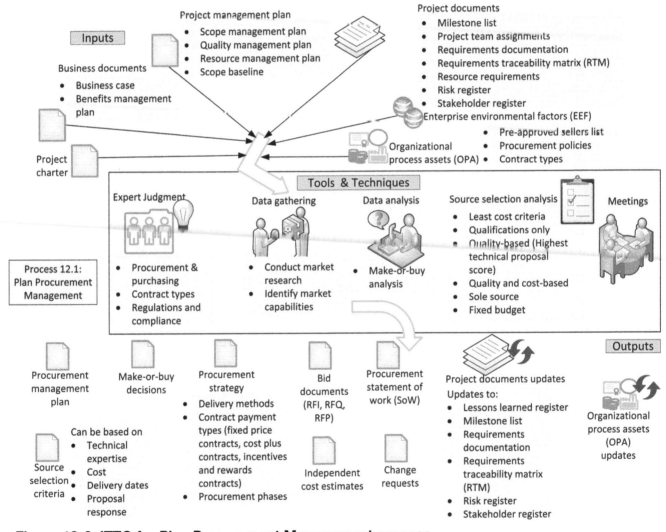

Figure 12-2: ITTO for Plan Procurement Management process

Types of Contracts

There are three broad categories of contracts (see Figure 12-4):

1. Fixed-price (FP),
2. Time and material (T&M), and
3. Cost-reimbursable (CR) or Cost plus (CP) contracts.

The procurement administrator and project management team must work together to decide on the most suitable contract type for each purchase. The decision is based on various factors such as the nature of goods or services to be purchased, whether the buyer is required to supervise the work and whether incentives are included in the contract fee. The legal department must also be involved so they can review the terms of reference (TOR) in the contract.

---

* For the Exam *

There are two categories of contract-related questions:

- Questions that describe a scenario and ask you to select the most suitable contract type to be used.
- Questions that provide a contract description and ask you to identify the name of the contract type.

A common goal of bid documents (RFI, RFP, etc.) is to ask the seller for the proposed cost and required time. In some contracts, the seller is incentivized to meet cost and schedule constraints. This is usually done via a fee or award-based contract.

Table 12-2 and Figure 12-3 have a few common contract terms that you could see in the exam. Also, know the difference between sale price and profit. The sale price is the larger amount. The profit is the smaller amount left after subtracting the expenses (such as costs of goods sold) from the sale price (revenue).

#	Term	Definition and formula
1	Target cost	Estimated cost for the work and agreed to by the buyer and seller. ▪ For a fixed price (FP) contract, the seller receives this fixed fee. ▪ For cost-reimbursable (CR) contracts, this amount, if exceeded, could result in fee reduction for the seller.
2	Actual cost	Actual expenses incurred by the seller.
3	Target fee	An extra amount (in the form of a fee or an award) that is given to the seller based on previously-agreed criteria such as early completion of project work, actual expenses being lower than the target cost, quality levels that exceed expectations, etc.
4	Target price	A pre-defined amount, that is given to the seller, if the work is completed at the target cost. Target price = Target cost + Target fee
5	Ceiling price	A pre-defined maximum amount that will be given to the seller, regardless of expenses incurred or other situations. It is higher than the target price.
6	Cost variance	Cost variance(CV) = Target cost - Actual cost ▪ If the actual cost is less than the target cost, we have savings. That is good for all parties and the seller may receive an incentive fee. ▪ If the actual cost is higher than the target cost, we have an overrun. That is bad for all and a fine may be subtracted from the amount due to the seller.

7	Share ratio	Share ratio is the ratio that the cost variance is divided between the buyer and seller. By default, it is written with the buyer's share first followed by the seller's share. For example, a 70-30 share ratio means that the buyer's share is 70% and the seller's share is 30% of the cost variance. ▪ Buyer's share (\$) = cost variance(\$) * buyer's share ratio ▪ Seller's share (\$) = cost variance(\$) * seller's share ratio
8	Point of Total Assumption (PTA)	This is the point at which the seller starts assuming and bearing all further costs for the project work.

Table 12-2: Terms used in contracts

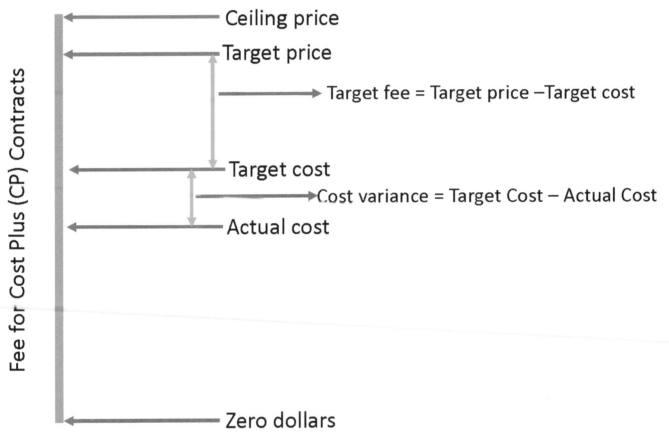

Figure 12-3: Target cost, target fee, target price and ceiling price

* For the Exam*

Distinguish between award/incentive fee and price (Figure 12-3):

(a) Award/incentive fee is the amount paid as award or motivation and it adds to the seller's profit. It excludes the fixed amount (for FP contracts) and the actuals (for CP or CR contracts) for the delivered goods or services.

(b) Price, on the other hand, is the larger amount and is the entire amount paid to the seller. It includes the fee, awards, incentives, reimbursable actuals, etc. It could also be a fixed or lump-sum amount that has been previously-agreed to, by all parties.

Figure 12-4 shows the three types of contracts:

1. Fixed price (FP) contracts,
2. Time and Material (T&M) contracts, and
3. Cost-reimbursable (CR) contracts, also called cost-plus (CP) contracts.

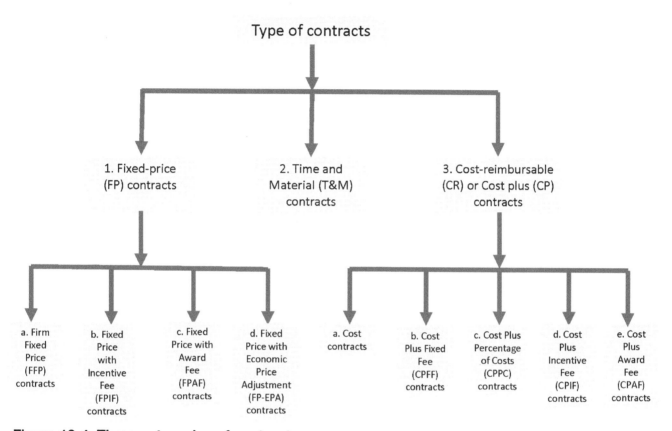

Figure 12-4: Three categories of contracts

1. Fixed-Price (FP) Contracts

These are contracts used when the work scope or product specifications are clearly defined. The buyer can estimate the amount to be paid and can budget in advance, and they need to specify the scope clearly in the beginning. Otherwise, there would be scope change requests, leading to additional expenses and time.

The seller also knows the assigned amount and is obligated to complete the scope within that amount. If any conditions in the contract are not met, the contract has penalties to be paid by the party that missed the conditions.

Table 12-3 describes the various FP contracts. The simplest type of FP contracts is a purchase order (PO), often used to buy commodity items. These can be unilateral, where it is signed by the buyer, only. In some cases, the buyer may require that the PO be signed by the seller as well (bilateral, since it is signed by both).

#	Type of contract	Acronym	Definition	Benefits and problems	Example(s)
a	Firm fixed-price contract (also called Fixed Price or Lump sum contract)	FFP	▪ These contracts have a firm fee. There are no opportunities for any additional amount, unless there is a change in the goods ordered or in the work scope. ▪ To protect everyone, the work scope in the contract must have all the details.	▪ These are less risky for the buyer as the amount can be budgeted. ▪ Usually, there are no changes. ▪ Any increase in raw material cost or increase in project time (for example due to labor inefficiencies) will negatively impact the seller.	▪ A contract given to a vendor to develop an application software (with detailed specifications) for a lump-sum fee of $450,000.00 ▪ A purchase order (PO) given to a seller to buy 2,500 six-feet copper cables at $5.50 each.
b	Fixed price with incentive fee contract	FPIF	▪ The price is fixed, but the seller gets an additional fee if the seller meets certain criteria such as completing the milestones earlier, achieving certain quality levels, etc. ▪ The contract has parameters to compute the incentive amount. ▪ The incentive amount is paid at project completion.	The incentive fee provides additional motivation to the seller to be more efficient and produce higher quality deliverables.	▪ A contract is drafted for software deployment for $280,000 over 8 months for 500 users and the seller will get $20,000 extra for each month that the project finishes earlier than 8-month span. ▪ A training contract for $40,000 to train 50 engineers and a fee of $10,000 if 75% of the trainees pass the certification exam (after training) and a fee of $20,000 if 100% of the trainees pass the exam
c	Fixed price with award fee contract	FPAF	▪ This is a fixed fee contract with a pre-determined award (bonus) at certain project milestones in case certain quality metrics are met. ▪ The award amount is decided by the buyer, is non-negotiable and is usually a flat amount.	▪ Enhances motivation and dedication for the seller ▪ Also improves the relationship between the seller and the buyer.	A contract to develop a software application in 9 months for a fixed fee of $900,000 and an award to be determined at project completion by the client and based on criteria such as meeting certain quality levels or early completion.
d	Fixed price with economic price adjustment contract	FP-EPA	This is a fixed fee contract with predetermined adjustments at certain project milestones for changes in financial parameters, economic indices, inflation, price of raw materials, currency fluctuations, etc.	Such contracts are used for multi-year engagements and help protect all parties against external dependencies that are beyond their control.	A three-year contract is awarded for $120,000 each year, with 5% extra in year 2 and 3, if inflation increases by more than 2%.

Table 12-3: The four types of Fixed-Price (FP) or Fixed Fee (FF) contracts

FP contracts are preferable for all parties since everyone knows the work scope and fee in advance. However, the scope, must be detailed and fixed. Any gaps in scope description could lead to new changes and additional fee requests by the seller.

EXERCISE TIME 1:

Question

A seller is awarded a 6-month FPAF contract to manage the networks for $30,000 each month and an award based on customer satisfaction scores and network uptime reports. The customer decides to provide an award of $5,000 for three of the 6 months. What is the total fee paid to the seller?

Solution:

Total price = fixed fee for 6 months + award for 3 months
    = ($30,000/month * 6 months) + ($5,000/month * 3 months)
    = $180,000 + $15,000
    = $195,000

The answer is $195,000.

If the final price (fixed fee plus incentive fee) is higher than the ceiling price, the seller will get the ceiling price and no more.

Here is a question on FPIF contract. Try to solve the problem, before reading the solution.

EXERCISE TIME 2:

Question:

A seller is awarded an application development and deployment contract for $1,800,000 for 30 months. However, for every month that the project finishes earlier, the vendor gets an incentive of $100,000. If the vendor gets the project completed in 27 months, what is the final price to the vendor? Note that the ceiling price in the contract is two million dollars.

Solution:

Final price = fixed fee + incentive for finishing 3 months earlier
    = ($1,800,000) + ($100,000/month * 3 months)
    = $2,100,000

But we have a ceiling of $2 million and the vendor is, therefore, paid $2 million.

Here is a question on FP-EPA.

EXERCISE TIME 3:

Question:
A seller is awarded an FP-EPA contract for an airport terminal development for $15 million with adjustments for changes in currency valuation, consumer price index (CPI) and raw material purchase prices. At the end of the development, an additional 3% needs to be paid to the seller for CPI changes and 4% for currency devaluation. What is the additional payment to the contractor (vendor)?

Solution:
The total increase is 7% of 15 million dollars, which is 1.05 million dollars. The additional payment to the vendor is, therefore, $1,050,000.

---

2. Time and Materials (T&M) Contracts (or Unit Price contracts)

This is a hybrid of fixed priced and cost reimbursable contracts. A T&M contract is often used when the deliverable is in man-hours and other associated expenses are reimbursed at actuals.

The seller profit may be included in the hourly rate but there is usually no additional fee. Cost-reimbursable (CR) contracts, on the other hand, sometimes have a fee that adds to the seller profits.

An example of a T&M contract would be a contract to conduct a training session at $120 per hour, but not to exceed 10 hours a day and a total of 400 hours with reimbursement for lodging expenses at $100 per day and for training material at actuals.

- It is like FP contracts since the rate is fixed (at $100/hour) with a maximum of 400 hours.
- It is also like CR contracts since the seller is paid for the actual number of hours, which is not fixed. Also, all costs related to training material are reimbursed at actuals and daily lodging expenses are also reimbursed.

EXERCISE TIME 4:

Question: A seller is awarded a T&M contract for a 150$/hour and actual for travel and lodging. What is the seller paid if he works for 15 hours and travel expenses come to $600?

Solution:
Total paid to seller = 15 hours * $150/hour + $600
= $2,250 + $600 = $2,850

---

3. Cost-reimbursable (CR) Contracts

These are also called cost-plus (CP) or cost-disbursable (CD) contracts. These contracts (see Table 12-4) involve reimbursement for all actual costs for completed work plus a fee representing seller profit. These are different from T&M contracts due to the fee, that is fixed or variable.

CR contracts could start with a high-level work description with the understanding that there would be scope changes as the work proceeds. The benefit for the seller is that the seller is paid for the actual time and material spent. The benefit for the buyer is the flexibility to modify work scope as and when required.

#	Type of contract	Acro-nym	Definition	Benefits and problems	Example
a	Cost Contract	-	A contract, where the seller is paid for all allowable costs for the project work.	These contracts are usually taken by non-profit organizations. There is usually no profit for the seller.	The seller is awarded a contract in which the seller will be reimbursed for all actual expenses labor, operating expense and capital purchases.
b	Cost Plus Fixed Fee contract	CPFF	The seller is reimbursed for all permitted costs for doing the project work. In addition, the seller receives a fee, which is either a ▪ A fixed **amount**, or ▪ A fixed **percentage** of the **initial** estimated project cost.	This is beneficial for the seller since the seller can estimate the fee in advance, regardless of the performance. The buyer can get more bidders (if needed) by increasing the fixed fee. But the buyer bears the risk since it is forced to pay the fixed fee at project completion regardless of the outcome, in addition to all actual expenses.	The seller is awarded a contract in which the seller will be reimbursed for all actual project costs plus $25,000.
c	Cost Plus Percentage of Costs contract	CPPC	The seller is paid for all incurred costs plus a percentage of the **final** project costs.	This contract is not good for the buyer since the seller is motivated to artificially increase incurred (actual) expenses to receive a higher fee.	The seller is awarded a contract in which the seller will be reimbursed for all project costs plus 20% of the final project costs.
d	Cost Plus Incentive Fee contract	CPIF	The seller is paid for all costs plus an incentive fee based on achieving certain performance goals. A common incentive is to split the difference between the initial estimates and actual incurred cost in a ratio (such as 80/20 or 50/50 split) between the buyer and seller. Another incentive would be a fee, if the seller completes the work before the target completion date.	Splitting the project savings is a motivation for both the buyer and seller. It encourages collaboration between the buyer and seller to successfully complete the project goals.	A contract for a project with an estimated budget of $60,000 where the seller is reimbursed for all costs plus 20% of the savings (or reduced by 20% of excess if actuals exceed $60,000). A second incentive fee would be of $1,000 for each week that the project completes earlier than the estimate of 32 weeks.
e	Cost Plus Award Fee contract	CPAF	The seller is paid for all costs plus an award fee. The award is based on meeting certain quality or performance objectives, described in the contract. The maximum award amount is sometimes mentioned in the contract.	The fee is a motivation for the seller. It could be based on ▪ Meeting or exceeding quality objectives ▪ Completing the work in advance ▪ Completing the work below the initial estimated budget.	A contract for a project with an estimated budget of $80,000 and ceiling of $120,000 where the seller is reimbursed for all actual costs plus an award fee not to exceed $20,000 if the project is under budget and takes less than 6 months.

Table 12-4: Five types of cost-reimbursable (CR) or cost-plus (CP) contracts

> *** For the Exam ***
>
> In the exam, there could be questions asking you to select if the described amount is an incentive fee or award. You must understand the difference between the two!
>
> - **Incentive** fee amount is based on certain agreed-upon parameters or formula. Does the seller know of the incentive amount in advance? Yes! The seller or buyer can **objectively** compute the incentives for different combinations of the criteria or parameters.
> - **Award** fee amount is decided by the buyer. Does the seller know of the award amount in advance? No! The seller is not able to compute the award amount. The criteria to provide an award could be specified in the contract, but the amount is **subjective** and depends on the satisfaction level of the buyer. Also, the amount is not subject to appeals by the seller.

Fixed Price contracts are the most common form of procurement contracts. Selecting the contract type is crucial as it determines the long-term working relationship between the parties. Long-term and large contracts could be a mix of the three types, where certain portions of the work are based on either FP, T&M or CR terms.

EXERCISE TIME 5:

Question:
A seller is awarded a CPIF (cost plus incentive fee) contract with an initial estimated project cost of $80,000, a target fee $15,000 and has a share-ratio of 60/40 between the buyer and seller for savings or overruns. What is the amount paid to the seller in case the actual expenses are $75,000? The ceiling price in the contract is $120,000.

Solution:
Since the actuals ($75,000) are less than the target cost ($80,000) the savings is $5000. 40% of the savings is passed on to the seller.

Total paid to seller = Actuals of $75,000 + target fee of $15,000 + (40% of $5000)
  = $75,000 + $15,000 + $2,000
  = $92,000

Distinguish between the final fee and final price. In this example, the final fee is $15,000 + $2,000 = $17,000. But the final price is $92,000 and is the amount paid to the seller.

The following problem is similar to the one above, but in this case, the actuals are more than the target cost. The overrun amount is divided between the buyer and seller. The seller's revenue is reduced by the share ratio of the overrun amount. Note that the first part of the share ratio is for the buyer.

EXERCISE TIME 6:

Question:
A seller is awarded a CPIF (cost plus incentive fee) contract with an initial estimated project cost of $80,000, a target fee of $15,000 to be paid in case, the actuals are below the ceiling price and a share-ratio of 60/40 between the buyer and seller for savings or overruns. What is the amount paid to the seller, in case the actual project costs are $100,000? Note that the contract ceiling price is $120,000.

Solution:
Since the actuals of $100,000 are higher than target cost ($80,000) the overrun is $20,000. 40% of the overrun is subtracted from the amount due to the seller. The target fee will still be paid to the seller since actuals are below the ceiling price.

Total paid to seller = Actuals of $100,000 + target fee of $15,000 - (40% of $20,000)
                       = $100,000 + $15,000 - $8,000
                       = $107,000

(Again, distinguish between the final fee and final price. In this example, the final fee is $15,000 minus $8,000 = $7,000. But the final price is $107,000 and is the amount paid to the seller.)

The contract has a ceiling price, which is the maximum that the seller can expect to get including all incentives and awards. If the calculated amount to be paid to seller is higher than the ceiling, the seller gets the ceiling price and no more.

EXERCISE TIME 7:

Question: A seller is awarded a CPAF (cost plus award fee) contract with an initial estimated project cost of $210,000, a ceiling of $250,000. The work is completed before time at actuals of $200,000, exceeds quality standards and the client wants to give an award of $60,000. How much can the seller get for the work?

Solution:
The seller gets the actuals ($200,000) plus the award of $60,000. That adds to $260,000 which is above the ceiling. As per the contract, the seller can get a maximum of $250,000 for the work. The answer is $250,000.

Note that the risks depend on project-specific conditions. Figure 12-5 shows a generalized view of the distribution of risks between the buyer and seller for different contract types.

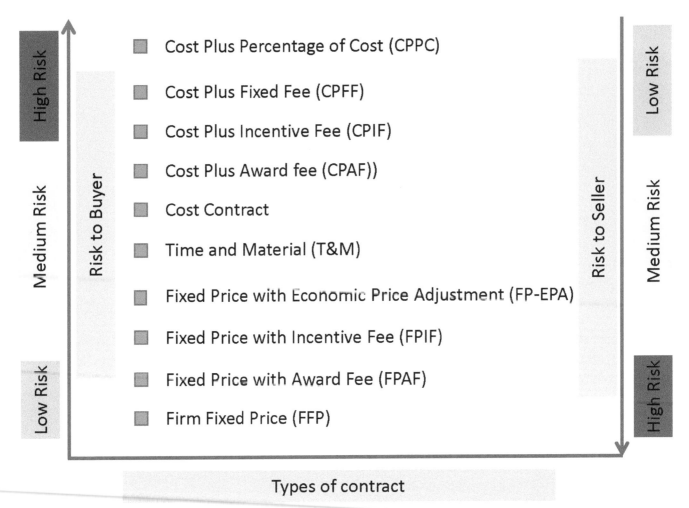

Figure 12-5: Typical distribution of risks to buyers and sellers for different contract types

Procurement Management Plan

You may think that the enterprise has an established process for procuring goods or services and you can safely rely on that for your project. While this is true for projects where you have simple or standard purchases, but you usually need to develop custom contracts for large procurements.

For example, if you are responsible for construction of a large housing complex or an airport and need to work with about 100 vendors and have a budget of 100 million dollars, you need to develop special contracts. It is possible that such work has never been undertaken by your organization. You would need a plan tailored to the project requirements for the procurement of goods and services.

The procurement management plan describes how the project team would manage the purchase of goods or services. It includes details on:

- Types of contract (FP or T&M or CR) that will be used for various purchases,
- The process to develop procurement or bid documents,
- Factors to help make buy-versus-build or lease-versus-buy decisions,
- The format for bid documents,

- Factors used to shortlist vendors who would be asked to provide solutions and quotes,
- Process to select a vendor, award a contract to the selected vendor and monitor the performance of the vendor,
- Bidder conferences to be conducted to provide information or clarifications to vendors, and
- Procurement risks related to long lead times or delay the delivery of services or goods.

Procurement Statement of Work (SOW)

A SOW is a document created by the buyer that describes the needs of the buyer and the service or product, including specifications, desired service level agreement (SLA), duration of the contract, etc.

SOW is provided to the seller, so the seller can respond if they want to take up the work and provide an asking price for the work. In some cases, the seller may create the SOW based on the sellers understanding of the needed tasks and work scope.

Procurement (Bid) Documents

Procurement (or bid) documents are those that are provided by the buyer to get proposal and price from one or more vendor. The buyer needs to consolidate all information in a bid document and provide that to vendors, asking for a response.

The proposal includes various things from the vendor such as the proposed approach and solution, asking price for the service or product, project duration, project management experience, technical skills, etc.

Figure 12-6 below shows the various types of bid documents, prepared and provided by the buyer to the seller for a response:

- Request for information (**RFI**): Vendor is not asked to provide a price, but provide only information on their skills, approach, product specifications,
- Request for proposal (**RFP**): This is also called a request for tender (RFT). It requires a detailed response such as technical qualifications, experience, skills, resumes, etc.
- Invitation for bid (**IFB**): This is also called a request for bid (RFB). The response from the vendor is simply a total lump-sum asking price for the service or product.
- Request for quote (**RFQ**): This is a request for providing price per unit (for example, $55 per pound) or for the entire quantity.

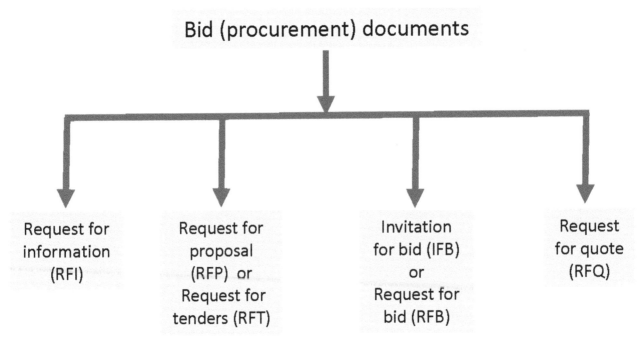

Figure 12-6: Types of procurement (or bid) documents

Source Selection Criteria

Source selection criteria are factors that you consider for selecting a vendor or seller. For various bids or SOWs, there will be multiple vendors who will want to win the contract and do the work. But you need to pick one. How do you select the most suitable seller?

An important part of the procurement management plan is to develop a vendor-selection process. An example of a vendor-selection process would be to request each bidder for a technical and commercial proposal, followed by an evaluation of the proposals and a bidder presentation of their solution and capability to undertake the work.

Steps for vendor selection for a fixed fee (FF) contract

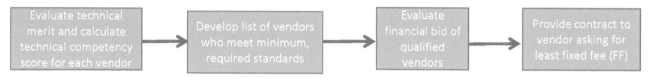

Plan A

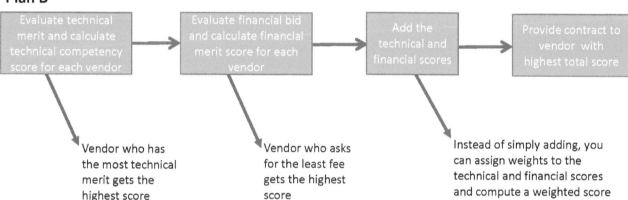

Plan B

Figure 12-7: Steps for technical and financial bid analysis to select a vendor for a fixed fee (FF) contract (note that the amount could be proposed by the vendor for a FF contract)

As a product or service buyer, you need to understand the factors or criteria for selecting a seller (vendor). Of course, the asking price for the work is an important criterion. But can you just pick the vendor who is asking the least price and give him the contract? No! You first need to qualify and see if the vendors meet the technical requirements. Once you have used the technical measures to shortlist the vendors and created a pool of qualified vendors, you can then look at the asking prices and select the vendor who is asking the least.

But what are the technical factors to create a pool of qualified vendors? Those are:

- Skills of the vendors and their technical prowess to complete the work,
- Quality of RFP response from the vendor, which consists of the vendor's understanding of the project requirements, skills, experience and proposed approach,
- The quality and relevance of the solution proposed by the vendor, and
- Post-completion support.

You also need to look at financial factors:

- Asking price or fee for the project scope,

- Duration of warranty for the product, and
- Cost of post-completion support.

There are other factors, such as:

- Past performance of the vendor,
- References,
- Financial capability to complete the project, and
- Interest and incentive of the vendor to meet the project commitments.

All the qualitative aspects mentioned above are relevant, but you need to quantify those to develop a numerical score for ranking the vendors. Table 12-5 is an example to quantify the strengths of the vendors and relevance to the project. The criteria are listed and a weight (from 0 to 1) is assigned to each criterion. The criterion weight is multiplied with the raw score to compute the weighted scores. The weighted scores are added and the sum is used as a factor during vendor selection. In Table 12-5, Vendor B has the highest sum of weighted scores, which is 75.5.

#	Criteria Description	Criteria Weight	Vendor A		Vendor B		Vendor C	
			Raw score (1- 100)	Weighted score	Raw score (1- 100)	Weighted score	Raw score (1- 100)	Weighted score
1	Technical experience & expertise of vendor	0.15	70	10.5	80	12	75	11.25
2	Project management competencies	0.15	40	6	90	13.5	65	9.75
3	Quality of proposed solution	0.30	60	18	60	18	90	27
4	Asking price by vendor (lower asking price earns higher raw score)	0.40	80	32	80	32	40	16
	Sum of Weighted Scores	**1.00**	--	**66.5**	--	**75.5**	--	**64**

Table 12-5: Quantitative evaluation of vendors using weighted scores

Build-versus-Buy Decisions

A build-or-buy analysis is a technique to decide whether to develop a product internally or buy that from the market. For services, it would be a decision to get the work done using internal resources versus outsourcing the work to a vendor.

What are the factors that influence a build-or-buy decision? Common factors are:

- Internal skills: Does the internal team have the skills needed to develop a product or do a particular work.

- Time commitments: You need to get a time estimate for doing the work internally. You also need a time estimate to find a suitable vendor, draft contract and get approvals, and get the vendor to do the work. How much time is there in the project to get the work completed? If you are crunched for time, which is quicker? Doing it internally or having an external vendor, do it?
- Budget constraints: You need to assess the costs involved in doing it internally versus having an external vendor do the work. Sometimes, it may be cheaper to outsource the work or buy an off-the-shelf product. If you decide to buy, you need to reduce the risks of exceeding the allocated time, budget and other resources. On the other hand, if you decide to build it internally, you need to make sure you have the required resources, skills and time. Building internally is usually necessitated by a need to maintain control and ownership, especially if the solution involves using intellectual property (IP) and copyright information.

You will have questions in the exam that will require you to compute and then decide on the most optimum option amongst buying, leasing, internally developing or outsourcing the development.

EXERCISE TIME 8:

Question:
You can buy an off-the-shelf application for $1,500,000 but it has a maintenance expense of $200,000 each year for a lifespan of 5 years. If you were to develop and maintain it internally, you will need 5 engineers at $100,000 each year for 5 years. Would it be financially less expensive to buy or develop the application?

Solution:
- Buy price = $1,500,000 + $200,000/year * 5 years = $2,500,000
- Internal development price = 5 engineers * $100,000/year * 5 years = $2,500,000

The expenses in both scenarios are identical over the life of 5 years. The data provided will not help you select an option. You will need to look at other factors such as ease-of-use for users, training costs, the possibility of using the application beyond 5 years, etc.

The following is an exercise to select between purchase and lease options.

EXERCISE TIME 9:

Question:
You need to decide whether to lease or buy machinery for your 36-month project. The lease cost is $4,000 per month. You can buy the equipment for $80,000 but the annual maintenance cost is $12,000. Which is a cost-effective choice?

Solution:
- Lease cost = $4,000 per month * 36 months = $144,000
- Purchase cost = $80,000 + $12,000/year * 3 years = $116,000

The choice would be to purchase the machinery due to savings of $28,000.

Process 2: Conduct Procurements

PMBOK®: Page 482
Process Group: Executing

This process involves asking for and getting responses from the vendor, selecting a vendor and providing a contract or purchase order to the vendor.

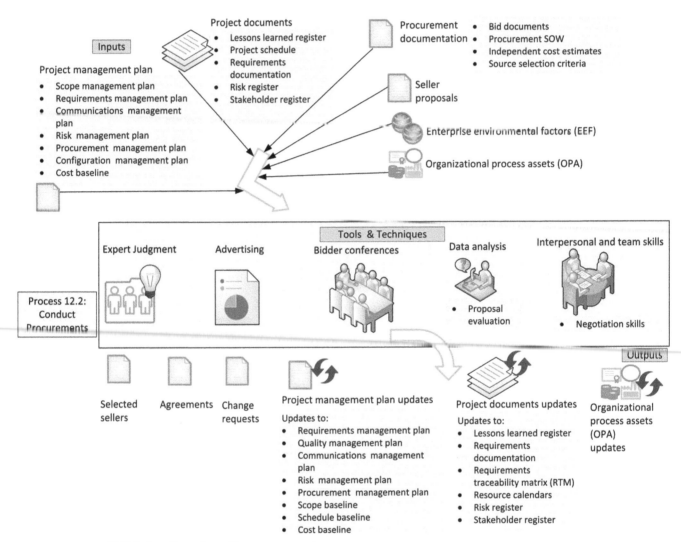

Figure 12-8: ITTO for Conduct Procurements process

Bidder Conferences

Let us assume that you (as a buyer) must select one from 10 bidders for a contract. The bidders are preparing a bid response and need clarifications. You can hold separate and independent meetings with each bidder. But what could be the potential problems with that approach? First, that would be too time-consuming for you. Secondly, the bidders would get different and inconsistent information. Then, there is a possibility of preferential treatment to certain bidders.

So, how do you get around these problems? The solution is to hold a conference for all the bidders. For this, you schedule a time and place for a conference and invite all the bidders. The conference could start with a brief overview of the desired service or product followed by a question-and-answer session. This provides an opportunity for all vendors to listen to the various answers. This also leads to consistency in the information provided to all the bidders, saves you time and helps avoid preferential treatment.

Procurement Negotiations

Negotiations are especially relevant for service contracts. The goal of negotiations is to:

- clarify grey areas and remove ambiguity in terms and conditions
- decide on changes to baselines namely scope, schedule and cost
- arrive a price point that is fair to the seller and to the buyer as well, and
- create a win-win situation for all parties, where the seller makes a rational profit and the buyer gets the work done on time and within budget.

A win-lose contract, that is in favor of one party, usually results in a lose-lose scenario for all. If the contract has terms favoring the buyer, the seller will gradually lose interest in completing the work, once it knows that it cannot make any profit. The seller may later try to get additional funds by proposing new enhancements or features. The seller may also try to prove that part of the work being done (or asked for) is not explicitly in the signed contract and hence requires a change request and additional funds.

There are several outputs of this process such as:

- a list of selected vendors,
- agreement documents,
- resource calendars,
- change requests, and
- updates to the project management plans, baselines and other project documents.

Note that all procurements do not require negotiations. For example, if you have a need to issue a purchase order (PO) for goods to be bought, you can simply provide the PO to the lowest bidder. If required, the procurement team can negotiate with vendors for lower prices, on behalf of the project team.

Agreement documents for sellers

You may think that the only important part of the contract or agreement is the work scope, timeline and offered price. But an agreement contains various important sections such as terms and conditions, incentives, payment schedule, etc. Figure 12-9 has the various sections within a contract. These can be categorized into two parts:

- Description of work to be done (or product to be delivered) along with technical specifications, and
- Financials including price, maintenance costs, warranty period, etc.

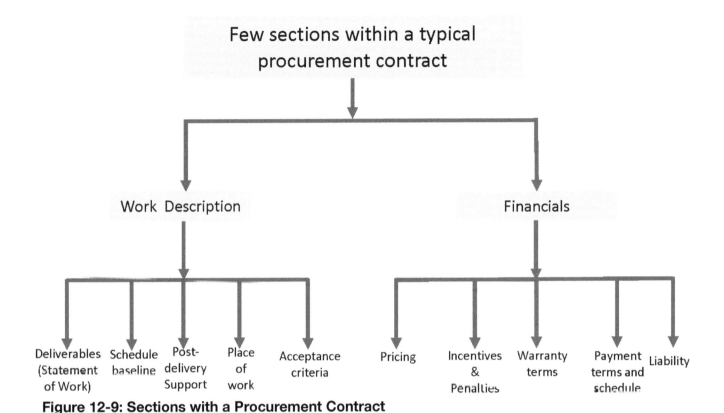

Figure 12-9: Sections with a Procurement Contract

A contract must also contain legal fine print such as intellectual property rights, indemnification statements, product ownership and force majeure statements to protect against natural disasters that are outside anyone's control.

Besides the parts of an agreement in Figure 12-9, an agreement also has termination clauses that describe actions to be taken in case any party wants to exit the contract. It also has steps called alternative dispute resolution (ADR) mechanisms that describe what must be done to resolve conflicts (if any) between the parties.

A contract is an important, legal document. Not conforming to any part of the contract, is a valid reason for the negatively-impacted party to take the other parties to court and ask for fines, penalties, refund of disbursement amounts, reimbursement of actual legal fees, etc.

Process 3: Control Procurements

PMBOK®: Page 492
Process Group: Monitoring and Controlling

Control Procurements is concerned with managing the work being done by and relationships with the vendors. The goal is that all the parties meet the requirements that have been agreed to in the contracts.

Changes (if any) to the contracts should be made using approved change requests or revisions to statement of work (SoW), service level agreement (SLA), master service agreement (MSA) or another contract. These changes could be related to the work scope schedule, fees, quality, product specifications, etc.

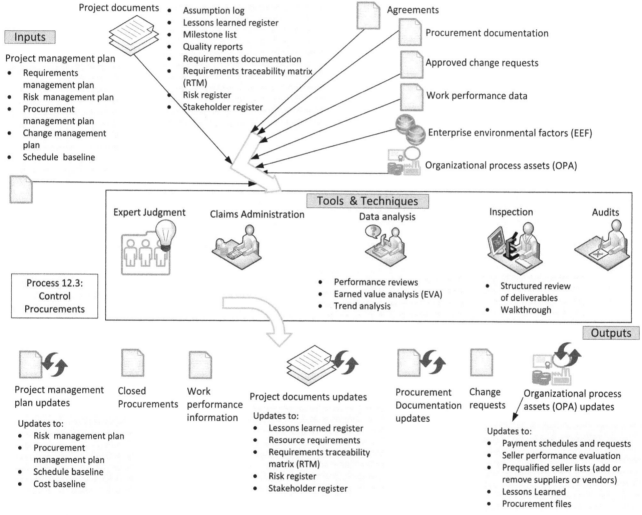

Figure 12-10: ITTO for Control Procurements process

How do you control procurements? On the surface, it may seem easy for a project manager to deal with vendors, monitor their performance and make changes, as needed, to the contracts. While it may be easy for small projects, imagine a project with $500M, 200 project resources and 50 vendors, working in 10 countries. The procurements would be impossible for a project manager to draft, get approvals and later monitor and control the deliverables. It would require collaboration with the procurement teams, including the procurement administrators, in each country. Changes to the contract must be approved and signed by the contract administrator or by the procurement administrator.

One way to control procurements is to conduct regular procurement performance reviews. The objective would be to:

- review the quality of the work completed till now,
- assess for compliance or non-compliance with the required terms in the contract,
- assess the project plans, in case there are procurement delays,
- make sure that the project can be completed within the assigned budget and time,
- review project documentation,
- identify performance failures or successes, and
- assess if the vendor has fulfilled the terms in the contract.

An important aspect of the **Control Procurement** process is to make sure that the vendor is paid as per the schedule of payments in the contract. Usually, the payment is based on completion of certain milestones and after demonstrating that the completed work has met the quality, as agreed in the contract. The assessment of satisfactory completion must be done by an authorized person in the project team.

More points for the exam:

- Assume that your client is external to the organization.
- A win-win situation for the buyer and seller must be built into procurement documents to ensure project success.
- All deliverables in the contracts must be completed and all terms must be followed.
- Changes to the procurement contracts are done by the procurement or contracts administrator.
- The seller cannot ask the buyer for something that is not in the procurement contract, unless a formal change order is approved in writing, by both the parties.
- Procurement practices are governed by regulations in each country. But, to answer exam questions, you do not need to know the country-specific regulations. You just need to follow the guidelines in the PMBOK.
- Contracts must be written in a formal manner so those can be used in a court of law to resolve disputes and estimate penalties.
- Verbal decisions or communications are usually not enforceable in a court of law.

Practice Questions for Chapter 12

1. Closed procurements are an output of:
   A. Control Procurements
   B. Conduct Procurements
   C. Close Project or Phase
   D. Plan Procurement Management

2. A type of contract that is a hybrid of cost-reimbursable (CR) and fixed-price (FP) contracts is:
   A. Purchase order (PO)
   B. Joint venture (JV) between buyer and supplier
   C. Time and material (T&M) contract
   D. Statement of work (SOW)

3. Which of the following is the most formal of all following documents with guidelines for sellers to provide technical solutions, price, project timelines, etc.?
   A. Request for information (RFI)
   B. Request for quotation (RFQ)
   C. Request for proposal (RFP)
   D. Invitation for bid (IFB)

4. Which of the following is typically not used for commercial or industrial construction projects?
   A. Build-own-operate-transfer (BOOT) contracts
   B. Design-bid-build (DBB) contracts
   C. Design-build-operate (DBO) contracts
   D. Cost-reimbursable (CR) contracts

5. You have a work scope that you need to outsource. You know that the work scope is not firm and will significantly change once the work starts. What would be the most suitable contract type to use?
   A. Cost-reimbursable (CR) contract
   B. Fixed-price (FP) contract
   C. Time and material (T&M) contract
   D. Statement of work (SOW)

6. You are developing a contract document for a vendor. The work duration is 3 months. The vendor will be paid on the cost incurred and will get 20% additional if the work is completed in two months or less. This is an example of:
   A. Cost Plus Fixed Fee (CPPF)
   B. Cost Plus Incentive Fee (CPIF)
   C. Fixed Price with Incentive Fee (FPIF)
   D. Cost Plus Award Fee (CPAF)

7. Alexa Simmons is a project manager for a natural gas driller in North Dakota. She has the signed project charter for a new drilling rig to be established. But the work is complex and she knows that developing and implementing the solution is not easy. Which is the right type of document to use to get vendors to provide a solution and quote?
   A. Request for information (RFI)
   B. Request for quotation (RFQ)
   C. Request for proposal (RFP)
   D. Bid document

8. Which of the following is not true for a procurement statement of work (SOW)?
   A. It is developed from the project scope baseline and contains the portion that is to be contracted out.
   B. It usually has a schedule of payment that will be followed for payments to be made to the seller.
   C. It requests the sellers to prepare and submit a technical solution.
   D. It contains details that will help prospective bidders decide for themselves if they have the skills to undertake the requested services.

9. Which of the following contracts are typically used for staff augmentation or to procure external services, especially when a precise statement of work cannot be developed?
   A. Time and material (T&M) contract
   B. Purchase Order (PO)
   C. Cost-reimbursable (CR) contract
   D. Fixed-price (FP) contract

10. Which one of the following processes, has bid documents (such as RFP, RFI or RFQ) and procurement statement of word (SOW) as outputs?
    A. Plan Procurement Management
    B. Conduct Procurements
    C. Control Procurements
    D. All the 3 processes in Procurement Management Knowledge Area

11. Susan Johnson needs to procure 25 desktops for an application development and testing project. What type of contract should she use?
    A. Request for Information (RFI) followed by a Purchase Order (PO)
    B. Invitation for Bid (IFB)
    C. Request for Proposal (RFP)
    D. Request for Quote (RFQ) followed by a Purchase Order (PO)

12. Which of the following documents or outputs will not help a project manager acquire goods or services from a vendor?
    A. Procurement management plan
    B. Procurement strategy
    C. Make-or-buy decisions
    D. Bid documents

13. Richard Ronald is looking for the right contract type to outsource a large cloud migration project to a vendor. Which one of the following contract types poses the most risk for Richard?
   A. Fixed Price with Award Fee (FPAF) contract
   B. Time & Material (T&M) contract
   C. Cost Plus Award Fee (CPAF) contract
   D. Cost Plus Fixed Fee (CPFF) contract

14. Which of the following processes has updates to the list of prequalified sellers (empaneled vendors) as an output?
   A. Plan Procurement Management
   B. Conduct Procurements
   C. Control Procurements
   D. Control Resources

ANSWERS

Question Number	Correct Answer	Explanation
1	A	In the **Control Procurements** process, the buyer, along with the procurement administrator, provides the seller with a formal written notice that the contract has been completed and can be closed.
2	C	T&M contracts are a hybrid of cost-reimbursable (CR) and fixed-price (FP) contracts.
3	C	An RFP requires the prospective seller to provide the technical solution, price, etc. and provide that they have the skills and experience to undertake the proposed scope.
4	D	Cost-reimbursable contracts are typically not used for commercial or industrial construction. The other choices are commonly used for construction and infrastructure projects such as for power plants, highways, airports, shipyards, etc.
5	A	A cost-reimbursable (CR) contract is best when the work scope is expected to change.
6	B	There is an incentive fee for early completion on top of reimbursement of actual expenses. Hence it is a Cost Plus Incentive Fee (CPIF) contract.
7	C	An RFP is used when the solution is complex and you need the vendors to provide a technical solution and supporting prices.
8	C	A SOW usually does not request the sellers to prepare and provide a technical solution. SOW typically contains a subset of the project scope and asks for a timeline and price for the proposed scope.
9	A	A time and material (T&M) contract is used for staff augmentation, vendor services, etc. when a firm SOW cannot be prepared.
10	A	Bid documents are an output of the **Plan Procurement Management** process. They are used as inputs for the **Conduct Procurements** process.
11	D	An RFQ is needed to get quotes from vendors. Once a vendor is selected, a PO is used to buy the equipment. Note that a PO is used to buy commodity items and also for customized services or goods.
12	C	Notice the keyword **not**. The make-or-buy decisions help decide whether to use a vendor or have the work done internally. It does not help a project manager acquire goods or services.
13	D	Cost Plus (CP) contracts are riskier than Fixed Price (FP) or T&M contracts for buyers. In the choices, there are two CP contracts: CPAF and CPFF. CPAF has an award that is determined by the buyer and is not subject to appeals. CPAF is less risky than CPFF for buyers. Thus, CPFF has the most risk for the buyer in the case.
14	B	The **Conduct Procurements** process has 'updates to list of prequalified sellers' as one of its output. Vendors are added or removed from the list of sellers, based on their ability to undertake the proposed work scope and meet the contract terms.

CHAPTER 13

Stakeholder Management

Why do most projects fail? It is usually not due to technical or logistical reasons, but due to people-related reasons such as lack of support from the project team or stakeholders.

Also, do you find that resource owners have removed their previously-committed resources from projects? There could be many reasons for their lack of support. The project costs may have become too expensive and not worth the expenses. The customer may be planning to cancel the order. Missed deadlines would have made the project deliverables irrelevant and useless.

Sometimes, the root cause may be outside the influence or responsibility of the project management team. Or it could be due to poor stakeholder management. The stakeholder interest and support may have reduced, but the project manager did not work in time, with the stakeholder to identify and remediate the root causes. As you can see, stakeholder management (like communication management) is crucial for project progress and success.

There are 4 processes in the **Stakeholders Management** knowledge area:

Initiating Process Group	Planning Process Group	Executing Process Group	Monitoring and Controlling Process Group
13.1) Identify Stakeholders	13.2) Plan Stakeholder Engagement	13.3) Manage Stakeholder Engagement	13.4) Monitor Stakeholder Engagement

Both communication and stakeholder management are vital responsibilities of a project manager. The stakeholders need to be aware of the project status and willing to extend their help. Stakeholder management is not complex for a project with a few stakeholders. But it is complex if you are the project manager for a project that has 200 stakeholders and a project team of 50+ members reporting to 10 functional managers.

You will need a good stakeholder management plan and strategy to enable smooth project progress. Here are guidelines to develop a good stakeholder management plan:

- Identify stakeholders at the start of the project.
- Find what they require? This may need several meetings with the stakeholders. They may guide you to someone else for more requirements. But all these must be done before you start the project. If you do not get all requirements towards the start, you will get to know those later. Your time estimates will slip. You will have to create change requests during execution, which will make everyone uneasy and wonder if work were even planned earlier!
- Understand the level of stakeholder interest in the project. Is the project crucial to their responsibilities and will that impact their direct reports? Do they want to participate in the project meetings?
- Understand if they are interested in contributing to or learning from the project
- Understand who can help in the tasks such as planning, execution, testing, communications, meetings, etc.
- Understand how they want to be updated on project status. Is that via emails, in-person meetings or by posting project status reports on a portal or shared folder?
- Also, need to document the frequency of status updates? Should the project manager provide updates each month, each week or each day?
- Determine their influence. Stakeholders can positively or negatively impact the project. How will you manage their influence on the project?
- Understand how you will measure if stakeholders support is deteriorating. How will you enhance their support for the project?

---

* For the Exam*

Good communications and relationships with the stakeholders are crucial throughout the project, not only during project initiation. It is therefore, important to monitor the stakeholder relationships and keep correcting for breakdowns, if any! You can answer exam questions correctly if imagine that you are managing a project with 100+ stakeholders in different countries.

Trends and Emerging Practices

A growing trend is to do a **thorough identification** of stakeholders and assessment of the degree of support from them. This is not something you do initially only but must be done continuously across the project life. Another trend is to involve more team members for stakeholder identification and assessment, instead of just being done solely by the sponsor, project manager and a few members of the project management team.

Another growing trend is to consider the stakeholders as **partners** for project progress. They are included in more project meetings. Again, this sense of partnership should not be limited to project initiation and planning but must remain active throughout the project life. The engagement can be viewed in a positive and negative stance.

- The positive stance is that active collaboration with stakeholders would help gain their support and guidance, thereby improving the quality of the deliverables.
- The negative stance is that if the stakeholders are not actively engaged, their indifference or apathy to the project can increase the likelihood that the final deliverables will neither be approved nor used by them.

There is a growing acceptance that the project is **co-created** by the project resources and stakeholders. The end-users and clients would be using the project deliverables, long after the project team has completed the project. There is a growing awareness that it is fair that the users, clients and other impacted stakeholders be considered and involved as co-creators of the project deliverables.

Tailoring Considerations

Like communications, managing stakeholders is also a significant responsibility of a project manager. To be effective and successful, the project manager must develop different approaches to manage different stakeholders. Obviously 'one approach fits all' will not work!

You need to tailor (customize) the details in the **Stakeholder Management** Knowledge Area based on **project-related factors** such as

- communication technologies used for the project,
- various project reports that are developed for the stakeholders,
- number of stakeholders in the project, and
- the diversity of the stakeholders.

You also need to tailor the processes based on **stakeholder factors** such as whether each stakeholder

- prefers detailed status reports or just a summary,
- wants to be involved in periodic (daily or weekly) status meetings or not, and
- wants to be part of discussions with other stakeholders.

If a stakeholder is involved in direct discussions with other stakeholders, there is a likelihood that he or she is getting information that has not been influenced by the preferences of the project manager.

The processes must be tailored to promote continuous assessment of the attitude and support of the stakeholder.

Considerations for Agile/Adaptive Environments

Projects with a high degree of changes in requirements and scope require aggressive transparency and stakeholder engagement. This can be done by:

- Inviting stakeholders to project meetings.
- Posting project documents and artifacts in public places.
- Active collaboration between users, engineers, client and other stakeholders by cutting through the hierarchical layers.

The advantages are that it builds trust, aligns the work done to stakeholder expectations and helps identify issues early on when changes and remediation are easier and less expensive.

Process 1: Identify Stakeholders

PMBOK®: Page 507
Process Group: Initiating

Identify Stakeholders is the second process in the **Initiating** Process Group. Here you make a list of all stakeholders and determine:

(1) how they can impact the project,
(2) how they are affected by the project outcome,
(3) their requirements and expectations from the project,
(4) how they want to be involved with the project, and
(5) how they want communications on project status.

All these factors enable the project manager to appropriately plan the work required for each individual stakeholder or each group of stakeholders.

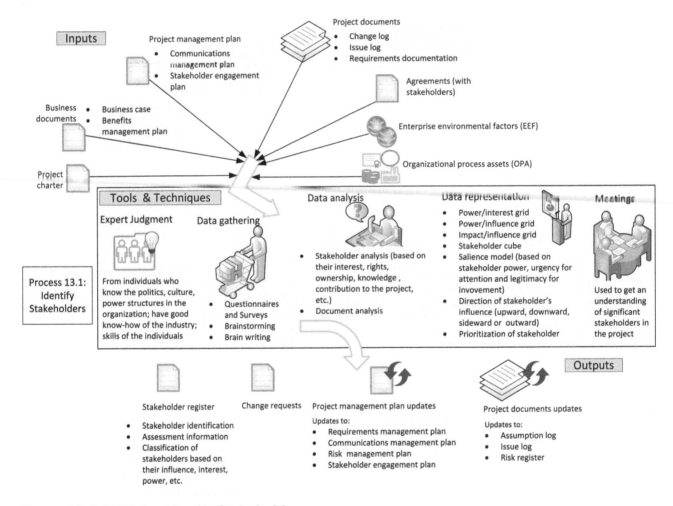

Figure 13-1: ITTO for Identify Stakeholders process

Stakeholder Analysis

This is a technique to identify stakeholders, their level of support towards the project, their areas of interest and how they can affect the project progress. An initial list of stakeholders can be found in the project charter. Also, you need to schedule meetings with them to understand their expectations and requirements and get names of other stakeholders.

You can then group the stakeholders in categories based on factors such as their:

- interest in the project,
- influence and impact on the project,
- political clout and power, and
- authority.

All these can be shown using a 2-D grid as in Figure 13-2.

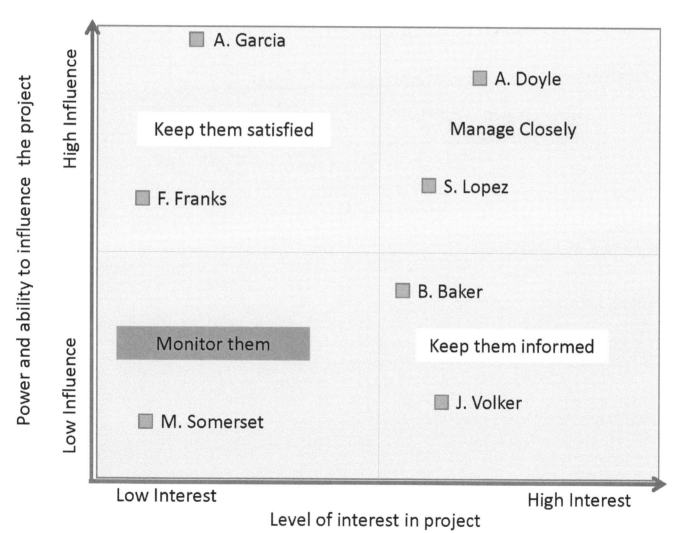

Figure 13-2: Grid of the influence of stakeholders and their interest in the project

Stakeholder Cube

A 2-D grid may not represent all the different factors (power, influence, impact, interest, etc.) about stakeholders. A stakeholder cube (as shown in Figure 13-3) is a 3-D representation that can depict three factors.

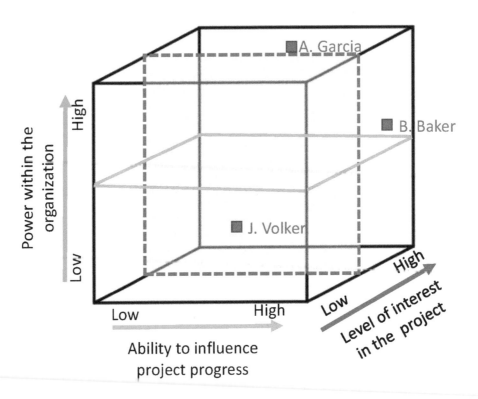

Figure 13-3: Stakeholder cube

Salience Model

Large projects may have tens or hundreds of stakeholders, who could be managing different business units or divisions. Stakeholders may have conflicting expectations from the project. Trying to meet such expectations and establish effective communications is a challenge for the project manager.

The salience model (Figure 13-4) is helpful, especially for large projects, to identify the status and relevance of stakeholders. It categorizes the stakeholders on their:

- Power: the ability to influence the project progress
- Urgency: the need for immediate communication and action for them
- Legitimacy: relevance and appropriateness of their involvement in the project

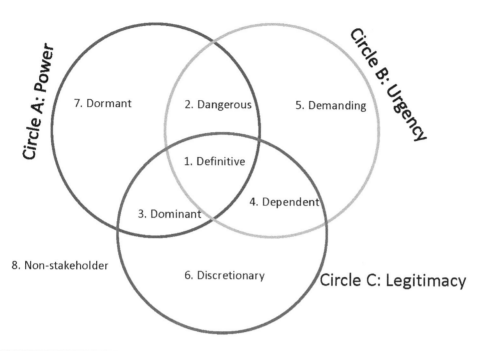

Stakeholder appears in number of overlapping circles	Type	Attention level that the project manager and project management team need to provide to the stakeholder
Stakeholders, who are in all 3 circles	(1) Definitive	High attention
Stakeholders, who are in any 2 of the circles	(2) Dangerous (3) Dominant (4) Dependent	Medium attention
Stakeholders, who are in only 1 of the circles	(5) Demanding (6) Discretionary (7) Dormant	Low attention

Figure 13-4: Salience Model of Stakeholders

Directions of Stakeholder Influence

Stakeholders can be categorized according to the direction(s) of their influence, as shown in Figure 13-5. Some stakeholders have an influence on **upward** management. Some would have an influence on the **downward** members, who contribute towards the technical know-how and perform hands-on activities for the project. Other stakeholders may have an influence on the **outward** or external stakeholders such as government agencies, vendors, industry leaders, etc. Some would have a **sideward** influence on peer managers.

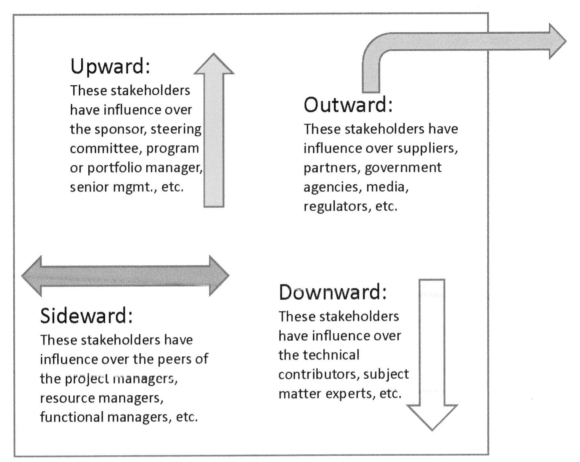

Figure 13-5: Directions of Influence of Stakeholders

Stakeholder Register (output of this process)

An important output of this process is the stakeholder register. It is usually in the form of a table. It records all the information you have collected about each stakeholder. Table 13-1 is an example. Examples of information recorded within the register are:

- Department of the stakeholder
- Title or position of the stakeholder
- Contact email address and phone number
- Level of interest in the project (can be qualitative such as high, medium or low interest or can be quantitatively ranked with a number between 1 and 10, where 10 shows the highest level of interest)
- Political clout and power
- Influence and impact on the project (high, medium or low or a number between 1 and 10)
- Requirements from the projects
- Key expectations (these are not hard requirements, but an outcome they hope to see). An expectation is a belief in what will happen in the future. Stakeholders will have different (and sometimes opposite) views of the future. That is why it is important to discuss their expectations and see if they are realistic! Also, discuss if those can be in-scope or not!
- Level of engagement (unaware, supporter, neutral or resistor to project progress)

You can have various fields related to each stakeholder in the stakeholder register. It is a living documnet and you do not need to fill each cell in the register towards the start of the project. Some fields can be left blank and filled later. The stakeholder register will help you in the next process, which is **Plan Stakeholder Engagement**.

Project Name: New Enterprise Resource Planning (ERP) Application Setup and Rollout							
Project Number: 20-203							
#	Stakeholder name	Key role in the project	Power and influence on the project (1 – 10, 10 being highest)	Interest in the project	Key Expectations	Communication preference	Classification
1	Boyden Brooks	Project Sponsor	8	High	On-time and under-budget completion	Weekly status report by email	Supporter
2	Keith Conrad	Customer Point of Contact	10	High	Successful test outcome; ease of use of new application; quick adoption by user community	Daily 30-minute meetings in a conference room	Resistor
3	George Garcia	Auditor for Project Success Checks (PSC)	8	Medium	Project documents follow the government compliance requirements; correct templates are utilized	Video conference each month	Neutral
4	Patrick Samson	Project Test lead	3	High	Successful user acceptance and integration testing	Weekly status report by email	Neutral

Table 13-1: Example of stakeholder register

Process 2: Plan Stakeholder Engagement

PMBOK®: Page 516
Process Group: Planning

This process is concerned with developing the plan and strategies to engage the stakeholders throughout the project. This is based on their expectations from the project, their interest in different project activities and their potential impact on the project progress.

This stakeholder engagement plan provides a plan to improve interaction with and support of the stakeholders. Stakeholder support is crucial for project progress.

Figure 13-6 shows the inputs, tools and techniques and outputs of the Plan Stakeholder Engagement process.

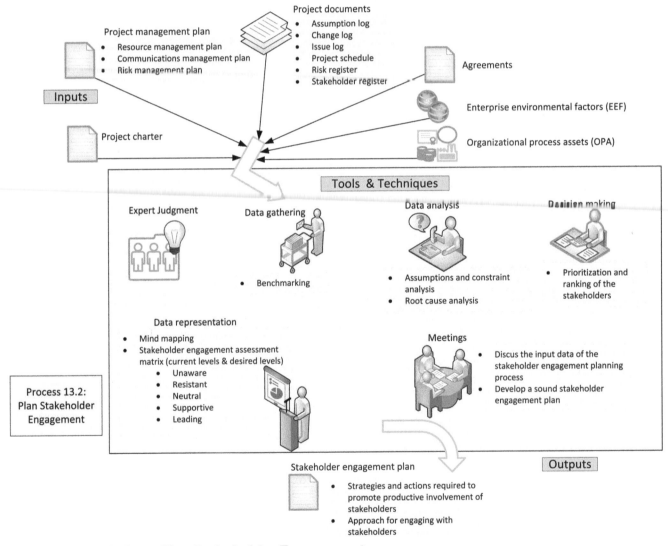

Figure 13-6: ITTO for Plan Stakeholder Engagement process

You need to also develop a stakeholder engagement matrix, as shown in Table 13-2, where:

- C denotes the current engagement status, and
- D denotes the desired engagement status.

C and D could be any of the following:

- **Unaware**: Stakeholder is not aware or knowledgeable about the project
- **Resistant**: Stakeholder knows the status but is resistant to the project progress. The project objectives are against what he or she stands for. Do you have such stakeholders who do not want to see your project move ahead? If yes, you cannot ignore them. They have political capital and influence. They will pull resources away from the project and the project may never see the light of day.
- **Neutral**: They are aware of the project status, but they are unbiased towards the project objectives and progress.
- **Supportive**: They support the project. You need to make sure they stay that way and do not become neutral or resistant.
- **Leading**: They are actively engaged in making sure that the project progresses steadily.

Project Name: New Enterprise Resource Planning (ERP) application Implementation and Rollout							
Project Number: 20-203							
#	**Stakeholder name**	**Key role in the project**	**Unaware**	**Resistant**	**Neutral**	**Supportive**	**Leading**
1	Boyden Bleu	Project Sponsor					C, D
2	Keith Conrad	Customer Point of Contact			C		D
3	George Garcia	Auditor for Project Success Checks (PSC)	C			D	
4	Patrick Simpson	Project Test lead		C		D	

Table 13-2: Stakeholder engagement assessment matrix (C=current status, D=desired status)

Table 13-2 is an example of a stakeholder engagement matrix with:

- as-is or current (C) and
- to-be or desired (D)

levels of engagement. If C and D are different for certain stakeholders, you need to move the C towards D. This requires strong interpersonal skills, planning and building good business relationships with the stakeholders.

With people having their own preferences and working style, politics and power plays cannot be ignored. It has prevailed since mankind started living together in the form of societies. It has prevailed for thousands of years and will continue, despite the well-known problems. It is not within your scope to prepare a politics-free organization or project team. Project managers need to work within and be a part of the existing system.

So, what do you do? Develop honest and transparent working relationships. Here are skills that you need to develop and use in order to build good relationships with stakeholders and get their support for the project:

- Sympathy
- Trust
- Honesty
- Transparency
- Good communication skills
- Interest in genuinely understanding the expectations and requirements of the stakeholder
- Respect for the stakeholder
- Understanding the concerns that the stakeholder may have on project status and outcomes

Figure 13-7 shows the strategy that you need to adopt and actions you need to plan for stakeholders, who will have varying levels of interest and influence on your project.

The output of this process is the stakeholder engagement plan. It is a document that has information about the stakeholders, their expectations from the project, strategies that the project management team can use to effectively engage the stakeholders and maintain their interest throughout the project life. The stakeholder engagement plan contains the following:

- Desired and current engagement level of each stakeholder.
- Your strategy to keep each stakeholder engaged through the project life (see Table 13-2).
- What they want to know about the project?
- What information needs to be provided to each stakeholder and why?
- Their preferred communication requirements such as frequency of communication (each week, each month, etc.) and preferred technique (email, in-person meetings, discussion, presentation).
- How you will update information related to existing stakeholders?
- How you will add more stakeholders to the plan?
- Strategy to resolve deadlocks in case two or more stakeholders have conflicting requirements.

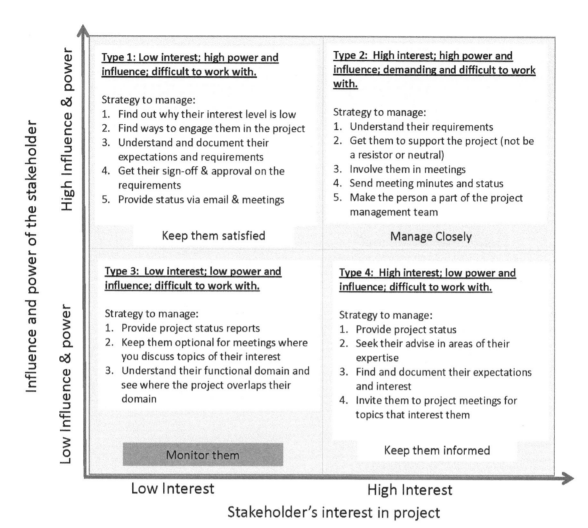

Figure 13-7: Strategy for managing stakeholders with different interest and power

Parts of the stakeholder engagement plan and communications management plan seem to overlap. But there are differences in their approach and objectives:

- The stakeholder engagement plan is about the reasons behind the communication structure and plan. It contains their status (whether they are supportive or resistant or 'do not care'), their stake in the project objectives, their need for the content, etc.
- On the other hand, the communications management plan is about the details such as frequency of communications (for example, status reports must be provided weekly or daily) delivery mode (written or oral), whether it should be conveyed via emails or meetings, etc.

Access to the stakeholder engagement plan must be restricted. It could have sensitive information about the behavior and attitude of the stakeholders towards the project. You need to be careful about who gets to access and edit the documents.

Should you write everything in the stakeholder engagement plan? No! Some information related to stakeholders may be too sensitive to be documented and distributed! You just need to remember the information and discuss discreetly (as required) during meetings!

Process 3: Manage Stakeholder Engagement

PMBOK®: Page 523
Process Group: Executing

This process deals with maintaining the support, interest and engagement of the stakeholders throughout the project. It is about actions that you take to meet the expectations of the stakeholders and address issues as they happen. All this will help reduce the resistance from the stakeholders, thus paving a path for the project success.

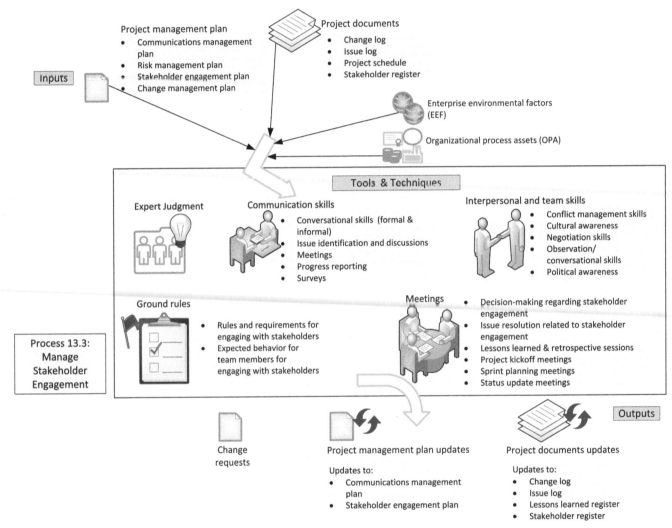

Figure 13-8: ITTO for Manage Stakeholder Engagement process

Engaging with and managing stakeholders requires good interpersonal and soft skills such as:

- Ability to foresee risks and plan agreeable workarounds
- Ability to resolve conflicts in an amicable manner, especially if stakeholders have conflicting requirements or expectations
- Ability to build trust

- Ability to overcome resistance to project and win resistors (to some degree at least) over to the project

Managing stakeholders requires managerial and leadership skills. You need to do the following:

- Be proactive in identifying issues and addressing those.
- Maintain trust with stakeholders.
- Pay attention to stakeholder needs while the work is in-progress.
- Keep stakeholders updated on the in-progress and future work so they have the right expectations.
- Be honest about expectations. If certain requirements or expectations are not being met, you cannot just ignore it. Instead, meet with the stakeholder to develop an alternate plan.
- Facilitate group consensus towards project goals.
- Influence stakeholders and resources to support the project.
- Negotiate and resolve conflicts (instead of avoiding conflict) and gain consensus for a certain goal.

The main takeaway is that you must work with and involve the stakeholders. Even though there may be lot of activities and issues to take care of, remember that the project has been funded by the stakeholders and exists to meet the business and stakeholder requirements. There may be a few stakeholders who are antagonistic or resistant to the project objectives and progress. But the project manager owns the responsibility to make the stakeholders acknowledge the organizational need for the project outcomes and get their support, necessary for progress.

Other outputs from the **Manage Stakeholder Engagement** process are:

- Feedback from stakeholders on project progress
- Change requests for corrective or preventative actions
- Updates to the project documents such as change log, issue log, lessons learned, stakeholder register, stakeholder engagement assessment matrix, etc.
- Updates to what reports you send to the stakeholders and how those are communicated (these result in updates to the communications management plan)
- Updates to the stakeholder engagement plan.

Process 4: Monitor Stakeholder Engagement

PMBOK®: Page 530
Process Group: Monitoring and Controlling

Monitor Stakeholder Engagement is the process of observing and monitoring the relationship with the stakeholders and then making required changes to the engagement plan. The objective is to make sure that you get the required support from stakeholders.

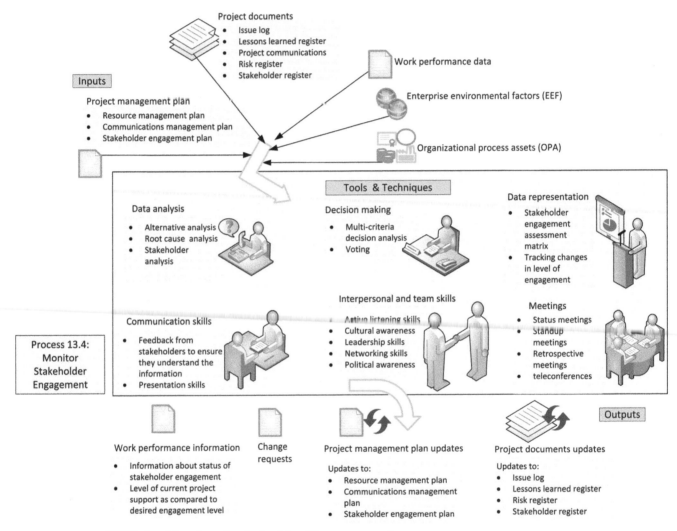

Figure 13-9: ITTO for Monitor Stakeholder Engagement process

The inputs to this process are project management plan, stakeholder register, issue log, change log, project schedule and work performance data related to completed work, cost, etc. The tools used include meetings, expert judgment and information management systems that use the work performance data to prepare visual representations, spreadsheets, presentations and charts which are in turn, consolidated into reports for stakeholders.

Once the stakeholders receive and review the reports, they will provide comments and feedback, which could lead to change requests. The change requests could be for corrective actions to bring the project deliverables or baselines (scope, schedule and cost) in-line with stakeholder requirements and expectations. There could also be change requests for preventive actions to help reduce the probability and impact of threats to project progress and deliverables.

Good communications are an important tool for controlling stakeholder engagement. You need to spend time in meetings with stakeholders. You will need to ask a set of previously-prepared questions and document the answers. Also, note the non-verbal cues and body language and their perceptions about the project.

Stakeholder engagement is a crucial activity. It starts with identifying all stakeholders early in the project life, starting from the stakeholder list in the project charter. You need to plan and manage the stakeholder engagement throughout the project duration.

Here are the benefits you will see, if you have been successful in stakeholder engagement:

- Improved relationships with the stakeholders,
- Better alignment of the project work with the planned goals and expectations,
- Stronger support for changes to the project plans, and
- Higher possibility that the final deliverables will be accepted by stakeholders.

More points for the exam:

- Stakeholders must be identified, as thoroughly as possible, towards the start of the project and documented in the stakeholder register.
- Stakeholder register must be updated throughout the life of the project.
- Stakeholders, who seem to show low interest in the project, but have high influence and stake, cannot be ignored. You must identify ways to get the requirements from them, document those requirements, get their approvals and sign-offs, send project status reports and actively seek their feedback.
- Skills such as honesty, sincerity, mutual respect, and concern for the project and organization are all required to develop and maintain good relationships with the stakeholders.

Practice Questions for Chapter 13

1. A document that contains the strategies and actions required to promote the involvement of stakeholders for project planning and execution is:
    A. Stakeholder engagement assessment matrix
    B. Salience model
    C. Stakeholder register
    D. Stakeholder engagement plan

2. Sam Sanders is developing a stakeholder engagement plan for his new project to develop a cloud-based training application for employees around that world. Which one of the following is not an objective for him now?
    A. Develop strategy and approaches to involve the stakeholders based on their interest, expectations and potential impact on the project.
    B. Identify the current and desired engagement level for each stakeholder.
    C. Develop an actionable plan to promote productive involvement of the stakeholders in decision-making and project execution.
    D. Identify stakeholders.

3. Change requests are not an output of:
    A. Identify Stakeholders
    B. Plan Stakeholder Engagement
    C. Manage Stakeholder Engagement
    D. Monitor Stakeholder Engagement

4. Stakeholder influence is typically highest during:
    A. Project Initiating
    B. Project Monitoring and Controlling
    C. Development of technical solution for the project deliverables
    D. Project Execution

5. Susan Simpson has set up a series of meetings with stakeholders for her project to deploy a new HR application across 40 offices in Europe and Asia. She plans to understand and document the interest and influence of various stakeholders and whether they are supportive, neutral or resistant to the project objectives. This activity is part of:
    A. Stakeholder analysis
    B. Stakeholder identification
    C. Stakeholder engagement
    D. Stakeholder monitoring

6. Shyla Sanders is involved in stakeholder analysis for a project with a large stakeholder community. She has developed a model that she can use to determine the relative importance of the stakeholders. The model has stakeholder categories based on their power, urgency and legitimacy of their involvement in the project. The model is called:
   A. Stakeholder power and influence grid
   B. Stakeholder cube
   C. Salience model
   D. Stakeholder engagement assessment matrix

7. A technique where the participants are provided questions and then given time to think and develop their responses, before the group gets together for discussions is called:
   A. Questionnaires and survey
   B. Mind mapping
   C. Brainstorming
   D. Brain writing

8. A document that describes the current level of engagement and the desired engagement levels for successful project delivery is:
   A. Stakeholder engagement assessment matrix
   B. Stakeholder cube
   C. Stakeholder register
   D. Stakeholder engagement plan

9. Andrew Ashton is working on a project to set up a gas drilling station in Alaska. There are several stakeholders spread out in North America, Europe and Asia. Some of the stakeholders are known to ask for many change requests, but only after the project gets well into execution mode. What is the best way to involve those stakeholders?
   A. Include those stakeholders in project initiation and planning and as early as possible.
   B. Speak with other project managers and find out how they have worked with these stakeholders in previous projects.
   C. Avoid including these stakeholders in the stakeholder register
   D. Ask the project sponsor to assign another project manager, who has better working relations with these stakeholders, to lead the project.

10. Which of the following is a technique that helps determine the relative importance of stakeholders based on their ability to influence, involvement in the project, need for immediate attention and stake in the project, especially for projects with a large community of stakeholders and complex relationship networks?
    A. Stakeholder engagement assessment matrix to determine the current and desired engagement levels
    B. Stakeholder analysis
    C. Salience model
    D. Impact/influence grid for stakeholders

11. In the salience model, stakeholders who have the urgency but have no power or legitimacy can also be described as:

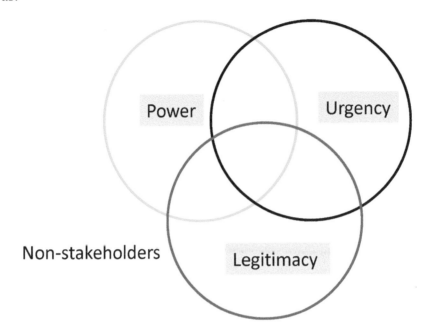

A. Stakeholders who are optional or discretionary
B. Stakeholders who are not too involved or interested in the project
C. Stakeholders who can be relied upon to get organizational support for the project
D. Stakeholders who need the information immediately but have no valid reason to be involved in the project

12. The directions of influence on a project by a stakeholder can be:
A. Upward or downward within the organizational hierarchy
B. Outward to suppliers, public, regulators, etc.
C. Sideward to peers of the project manager, functional managers, etc.
D. All of the above

13. Britney Blyton is identifying stakeholders for her new project to develop and implement a new training curriculum for employees and customers. Which of the following would not be a stakeholder for her?
A. Clients
B. Internal pilot team members
C. Training content reviewers
D. Others in the industry who are offering similar training programs

14. A technique to plan stakeholder engagement where you visually organize the information about the stakeholders and their relationships with the organization and with other stakeholders is called:
A. Mind mapping
B. Stakeholder engagement analysis
C. Multicriteria decision analysis
D. Expert judgment

15. Herman Reader is reviewing the stakeholder register for a new project to develop a cloud-based software application for the workplace and facility teams. He is interviewing potential stakeholders to collect business requirements. Who can Herman not contact for the requirements?

    A. Those who will use the application.
    B. Those who will administer the application after rollout.
    C. Managers whose direct reports will be responsible for resolution of the open trouble tickets for the new application.
    D. Those who know about the need for the application and can help develop test scenarios.

ANSWERS

Question Number	Correct Answer	Explanation
1	D	Stakeholder engagement plan has the strategies, approaches and action items to involve the stakeholders in a productive manner for decision-making, planning and execution.
2	D	Sam is in **Plan Stakeholder Engagement** process and preparing the stakeholder engagement plan. All the choices, except for Choice D, are required to develop the stakeholder engagement plan. Identifying stakeholders is done during the previous process (**Identify Stakeholders**).
3	B	All these processes have change requests as one of their outputs except for the **Plan Stakeholder Engagement** process.
4	A	Stakeholder involvement and input are high during project initiation. At this time, they provide their requirements and a high-level timeline and budget for the project.
5	A	Stakeholder analysis is about understanding their interest in and support for the project, which is documented in the stakeholder register. It is part of the **Identify Stakeholders** process.

6	C	A salience model describes classes of stakeholders based on their
		  ▪ power,
		  ▪ urgency for need of project information, and
		  ▪ legitimacy of involvement in the project.
		It is used to determine the relative importance of stakeholders and their involvement.

7	D	Brain writing is a technique, where the individual participants are given time to consider the questions and form their responses before they get together to discuss the responses. Brain writing is a modification of brainstorming.

8	A	Stakeholder engagement assessment matrix has the current (C) and desired (D) engagement levels. The five levels of stakeholder engagement are
		  ▪ Unaware
		  ▪ Resistant
		  ▪ Neutral
		  ▪ Supportive and
		  ▪ Leading.
		The objective is to identify lack of stakeholder support (if any) and improve their support levels, as needed.

9	A	It is best to include the stakeholders (who ask for many change requests) as early as possible and include the relevant points in the project plan. It is not beneficial to avoid the stakeholders. The stakeholders may have good points to contribute to the project planning and progress.

10	C	The salience model depicts the
		  ▪ Power (authority level)
		  ▪ Urgency (need for immediate attention/information)
		  ▪ Legitimacy of level of involvement in a project
		Salience model can represent three factors and is suitable when there are complex relationships with a large stakeholder community.
		On the other hand, impact/influence grid is limited to two factors and is suitable for projects where you have simple relationships and a small number of stakeholders.

11	D	These are stakeholders who have no power or valid reasons to be involved in the project but have an urgent need for information. This group of stakeholders is demanding and an overhead.

12	D	The direction of influence can be outward (towards vendors, clients, regulators, and competitors) or upward, downward or sideward within the organization.
13	D	Others in the industry may be offering similar training curriculum but they are not involved in the project and will not contribute to the project. Hence, they are not stakeholders.
14	A	Mind mapping is used to visually organize the information about the stakeholders and their relationships with other stakeholders and with the organization.
15	D	The best answerer is D. The group that knows about the need and can help develop test scenarios may not be impacted by the project outcome. They can be just contributors for the test scenarios.

CHAPTER 14
Ethics and Professional Responsibility

There are no chapters dedicated to Ethics and Professional Responsibility in the PMBOK®. However, there may be questions or parts of questions in the exam to test your professional judgment and ethics. PMI has two documents that describe their position on ethics and its implementation:

- **Code of Ethics and Professional Conduct**.
- **Ethical Decision-Making Framework**.

You must download and read these two in preparation for the exam.

Code of Ethics

Responsibility	Respect
Fairness	Honesty

Figure 14-1: The Four Tenets of Ethics (Source: PMI Code of Ethics and Professional Conduct®)

Who is required to know and follow the PMI code? The code is for those who are working with PMI for volunteer opportunities, certification, training, or in any other capacity or relationship. It applies to:

- All PMI members, regardless of whether they are certified or not.
- All those who have started the PMI application process for certification.
- All PMI certification holders, regardless of whether they have PMI membership or not.
- All those who work (in paid or unpaid positions) for PMI.

How did PMI come up with the **Code of Ethics and Professional Conduct**? PMI conducted a survey among various project management practitioners across the world. They were asked to identify the values that helped them decide and guide their actions. This led to four areas that later became the cornerstones (see Figure 14-1) for **PMI Code of Ethics and Professional Conduct**:

- Responsibility
- Respect
- Fairness
- Honesty

Responsibility

Responsibility means that you take ownership for the making (or not making) the decisions and completing (or not completing) the actions. It also means that you take ownership of the consequences of those decisions and actions.

Are you responsible for what happens in your project? The common answer is yes. We all mean to take responsibility. But there is more. Taking responsibility is an attitude to actively taking ownership of the actions and its consequences. For example, if you inherit a project that is in execution mode, but the project requirements and plans, which have been approved, are incomplete. Are you responsible enough, to bring this up with the stakeholders for discussion? Can you tell them, "Well, the project activities are in-progress, but the scope and plans are incomplete? If I should own and complete this project, I must now stop all activity, until the project requirements and plans are revised and approved again!"

Being responsible requires that you do (or not do) the following:

- Understand what is good for society, environment and safety and use that understanding to guide decisions and actions.
- Fulfill all that you undertake or promise. A person is only as good as his words.
- When you make errors, own up to the errors. Let the impacted stakeholders know. Do not hide! Then take steps to remediate the errors.
- When others make mistakes, do not ignore or look away. Ask and help the person report the mistakes to the management. If the person is unwilling to report, you must be responsible enough to step up and report those to the management. Knowing and then hiding other's mistakes is same as hiding your own mistakes.
- File complaints, only after you have collected the facts to support your complaint.

Respect

Respect is your regard for yourself and others, and for the resources that have been allocated to you. The resources could be money, equipment, people's time, environment, safety, etc. Why is respect so important? It is because respect develops a sense of trust and confidence and encourages everyone to cooperate for success.

Showing respect requires that you do (or not do) the following:

- Acknowledge that others have certain rights.
- Respect the rights of others.
- Take the time to listen to others. They usually have valid reasons for their suggestions or views and once you understand those reasons, you may tend to agree with them.
- If you have a disagreement or conflict, go ahead and approach the other party directly (and not indirectly through someone else).
- Do not act in an abusive manner to others.
- Do not use your powers and knowledge for your gains.
- Do not try to create a win-lose situation where your project gains but at the expense of someone else's project.

Fairness

Fairness means that our decisions and actions are free from self-interest or favoritism and we must act impartially and objectively. We should not do, what would later lead to a conflict of interest.

Being fair requires that you do (or not do) the following:

- Show a high degree of transparency in decision-making.
- You will be in positions, where you must decide about and provide bonus, rewards, or contracts. You will sometimes have to penalize others as well. Do not base your decisions or actions on favoritism or personal preferences.
- Do not discriminate because of gender, race, nationality, religion, or disability.
- You may also be in a situation, where you have a conflict of interest. In that case, do not try to influence the decision or action. If you think have a conflict of interest and yet must be involved, let the impacted stakeholders know your situation. Proceed only if the impacted stakeholders have provided their approval to go ahead.
- Make information and opportunities available to everyone who may have a need for those. Do these without any bias or favoritism For example, if you are providing information to one of the bidders (vendors) for a contract, make the same information available to all the bidders. An efficient way to do this is to organize a bidder's conference where all the bidders are invited.

Honesty

Honesty is about knowing and acknowledging the truth and then acting in a truthful manner.

Being honest requires that you do (or not do) the following:

- Attempt to identify and understand the truth!
- Do not engage in actions, where you may have to deceive others or make false statements.
- Be truthful in your communications.
- Provide information that is accurate as per your understanding. Will you always know everything? No! In that case, say something like, "I have limited knowledge now, but as far as I know, I have not heard of any serious problems with going ahead with the work."

To summarize, you need to think, if you will be okay if the organization or community were to find the real reasons for your decision or actions. You must have an attitude to do what is right, even if no one will ever get to know about your plans or actions. This attitude and mindset will also help you select the correct choices in the exam.

Practice Questions for Chapter 14

1. Your project scheduler is away for three weeks. She has asked you to fill-in. You need to present a prepared report to the PMO and program manager. You notice that schedule variance (SV) is specified as being positive in the report. But you have checked the details in the project documents and you have estimated that the SV to be negative in the real project data. What should you do?
   A. Wait for the project scheduler to return and then discuss the matter with her.
   B. Bring this up in the meeting and let the PMO and program manager decide whether to make the SV changes in the report.
   C. Discuss the matter with the PMO and see what they suggest, while you let the manager of the project scheduler know of the situation and escalation to the PMO.
   D. Modify the report to make it consistent with the real project report data, and report the changes and contradiction to the PMO and program manager.

2. You have completed development of a major enterprise resource planning (ERP) application project at a software product firm. The product had a very successful launch. There are lots of media coverage. Several competitors have been trying to develop and market a similar product for the last three years. You have been approached by a competitor to lead a similar effort at their firm for better perks and salary. What would be your best response to the offer?
   A. Decline the offer because the current employer has high-quality projects for you in the pipeline.
   B. Decline the offer since there are confidentiality issues.
   C. Ask the competitor to wait until the media euphoria subsides and people stop taking note of changes
   D. Take the offer since the competitor has told you that their new product will be slightly different.

3. At your workplace, Kim is a diligent project manager. She follows the PMI processes, does detailed documentation and has professional relationships with her project resources and stakeholders. However, once when she was at an after-hours corporate get-together, she complains about PMI's requirements for professional conduct not having any value or use! How would you explain the benefits of PMI standards for ethics and professional conduct?
   A. Explain that the standards would help her improve her image as a professional within the organization and outside.
   B. Explain that it will help her get more respect from project resources, who are working for her projects.
   C. Explain that it will help her gain and maintain trust and confidence with project stakeholders, customers and the public.
   D. Explain that it will help her improve the professional image of her own and the project management community.

4. You have been working on four projects. The work pressure has rapidly increased. To help out, the program manager has temporarily assigned a project coordinator to help you. The program manager asks for a status report, which you further delegate to the new coordinator. He ends up writing a brilliant status report for the project. You are tempted to change some text and send that to the program manager, claiming to have done it all by yourself. Should you do so?
   A. No! Because that would be failing to respect intellectual property and claiming what is rightfully someone else's work.

B. No! Because you want to encourage a junior colleague and boost his confidence!

C. No! You need to give credit to where it is due!

D. No! Because the project coordinator may directly go to the program manager and show the status report he wrote for you!

5. You have completed a cost-benefit analysis for two projects. Project A has less return on investment (ROI) than Project B. But your boss wants to get approval for Project A. He asks you to increase the benefits for Project A, so that it gets approved for intake. What should you do?

A. Explain that you cannot do so, since it is unethical to change numbers without supporting facts.

B. Explain that the program team can question the data and consider the analysis as materially incorrect.

C. Explain that you will find another metrics that can show Project A as being a better choice.

D. Explain that the project sponsors may review various factors besides the cost-benefits analysis. To gain approval for Project A, you and the project sponsor should identify the strategic and soft benefits of Project A and include those for consideration.

6. You are managing a project to design and produce 20 sets of 1,000 steel gears for a crane manufacturer. You have sent the first set to the manufacturer. They find that the gears are slightly below the lower specification limit. The use of such gears will cause excessive wear and tear and lead to recalls and warranty expenses. The manufacturer is threatening to return the entire set of gears to you. What should you do?

A. Explain to the manufacturer that your company can set up a joint program to share the warranty expenses.

B. Accept the set, back from the manufacturer. Explain to the stakeholders that the internal quality process has missed checking the gears and that it will be corrected in the next set.

C. Insist that the manufacturer accept the first set and you will have correct specifications in subsequent sets.

D. Explain to the manufacturer, that they should have proactively helped out during the quality control phases of the production.

7. Which of the following groups is supposed to follow and abide by the PMI Code of Ethics and Professional Conduct?

A. All PMI members.

B. Non-members who hold PMP certification or have applied to get one.

C. Non-members who serve PMI as a volunteer.

D. All the above.

8. Timothy Timken, a Canadian citizen, and a senior project manager, has been sent to Uganda to manage an ERP application deployment project for the central water division of the government. He is however unfamiliar with the norms, expectations and culture. Which of the following documents should he use to understand the business practices in the new workplace?

A. Company policies and procedures

B. Project management plan

C. Project charter

D. PMI Code of Ethics and Professional Conduct

9. Tom, a PMP-credential holder, is working for a telecom services provider. He is responsible for recruitment of new engineering resources for current projects. The new candidates need to have four or more years of relevant experience. He interviews Mike, who is aspiring for a new job. Tom realizes that Mike's technical knowledge and skills will prove beneficial for the projects. Mike says that he does not meet the 4-year experience requirement but he can provide the necessary experience certificate. Should Tom go ahead and recruit Mike for the active projects?
   A. No! Mike will not be able to contribute effectively to the active projects.
   B. No! Even if Mike is recruited now, it will later be publicly revealed that Mike does not have the minimum qualifications. That is bound to lead to serious consequences for many employees in the recruitment team.
   C. No! Mike is too young and may not gain respect from senior resources in the engineering team.
   D. No! Tom has a responsibility to recruit the right candidates and he must be honest and fair.

10. Your ex-colleague, Christopher, is a PMP-certification holder. He is now looking for work and advertising his skills as a consultant in enterprise resource planning (ERP) application. He is also claiming to have completed projects, which you know he has not done. What should you do?
    A. Reach out to potential clients that Christopher has approached. Let them know that claims made by Christopher are false!
    B. Confront Christopher! Tell him to stop making false claims! Or else, you will report the incidents to PMI.
    C. Collect evidence of the claims that Christopher is making. Once you have enough evidence, send those to PMI.
    D. Make postings on social media sites that Christopher is making false claims about his expertise and background.

11. Zamir Hussain works in a country in eastern Africa as an employee of a US firm. He is trying to win a state government contract for sanitation system development for certain towns. Zamir has been asked to pay a sourcing fee for $20,000 but it is optional. Other bidders are also asked the same. When he joined the firm six years ago, he was instructed by the HR team that providing or accepting bribes has been banned by the firm. What should Zamir do?
    A. Have a candid discussion with the project sponsor, Sam. It is also in Sam's interest to win the contract. Sam can escalate to senior management for suggestions, if he prefers.
    B. Provide the fee. US requirements are applicable within the US.
    C. Be honest, with the client. Tell them that the sourcing fee cannot be paid. But the amount can be padded to the bid price.
    D. Decline to make the payment. Zamir may, therefore, risk losing the contract and that is okay!

ANSWERS

Question Number	Correct Answer	Explanation
1	D	Since you have taken over the project and reporting, it is your responsibility to make sure that the information is accurate. Also reporting the contradiction is important because the audience may notice inconsistencies between various reports for the same project.
2	B	This is a case where the new role will require you to use the experience and knowledge to create a competing product. There are confidentiality clauses in employment terms, which you need to honor.
3	C	All options are correct but Choice C is the best answer. An important objective of the PMI standards is to improve the professional image of the project management community. This, in turn, increases the confidence and trust of project teams and stakeholders towards project managers.
4	A	Claiming that the majority of work was done by you, would be a lie. You need to be truthful and show integrity.
5	D	These types of situation do arise in real life. Remember that your integrity and ethics should be more important to you than a job! The numbers that you present can be questioned and you should have facts and evidence to back those numbers. There are various soft and strategic benefits (besides quantitative metrics) that can influence the decision to initiate a project.
6	B	Accepting responsibility is one of the four values in the **PMI Code of Ethics and Professional Conduct**. You need to take ownership and responsibility for actions. That helps instill and improve trust and loyalty amongst clients.
7	D	The code applies to all members and non-members who are associated with the PMI in any manner. See Page 1 of the **Code of Ethics and Professional Conduct** at www.pmi.org.
8	A	The company policies and procedures should be used to understand how decisions are made in a foreign country. Project charter and plans pertain only to the project. They do not describe the government regulations and business practices that are expected in the country.
9	D	Tom is bound by the mandatory standards for responsibility and honesty, while performing his assigned work.
10	B	As a PMI member, you cannot ignore a violation of the PMI code. But you need to show respect and fairness and give an opportunity to your ex-college for him to stop falsifying his experience.
11	D	He needs to follow the requirements of the US firm. Abiding by the firm's requirements and being ethical is more important than winning a contract.

Practical Suggestions for Real-World Project Management

Here are tips for day-to-day project management at your office or workplace. These suggestions come from 50+ years of our experience in managing projects.

1. Here is a list of project documents that will help you plan and track progress:
   a) Project charter (usually in Microsoft Word)
   b) Project schedule (usually in Microsoft Project)
   c) Project budget (usually in MS Excel)
   d) Activity log (in MS Excel). This may seem like a duplicate of the project plan, but the activity log has more details. Each line in the project plan can be broken into various activities in the activity log. Another benefit of maintaining an activity log is that you can share this with the project team for their review and edits. They may be more familiar with MS Excel and Word, rather than MS Project.
   e) Project communications plan (in MS Word or Excel)
   f) Business requirements document (in MS Word or Excel)
   g) Solution and technical requirements document (in MS Word or Excel)
   h) Stakeholder registers (usually in Excel)
   i) Risk register (usually in Excel)
2. For each project, maintain a personal "to-do" list. This is different from the activity log mentioned above.
3. Look at and update your personal "to-do" list throughout the workday. This is your first go-to place when you think about what you ought to be doing for your project.
4. Develop a checklist of project management tasks that must be done routinely (each week, month and quarter). This will include tasks such as
   a) updating financial forecasts,
   b) reviewing invoices that need to be paid by accounts payable team and charged to your project budget,
   c) sending status reports,
   d) reviewing hours charged by the resources to your project,
   e) conducting project status calls, etc.

5. Maintain weekly calls for each project. However, if a project is busy (e.g., during execution) schedule daily review meetings (15 to 30 minutes should suffice).
6. During project meetings:
   - start with a list of agenda items.
   - use the online display to show the project schedule, activity log, project artifacts, etc.
   - capture ideas in either an online document or on a whiteboard.
   - encourage others to open up and discuss their portions of the project.
7. Start and end meetings on time!
8. A detailed project plan is required for success! Spend time each day updating the project plan.
9. Look at the end activities of the project and work backward.
10. For 1:1 or small-team meetings, 15 minutes may be adequate. There is no need to default to 30-minute time slots for every meeting.
11. Set up a reward policy to motivate project resources.
12. Learn how to understand people and acknowledge what they are attempting to convey – body language and non-verbal communication cannot be ignored.
13. You do not have to like office politics or power games, but such behavior is not going to go away within your project duration! Acknowledge it and work within the system!
14. Remember, projects do not fail due to technical causes! They fail due to people reasons! Keep your project team and stakeholders adequately engaged to the project.
15. Know the power players and those who are influential in the organization!
16. Build political capital within the organization.
17. Help others! Someday, the going will could get tough. At that time, you will need help from others!
18. If opportunities arise, volunteer to take more responsibility.
19. Focus on the big picture, but care about the details as well. No one else will!
20. Keep your cool. There is no need to overreact to minor details and mini-crises! Many of these get resolved without a project manager's help or intervention.
21. Keep your promises!
22. Be genuine! Be honest! Acknowledge that people can see through pretense and cover-ups!
23. In this global and virtual workplace, get to know people! Hold 1:1 meetings with key project team members and stakeholders.
24. Meet them face-to-face, whenever possible.
25. Be proactive. This is the single important quality of a project manager.
26. Follow up on action items (critical requirement and responsibility of a project manager). Accept that project team members are busy with commitments for several projects. They have a long list of operational and project tasks!
27. Soft skills are vital for project progress.
28. Build rapport and trust with stakeholders and project resources.
29. Your project team needs a leader more than one more friend! Provide challenges and motivation!
30. Managing documentation is good but leading with confidence and managing the project resources and stakeholders are what makes or breaks a project.
31. Protect the team members. They, in turn, will protect the project.
32. Methodologies are good but know that you are working with humans. Their responses are sometimes not predictable or logical.
33. Leave egos at the meeting doorstep. Be aware of your weaknesses and work to reduce their impact. The room for growth is the biggest room in the world.
34. Do not be afraid to fail. Fail fast; recover fast.

35. Support your project team and challenge them in equal measures. It helps bring out the best in them and builds a progressive team.

36. Learn to ask for help! An expert and experienced project manager knows that each project is unique. Asking for help increases trust and openness.

Tips for Preparing for the PMP® Exam

Here are some tips to help you prepare for the exam:

1. First, commit to yourself that you must work towards the certification.
2. Set a deadline for taking the exam. In fact, register on pmi.org and block an exam date that is four to eight weeks away. That gives you a deadline to prepare towards.
3. Treat the PMP preparation as your personal project, whose output will help you possibly for your entire career.
4. The PMP exam is tough and you are going to need more preparation in addition to taking the 35 or 40-hour training class (boot camp).
5. Give yourself at least two weeks (ideally four weeks) after completing your training (35 hours).
6. After the training you will be mentally fatigued and been introduced to many new concepts, formulas, diagrams, etc. You need to time to let the learnings sink in and solidify.
7. Also you need the time to take additional practice tests, identify gaps in your understanding of the PMBOK and review those sections.
8. The exam has situational questions or case studies that are meant to test your understanding of the concepts (and not memorization).
9. Read the PMBOK® Guide two times, in conjunction with this book. The sequence of chapters in this book and PMBOK are identical.
10. You need to be very familiar with the PMBOK Guide. It is the basis for most of the exam questions. Candidates, who take the exam without understanding the PMBOK guide, have a high possibility of failing.
11. Keep the Process Group/Knowledge Area table (Page 25 of the PMBOK) in front of you during your preparation. It has 49 processes. Memorize the process names and the Process Group and Knowledge Area they fit in.
12. For each process, you should be able to write one sentence on the objective and key output. Later, you should understand the requirements (inputs) and how the process is conducted (tools and techniques).
13. Make your study notes (in Microsoft Word, for example) for each chapter. This is your go-to notes just before the exam.

14. Learn the charts and figures (such as the cause-and-effect diagram, control charts, etc.) Know their purpose, knowledge area and various names used to identify those.

15. From the study notes, decide what you will write down on the scratch paper given to you at the start of the PMP exam (if writing notes on that paper is permitted). This must include the formulas (Appendix C) and the 49-process grid. Practice writing these from memory at least five times.

16. After you have read each chapter, do the practice test at the end of each chapter in this book.

17. Identify the root cause for questions that you answered incorrectly. This is an opportunity to identify your knowledge gaps. Was the wrong answer due to not reading the question and choices correctly? Or was that due to a lack of understanding of the material? If you do not understand the material, go back and review the content.

18. Review the questions that you answered correctly. Was the correct answer a lucky guess? Did you select that for the wrong reasoning? This is also an opportunity to identify your gaps and learn the material. It is better to make the mistakes now rather than in the exam.

19. PMI does not publish the required score to pass, but you must get 85 percent or more in the practice or mock tests before you go for the exam.

20. The PMBOK is a good reference book for the PMP exam. But there may be questions on concepts and terminology that are outside the PMBOK. Therefore, you will need an exam-preparation guide such as this book.

21. Toward the end, do the full mock exam of 200 questions (in 4 hours), which is at the end of this book.

22. One of the biggest PMP challenges is answering 200 questions in one stretch. Doing questions in batches of forty or fifty at home is easy.

23. You must practice at least three full 200-question tests at home to build your test-taking tenacity. You should get 85% or more in these tests at home. Many online practice questions are easier than what you will see in the exam.

24. Visit the exam center, if possible, before the exam day.

25. On the day before the exam, do not study a lot. Just review your study notes and take rest. You will need your energy to focus for four hours during the exam.

APPENDIX C
Formulas for the PMP® Exam

Here are important formulas for the exam. This is an essential table to include in your review just before the exam day.

Chapter	Formula

Chapter 4: Integration Management	PV = FV / (1+r)^n
	    ▪ PV = present value
	    ▪ FV = future value
	    ▪ r = rate of interest per time period
	    ▪ n = number of time periods (one-time period is usually one year or 6 months)

Chapter 6: Schedule Management	EAD (estimated activity duration) using beta (PERT) distribution = (P+4*M+O)/6
	
	EAD using triangular (average, simple or 3-point) distribution = (P+M+O)/3
	    ▪ P = pessimistic estimate
	    ▪ M = mean estimate
	    ▪ O = optimistic estimate
	
	Standard deviation or SD = (P – O) /6
	
	Lower side of the Range = (EAD) - (standard deviation)
	
	Upper side of the Range = (EAD) + (standard deviation)

Chapter 6: Schedule Management	There are two ways to estimate Total Float:
	    ▪ Total Float = Late Start – Early Start = LS – ES
	    ▪ Total Float = Late Finish – Early Finish = LF – EF

Chapter 7: Cost Management	▪ CV (cost variance) = EV – AC
	    ▪ CPI (cost performance index) = EV/AC
	    ▪ SV (schedule variance) = EV – PV
	    ▪ SPI (schedule performance index) = EV/PV
	
	where:
	    ▪ EV = earned value
	    ▪ AC = actual cost
	    ▪ PV = planned value

Chapter 7: Cost Management	VAC (variance at completion) = BAC – EAC
	
	where:
	  ▪ BAC = budget at completion
	  ▪ EAC = estimate at completion

Chapter 7: Cost Management	There are four ways to estimate EAC (estimate at completion)
	  ▪ EAC = BAC / CPI
	  ▪ EAC = AC + BAC – EV
	  ▪ EAC = AC + Bottom-up ETC
	  ▪ EAC = AC + (BAC – EV) / (CPI * SPI)

Chapter 7: Cost Management	There are two ways to estimate ETC (estimate to completion)
	  ▪ ETC = EAC – AC
	  ▪ ETC = (Bottom-up re-estimation of the remaining work)

Chapter 7: Cost Management	There are two ways to estimate TCPI (To complete performance index)
	  ▪ TCPI = (BAC -EV) / (BAC – AC)
	  ▪ TCPI = (BAC -EV) / (EAC – AC)
	
	TCPI = Work remaining / Funds remaining
	  ▪ Work remaining = BAC – EV
	  ▪ Funds remaining can be (BAC – AC) or (EAC – AC)

Chapter 8: Communications Management	Number of communication channels = N * (N – 1)/2 ▪ N = number of people (remember to include the project manager if he or she is part of the communication)

Chapter 11: Risk Management	EMV (expected monetary value) = P * I
	
	where:
	  ▪ P = probability of occurrence of the risk
	  ▪ I = Total impact if the risk occurs

Chapter 11: Risk Management	NPV (net path value) = (payoffs from opportunities) – (losses from threats) – (invested amount or cost)
Chapter 12: Procurement Management	PTA (point of total assumption) = Target price + (ceiling price – target price) / (buyer's share ratio)

Table C-1: Formulas for Review before the Exam

Tips for Taking the PMP® Exam

Here are some tips to help you during the four-hour exam.

1. Bring a printout of your test appointment and two IDs (driver's license, passport, etc.)
2. Bring a sweater or jacket for yourself. The room may get cold. Also, bring water and light snacks. You will have to keep everything in a locker outside the exam room.
3. Before the exam, drink water. Also, locate and use the washroom.
4. At the beginning of the exam, you may be provided with blank (scratch) sheets. Find out if it is acceptable that you write certain formulas on that sheet. In that case, write down the hard-to-recall formulas. That will free your mind and serve as a reference during the exam.
5. Toward the start, you will have a fifteen-minute tutorial that will get you familiar with the exam-taking functionality.
6. If you need extra paper, you can ask for that, but the previous papers will be taken away in exchange.
7. Some exam centers provide a physical calculator for you. Other centers have an online calculator on the computer.
8. Use the calculator (online or physical). It will help you avoid careless errors, especially since you may be short on time
9. During the exam, you will see only one question and its four choices at one time. You can mark a question for later review.
10. The exam has 200 questions to be answered in four hours (240 minutes).
11. Each question has four choices, out of which only one is correct.
12. If a question has two or more choices that seem correct, choose the best answer. There are no negative marks, so answer every question.
13. Do two passes:

   - Pass 1: Do the easy and quick problems. Mark the rest for Pass 2. If a question seems to take more than two minutes, mark those for Pass 2.
   - Pass 2 (later review): Now you do the ones that you have marked.

14. Pace yourself to complete one question per minute. That way you can complete 200 questions in 200 minutes (Pass 1). You will have 40 minutes for questions which you have marked for later review (Pass 2)

15. Do not be worried or upset if you see problems that seem completely unfamiliar. Mark those for Pass 2!

16. You can take breaks in the middle but remember that break time counts toward your four hours.

17. After you have read the question, think of the following three ways:

    a) How would the author of the PMBOK® answer the question?

    b) If the above does not help you answer the questions, think about how the contents of this book would have you answer the question.

    c) If both of the above do not help you, think about your real-world experience.

    Do the above in the specified sequence.

18. As mentioned earlier, assume that you are the project manager for a large project with resources and stakeholders around the world.

19. Assume that proper project management practices have been followed, which means you have an approved charter, project plans, risk register, quality metrics, change log, etc.

20. Watch for these:

    - Global words like "never" and "always." Choices that have "never" or "always" are often false.
    - Questions that ask you "which of the following is **not** true."
    - If you have long-winded questions, quickly identify and skip irrelevant points.

21. During the test, breathe well! It helps you focus and relax.

APPENDIX E
Changes in the PMBOK® 6th Edition

The 6th Edition was published by PMI in September, 2017. This Appendix describes the changes in the 6th Edition, as compared to the 5th Edition.

This appendix will **not** help you answer exam questions. This content is **not** relevant if you are unfamiliar with the PMBOK 5th Edition. But if you are familiar with the 5th Edition, this appendix will help you know the differences in the 6th Edition.

What has not changed?

1. The number of knowledge areas remains the same. We still have ten knowledge areas. The sequence, of the Knowledge Areas, has not changed. However, the names of two of the Knowledge Areas have changed.
2. The number and names of the Process Groups remain the same. We still have five Process Groups, namely:

   - Initiating
   - Planning
   - Executing
   - Monitoring and Controlling
   - Closing

What has changed?

1. The 5th Edition had 47 processes. The 6th Edition has 49 processes.
2. There are three new processes:

   - **Manage Project Knowledge** process in chapter 4 (Project **Integration** Management).
   - **Control Resources** process in chapter 9 (Project **Resource** Management).
   - **Implement Risk Responses** process in chapter 11 (Project **Risk** Management).

3. One process has been deleted. In the 5th Edition, Chapter 12 (Project Procurement Management) had a process named **Close Procurements**. This process has been removed.

4. Two of the Knowledge Areas have new names:

    a) **Time** Knowledge Area (Chapter 6) is now renamed to **Schedule** Knowledge Area.

    b) **Human Resources** Knowledge Area (Chapter 9) is now renamed to **Resources** Knowledge Area, to reflect that project resources are not limited to people, but need to include hardware, software, leased or purchased equipment, office space, etc.

5. The **Estimate Activity Resources** process was previously part of Chapter 6, Project **Time Management**. In the 6th Edition, this process has been moved to Chapter 9, Project **Resource Management**.

6. The names for three processes have been changed, where the word control has been replaced by monitor:

    a) **Control Communications** process is now **Monitor Communications**.

    b) **Control Risks** is now **Monitor Risks**.

    c) **Control Stakeholder Engagement** is now **Monitor Stakeholder Engagement**.

    Why this change? This reflects the need for project managers to monitor the processes rather than trying to control those. It is also not realistic to expect a project manager to completely control the communications, risks and stakeholder engagement for a project. But monitoring those is realistic.

7. Each chapter on Knowledge Areas (Chapter 4 to 13) has four new sections toward the start of the chapter. The sections are:

    ▪ Key Concepts
    ▪ Trends and Emerging Practices
    ▪ Tailoring Considerations
    ▪ Considerations for Agile/Adaptive Environments

8. In the 5th Edition, the ITTO figures for the processes did not have bulleted subheadings (or sub-bullets). But in the 6th Edition, some of the ITTO figures have bulleted sub-lists.

Basics of Using Microsoft Project®

Microsoft Project (or MS Project) is a project management application used to develop a work schedule, track the progress of activities, and assign resources and cost. It also helps you analyze workloads on the resources and manage the project budget.

There are several other competing applications, such as:

- Primavera application from Oracle Corporation (in California)
- Planview application from Planview (based in Texas)

In case, you are starting with MS Project; this appendix can help. Also, there are many features and functionalities in MS Project that are not covered in this appendix.

A Brief History of Microsoft Project®

The first commercial version was launched in 1983 for DOS operating systems, primarily written in Microsoft C. In 1984, Microsoft bought all rights for the application and soon after that released Version 2. The first Windows version was released in 1990 and called "Version 1 for Windows."

The popular versions are:

- MS Project 2010
- MS Project 2013
- MS Project 2016
- MS Project 2019

The above are available in **Standard** and **Professional** editions. The examples and figures in this appendix are for MS Project 2013 Professional Edition.

Opening and Closing MS Project® Application

To launch MS Project, click on **Start → Microsoft Project.**

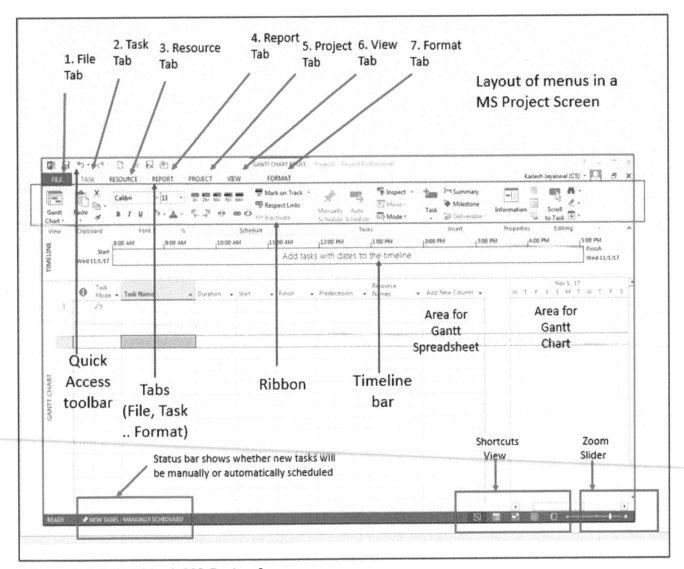

Figure F-1: Initial blank MS Project® screen

How to Create a Simple Schedule in Microsoft Project®
Step 1: Create a New Project Plan

Launch MS Project. Click **File → New**. Project displays your options for creating a project plan. Double-click on **Blank project** to create a new project plan.

MS Project® provides various ways to start a new project plan:

- From a blank project file.
- From a template project plan file.
- From an existing project plan file.
- From an Excel file.

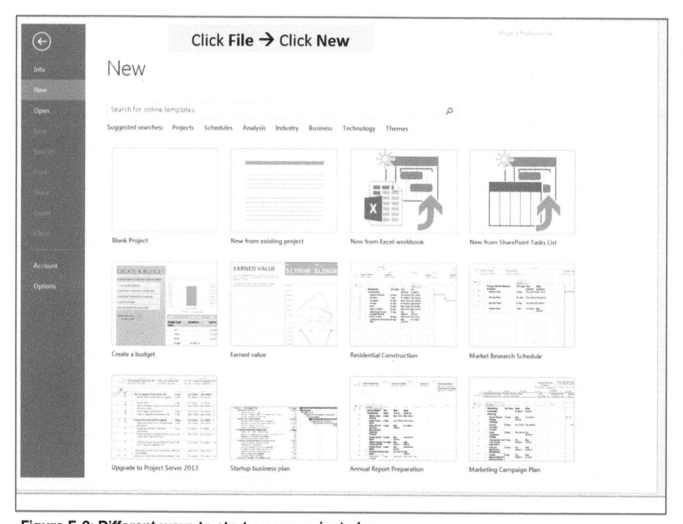

Figure F-2: Different ways to start a new project plan

You will see the screen as in Figure F-3.

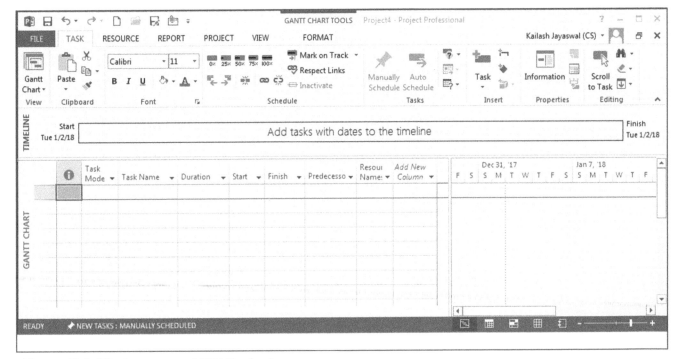

Figure F-3: First screen of MS Project

Click on **Project** tab. Then click on **Project Information**.

Type in the **Start date** or click the down arrow to display the calendar and click 11/30 (or any other date). Click **OK.** The format is MM/DD (for example 11/30).

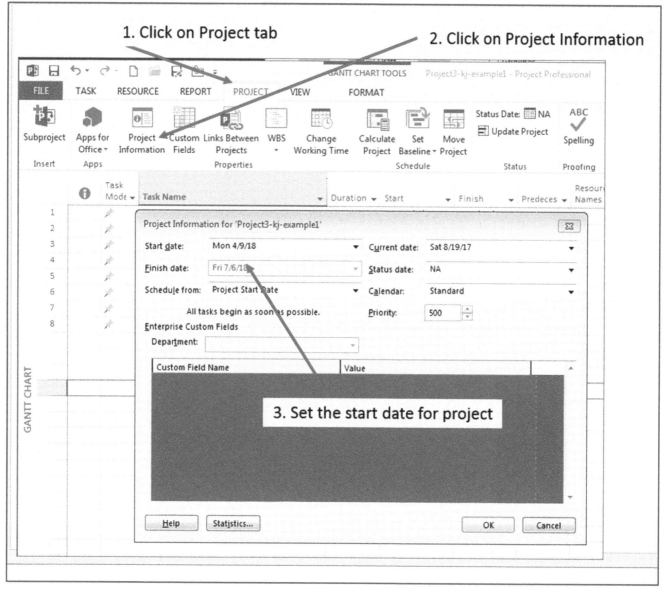

Figure F-4: Setting a start date for a project

To save the project plan, click on the **File** tab and click **Save As**. In the Windows Explorer, locate the folder where you want to save the file and type in the file name.

Step 2: Enter Activities or Tasks

Click on the cell directly below "**Task Name**" and type in "Develop building architecture." Activities are called **Tasks** in MS Project. As soon as you type in a description in the task field, it gets a unique ID number, which is used to specify dependencies.

Enter the following tasks:

1. Develop building architecture
2. Discuss with client

3. Prepare revised architecture
4. Provide request for quote to vendors
5. Get vendor bid prices
6. Conduct vendor meetings

Once you have entered the six tasks mentioned above and in Table F-1, you will see the screen shown in Figure F-5.

Note that MS Project automatically assigns an ID number to each task. You can later use the ID numbers in the **Predecessor** column to specify dependencies.

Step 3: Enter the Durations for the Tasks and Specify Start or Finish Dates

We will now enter the time in the **Duration** column (next to the "Task Name". You can enter the duration in:

- Minutes (m)
- Hours (h)
- Days (d)
- Weeks (w)
- Months (mo)

For manually scheduled tasks, you need to specify two of the following three things:

- Duration
- Start date
- Finish date

MS Project then uses those two specified values to compute the third value.

Enter the duration and start dates, as in Table F-1.Click on the cell in the **Duration** column and type **10d** for ten days for the first task.

ID number (assigned by MS Project)	Task Name	Duration	Start date	Finish Date
		You need to specify two of these three values. **MS Project** will compute the third.		
1	Develop building architecture	10 days	Mon 4/9	Fri 4/20
2	Discuss with client	1 week	Tue 4/17	Mon 4/23
3	Prepare revised architecture	2 weeks	Mon 4/30	Fri 5/11
4	Provide request for quote to vendors	1 month	Mon 5/21	Fri 6/15
5	Get vendor bid prices	10 days	Mon 6/11	Fri 6/22
6	Conduct vendor meetings	10 days	Mon 6/25	Fri 7/6

Table F-1: Task names and their Duration and Start and Finish dates

To specify the **Duration**, you can click on the cell in the **Duration** column and type duration for example, "10d" for ten days, "1w" for one week or "1 mo" for one month. You can alternatively use the up-down wheel to change the duration.

Once you have specified the duration for all tasks, you now need to specify the **Start Date** for each task. To enter the start dates, click on the cell in the **Start** column and type in 4/9. You can use the triangle to see a month-view and select a date. Alternatively, you can specify a finish date in the **Finish** column and MS Project will compute the start date.

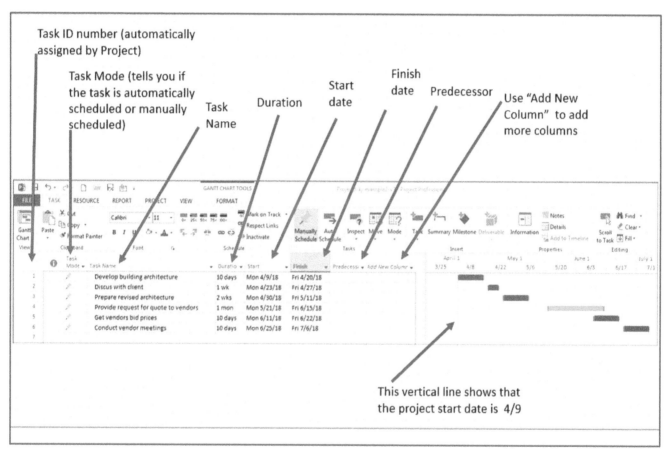

Figure F-5: Project with various Tasks along with Duration and Start and Finish dates

For automatically scheduled tasks, MS Project uses the **Predecessors** column to compute the start date. Then it uses the duration (that you provide manually) to compute the finish date.

Step 4: Creating Milestones

In addition to specifying tasks, you may want to specify milestones in your project. Note that a milestone is not an activity or work. It just signifies the completion of a deliverable. Hence, the duration is zero days.

How do you create a milestone?

Method 1: There is a column titled **Add New Column**. It is the last column. Click on the inverted triangle icon, scroll down and select **Milestone**. That will give you a new column called **Milestone**, where you can have No or Yes. Right now, you will see No for all cells because we do not have a milestone yet.

Let us insert a new task and label that as a milestone. Click **TASK** tab on top and then click **Task** icon and type "**Completed Architecture Phase**" in the Task Name column.

Select the task row, enter Yes in the **Milestone** column for that task, zero days for **Duration**, and a start date of 5/11.

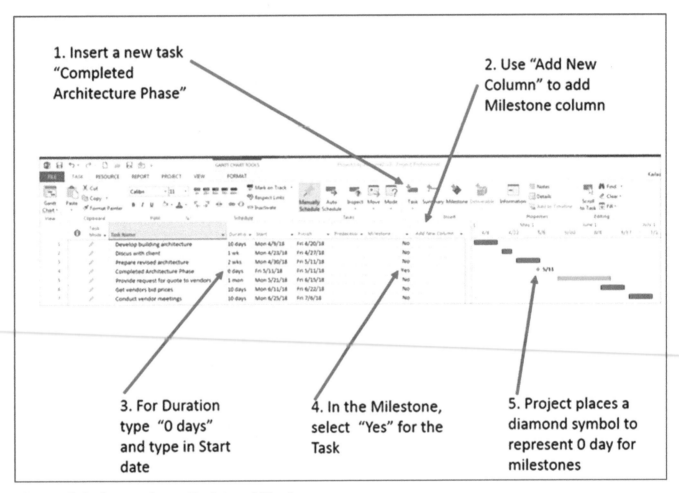

Figure F-6: Converting a Task to a Milestone

Method 2: This method works if you have an existing task which you want to change to a Milestone. Select the task row and then click on **Information** (part of **TASK** tab). Alternatively, you can open the Task Information window by double-clicking on the Task cell. In the **Task Information** pop-up window, select the **Advanced** tab and enter zero days for **Duration** and check "**Mark Task as Milestone**".

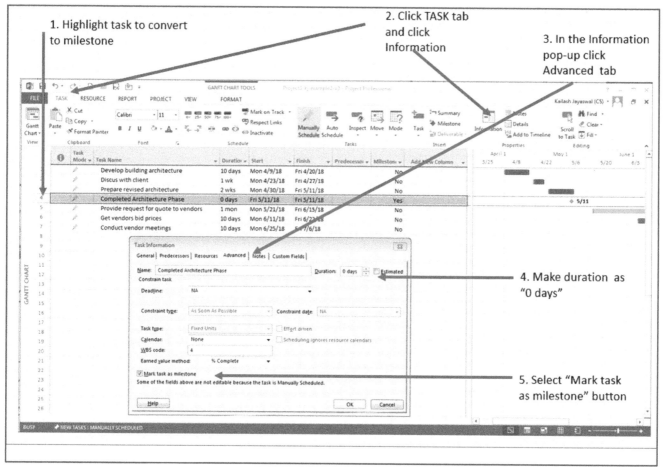

Figure F-7: Converting an existing task to a milestone using Task Information window under TASK tab

Step 5: Linking Tasks

So far, we have worked with various tasks. But these are not independent tasks. There is a sequence for completing the tasks. The tasks have relationships. Table F-2 shows the four types of relationship.

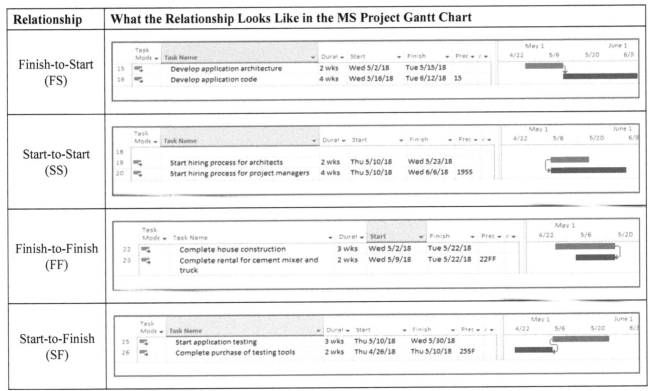

Table F-2: Relationships between tasks (AppF-TableF2-FigA, FigB, FigC and FigD)

The most common relationship is the FS relationship, where the predecessor activity must finish before the successor activity can start. You can also setup a lead or lag time. If the successor must start after ten days, the relationship is FS+10 days, as shown in the figure below.

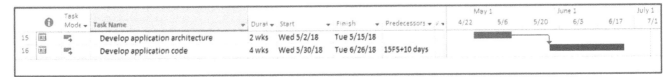

Figure F-8: FS + 10 days lag relationship between two Tasks

To establish an FS-relationship, you need to type the ID number of the predecessor in the **Predecessor** column. We need to link tasks 1, 2 and 3, so Task 1 must finish before Task 2 can start. Also, Task 2 must finish before Task 3 can start. Here is the process to link the tasks:

- For Task 2 row, enter "1" in the **Predecessors** column. This signifies that Task 1 is the predecessor and must finish before Task 2 can start.
- For Task 3 row, enter "2" in the **Predecessors** column.

Figure F-9: Entering predecessor task number in the Predecessor column

You can also use the **Task Information** window to enter a new or edit an existing relationship. Highlight the task for which you need to set the relationships. Then, click the **Task** tab and **Information**. This will bring up the Task Information window. Alternatively, you can double-click on the task row to bring up the Task Information window.

In the window, click on the **Predecessors** tab. In this tab, you enter the ID number of the predecessor task and type of relationship. You can enter lag or lead (if any). A task may have two or more relationships. If so, you need to have one row for each relationship.

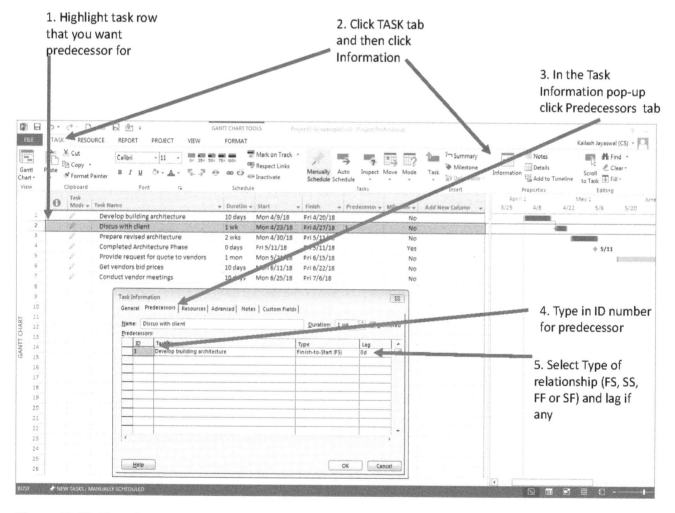

Figure F-10: Entering predecessor in the Task Information pop-up window

Step 6: Manual and Automatic Scheduling of Tasks

On the bottom left side of the MS Project window, you see **New Tasks: Manually Scheduled** or **New Tasks: Automatically Scheduled**. This signifies what new tasks will default to. You can set it to "automatic scheduling," and then the new tasks will calculate the start date using the predecessor information.

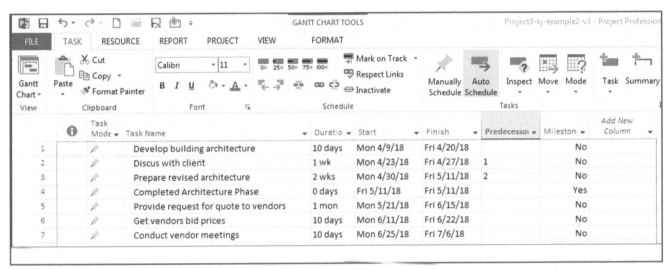

Figure F-11: Spreadsheet section where all Tasks are Manually-Scheduled and Tasks 1 through 3 are linked

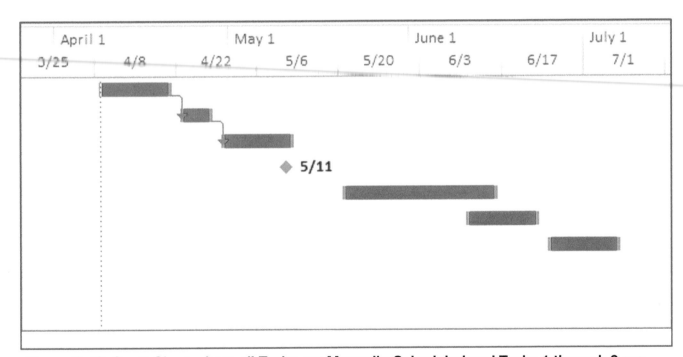

Figure F-12: Gantt Chart where all Tasks are Manually-Scheduled and Tasks 1 through 3 are linked

Now you can select Task 1 through Task 7 and click Auto Schedule. You will see that the icons in the **Task Mode** column change from push pins to an auto-scheduling bar. Also, note the change in the Gantt chart. Tasks 1, 2, and 3 are linked and hence appear as a sequence.

However, all the other tasks are lined up with the project start date. If you click on the **PROJECT** tab and then on the **Project Information**, you will see that the start date is set to 4/9. Tasks 2 and 3 know their dependencies, and they can compute their start date. However, the other tasks start on the Project Start date which is 4/9 because by default those are set to start **As Soon As Possible** in the **Task Information** window.

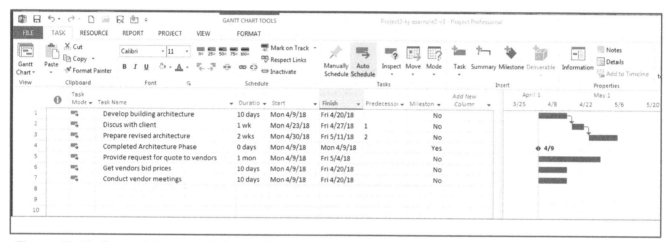

Figure F-13: Spreadsheet and Gantt chart where all tasks are automatically scheduled and Tasks 1, 2, and 3 are linked

Now let us set dependencies for the remaining tasks, where Task 4 is a Milestone and Tasks 5, 6, and 7 can start only if the previous task has completed. A simple way to do this is to enter the ID number of the predecessor in the **Predecessor** column.

	Task Mode	Task Name	Duratio	Start	Finish	Predecesso	Mileston	Add New Column
1		Develop building architecture	10 days	Mon 4/9/18	Fri 4/20/18		No	
2		Discus with client	1 wk	Mon 4/23/18	Fri 4/27/18	1	No	
3		Prepare revised architecture	2 wks	Mon 4/30/18	Fri 5/11/18	2	No	
4		Completed Architecture Phase	0 days	Fri 5/11/18	Fri 5/11/18	3	Yes	
5		Provide request for quote to vendors	1 mon	Mon 5/14/18	Fri 6/8/18	4	No	
6		Get vendors bid prices	10 days	Mon 6/11/18	Fri 6/22/18	5	No	
7		Conduct vendor meetings	10 days	Mon 6/25/18	Fri 7/6/18	6	No	
8								
9								
10								

Figure F-14: Spreadsheet section where all tasks are automatically-scheduled and linked

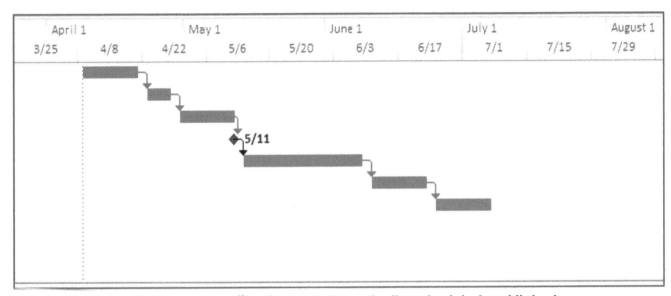

Figure F-15: Gantt chart where all tasks are automatically-scheduled and linked

Step 7: Grouping Tasks into Summary Tasks (or phases)

In MS Project you can group tasks into phases. This makes it easier to visualize and discuss with stakeholders who may want to look at only high-level phases and their dates.

In this step, we will look at the **bottom-up approach** to developing phases. We have the individual tasks, and we can group the tasks into phases.

Let us create the following two phases:

- Phase 1: Architecture phase
- Phase 2: Vendor interaction phase

There are two ways to create phases or summary tasks.

- Method 1: You insert a new task, and in the **Task Name** column describe that as a phase or summary. This new task needs to be immediately above the tasks that will become the subtasks (which need to be as a contiguous block). Then, you select the tasks that need to be part of the summary and click on the **Indent Task** (part of **TASK** tab). The selected tasks will become sub-tasks within the summary task. The dates for the summary task are the time span for all its sub-tasks.
- Method 2: You select the tasks that need to be part of the summary and click on **Insert Summary Task** (part of the **TASK** tab). That gives you a new Task line immediately above the selected tasks. The new line now says **<New Summary Task>** and you can change the text.

Figure F-16 and Figure F-17 show the tasks with no summary.

	Task Mode ▾	Task Name ▾	Duratio ▾	Start ▾	Finish ▾	Predecessoı ▾	Mileston ▾	Add New Column ▾
1		Develop building architecture	10 days	Mon 4/9/18	Fri 4/20/18		No	
2		Discus with client	1 wk	Mon 4/23/18	Fri 4/27/18	1	No	
3		Prepare revised architecture	2 wks	Mon 4/30/18	Fri 5/11/18	2	No	
4		Completed Architecture Phase	0 days	Fri 5/11/18	Fri 5/11/18	3	Yes	
5		Provide request for quote to vendors	1 mon	Mon 5/14/18	Fri 6/8/18	4	No	
6		Get vendors bid prices	10 days	Mon 6/11/18	Fri 6/22/18	5	No	
7		Conduct vendor meetings	10 days	Mon 6/25/18	Fri 7/6/18	6	No	

Figure F-16: List of tasks with no Summary Tasks

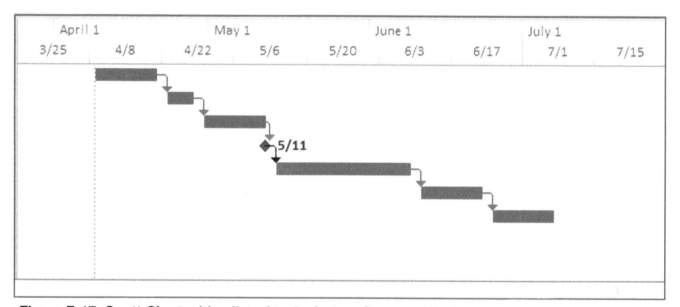

Figure F-17: Gantt Chart with a list of tasks but no Summary Tasks

We will use Method 1 to create Summary Tasks. We will set tasks 1 through 4 as part of a new Summary Task called **Phase 1: Architecture phase**. We will then set Tasks 5 through 7 as part **Phase 2: Vendor interaction phase** Summary Task

- For Phase 1, insert a new task above Task 1 and name it **Phase 1: Architecture phase.** Then select the four tasks below that line and click on the **Indent Task** (part of the **TASK** tab). The four selected tasks will become sub-tasks.
- For Phase 2, insert a new task above the planned sub-tasks and name that as **Phase 2: Vendor interaction phase**. Then select all the tasks below that and click on **Indent Task**.

Figure F-18 and Figure F-19 show the tasks split into two phases (summary), each headed by a Summary Task row. Each summary task row automatically gets dates, which span the duration for the sub-tasks in that summary.

	❶	Task Mode ▾	Task Name	Duratio ▾	Start ▾	Finish ▾	Predecessoɪ ▾	Mileston ▾	Add New Column ▾
1		▰	▴ Phase1: Architecture Phase	25 days	Mon 4/9/18	Fri 5/11/18		No	
2		▰	Develop building architecture	10 days	Mon 4/9/18	Fri 4/20/18		No	
3		▰	Discus with client	1 wk	Mon 4/23/18	Fri 4/27/18	2	No	
4		▰	Prepare revised architecture	2 wks	Mon 4/30/18	Fri 5/11/18	3	No	
5		▰	Completed Architecture Phase	0 days	Fri 5/11/18	Fri 5/11/18	4	Yes	
6		▰	▴ Phase 2: Vendor Interaction Phase	40 days	Mon 5/14/18	Fri 7/6/18		No	
7		▰	Provide request for quote to vendors	1 mon	Mon 5/14/18	Fri 6/8/18	5	No	
8		▰	Get vendors bid prices	10 days	Mon 6/11/18	Fri 6/22/18	7	No	
9		▰	Conduct vendor meetings	10 days	Mon 6/25/18	Fri 7/6/18	8	No	

Figure F-18: List of tasks split into two Summary Tasks

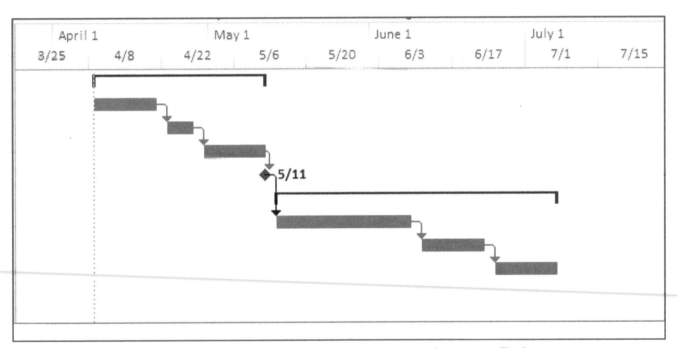

Figure F-19: Gantt chart showing a list of tasks split into two Summary Tasks

Note that it is common to have project plans with a mix of manually-scheduled and automatically-scheduled tasks. Also, a summary task can have a mix of sub-tasks. However, the summary task row must be automatically-scheduled so that it can automatically compute its own start and finish dates from the sub-task dates.

Full-Length Practice Test
(with 200 questions)

Distribution of 200 questions amongst the 5 Process Groups

Process group	Percentage of questions in the exam	No of questions in the exam
Initiating	13%	26
Planning	24%	48
Executing	31%	62
Monitoring and Controlling	25%	50
Closing	7%	14
TOTAL	**100%**	**200 questions**

Section 1 of 5: Questions on Project Initiating Process Group (questions 1- 26)

1. Which of the following authorizes you to start a project?
   A. Getting buy-in from senior stakeholders on the project constraints of scope, time and resources
   B. Getting sign-off on the project charter
   C. Developing the project scope document
   D. Developing a cost-benefit analysis that clearly shows the project benefits

2. At which stage, in a typical project do stakeholders have maximum influence?
   A. Towards the beginning of the project
   B. In the middles phases
   C. Towards the close of the project
   D. Stakeholders have uniform influence across all phases.

3. Jessica Johnson has been asked by her program manager to develop the charter and identify stakeholders for a new project. Defining a high-level scope and timeline for a new project is part of:
   A. Identify Stakeholders process
   B. Planning Process Group
   C. Define Scope process
   D. Initiating Process Group

4. Which of the following is not true about project initiation?
   A. Your project expenses are the highest during initiation.
   B. Your stakeholders have the most input and influence during this phase.
   C. Of all the phases, initiation has the most uncertainty.
   D. You have an unclear idea of the details and how the project will progress.

5. Which is true about product lifecycle?
   A. A product lifecycle is managed within a project lifecycle.
   B. Various projects can be associated with the lifecycle of a single product.
   C. Adding a feature to an existing product, that is being manufactured and sold, is an ongoing operational task.
   D. Initiation of a product is similar to initiating a project.

6. Which of the following processes does not use data analysis as a tool or technique?
   A. Plan Scope Management
   B. Monitor and Control Project Work
   C. Develop Project Charter
   D. Perform Integrated Change Control

7. Alex Mason has been asked to select a project with the least payback period after subtracting for operating expenses. The capital, as well as operating expenses each month, is noted in the table below. Which project should Alex choose?

Project	Initial Capital Expense	Incoming revenue each month	Operating and maintenance (O&M) expense each month
Project A	$300,000	$25,000	$ 5,000
Project B	$400,000	$35,000	$10,000
Project C	$180,000	$15,000	$ 5,000
Project D	$300,000	$20,000	$ 5,000

   A. Project A
   B. Project B
   C. Project C
   D. Project D

8. Brooks Bernstein has joined a datacenter monitoring and management firm in Austin, Texas and is in-charge of a project for installing a new application monitoring software for global clients. When should she expect to get most inputs from stakeholders for her new project?
   A. Throughout the project, especially to develop change requests that have a potential impact on the project cost, schedule or scope baselines
   B. Towards the end of the project
   C. Towards the middle of the project
   D. Toward the start of the project

9. A project to develop a highway in Uganda is expected to cost $5,000,000. The highway will take 2 years to develop and complete and is expected to return $200,000 per month in road tolls. What is the payback period including the development time?
   A. 24 months
   B. 25 months
   C. 49 months
   D. 50 months

10. Which of the following is part of enterprise environmental factors (EEF) needed to initiate a new project?
   A. Organizational policies and procedures
   B. Project governance framework for projects, programs and portfolio that help provide guidance and decision-making
   C. Project monitoring and reporting methods
   D. Organizational governance framework that provides direction and coordination through people and policies to meet organizational goals

11. Which of the following is an output of the Develop Project Charter process?
    A. Issue log
    B. Assumption log
    C. Change log
    D. None of the above

12. Stakeholder register is the result or output of the:
    A. Identify Stakeholders process
    B. Manage Stakeholders process
    C. Plan Stakeholder Management process
    D. Develop Project Charter process

13. Which of the following process groups requires you to complete a project charter?
    A. Executing
    B. Planning
    C. Initiating
    D. Monitoring and Control

14. Which of the following is not true for projects, programs or portfolio?
    A. A portfolio comprises of projects and program that are inter-related and aim to achieve a strategic objective.
    B. A program comprises of a group of related projects managed in a coordinated way to obtain larger control and benefits.
    C. A project, within an enterprise, may not be part of any program.
    D. It is possible that a program contains related work that is outside the scope of the discrete projects within it.

15. Which of these is not correct about a project charter?
    A. A project charter is developed by the project manager with help from the project team and stakeholders.
    B. A project charter authorizes the project manager to use the corporate resources.
    C. A project charter lists the project approvers and project manager.
    D. A project charter contains an exhaustive list of all possible risks, constraints and assumptions.

16. Which project document has a list of high-level requirements for the project and/or product?
    A. Functional and non-functional requirements document
    B. Requirements management plan
    C. Project charter
    D. Requirements traceability matrix

17. Who owns the business case for a project that needs to be initiated?
    A. The project manager
    B. The customer
    C. The project sponsor
    D. The person who requested the project

18. Which of the following is an input to the business case?
    A. Project charter
    B. Requirements documentation
    C. Benefits management plan
    D. Needs Assessment

19. Stakeholders should ideally be identified during which of the following project stages?
    A. They should be identified throughout the project
    B. During project planning
    C. During project execution
    D. During project initiation

20. Which of the following is an input for the Identify Stakeholders process?
    A. Communications management plan
    B. Issue log
    C. Requirements documentation
    D. All the above

21. Which of these is an input for identifying stakeholders?
    A. Stakeholder engagement plan
    B. Stakeholder engagement assessment matrix
    C. Stakeholder register
    D. Change requests

22. You are asked to select one of the following projects based on the internal rate of return (IRR) but without any consideration for the wait period. Note that the initial capital investment is considered as the sunk cost. Which project would you select?
    A. Project A: The initial investment is $200,000 and you will get $20,000 per month after 6 months.
    B. Project B: The initial investment is $300,000 and you will immediately start getting $30,000 per month
    C. Project C: The initial investment is $400,000 and you will get $40,000 per month after 12 months
    D. Project D: The initial investment is $500,000 and you will get $25,000 per month without any wait time.

23. Which of the following is not included in the stakeholder register?
    A. Stakeholder classification based on his influence within and outside the organization
    B. Stakeholder's ability to influence the project objectives
    C. Project phase where the stakeholder can impact or influence the project
    D. Engagement level of the stakeholder

24. Jim Juarez has been asked to develop a project charter to start a new project to migrate 1,000 users to another office building in the next 4 weeks. Which of the following should he not include in the project charter?
   A. A high-level schedule
   B. Quantifiable objectives
   C. Criteria for canceling the project
   D. A list of change requests that will be needed. This will provide advance information to the change control board and key stakeholders.

25. You have been asked to select one of the following projects based on payback period including the wait time. Which would you select?
   A. Project A: The initial investment is $200,000 and you will get $20,000 per month after 6 months.
   B. Project B: The initial investment is $300,000 and you will immediately start getting $30,000 per month
   C. Project C: The initial investment is $400,000 and you will get $40,000 per month after 12 months
   D. Project D: The initial investment is $500,000 and you will get $25,000 per month without any wait time.

26. Which of the following is true about stakeholders?
   A. Someone who is involved in the activities of the project.
   B. Someone who is interested in the planning and progress of the project.
   C. Someone who can impact or can be impacted positively or negatively by the project.
   D. Someone who can positively or negatively influence the progress of the project.

Section 2 of 5: Questions on Project Planning Process Group (questions 27 – 74)

27. Email is an example of:
   A. Mass communication
   B. Network communication
   C. Public communication
   D. Push communication

28. Which one of the following is true for a project?
   A. A project can be done by a single person.
   B. A project is usually given to a team that has prior experience delivering similar project objectives, regardless of success or failure of the prior projects.
   C. A project requires involvement from multiple departments from the same organization or involvement of external organizations or partners.
   D. A project needs to go through planning and execution phases before it can be terminated.

29. Which of the following contract type poses the least risk for the buyer?
   A. Time & Material (T&M) contracts
   B. Cost Plus Fixed Fee (CPFF)
   C. Cost Plus Incentive Fee (CPIF)
   D. Fixed Price with Incentive Fee (FPIF)

30. You are reviewing documents related to risks for your new project. One of the risk documents contains a section that has all the risks and their sources in a hierarchical order. What is the section referred to as?
    A. Risk breakdown structure (RBS)
    B. Risk categories
    C. Risk management plan
    D. Risk strategies

31. Which is the most common type of precedence dependency used when sequencing activities?
    A. Finish-to-start (FS)
    B. Finish-to-finish (FF)
    C. Start-to-start (SS)
    D. Start-to-finish (SF)

32. Which of the following risks can be mitigated by Monte Carlo analysis?
    A. Non-event risks
    B. Event-based risks
    C. Variability risks
    D. Ambiguity risks

33. In the salience model shown in the figure below, which one of the following choices best describes the position of Albert Jameson as a stakeholder?

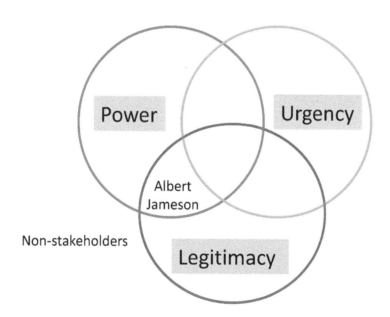

    A. He needs attention, should be kept informed and can be relied upon to get help from other stakeholders.
    B. All his needs must be met and he is crucial for continued existence and progress of the project.
    C. He needs close attention and you need to provide information as and when Mr. Jameson asks for that.
    D. He needs close attention and can potentially be dangerous for the project.

34. You have developed activities and their sequences with help from the project team. Activity B needs to start 20 days after Activity A has been completed. Which of the following represents this scenario? (F is for finish and S is for start).
    A. FS – 20 days
    B. FS + 20 days
    C. SF - 20 days
    D. SF + 20 days

35. Which of the following is used to acquire more information about services or goods from the sellers?
    A. Request for information (RFI)
    B. Request for quotation (RFQ)
    C. Request for proposal (RFP)
    D. Bid document

36. A technique that is used to find the strength of relationships between various causes (factors) and the outcome is called:
    A. Logical data model
    B. Mind mapping technique
    C. Matrix diagram
    D. SIPOC (suppliers, inputs, process, outputs, customers) model

37. You have a choice to purchase or internally develop a software product. If you develop it internally, the added advantage is that you can sell subscriptions in the open market which can be profitable given strong demand.

    The software purchase price is $2 million. If developed internally and sold in strong market conditions (25% possibility) it will provide a net profit of $20 million after subtracting for development expenses. But given weak market conditions (75% possibility) it will result in a net loss of $10 million. What is the net path value (NPV) of developing internally followed by strong market conditions?
    A. Loss of $2M
    B. Loss of $10M
    C. Gain of $18M
    D. Gain of $20M

38. You are managing a project team meeting where you have 6 members, besides yourself. How many potential communication channels exist during the meeting?
    A. 42
    B. 6
    C. 7
    D. 21

39. Lisa Samuelson is a project manager for a global facilities management firm in Budapest, Hungary. She is managing the renovation for a large government office complex. She has come to be aware of risks to the building primarily due to it being a very old structure. She discusses this with her program manager and they agree to get additional property insurance. What type of risk response is being implemented?
    A. Mitigate
    B. Transfer
    C. Avoid
    D. Escalate

40. You have a choice to buy or internally develop a software product. If you develop it internally, the added advantage is that you can sell subscriptions in the open market and it can be profitable if there is strong demand.

    The software purchase price is $2 million. If developed internally and sold, a strong market (25% possibility) will get you a net profit of $20 million after subtracting for development expenses. But a weak demand (75% possibility) will result in a net loss of $10 million. What is the net path value (NPV) of developing internally followed by a weak demand?
    A. Loss of $2M
    B. Loss of $10M
    C. Gain of $18M
    D. Gain of $20M

41. Which of the following is required for the Plan Resource Management process?
    A. A basis of estimates for the project budget
    B. Work performance information and reports
    C. Geographical distribution of your project resources, facilities, and equipment
    D. Contracts and agreements with vendors and suppliers

42. Max Molnar is a project manager for a pharmaceutical firm. He is managing a project with several research activities with his project team of scientists. He has prepared a diagram using critical path method (CPM) with various activity nodes.

    One of his research activities on the non-critical path has an early start of 90 days and early finish of 105 days. The same activity has a late start of 120 days and a late finish of 135 days. Which of the following is true about that activity?
    A. The activity has a free float of 30 days
    B. The activity has a total float of 30 days
    C. The activity has a total float of 15 days
    D. The activity has a free float of 15 days

43. Emily Emerson is a project manager for an aircraft manufacturer. She is preparing a contract for work scope to be outsourced. The scope well-defined and not likely to change. What would be the most appropriate contract type to use?
    A. Time and material (T&M) contract
    B. Statement of work (SOW)
    C. Cost-reimbursable (CR) contract
    D. Fixed-price (FP) contract

44. Alex Anderson has developed a time estimates based on PERT weighted average of optimistic, pessimistic and most likely values. The estimates and dependencies between the activities are listed below. All the dependencies are mandatory, have an FS relationship and have no lags or leads. What is the project duration?

Activity	Predecessor	PERT duration (weeks)
A	None	10
B	A	20
C	None	40
D	None	50
E	B, C, D	20

   A. 80 weeks
   B. 50 weeks
   C. 70 weeks
   D. 90 weeks

45. A project has a 70% chance of a profit of $200,000 and a 30% chance of a loss of $100,000. What is the expected monetary value (EMV) of the project?
   A. $140,000
   B. $30,000
   C. $110,000
   D. $200,000

46. Which of the following is not true for contingency reserves?
   A. It is kept for cost uncertainty, rework for project deliverables and other identified risks.
   B. It is meant to cover for known-unknowns.
   C. It is a percentage of the estimated cost or a fixed amount.
   D. It is not part of the cost baseline

47. Which of the following is not true about the critical path in a project?
   A. It is the shortest time required to complete the project.
   B. It represents the longest path within the project schedule network.
   C. All activities on the critical path have a float (slack) of zero
   D. There can only be one critical path in a project schedule.

48. A procurement document that has the procurement phases, delivery techniques and agreement types to be used is:
   A. Procurement strategy
   B. Procurement statement of work (SOW)
   C. Procurement terms of reference (TOR)
   D. Procurement management plan

49. Susan Simpson is developing dependencies for activities in her new project for remodeling the office building. She wants to schedule final painting after electrical work is completed. However, she is dependent on the contracting agency that is responsible for scheduling time with the vendors. The VP, Facility tells Susan that the sequence is not critical. Any problems created by the electricians can be resolved quickly even after the final painting. This dependency is an example of:
   A. Mandatory external dependency
   B. Mandatory internal dependency
   C. Preferential external dependency
   D. Soft internal dependency

50. Which of the following is not true for resource smoothing?
   A. The activity schedule is updated to make sure that the resource demand does not exceed preset limits.
   B. The critical path and project end date usually do not change
   C. Activities are delayed only within their free or total float.
   D. It helps in always optimizing resource utilization

51. Kim Amberley, a project manager for a cloud service provider, needs to purchase licenses for a software application, but is not sure of the quantity. She develops a contract where the price per license is fixed but the total amount can be later changed. Such a contract is called:
   A. Fixed price contract
   B. Cost reimbursable contract
   C. Unit price contract
   D. Time and material contract

52. Which one of the following is a contract type where the seller is paid for admissible costs plus 80% of the difference between the actual expenses and a pre-determined project cost if the actuals are lower than the pre-determined project cost? However, in case the actuals are higher, the total fee is reduced by 50% of the difference.
   A. Cost Plus Incentive Fee (CPIF)
   B. Cost Plus Award Fee (CPAF)
   C. Fixed Price with Award Fee (FPAF)
   D. Fixed Price Incentive Fee (CPIF)

53. Dave Dickenson has collected optimistic (O), most likely (M) and pessimistic (P) time estimates for different activities. He wants to use the weighted average technique to compute the duration of the activities. Which of the following techniques can he use? He plans to later use the computed durations to develop a project schedule using critical path method (CPM).
   A. Triangular distribution
   B. Program Evaluation and Review Technique (PERT)
   C. Mean or average distribution
   D. Parametric estimation

54. Matthew Mueller is preparing a scope baseline for his new office modernization project. Which of the following would not be part of his new scope baseline?
    A. Project scope statement
    B. Work breakdown stricture (WBS)
    C. WBS dictionary
    D. All the above needs to be included in Matt's new scope baseline

55. Tim Tillerson is setting up a new firewall and a new Enterprise Resource Planning (ERP) application in a dedicated internal network. One of the requirements is that the new network is logically separated from the network that hosts user productivity applications such as email, shared folders, etc. Which one of the following is a non-functional requirement for the new firewall and ERP setup?
    A. The requirements documentation must be approved and signed by the sales head.
    B. The user interface must be intuitive for business heads to navigate through the information and get the planned and actual sales each week.
    C. The application response time must be less than 3 seconds for users who need to enter production data.
    D. The application must have a module to capture location and stage in the workflow process for each product.

56. Kevin Keith has developed a network diagram for the activities in his application development project. What is the time duration of the project?

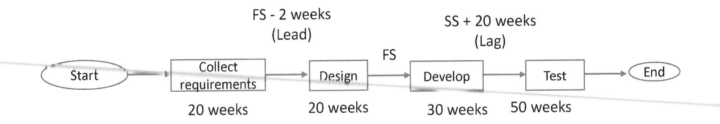

    A. 120 weeks
    B. 112 weeks
    C. 108 weeks
    D. 102 weeks

57. Scope baseline is an output of:
    A. Collect Requirements
    B. Define Scope
    C. Create WBS
    D. Plan Scope Management

58. Janet Jacobson, a project manager, oversees about 10 projects. Most of the projects have a duration of less than 6 months and have less than 5 project team resources. She wonders if she should follow all the processes mentioned in the PMBOK® for her projects. You explain to her that for each project she needs to 'pick-and-choose' or tailor which processes are applicable, and select the tools and techniques, relevant for each process. Why is there a need for tailoring?
    A. The customization or tailoring is needed because each project is unique.
    B. The resources working on the projects are different and processes need to be adapted as to the skills of the project team resources for project success.
    C. The projects are of different duration. The projects which need more time to complete will have more processes than the projects of shorter duration.
    D. The customization needs to be done as per the understanding and needs of the project sponsor and the division that provided funding for the project.

59. Which of the following is not included in a scope management plan?
    A. Process to create a work breakdown structure (WBS) from details in the project scope statement
    B. Process to get approval and updates to the scope baseline
    C. Process to plan and update activities related to project requirements and provide activity status
    D. Process to obtain formal acceptance of the completed project deliverables

60. Jerry Jackson has been hired as a project risk analyst. His manager tells him that risks must be identified but more importantly, risks must be tracked and updated in the risk register. Which of these processes is not something that Jerry can use to identify new risks or update existing ones?
    A. Plan Risk Management
    B. Direct and Manage Project Work
    C. Monitor and Control Project Work
    D. Perform Integrated Change Control

61. Samuel Simpson needs to assess whether the required software modules can be developed internally or must be outsourced to a consulting organization. His project sponsor suggests that in the interest of time, they look at available software products and purchase one off-the-shelf. When Samuel presented the purchase option to the engineering manager, the manager raised several questions about required customization. Which of the following techniques can Samuel use to identify the most suitable option? Note that he cannot ignore the constraints specified in the project charter.
    A. Cost-benefit analysis
    B. Multi-criteria decision analysis
    C. Expert judgment
    D. Alternatives analysis

62. Rick Robertson has identified various risks in his project. He and his project sponsor realize that if the risks were to happen the project would be delayed and they want to be transparent to the client. But Robert needs to document the impact of the risks on the schedule (in case those situations were to happen) and identify required schedule reserves. What is this analysis referred to as?
    A. Risk impact analysis
    B. Earned value analysis
    C. What-if scenario analysis
    D. Trend analysis

63. Max Moses is collecting requirements from the stakeholders and the customers. The different types of requirements would be:
    A. Low and high priority requirements
    B. Stakeholder, sponsor, tester and customer requirements
    C. Technical, functional, non-functional, business and quality requirements
    D. Optional and mandatory requirements

64. You are managing a project to set up and deploy a new datacenter for a client, who wants to offer cloud-based ERP services. One of your project activities is to develop the cloud architecture. You contact experts and get the optimistic (O), most likely (M) and pessimistic (P) estimates for the architecture as 50, 60 and 100 days, respectively.

    What is the expected number of days, based on beta distribution, that it would take to architect the datacenter?
    A. 64 days
    B. 70 days
    C. 65 days
    D. 75 days

65. You are preparing activity estimates for a new Demilitarized Network Zone with six firewalls. From a previous, similar project, you see that it had taken 2 days to setup a similar network with three firewalls. You, therefore, estimate the activity to take 4 days. This is an example of:
    A. Parametric estimation
    B. Analogous estimation
    C. Bottom-up estimation
    D. Data analysis

66. You are managing a project to setup and deploy a new datacenter for a client, who wants to offer cloud-based ERP services. One of your project activities is to develop the architecture. You contact experts and get an optimistic (O), most likely (M) and pessimistic (P) time estimates for the architecture as 60, 80 and 100 days respectively. What is the standard deviation?
    A. 10 days
    B. 5 days
    C. 6 days
    D. 9 days

67. What is the time duration for a milestone?
    A. 1 day
    B. Depends on the time taken for the milestone activity
    C. Depends on the time take for the set of activities that lead to the milestone
    D. 0 days

68. Julian Jones is conducting a requirements workshop with stakeholders, users and the project team to develop functional and non-functional requirements for the application, which he is managing as a project manager. For each required feature, Julian documents:
   - the role of the stakeholder who benefits from the feature (role),
   - what the stakeholder needs to accomplish (goal) and
   - the benefits that the feature provides to the stakeholder (motivation).

   Such a format for recording requirements is referred to as:
   A. User stories
   B. Mind maps
   C. Story points
   D. Micro-deliverables

69. Sam Simpson is collecting requirements for his new project to develop the architecture for a new power-generating plant in Nevada. Which of the following documents will he need?
   A. Project charter and scope statement
   B. WBS and activity list
   C. Budget and stakeholder management plan
   D. Project charter and stakeholder register

70. Which of the following is not part of a scope baseline?
   A. Work breakdown structure (WBS) and its dictionary
   B. Work packages, control accounts and planning packages
   C. Project scope statement
   D. Project requirements documentation

71. Richard Reskins is a project manager for a mining company in Angola in southern Africa. He is developing a risk management plan for a project to develop a new mine near Luanda, the capital of Angola. Which of the following is not an input for him at this time?
   A. Project Charter
   B. Lessons learned register for this project
   C. Organizational risk policy
   D. Templates of risk register, risk management plan and risk report

72. Mary Meyers is a project manager for a global facilities management corporation. She is preparing a project schedule network diagram for a new project using the precedence diagramming method (PDM). This technique is also known as:
   A. Activity-on-Arrow (AOA)
   B. Critical path method (CPM)
   C. Activity-on-Node (AON)
   D. Schedule network analysis

73. Which of the following is not true for variability risks?
    A. Variability risks are a type of non-event based risk, borne due to uncertainties related to certain key characteristics of project activities or decisions.
    B. Delay in construction schedule due to unseasonal weather conditions is an example of variability risk.
    C. Variability risks can be addressed using Monte Carlo analysis.
    D. All of the above choices are true for variability risks.

74. Kris Kelvin is a project manager for a cloud-based backup project. One of the requirements is that any data residing on the in-house disks and not used for 30 consecutive days, should be moved to the cloud. This is an example of:
    A. Project requirement
    B. Non-functional requirement
    C. Transition requirement
    D. Quality requirement

Section 3 of 5: Questions on Project Executing Process Group (questions 75 – 136)

75. A process where you compare the actual project quality standards to those of comparable projects in another industry is called:
    A. Benchmarking
    B. Expert judgment
    C. Brainstorming
    D. Data gathering

76. Lucy Simpson is managing a project with about 20 stakeholders. One of the stakeholders, Jill Peterson, needs to sign-off and accept the project deliverables. Which of the following is a hint that Jill needs more work and communication from the project manager?
    A. The stakeholder, Jill Peterson, does not attend the project meetings.
    B. The stakeholder used to be earlier participate in the discussions but lately, she has been too silent.
    C. The stakeholder has asked that she not be included in the project meeting notes.
    D. The stakeholder engagement level was 'leading' earlier but is now 'neutral'.

77. You are going through the steps of forming, storming, norming, etc. with a new project team. You realize that the project team members have not worked together in any project earlier. Which process are you in, now?
    A. Plan Resource Management
    B. Develop Team
    C. Manage Team
    D. Control Resources

78. What should drive the level of communications needed to effectively engage stakeholders in the project?
   A. The position of the stakeholder in the power/interest grid or the impact/influence grid.
   B. The direction (upward, downward, sideward, outward) of the influence of the stakeholder.
   C. The position of the stakeholder in the salience model which describes stakeholder classes based on their level of authority, their need for immediate attention and the legitimacy of their involvement in the project.
   D. The gap between the current (C) and desired (D) engagement levels as documented in the stakeholder engagement assessment matrix

79. You are managing a project team where you have 11 members, including yourself. How many potential communication channels exist in the project?
   A. 66
   B. 10
   C. 11
   D. 55

80. A seller is awarded a fixed price with award fee (FPAF) contract for $100,000 per month for 12 months. The award is for $25,000 for the month that the SLA expectations are met or exceeded, which actually happened for 4 out of 12 months. What is the amount paid to the service provider?
   A. $1,200,000
   B. $1,300,000
   C. $1,000,000
   D. $1,100,000

81. Emily Laurens is a project manager for a natural gas drilling firm in Algeria. The firm is engaged in traditional vertical drilling as well as non-traditional hydraulic fracturing in various regions across Algeria. Emily needs work performance information to prepare a production variance report. Which of the following processes would provide work performance information?
   A. Control Scope
   B. Define Scope
   C. Estimate Activity Durations
   D. Direct and Manage Project Work

82. Which of the following is true for the Tuckman ladder model in human resource management?
   A. The stages must be done in the same sequence as mentioned in the model.
   B. You must not skip or bypass any stage.
   C. It is common for each of the five stages to take the same amount of time.
   D. It is possible that your project team may get stuck at a particular stage or need to go back to a previous stage.

83. You are explaining the difference between fitness for use and conformance to requirements. Which of the following would be true?
    A. Fitness for use is about making sure that the product or service satisfies real needs. Conformance is about meeting product requirements.
    B. Fitness for use is about making sure that the user experience is positive and ease-of-use is high.
    C. Fitness for use and conformance are about making sure the product meets the stated requirements.
    D. Fitness for use is about user-friendliness. Users will tend to avoid using a product if it is difficult or cumbersome to use.

84. A set of techniques that aim to improve the quality by identifying and removing the causes of defects and minimizing variability in manufacturing or business processes is called:
    A. Total Quality Management (TQM)
    B. Plan-do-check-act (PDCA) model
    C. SIPOC (suppliers, inputs, process, outputs and customers) model
    D. Six Sigma

85. A vendor is awarded a T&M contract for a 250$/hour and actuals for travel. What is the seller paid if the seller has a team of 4 persons who work for 20 hours each and travel expenses total to $1,500 per person?
    A. $20,000
    B. $25,000
    C. $26,000
    D. $30,000

86. Andrew Johnson is managing a project with 20 stakeholders across 10 countries. Which would be a good way to manage the stakeholder?
    A. Travel to those countries and meet them in-person to understand their concerns, expectations and engagement levels
    B. Keep the stakeholders informed of status via emails, weekly meetings and by sharing information and reports on an internal portal.
    C. Prepare and send project variance reports each week
    D. Schedule and conduct meetings with all stakeholders at completion of each milestone

87. A technique that is used to optimize or improve a specific aspect, such as reliability, ease of use, safety or quality, during product design, is known as:
    A. Design for X (DfX)
    B. Root case analysis (RCA)
    C. Alternative analysis
    D. Cause-and-effect (fishbone) diagram

88. Painting a fence can start 5 days after fence installation has begun. This is an example of:
    A. Start-to-start dependency with a lead of 5 days
    B. Start-to-start dependency with a lag of 5 days
    C. Start-to-finish dependency with a lead of 5 days
    D. There is not enough information to determine lead or lag since the work duration of painting or installation is not specified.

89. Responsibility for quality of project deliverables lies with the:
    A. Project manager
    B. Project team members
    C. Project sponsor
    D. Senior management

90. Jeremy Reader is a project manager for a large construction firm. He has developed a project schedule for a client in Singapore who wants a design for a new sewage plant. The high-level activities, represented in alpha-numeric code, are shown below.

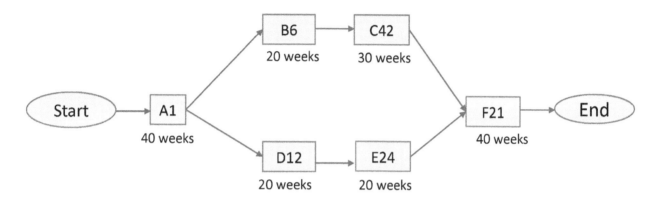

The client wants to now insert another activity which would take 20 weeks after A1 and before the start of D12. What is the increase in project duration due to this change?
    A. 10 weeks
    B. 20 weeks
    C. 5 weeks
    D. It is not possible to estimate the change in project duration given the information.

91. Which of the following must the project manager be aware of, for effective communication of project progress, risks and issues to the stakeholders?
    A. Aware of the gaps in stakeholder engagement
    B. Aware of the power relationships and political environment within the organization.
    C. Aware of the cultural differences within the stakeholder community.
    D. All of the above

92. Which of the following is a key output of the Manage Project Knowledge process?
    A. Lessons learned register
    B. Updates to the project management plans
    C. New change requests or updates to existing change requests
    D. Update to project baselines for cost, scope or schedule

93. Which one of the following processes, helps reduce the risk of project failure?
    A. Manage Communications
    B. Monitor Communications
    C. Manage Stakeholder Engagement
    D. Monitor Stakeholder Engagement

94. Alex Albertson is a program manager. He is delivering a presentation on project management best practices at a conference organized by his local PMI chapter. Which of the following statements are correct?
    A. He emphasizes correctly that most of his projects have been an elaborative progression.
    B. Various project processes have provided him valuable experience, templates and lessons that are bound to help him in future projects.
    C. Communication and stakeholder management are the two critical responsibilities for a project manager.
    D. All of the above are correct.

95. You have just joined as a project manager in a balanced matrix organization. You have five project team members. You are working to develop a stakeholder register. You need to understand the stakeholder engagement levels. You can expect that communications within the organization to be:
    A. Easy
    B. Complex
    C. Transparent
    D. Primarily in the form of in-person meetings

96. You are taking over a project from a project manager, who is being assigned to another project, but within the same program. You have been told by the program manager that you can later consult with the previous project manager, if he has time. He will continue to be around, and his new project will use the same engineering resources as the project you are taking over. The project manager has told you that the project team members are cooperative but need to be continuously reminded to complete their project deliverables. What is the first thing that you should do?
    A. Check the schedule performance index for the team members.
    B. Check schedule variance for the work completed so far.
    C. Explain project significance and objectives to the project team.
    D. Understand and discuss the risk status with the program manager.

97. At which stage does a typical project incur the maximum expenses?
    A. Initial or planning stage
    B. Middle or project execution stage
    C. Final and closing stage
    D. Cost is almost identical across all stages.

98. You are working as a project manager at an IT product development firm. Your cousin, Albert, is actively looking for a job as his company has moved various application development roles to Eastern Europe. Albert has given his resume to submit for an open position in your firm. You also realize that the candidate for this open position will be working on your project about 25% of the time. What should you do?
    A. Do not submit the resume. It is a conflict of interest. Advise your cousin to look elsewhere.
    B. Advise your cousin to submit the resume through the external website
    C. Submit the resume. Also, speak with the hiring manager and let him know that the candidate is your relative and that you cannot be in the interview panel.
    D. Ask a colleague to submit your cousin's resume.

99. Which of the following is represented by the outline in the figure below?

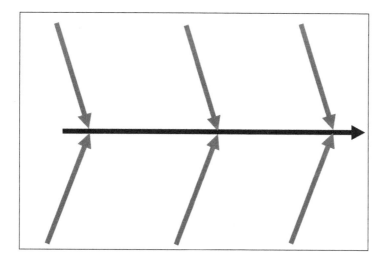

    A. Ishikawa diagram
    B. Scatter diagram
    C. Affinity diagram
    D. Flowchart

100. Which of the following cannot be done using a cause-and-effect diagram?
    A. Identify the root cause of problems.
    B. Identify the effect of certain errors or defects.
    C. Breakdown the cause of problems into discrete branches.
    D. Develop a timeline to resolve the root cause of a problem.

101. A bar chart that provides a graphical representation of numerical data is:
    A. Pareto diagram
    B. Affinity diagram
    C. Histogram
    D. Matrix diagram

102. A diagram that shows the correlation or relationship between two variables is called:
    A. Fishbone diagram
    B. Relationship diagram
    C. Affinity diagram
    D. Scatter diagram

103. Mary Morales is a project manager for a large oil and gas exploration and production (E&P) firm in Lima, Peru. She is trying to get to the root cause of certain problems in the oil rig stations. Which would be the best technique to be used?
    A. Affinity diagrams
    B. Fishbone diagrams
    C. Pareto diagrams
    D. Scatter diagrams

104. How should you involve and manage a stakeholder, who has high power and influence within the organization, is usually difficult to work with and is not particularly interested in the project progress or status?
A. Keep him informed
B. Manage him closely
C. Monitor his level of interest in the project
D. Keep him satisfied and provide project status via emails.

105. A seller is awarded a fixed price with incentive fee (FPIF) contract for $2M for 24 months. However, if the seller can complete the project in less than 24 months, the seller will get an incentive of $200,000 per month that it finished earlier. The seller was able to complete the project in 18 months. What is the amount paid to the seller?
A. $2.0M
B. $3.0M
C. $3.6M
D. $3.2M

106. When a risk becomes an issue, which document(s) should you refer for actionable tasks that must be done?
A. Risk register and risk report
B. Risk register
C. Risk report
D. Risk management plan

107. Sarah Jacobson is a project manager for a manufacturer in Richardson, Texas, that produces and markets machinery for power-generation firms. She needs to purchase equipment from a vendor in Rome. Fortunately, due to recent currency fluctuations between US Dollars and Euros, it is advantageous for her to quickly purchase the equipment from Italy and get that delivered to Texas. She works with the procurement administrator to place the order as quickly as possible. What type of risk response is this?
A. Escalate
B. Accept
C. Exploit
D. Enhance

108. Change requests are a possible output of which one of the following processes in Risk Management?
A. Plan Risk Management
B. Identify Risks
C. Perform Qualitative Risk Analysis
D. Implement Risk Responses

109. James Jacobson is a project manager for a large project in which he has 8 bidders, who have been pre-selected and invited to submit responses for a request for proposal (RFP). Several bidders have questions and need clarifications. James organizes a bidder conference to make sure that everyone gets the same information. Which process is James in now?
   A. Plan Procurement Management
   B. Conduct Procurements
   C. Control Procurements
   D. Manage Stakeholder Engagement

110. Rick Petersen is a project manager at a global training organization. He is dealing with complex issues arising due to lack of commitment from skilled resources that are needed for short duration projects. Which of the following communication techniques would best help him resolve the issues?
   A. Formal and written communications
   B. Verbal, unofficial and informal communications
   C. Verbal but official communications
   D. Unofficial but written communications

111. Which of the following is most crucial to managing a multi-cultural project team with members in various countries such as Argentina, Algeria, Brazil and Indonesia?
   A. Having a detailed project schedule and making sure that you have resources assigned for each WBS
   B. Strong interpersonal and communication skills
   C. Use of video conferencing to get the team members familiar to and comfortable with each other
   D. Having a cloud-based repository to store all project artifacts so project team members can review and update those at any time

112. Samuel Nicholson, a senior project manager at a pharmaceutical firm, has a conflict between two project resources. They need to come to a consensus but do not want to discuss or resolve their differences. Which of the following is the best technique for Samuel to use to resolve this?
   A. Formal and written communication
   B. In-person and private discussion with the two project resources
   C. Small group communication with key stakeholders of the project, including the project sponsor
   D. Informal, but written communication with the two project resources, and their functional managers but no one else.

113. Kevin Christensen is managing an office downsize project in Norway with 30 stakeholders and 10 project team members spread across 5 countries in Europe. Employee morale is low since many of the employees in Norway and neighboring countries is being let go. During a project weekly call, Kevin senses strong resistance by the project team to executing the activities in the project plan. What is the first thing that Kevin should do?
   A. He should report such opposition to the project sponsor and then seek to gain support from stakeholders to move the project execution forward.
   B. He should let the functional managers know all this and seek their buy-in to prioritize the project activities.
   C. He must try to understand the reasons why the team members are unwilling to execute the project activities and address their concerns.
   D. He should explain how the project objectives will benefit the staff members in Norway to motivate the team members.

114. Which of the following gives a quick review of the project status?
    A. Project progress report
    B. Project variance report
    C. Project status report
    D. Project schedule and the work completed so far.

115. Rick Rupert is a project manager for a global facility management services (FMS) firm. He has been asked by his firm to maintain formal communication for all important project decisions. Which of the following should Rick not use for documenting key decisions related to project baselines?
    A. Project status reports
    B. Weekly project meeting notes
    C. Project change requests
    D. 1:1 emails

116. Which of the following is most effective in motivating project resources in today's hyper-connected, virtual and fast-paced work environment, where resources are usually involved in multiple projects?
    A. Theory X
    B. Maslow's Hierarchy of Needs
    C. Expectancy Theory and Theory X
    D. Theory Y and Herzberg's Motivation-Hygiene Theory

117. You are interviewing for a new project manager. Which one of the following factors should you look for in the candidate?
    A. Technical and management degree from a reputed university and work experience as a project manager.
    B. Good technical know-how of the products that will be developed by the projects that the candidate will initially manage.
    C. Prior experience as a functional or line manager.
    D. Prior experience as a project resource, project coordinator and later promoted to work as a project manager.

118. Jerry Jacobson is a project manager in South Africa for an automotive manufacturer. He is evaluating design alternatives for a new project. Two of his engineers are arguing about various parameters for the engine cooling system. Jerry has given them adequate time to come up with a consensus. But they still do not have a consensus. He calls for a meeting with the two engineers, where they use certain points from each of the proposals to arrive at a solution that is acceptable to both the engineers. This strategy for resolving a conflict is:
    A. Withdraw/avoid
    B. Smooth/accommodate
    C. Compromise/reconcile
    D. Collaborate/problem solve

119. Chris Chung has joined a circuit-board manufacturing contract firm in North Carolina as a program manager. He notices that the firm focusses on keeping all equipment in top working condition to avoid breakdown and delays. There is a lot of focus on improving processes, employee morale and condition of all manufacturing and test equipment. Such a system is referred to as:
    A. Total Productive Maintenance (TPM)
    B. Total Quality Management (TQM)
    C. Continual Improvement
    D. Theory of Constraints (TOC)

120. Manage Quality process uses diagrams that break down the causes of a particular problem into discrete branches to identify the root cause. Which of the following is not the name of such diagrams?
    A. Ishikawa diagrams
    B. Fishbone diagrams
    C. Why-why diagrams
    D. Affinity diagrams

121. Which of the following processes has lessons learned register as an output?
    A. Perform Integrated Change Control
    B. Manage Project Knowledge
    C. Close Project or Phase
    D. Monitor and Control Project Work

122. Jim Johnson is a project manager for a consulting firm. He is developing a project schedule for a client and gets advice on duration estimates for an activity. The pessimistic estimate is 32 days and the optimistic estimate is 24 days. What is the most likely estimate?
    A. 28 days
    B. 26 days
    C. 30 days
    D. It is not possible to compute the most likely estimate.

123. Amelia Augustus is reviewing and updating the stakeholder engagement assessment matrix to understand the level of communications that she must plan for, to effectively engage the project stakeholders. Which of the following is not a desired or existing level in the matrix?
    A. Leading
    B. Supportive
    C. Active
    D. Resistant

124. Rita Wright is a project manager for a global office construction and facilities management firm in Paris. She is working on a project that is in the execution stage. She is updating a project document that has information on sources of overall project risk and summary of individual project risks. Such a document is called:
    A. Risk register
    B. Risk report
    C. Risk management plan
    D. Risk breakdown structure (RBS)

125. A work display method, that helps the team visualize the workflow and blockers and limit the amount of work required at each stage (such as to-be Backlog, Up-next, In-progress, Waiting, Done) is known as:
    A. Kanban boards
    B. Just-in-time charts
    C. Schedule variance charts
    D. Work progress charts

126. You are managing a project to setup and deploy a new datacenter for a client, who wants to offer cloud-based ERP services. One of your project activities is to develop the required architecture. You contact experts and get the optimistic (O), most likely (M) and pessimistic (P) estimates for the architecture as 60, 85 and 100 days, respectively. What is the activity variance?
    A. 42 days
    B. 45 days
    C. 50 days
    D. 60 days

127. Lisa Lee has joined a global commodity trading firm in Korea. She notices that the firm has various events aimed at continual improvement of the processes. These events are usually hosted by service or process owners and they discuss how they can improve the process. What are these events called?
    A. Continual Improvement Events
    B. Knowledge Sharing and Process Improvement Events
    C. Kaizen Events
    D. Six Sigma Events

128. Which of the following often leads to a win-lose situation?
    A. Compromise/reconcile
    B. Smooth/accommodate
    C. Force/direct
    D. Collaborate/problem solve

129. Emily Emerson is a project manager for a workplace relocation firm. She needs to assign roles to project resources for a large office move in Stockholm, Sweden for a new client, that does oil and natural gas exploration and production. She urgently needs a particular talent that she cannot find internally and has asked the HR and PMO departments, but to no avail. What should she do?
    A. She should herself learn the required skills and do the work. This will help reduce the project expenses and provide increased monitoring and control of the project.
    B. She should identify the most suitable person and then send him/her for further training.
    C. She should contact HR once again, but this time with a slightly modified description of the "Required Skills" section.
    D. She should look outside for an external vendor resource.

130. Dave Dillon is a project manager for a global commodity shipping and trading firm. He has just completed a project with a team of 20 team members spread in 5 countries. Dave gets an assessment of individual performances from peers, managers and end-users. Performance assessments are part of which of the following processes?
   A. Develop Team
   B. Control Resources
   C. Plan Resource Management
   D. Manage Team

131. Which of the following is usually the most suitable technique for resolving conflicts?
   A. Withdraw/avoid
   B. Smooth/accommodate
   C. Compromise/reconcile
   D. Collaborate/problem solve

132. For which one of the following situations is it best to use formal, written communications?
   A. Defects have been found during the inspection process and you need to get to the root cause.
   B. One of the project resources is certain there will be delays in meeting deliverable deadlines.
   C. The cost performance index (CPI) has exceeded the threshold that the customer had provided for alerting them.
   D. The customer has requested a change in the product features.

133. Albert Gonzales is a project manager engaged in developing commercial complexes for clients. For which of the following situations should he use formal and written communications?
   A. Provide cost and schedule variance
   B. Send a status report at the end of each week
   C. Make a scope change to a signed contract
   D. Provide details of construction material used for the roofs and walls

134. You have come to know that a few key resources in your project team are planning to leave the company for another job. It is important for you to retain them since their activities are on the critical path and the project schedule has no slack or float. You work with the sponsor to arrange for project-end performance bonuses for those members. What type of risk response is this?
   A. Escalate
   B. Avoid
   C. Transfer
   D. Mitigate

135. Alexa Anderson is a project manager for an electric car company. She is reviewing the cost of failures. Which of these would not be considered as external failure costs?
   A. Costs to recall and inspect cars for defective airbags.
   B. Cost for recovery from bad publicity due to defective airbags in the sold cars.
   C. Cost for 100% inspection of the airbags in the next batch of cars that are ready to be sent to the distributors.
   D. Warranty costs.

136. Dorothy Donaldson is working on an urgent project. The critical path duration is 25 working days. The delivery of equipment from the vendor has been delayed by 10 days and is on the critical path. What is the first thing that Dorothy should do?
    A. Look for ways to crash or fast-track activities on the critical path.
    B. Brainstorm with the project team and sponsor on options to reduce the scope and get additional resources.
    C. Inform the client, project sponsor and stakeholders that the delivery has been delayed and that it will impact the schedule.
    D. Prepare a change request to extend the project schedule.

Section 4 of 5: Questions on Project Monitoring and Controlling (questions – 137 – 186)

137. Change requests is an output of:
    A. Control Procurements
    B. Conduct Procurements
    C. Plan Procurement Management
    D. All the 3 processes in Procurement Management Knowledge Area

138. Which of the following is a part of internal failure cost?
    A. Cost for statistical sampling for parts and inspection of the sample set
    B. Cost for inspecting the entire lot or batch of parts
    C. Cost for correcting the defects identified during inspection prior to shipping the products
    D. Cost for calibrating the test instruments that failed inspection

139. Sarah Johnson is managing a project in which the client has returned various delivered products with a long list of defects found by the client. The client is waiting for defect-free products. The project sponsor asks Sarah to closely monitor the internal quality processes done by the project team. What should Sarah do to ensure that the next batch of deliverables is accepted by the client?
    A. Make sure that the stated requirements are met
    B. Exceed client expectations in a few areas
    C. Work with the project team to identify additional features that can be added
    D. Make sure that the defects are less than the product benefits

140. For a given project, the estimate at completion (EAC) is $100,000 and the budget at completion (BAC) is $75,000. What is the variance at completion (VAC)?
    A. -$25,000
    B. -$75,000
    C. -$20,000
    D. $25,000

141. Eric Edger is a project manager for development of the city infrastructure. He is developing a Pareto diagram to categorize the issues and risks facing the city. What would be the best description of the Pareto diagram?
    A. It is a fishbone diagram that helps identify causes of the existing issues and risks and categorize the causes.
    B. It is a chart that represents individual values and a cumulative total.
    C. It is similar to a scatter chart and shows correlation.
    D. It is based on Ishikawa cause-and-effect diagram.

142. What is the difference between a checklist and a check sheet?
    A. A checklist is a set of action items used as a reminder to be done in sequence and check sheet is used to record the findings in a structured manner.
    B. A checklist is a set of points to be considered and a check sheet is used to document the frequencies or consequences of identified defects.
    C. A checklist is a result of lessons learned from previous projects and a check sheet is a result of the quality assurance team needing to document problems and identify root causes.
    D. A checklist helps in managing the activities in a structured manner. Check sheets are used to collect and document product attributes to identify defects or trends.

143. Tom Timmins has taken over a project. When reviewing the WBS and a set of completed deliverables, he finds that four of the completed work packages do not meet the quality metrics that are in the statement of work (SOW). He discusses this with the project sponsor, who is surprised but asks Tim to create a change request for additional funding to fix the issues. The additional funding is part of:
    A. Prevention cost
    B. Inspection and quality control cost
    C. Appraisal cost
    D. Internal failure cost

144. Your product incurs additional cost in the field to fix certain defects in the parts. The problems due to defective parts were found and reported by various customers. This cost is part of:
    A. Customer service cost
    B. Cost of non-conformance
    C. Rework cost
    D. Break-fix cost

145. A technique to reduce the project duration by adding resources is an example of:
    A. Fast tracking
    B. Schedule compression
    C. Crashing
    D. Resource smoothing

146. You are managing a project, where the allocated budget at completion (BAC) is $300,000 and the assigned duration is 4 months. After two months, you see that you have completed work that is worth $100,000. But you have spent $125,000 so far. What is the cost variance (CV)?
    A. $-25,000
    B. $125,000
    C. $100,000
    D. $25,000

147. Kimberly Ramirez is moving resources from activities on the non-critical path to the critical path for her new project, which is in the planning stage. This is an example of:
    A. Resource leveling
    B. Schedule compression
    C. Resource smoothing
    D. Fast Tracking

148. The figure below shows the activity duration in weeks. It is mandatory, that you complete Activity, A before you start any other work. However, the other dependencies are discretionary. How can you reduce the project duration by 8 weeks?

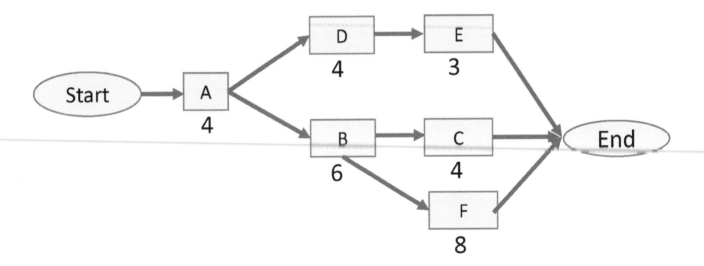

    A. Fast track activities D and E
    B. Fast track activities B and C
    C. Fast track all the activities except for A
    D. It is not possible to reduce the project duration by 8 weeks.

149. Your project has a budget of $50,000. Halfway down the project duration, you see that you have completed only 20% of the work and spent $20,000 so far. What is the cost performance index (CPI)?
    A. 0.25
    B. 0.60
    C. 0.40
    D. 0.50

150. Sam Simpson is managing a 2-month project. He has baselines for cost, schedule and scope. But due to application testing resources, being taken away from the project, the project has a delay of 4 weeks. Sam prepares a change request to extend the project duration. Who should he seek approval from?
    A. Project sponsor
    B. Client
    C. Impacted end-users who are waiting for the project deliverables
    D. Change control board (CCB)

151. You have been asked to reduce the project schedule but without increasing costs. The client is not particular about getting all the non-functional requirements that were initially agreed upon. Which of the following can you not do?
    A. Resource leveling
    B. Reducing scope
    C. Crashing
    D. Fast tracking

152. Which of these would not be considered as prevention cost?
    A. The cost to train employees to improve quality during manufacturing processes.
    B. The cost to make sure that the equipment is properly maintained and calibrated.
    C. The cost for proper documentation of the processes.
    D. The cost for reviewing the quality of a selected sample to make sure that the batch complies with the required quality objectives.

153. Tim Dylan has developed a project cost for normal modes of completing the activities. However, the project sponsor needs the work completed earlier by adding more resources. The work cannot be fast tracked due to high-quality requirements by the client. Tim has computed the additional cost for crashing each activity. The additional cost is needed for more resources at overtime rates. What is the least additional amount, required to crash by 4 weeks?

Activity	Original duration (weeks)	Duration if crashed (weeks)	Original cost ($)	Cost if crashed ($)
Design (A)	15	13	$20,000	$24,000
Development (B)	20	18	$40,000	$50,000
Testing (C)	11	9	$55,000	$75,000

    A. $14,000
    B. $24,000
    C. $12,000
    D. $10,000

154. Sam Dillon has developed a project duration and cost table as shown below. He needs to reduce the total project duration by 2 weeks while keeping expenses as low as possible. Which are the activities that Sam must crash and what would be the least additional cost that he must incur?

Activity	Predecessor	Original duration (weeks)	Original cost ($)	Additional cost per week for crashing ($/week)
A	None	40	$70,000	$2,000
B	A	20	$40,000	$1,000
C	B	10	$15,000	$ 500
D	A	30	$20,000	$1,000
E	C, D	80	$220,000	$3,000

A. Crash Activity C and D by 2 weeks, which incurs an additional $3,000
A. Crash Activity A by 2 weeks, which incurs an additional $4,000
B. Crash Activity C by 2 weeks, which incurs an additional $1,000
C. Crash Activity B by 2 weeks, which incurs an additional $2,000

155. John Dickerson is a project manager for a datacenter buildout project. He has a meeting with the client and finds out that he must complete the work 3 months in advance and without adding any more cost or resources. John reviews the project schedule with his project team and they are able to identify several discretionary dependencies. What is a viable option to reduce the project schedule?
A. Fast tracking the project activities
B. Identifying lead time to start the activities earlier.
C. Crashing the project activities
D. Resource smoothing

156. What is the relationship between specification and control limits in a control chart?
A. The range defined by control limits is less than that for specification limits.
B. The seller (or manufacturer) needs to make sure that all deliverables, provided to the customer, are within the control limits, even if they happen to exceed the specification limits.
C. Specification limits, along with control limits, are used to establish the natural capability for a stable process.
D. The range defined by control limits could be greater or less than that for specification limits.

157. You have a project budget of $500,000. Halfway down the project duration, you see that you have completed only 20% of the work and spent $400,000 so far. You re-estimate that you will need an additional $300,000 on top of the project budget, to complete the remaining work. What is the TCPI (to-complete performance index) that must be maintained in the future to complete the project?
A. 1.50
B. 0.40
C. 0.25
D. 1.00

158. Which of the following processes have change requests as an output?
    A. Monitor and Control Project Work
    B. Control Scope
    C. Validate Scope
    D. All of the above

159. For a given project, the estimate at completion (EAC) is $100,000 and the budget at completion (BAC) is $75,000. The actual cost (AC) has been $80,000. What is the estimate to complete (ETC)?
    A. $75,000
    B. $25,000
    C. $20,000
    D. -$20,000

160. Which one of the following has approved change requests as an output?
    A. Perform Integrated Change Control
    B. Monitor and Control Project Work
    C. Manage Project Knowledge
    D. Project Monitoring and Controlling

161. You have a project, where the PV (planned value) for the completed work is 200 hours but, the EV (earned value) is only 100 hours. What is the scheduled performance index (SPI)?
    A. 1.5
    B. 0.5
    C. 0.1
    D. 1.0

162. In a meeting, there is a discussion about outsourcing the application testing to a third-party. After an hour of discussion of the costs and benefits, the project sponsor made the decision for the group to not outsource the testing. This type of decision-making is referred to as:
    A. Dictatorship or autocratic
    B. Unanimity
    C. Majority
    D. Plurality

163. The figure below shows the number of days for each activity. The total project duration is 105 days. If you can fast track all the activities, what would be the project duration?

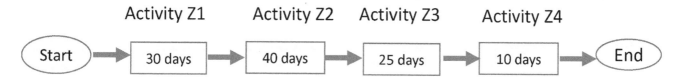

    A. 30 days
    B. 40 days
    C. 70 days
    D. 105 days

164. Cary Catherin has a vocal, unfriendly and argumentative set of stakeholders for a cross-country office-relocation project. Which of the following would not be a suitable technique or skill for her to use for managing stakeholder engagement?
    A. Interpersonal and team skills.
    B. Communications skills.
    C. Negotiation and conflict resolution skills.
    D. Project schedule management skills to help with crashing and fast-tracking various activities.

165. The figure below shows the number of days for each activity. If you fast track Activity B and Activity C, what would be the reduction in project duration?

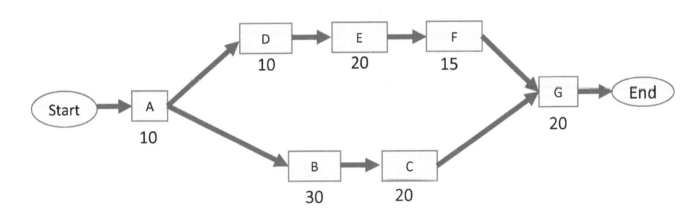

    A. 15 days
    B. 10 days
    C. 5 days
    D. There is no reduction in project duration since the activities that were fast tracked were not on the critical path.

166. Johanna Graves has started a new project that has a schedule of 10 months, a diverse stakeholder group comprising of 10 senior executives and 20 engineers in 6 countries and a budget of $6 million. The project objective is to identify, procure, and roll out a new supply chain management (SCM) application across all 10 manufacturing units within the company and train the end-users. Which of the following could be the most important success criterion for her project?
    A. The fitness of the identified SCM application to meet the stakeholder requirements.
    B. The ability of the end-users to use the application for their operational work and their increase in work efficiency.
    C. Satisfaction of the stakeholders.
    D. Completing the scope without exceeding the allocated budget and timelines.

167. You have a project, where the PV (planned value) for the completed work is 200 hours but the EV (earned value) has been only 100 hours. What is the schedule variance (SV)?
    A. -100 hours
    B. -200 hours
    C. 200 hours
    D. 100 hours

168. Which of the following is used to determine whether a process has predictable performance?
   A. Control chart
   B. Histogram
   C. Scatter diagram
   D. Affinity diagram

169. Berbers Mojave is a project manager and she needs to complete her project. However, only about 25% of the work has been finished. But $800,000 out of 2 million dollars has been spent. She realizes that budget at completion will not be sufficient to complete the project. Her program manager has asked her to estimate the amount needed to complete the project. She has computed the new estimate at completion (EAC) using a bottom-up estimation. What performance index must Berbers maintain for the remainder of the work to ensure that the project does not need any more funds?
   A. Cost performance index (CPI)
   B. Schedule performance index (SPI)
   C. The required future performance index depends on how Berbers Mojave computed estimate at completion (EAC)
   D. To-complete performance index (TCPI)

170. Which of the following is discussed during retrospective/lessons-learned meetings?
   A. Successful elements and events in the project or sprint.
   B. Things that can be improved.
   C. Things that must be included in the ongoing project to improve efficiency.
   D. All of the above choices are discussed during retrospective meetings.

171. When should quality control be done for the product and project deliverables?
   A. When the deliverables have been internally tested and are ready for the client or user
   B. When the scope of work has been completed and the test team is doing internal testing to verify functionality and going through the quality checklist
   C. When the client or user provides an issue list
   D. Throughout the project

172. Your project has a budget of $50,000. Halfway down the project duration, you see that you have completed only 20% of the work and spent $20,000 so far. What is the estimate at completion (EAC) assuming the cost performance index (CPI) will be maintained for the remainder of the project?
   A. $50,000
   B. $80,000
   C. $100,000
   D. $150,000

173. A chart that tracks the work that remains to be completed and is often used to identify the variance between the completed work and committed work is called:
   A. Scheduled Variance chart
   B. Gantt chart
   C. Iteration burndown chart
   D. Bubble chart

174. You have developed the following critical path diagram using the finish-start (FS) relationship. All relationships are mandatory. You are now asked to reduce the project duration by 8 weeks.

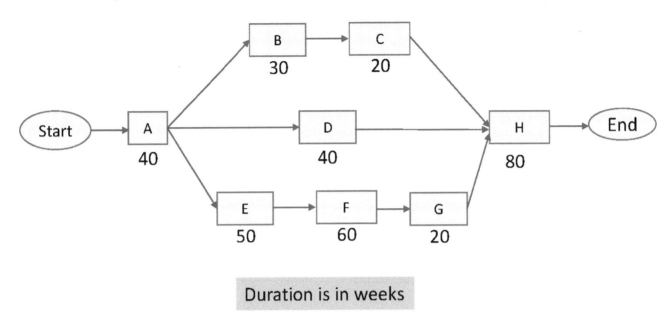

Duration is in weeks

The table below shows the activity duration (in weeks), cost for normal and crash mode execution of the activities and additional cost per week for crashing.

What would be the least additional cost incurred to reduce the project duration by 8 weeks?

Activity	Normal (weeks)	Crash (weeks)	Normal Cost ($)	Crash Cost ($)	Additional cost / week if crashed ($/week)
A	40	36	$40,000	$ 50,000	$2,500
B	30	26	$30,000	$ 50,000	$5,000
C	20	16	$20,000	$ 30,000	$2,500
D	40	30	$40,000	$ 50,000	$1,000
E	50	46	$50,000	$ 60,000	$2,500
F	60	56	$60,000	$ 80,000	$5,000
G	20	16	$20,000	$ 30,000	$2,500
H	80	76	$80,000	$100,000	$5,000

A. $5,000
B. $10,000
C. $20,000
D. $30,000

175. You have developed a project schedule as shown below with mandatory and discretionary FS (finish-start) dependencies. The duration is in days. Your project sponsor and client need the project completed as soon as possible to meet the period of peak demand in the market. What is the maximum reduction possible in the total project duration?

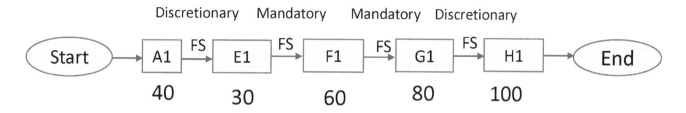

A. 80 days
B. 100 days
C. 110 days
D. 120 days

176. The diagram below shows the work completed versus the planned work.

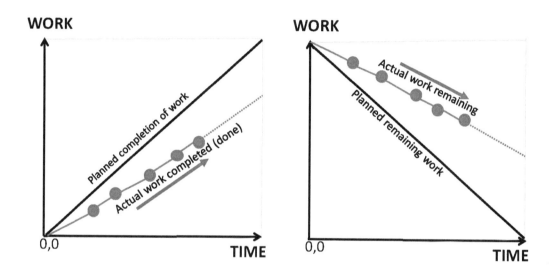

Such a diagram is an example of:
A. Schedule variance and feature charts
B. Earned value and work completed charts
C. Product backlog and progress charts
D. Burnup and burndown charts

177. The budget at completion (BAC) for your 10-month project is $40 million. After a month of execution, you assess that the completed work is worth $3,800,000. The planned value (PV) is now $4 million. The incurred cost has been $5M. What is the cost variance?
A. - $5 million
B. - $1.2 million
C. $1.2 million
D. - $3.8 million

178. You are developing a control chart with upper and lower specification and control limits. Which one of the following choices, indicates that the process is out of control?
    A. A point is outside the control limits
    B. Seven consecutive data points are all below the mean line
    C. Seven consecutive data points are all above the mean line
    D. One or more of the above three choices are true

179. The budget at completion (BAC) for your 10-month project is $40 million. After a month of execution, you assess that the completed work is worth $3,800,000. The planned value is now $4 million. The incurred cost has been $5M. What can you say about this project?
    A. The project is ahead of schedule
    B. The project is behind schedule
    C. The project is over budget
    D. The project is behind schedule and over-budget

180. You are in a meeting with two project resources to discuss the proposed Disaster Recovery (DR) solution for a new application. You know that these two usually disagree. During the discussion, what should you focus on?
    A. Pay attention to the words that they speak.
    B. Ensure they try to accommodate each other's solution and arrive at a consensus.
    C. Observe their non-verbal communication and focus the discussion on the merits and demerits of each proposal.
    D. Make sure that they honestly discuss the advantages and problems about their proposed solution without trying to force their point or withdraw from the discussion.

181. Validate Scope is a process, where you:
    A. Make sure that what you have documented during the Define Scope process meets the stakeholder requirements as captured during the Collect requirements process.
    B. Get the scope statement and baseline reviewed by the stakeholders to make sure they are okay with the scope.
    C. Formalize the acceptance procedures for the completed deliverables.
    D. Compare the requirements to the features of the completed product to find variances, if any.

182. You have a project, where the allocated budget at completion (BAC) is $300,000 and the assigned duration is 4 months. After two months, you see that you have completed work that is worth $100,000. But you have spent only $75,000 so far. What is the cost performance index (CPI)?
    A. 0.66
    B. 1.50
    C. 1.00
    D. 1.33

183. What is the comparison between Validate Scope and Control Quality?
    A. Control Quality is done before Validate Scope.
    B. Control Quality is primarily for product-related deliverables while Validate Scope is meant for service-related deliverables.

C. Validate Scope is mandatory and conducted for all projects, but Control Quality is performed only for products where the customer has provided specification and control limits.

D. Validate Scope is concerned with acceptance of the deliverables while Control Quality is about meeting the quality requirements.

184. You have a project resource, who is always late with his deliverables. What would be the first thing to do to motivate him?
  A. Have a 1:1 discussion either in-person or over the phone to understand the reasons for the delay.
  B. Escalate to his functional manager.
  C. Reduce the workload on the project resource.
  D. Have a formal, written communication with the project resource in privacy and without involving any other resource or stakeholder.

185. Which one of the following processes, has change requests as an output?
  A. Validate Scope
  B. Plan Scope Management
  C. Collect Requirements
  D. Define Scope

186. Rita Samuelson is in the middle of executing and monitoring stages for a project to deploy single sign-on (SSO) authentication for cloud applications. She needs to report variances to stakeholders. Which of the following has not been initiated?
  A. A. Develop Risk Responses process
  B. B. Develop Stakeholder Communication process
  C. C. Get signoff from the stakeholders for the completed deliverables.
  D. D. Create the lessons learned document

Section 5 of 5: Questions on Project Closing Process Group (questions 187 – 200)

187. Susan Simpson is starting work on a new project. Her program manager has provided various project documents and lessons learned from previous projects and explained to Susan that she must go and meet the project managers of the previously-completed projects and get tacit (implicit) knowledge about those projects. Which of the following is not a difference between explicit and tacit knowledge?
  A. Explicit knowledge is easy to document but tacit knowledge is not.
  B. Explicit knowledge lacks context but tacit knowledge has context.
  C. Explicit knowledge is not always understood or applied in the right way but tacit knowledge can be explained in informal communications and settings and it can be applied in the right way.
  D. Lesson learned register is an example of an explicit document, since all lessons learned from a project can be documented.

188. Donald Dickenson is delivering a presentation on emerging practices in integrating project activities. Which of the following should not be included in the presentation?
  A. There is a growing trend of using agile (iterative and incremental) methodologies in large projects, for certain sections which cannot be initially planned due to lack of visibility.

B. There is a growing need to use automated tools to analyze the rapidly-expanding volume of data.

C. Identifying project knowledge and transferring that to the proper target audience is critical since the workforce is becoming more and more transitory.

D. There is a new and growing trend to document lessons learned in a project and use those for similar projects in the future.

189. One of the key outcomes of a project is the 'lessons learned' document. It is part of organizational process assets and includes important recommendations for future projects. Lessons learned are assembled and documented during which project phase:
A. Planning and execution process groups
B. Closing process group
C. Throughout the project
D. In the middle of a project

190. The closure of a project phase provides a hand-off of the deliverable to the next project phase. It also serves as a natural point to assess the project progress and make alterations. This natural point is referred to as:
A. Stage gate
B. Kill point
C. Milestone phase review
D. All of the above are valid references

191. Beverley Baker is in the process of completing the deliverables for an application project rollout to 500 internal users across the world and getting approvals from the project sponsor. Which one of the following would be remaining for her to do?
A. Close vendor contracts.
B. Start the process to get acknowledgment and acceptance of the deliverables from the sponsor.
C. Complete lessons learned document.
D. Finalize requirement documentation.

192. Kevin Karson is a project manager for a large battery manufacturer in Egypt. He has completed setup for a battery manufacturing and waste recycling center in Egypt. The firm exports battery from Egypt to various electrical car manufacturers in Europe and North America. Towards the close of the project, Kevin needs to dispose electronic waste, furniture and toxic liquid. The car manufacturers (customers) have a requirement that vendor must dispose all e-waste and toxic material in a proper manner. Amir has contacted an e-waste vendor for his electronic equipment. A local furniture store is scheduled to pick-up the leftover furniture. But Amir cannot get a solution to dispose the toxic liquid. He discusses options with his project resources. The local project resources suggest that the liquid be disposed of in the local sewage system since that will be quicker and help meet deadlines for project closure. That has been a common and acceptable practice adopted by other manufacturing firms in that region. What should Kevin do?
A. Let the project resources give the material to a local recycling agency.
B. Do not improperly dispose of the toxic liquid.
C. Dispose of the liquid in the local sewage system! Others are doing the same.
D. Leave the material as is. The operation team can dispose that later.

193. Which of the following process groups is least likely to overlap?
    A. Initiating and Closing
    B. Planning and Closing
    C. Planning and Executing
    D. Initiating and Monitoring and Controlling

194. Mark Molson is late on a project. The functional managers are pressing him to release the project team members for other initiatives within the organization. Which of these must be completed before Mark can start project closure?
    A. Develop and send formal communication that the project will be closed and the deliverables are ready for use.
    B. Get formal acceptance from stakeholders and customers for the deliverables.
    C. Make sure vendors are paid for the completed scope.
    D. Close all open change requests for the project.

195. Which of the following activities contribute to the lessons learned document?
    A. Root cause analysis of issues
    B. Post-project review of completed activities
    C. Quality audit of completed deliverables
    D. Validation of project deliverables or products

196. Susan Kimberley is closing a natural gas discovery project in Queensland, Australia. Which of the following would not be a key activity for her during project closure?
    A. Archive project information for future use.
    B. Finalize project documents.
    C. Conduct cost-benefit analysis (CBA) for the completed work.
    D. Assign project resources to other projects or let them go from the organization.

197. You are managing a project with 20 stakeholders to develop a new server and data storage farm for a cloud services provider in Tokyo and e-waste the old equipment from the datacenter. Which of these should not be part of the Close Project process?
    A. Gain acceptance and signoff from the stakeholders for the completed deliverables.
    B. Complete project documents.
    C. Close accounts related to the project with the suppliers.
    D. Get a certificate of recycling (COR) from the e-waste vendor.

198. Gary Gibson is the project manager for an airline with flight services across the globe. He is managing a project to upgrade the aircraft service platforms at the headquarters in Dallas, Texas. He is working with the global procurement team to purchase the identified equipment for aircraft servicing and inspection. Which of the following would be the last activity for the project?
    A. Complete and archive lessons learned.
    B. Measure customer satisfaction for the installed aircraft service stations.
    C. Complete equipment maintenance training for the operations team.
    D. Make sure that the vendor invoices are paid and the purchase orders are closed.

199. Which of these is an input for Close Project or Phase process?
     A. Work performance information
     B. Final product or service
     C. Completed change requests
     D. Accepted deliverables

200. If a project is terminated early and before completion of deliverables, one of the key activities during project closure would be to:
     A. Develop lessons learned from the early termination of the project.
     B. Conduct root cause analysis to understand and document the reasons for project closure.
     C. Establish procedures to investigate and document the reasons for actions taken.
     D. Close project documents and reassign resources.

Answers for 200-Question Test

Answers for Initiating Process Group (Questions 1 – 26)

Question Number	Correct Answer	Explanation
1	B	To start a project, you need an approved project charter. It includes various sections such as cost-benefit analysis, project constraints, risk and assumptions and a high-level description of allocated resources and time and assigned scope.
2	A	Stakeholders provide input to developing the project constraints towards the beginning. They help develop the charter. In the planning and subsequent phases, you work with the project staff members and engineers.
3	D	Documenting high-level scope and timeline are part of Develop Charter process, which is part of the **Initiating** Process Group.
4	A	During initiation, you are involved in developing the project charter with stakeholders. The expenses are low. Most of the expenses will happen during execution.
5	B	A product lifecycle can have various projects such as product feasibility study project, launch project, marketing project, feature addition project, etc.
6	C	The **Develop Project Charter** process does not use data analysis as a tool or technique. However, data gathering is one of the tools and techniques. Develop Project Charter is one of the initial processes in a project and the main task is to gather information and data, rather than data analysis.
7	A	For each project, you first compute the net revenue, which is incoming revenue minus the O&M expense each month. You then divide the capital expense by the net revenue to get the payback period. The project with the least payback period is the correct answer. ▪ For Project A: The payback period is $300,000/$20,000 or 15 months ▪ For Project B: The payback period is $400,000/$25,000 or 16 months ▪ For Project C: The payback period is $180,000/$10,000 or 18 months ▪ For Project D: The payback period is $300,000/$15,000 or 20 months The payback period is the least for Project A and hence that is the correct answer.
8	D	Most of the inputs from stakeholders come towards the start of the project. At that time, the charter, requirements and project baselines (budget, scope and timeline) are being developed.
9	C	The payback period is the time to build the highway (which is 24 months) + the time to recover the capital expense (which is $5,000,000/$200,000 or 25 months). The total time = 24 + 25 = 49 months.
10	D	The first three choices are part of organizational process assets (OPA). It describes governance functions to help with guidance and decision-making within a project, program or portfolio. The last choice (organizational governance framework) is part of enterprise environmental factors (EEF). It describes how you can use resources, people and policies to meet organizational goals.
11	B	The assumption log is created in the **Develop Project Charter** process with various high-level assumptions on strategy and operational situations. Later, when the project is in-progress, details (about activities, resource availabilities, etc.) are added to the assumption log. See Page 81 of the PMBOK®.

12	A	One of the outputs of the **Identify Stakeholders** process is the stakeholder register. It contains stakeholders information such as: <ul><li>their contact details</li><li>their role in the project and expectations</li><li>their potential for influencing project outcomes</li><li>their impact, power and interest in the project progress and outcomes</li><li>their direction of influence within the organization (upward, downward or sideward) or outside the organization.</li></ul>There will be questions that require you to remember the process names that have key project documents such as the charter, risk register, baselines, etc., as an output.
13	C	The project charter is part of the **Initiating** Process Group.
14	A	It is possible that different programs or projects within a portfolio are not related to each other. But these programs or projects meet a strategic objective of "maximizing shareholder value". All projects within a program, however, are related and managed in a coordinated manner. The other options are all true. See Page 13 of PMBOK® Guide, Table 1-2 (Comparative Overview of Portfolios, Programs and Projects).
15	D	Charter has an initial list of risks, constraints and assumptions. These are later updated in other project documents such as risk register, and assumption log
16	C	The project charter has high-level requirements. Further details are gathered and documented during the **Collect Requirements** process.
17	C	The project sponsor owns the business case and may also be the requestor. There are others who also help with the role: <ul><li>The program manager</li><li>The analyst (also helps with project requirements)</li><li>The customer or requestor helps define the project needs and project.</li></ul>
18	D	The best answer is the needs assessment document. The benefits management plan and business case document may be developed in parallel. All these happen in the pre-project work and are used for a go/no-go decision for the project. See page 30 of the PMBOK®. Note that the other choices such as charter and requirements documentation are developed later, during the **Initiating** and **Planning** Process Groups, respectively.
19	D	Again, notice words such as never, almost, always, ideally in the question. Identification of stakeholders and changes to the stakeholder engagement assessment matrix can happen throughout the project. But ideally, identifying the stakeholders should happen during project initiation. Then during planning, the stakeholder needs can be captured in the requirements documents. This helps prevent changes to the project during execution phase when such changes are difficult and expensive to implement. If new stakeholders are identified and added during execution stages, the stakeholders will provide their requirements which will lead to new change requests.
20	D	These documents are required to identify stakeholders and prepare the stakeholder register. <ul><li>Communications management plan provides knowledge about the stakeholders.</li><li>Issue log provides insight to new stakeholders and how the engagement level of the existing stakeholders may be changing.</li><li>The requirement documents refer to the stakeholders who provided the requirements for the project.</li></ul>

21	A	The activity in the question is part of the **Identify Stakeholders** process. The stakeholder engagement plan (part of the project management plan) is an input and the information is documented in the stakeholder register. Note that during project initiation, the stakeholder engagement plan is not available, but once it is available later, it is used to identify more stakeholders and update the stakeholder register.
22	A	You need to compute the IRR (internal rate of return). ▪ For Project A: rate of return is 10% ($20,000/$200,000) ▪ For Project B: rate of return is also 10% ($30,000/$300,000) ▪ For Project C: rate of return is again 10% ($40,000/$400,000) ▪ For Project D: rate of return is 5% ($25,000/$500,000) The higher the IRR, the better. The IRR is the same for Projects A, B and C. The next factor to consider would be the investment, which is considered as a sunk cost. This sunk cost is least for Project A, which is therefore the correct answer.
23	D	The engagement level (desired and current) of the stakeholder is specified in the stakeholder engagement assessment matrix, and not in the stakeholder register.
24	D	Change requests happen after the charter is approved and usually after project execution has started. See Page 81 of the PMBOK® Guide for information that is included in the project charter.
25	B	Payback period is time needed to recover the capital costs. You will need to compute the months needed to recover the initial expenses. ▪ For Project A: You will need 10 months to recover the initial investment of $200,000 ($200,000/$20,000) but that is after a wait of 6 months. Hence the payback period = 6 + 10 = 16 months. ▪ For Project B: You will need 10 months ($300,000/$30,000) to recover the initial investment and there is no wait time. Hence the payback period is 10 months. ▪ For Project C: You will need 10 months ($400,000/$40,000) to recover the initial investment of $400,000 but that is after a wait of 12 months. Hence the payback period = 12 + 10 = 22 months. ▪ For Project D: You will need 20 months ($500,000/$25,000) to recover the initial investment of $500,000 and there is no wait time. Hence the payback period is 20 months. Project B has the least payback period (10 months) and is the correct answer.
26	C	All the stated choices are true about stakeholders but choice (C) is the best answer because it is true for all stakeholders. The other stated choices could be true for some but not all stakeholders.

Answers for Planning Process Group (Questions 27 - 74)

Question Number	Correct Answer	Explanation
27	D	Push communication is one that is sent directly to specific recipients who need to know about that. But there is no guarantee that the communication eventually reached the audience and whether they understood the message.
28	A	A project can be done by a single individual. At first glance, all four choices seem correct, but choices (B) through (D) are not always true! A project can be given to a team that has never done the work before. Most project deliverables are new for the project team. A project need not involve multiple departments or vendors. Also, a project can be terminated immediately after or in the middle of the initiation phase.
29	D	Contracts with Fixed Fee (FF) are least risky for the buyer because that the buyer is paying is not going to increase in the future.
30	A	Risk breakdown structure (RBS) is a hierarchical representation of the potential sources of risks. It is part of the risk management plan document.
31	A	Finish-to-start (FS) is the most common relationship. It is used as default by most schedule development application such as Microsoft Project.
32	C	Monte Carlo analysis can be used to mitigate variability risks. The range of variation is reflected in probability distributions. Variability risks are a type of non-event risks, but non-events risks is not the best answer. See Page 399 of the PMBOK®.
33	C	Power and Legitimacy are two factors for this stakeholder. He has no urgency but has legitimate needs to know about the project and he can influence the progress or even the existence of the project.
34	B	This is a Finish-to-start relationship with a lag of 10 days. Remember lags are shown as a positive value. Leads are shown as a negative value.
35	A	An RFI is used when more information is required from the sellers.
36	C	A matrix diagram is used to identify the strength of relationships between inputs (causes or factors) and the outcome. For example, a matrix diagram can have factors (inputs) on the row and it can have effects (outcomes) on the columns. The cells represent the strength of relationships between the items on the rows and columns. It helps to identify the factors that would have the most influence on the outcomes.
37	D	The net path value (NPV) of internally developing the software followed by a strong demand is a gain of $20M. Remember that NPV is the total loss or profit (sales minus expenses) for a path assuming that path occurs. You do not adjust for the percentage (possibility) of occurrence since that path is assumed to happen.
38	D	The number of communication channels is $(n)*(n-1)/2$ where n is the number of persons. In this case, the number of persons is 7 including the project manager. Therefore, the number of communication channels = $7*6/2 = 21$ channels. A common mistake in the PMP exam is to not include the project manager when estimating the value of **n**. Watch if the project manager should be included in the value or not!
39	B	Transfer is a response in which you move the ownership of the threat to another party by use of insurance, bonds, warranties, agreements, guarantees, etc.
40	B	The net path value (NPV) of internally developing the software followed by a weak demand is a loss of $10M. NPV is the total loss or profit (sales minus expenses) for a path assuming that path occurs.

41	C	The **Plan Resource Management** process is about defining how you will use estimate, acquire, manage and control the resources that you need for the project. For this, one of the key required information is the distribution and location of the resources (facilities, equipment, etc.).
42	B	The total float = late start – early start = 120 – 90 = 30 days. The total float can also be calculated using "late finish – early finish" = 135 – 105 = 30 days.
43	D	A fixed-price (FP) contract is best when the work scope is well-defined and not likely to change.
44	C	You need to quickly sketch a schedule network and write the activity durations. The path with the longest duration (critical path) is D-E which adds to 50 + 20 = 70 weeks.
45	C	The EMV = (70% of $200,000) – (30% of $100,00) = $140,000 - $30,000 = $110,000
46	D	Contingency reserve is part of the cost baseline. Management reserve is not part of the cost baseline. See Page 245 of the PMBOK®.
47	D	There can be multiple critical paths in a project schedule. All the critical paths have the same duration which is also the highest amongst all paths. For example, if a schedule has 10 paths and 3 of those have duration of 90 days each and the other 7 fewer than 90 days, the project has 3 critical paths and the project duration is 90 days.
48	A	A procurement strategy has the procurement phases, delivery methods and types of agreements. See the table on Page 481 of the PMBOK®.
49	C	The dependency is not hard or required. There are easy workarounds. It is preferential (also called discretionary, soft or preferred logic) dependency. Since it depends on the schedule created by the contracting agency, it is an external dependency. See Page 191 of the PMBOK®.
50	D	Resource smoothing may not be able to optimize resource utilization. See Page 211 of the PMBOK®.
51	C	Since the price per unit is fixed, it is a unit price contract.
52	A	The seller is paid the actuals and hence this is a cost-plus contract. In addition, the seller will receive an incentive fee if the actuals end up being less than the pre-determined project cost. Thus, it is a CPIF contract.

53	B	PERT uses a weighted average to compute the duration. The formula is $(O + 4*M + P)/6$. That computed duration can be used by CPM technique to develop a project schedule and a schedule baseline. Remember that triangular distribution (also called mean or simple average) uses the formula $(O + M + P)/3$. But this is not a weighted average.
54	D	Scope baseline consists of: ▪ Project scope statement ▪ WBS ▪ WBS dictionary ▪ Work packages ▪ Planning packages See Page 161 of the PMBOK®.
55	C	Being able to get a response in less than three seconds a supporting feature to enhance ease-of-use and get quick application response. It is a performance criterion and a non-functional requirement. It is not a functionality or feature. In the given choices in the question: ▪ A is a project requirement, ▪ B is a stakeholder requirement, ▪ C is a non-functional requirement, ▪ D is a functional requirement,
56	C	If all activities would have FS relationship, the project duration would then be $20 + 20 + 30 + 50 = 120$ weeks. But we need to subtract time because of overlaps caused by the leads (or add the weeks if the activities are distanced away). ▪ For FS -2, there are 2 weeks of overlap between 'collect requirements' and design. We need to subtract 2 weeks. ▪ For SS+20, test starts 20 weeks after development has started. Development has a duration of 30 weeks and it has an overlap of 10 weeks with 'test'. Hence, we need to subtract 10 weeks. The total duration, therefore, is $120 – 2 - 10 = 108$ weeks.
57	C	The key output of the **Create WBS** process is the scope baseline.
58	A	The project manager needs to tailor or customize the processes because each project is unique. Processes needed for a particular project will be different from the those needed for another project.
59	C	Tasks and processes related to requirements are in the requirements management plan (not in the scope management plan). All other listed choices are components of the scope management plan.
60	A	The **Plan Risk Management** process is not used to identify or update risks. It is used to develop a plan for identifying and managing risks. The other processes are used to identify, track and update risks in the risk register or risk report.
61	D	All the provided choices are good techniques to select the vendor. But alternatives analysis is the best answer. It is used to evaluate various options and then select the optimum (most suitable) solution.
62	C	What-if scenario analysis is the process of understanding the impact of various scenarios (that are likely to occur) on the project schedule, cost, quality and other constraints. Here you ask the question "If Scenario A were to happen, what would be the impact on the project". See Page 213 of the PMBOK®.

63	C	The various requirements are business, technical, solutions (functional and non-functional), quality, project, etc. The other choices show how the requirements can be qualified based on ▪ its urgency of implementation, ▪ stakeholder who provided the requirements, and ▪ end-user needs that led to the requirement.
64	C	This question asks for beta (or PERT or weighted) average, which is $(P + 4*M + O)/6 = (100 + 4*60 + 50)/6 = 390/6 = 65$ days.
65	A	This is an example of parametric estimation, which is a technique to estimate cost or duration using parameters and data from a previous, similar project.
66	C	The table below has the formulas related to optimistic (O), most likely (M) and pessimistic (P) estimates. |	Term	Formula
---	------	---------
1	Standard deviation (SD)	$(P-O)/6$
2	Variance (that is square of SD)	$SD*SD$
3	Weighted average (PERT or beta average)	$(P + 4*M + O)/6$
4	Simple average (triangular or 3-point)	$(P + M + O)/3$ | This question asks for SD, which is $(P-O)/6$ or $(100 - 60)/6$ or $40/6$ or 6.66 days. The closest answer is 6 days and hence it is the correct choice.
67	D	A milestone has zero time associated with it. It signifies that a deliverable or task has been completed.
68	A	A user story is a short description of the required functionality. This is usually developed during a requirement workshop. There is also an implicit promise that more details will be discussed and documented later. See Page 145 of the PMBOK®.
69	D	This question is related to **Collect Requirements** process where you identify, document and manage project requirements. The requirements come from the stakeholders. The project objectives are in the project charter. Hence you need the stakeholder register and project charter, which are outputs of the processes in the **Initiating** Process Group. **Collect Requirements** is the first process in the **Planning** Process Group other than developing plans. The other choices (WBS, activity list, budget, scope statement, etc.) need the requirements documents as an input are usually done later in the planning stage.
70	D	Scope baseline does not contain the requirements documentation. The other mentioned choices are part of the scope baseline.
71	B	Richard can refer to the lessons learned register from similar previous projects. But the one for this project has not been created yet.
72	C	Activity-on-node (AON) is a technique where activities are represented by nodes and dependencies (such as FS, FF, SF and SS with optional leads or lags), are represented by arrows. It is a precedence diagramming method (PDM).
73	D	All the choices are true for variability risks. These are caused by uncertainties related to project activities or decisions. For example, rainfall will impact the schedule of a construction project. But the amount of rain or schedule delay is not known at the start of the project. The amount of delay will vary. Hence it is a variability risk. See Page 398 of the PMBOK®.
74	C	This is a transition requirement because it specifies the criteria for transition of the data from internal disks to cloud storage.

Answers for Executing Process Group(Questions 75 – 136)

Question Number	Correct Answer	Explanation
75	A	Benchmarking is comparing the project plans, performance and quality to that of comparable projects within the organization or outside.
76	D	If the current and desired engagement levels are different, that is a distinct indication that the stakeholder is not engaged as he or she should be. The project manager needs to take actions and improve the engagement of the stakeholder.
77	B	The **Develop Team** process includes the phases of improving team dynamics. The 5 phases are forming, storming, norming, performing and adjourning. This is known as Tuckman ladder model.
78	D	The salience model, power/interest grid or the direction of influence does not tell you if you need to improve relationships and communications with any stakeholder. These show the significance of the stakeholder on the project. The gap between the current (C) and desired (D) engagement levels dictates the need for developing relationships. For example, if the current (C) engagement level is resistant, and the desired (D) level is supportive, you must work on communications to get the stakeholder to the desired level.
79	D	The number of communication channels is (n)*(n-1)/2 where n is the number of persons involved in the communications. In this case, the number of persons is 11 including the project manager. Therefore, the number of communication channels = 11*10/2 = 55 channels.
80	B	Total price for the FPAF contract = fixed fee for 12 months + award for 4 months = ($100,000/month * 12 months) + ($25,000/month * 4 months) = $1,200,000 + $100,000 = $1,300,000 The answer is $1,300,000
81	A	Work performance information is usually an output of processes in the **Monitoring** and **Controlling** Process Group. The **Control Scope** process is part of the **Monitoring and Controlling** Process Group and its output is work performance information. The other choices belong to the **Planning** or **Executing** Process Groups. Most questions in the exam will not be as hard as this. But, you do need to know the key output of each of the 49 processes.
82	D	The project team can get stuck at one of the five phases (forming, storming, norming, performing and adjourning). For example, performing (project execution) may take longer than any of the other stages. Will you need to go back? Yes! If you are not getting past the storming phase and it seems impossible to make the team perform in harmony, you may go back to forming stage and change team membership. You can also skip a stage. Storming and norming may not be needed if the team members have worked together earlier. You can go directly from forming to performing. Also you do not need to follow the prescribed sequence. If during execution, you find you need more resources, you may have to go back to forming and add new members. If conflicts happen during performing, you must go to norming again to try and resolve the conflicts.

83	A	Fitness for use is that the service or product meets real needs for the user. Conformance is about making sure that the product or service meets the objectives and requirements.
84	D	Six Sigma is a set of tools and techniques for process improvement by removing causes of defects and by minimizing variability. Each Six Sigma project has a specific goal such as to reduce manufacturing costs, increase customer satisfaction, increase profits, etc.
85	C	Total price for the T&M contract = fee for the man-hours + reimbursement for travel expenses = (4 persons * 20 hours * $250/hour) + ($1,500/person * 4 persons) = $20,000 + $6,000 = $26,000
86	B	The best way to manage remote stakeholders is to communicate frequently (as required by the stakeholder management plan) by emails, virtual meetings and sharing project documents and status reports.
87	A	Design for X (DfX) is a set of guidelines to optimize, improve or control a product's feature such as its scalability, serviceability, cost-effectiveness, ease-of-use, etc. DfX helps reduce cost and improve quality and performance. See Page 295 of the PMBOK®.
88	B	The start of painting is 5 days after the start of installation. Hence the dependency is SS + 5 days.
89	A	The quality of the project deliverables is for the project manager to own and control. He or she in turn, needs to work with the management, sponsor and project team to deliver the required quality. Note that the ownership of the quality at the organizational level is with the senior management.
90	A	Before the change, the critical path as shown in the diagram is A1-B6-C42-F21 and the duration is 130 weeks. After the client adds the new activity, after A1 and before D12, this path (A1 – new activity of 20 weeks – D12 – E24 – F21) becomes the critical path with a total duration of 140 weeks. The increase in project duration = 140 – 130 = 10 weeks.
91	D	The project manager needs to be aware of all the mentioned factors. They are all needed for effective communications with the stakeholders.
92	A	Lessons learned register is an output of **Manage Project Knowledge** process. Updates to the document are an output of many processes. See Page 104 of the PMBOK®.
93	C	At first glance, all 4 choices appear correct. But **Manage Stakeholder Engagement** process is the correct answer. In this process, you work with the stakeholders to address issues, meet their expectations and build required stakeholder involvement. These also help in effectively managing and monitoring the communications with the stakeholders. The benefit is improved support and reduced resistance from the stakeholders.
94	D	All the statements are correct and are similar to recommended practices in the PMBOK®.
95	B	Communications in a matrix organization is complex since there are hard-lined and dotted-line reporting structures. The project team members report directly to the functional managers. The project managers have moderate authority.

96	D	You need to assess why the team was in danger of missing schedule deadlines. The risk register may point to expected problems and team behavior which you first need to understand.
97	B	Expenses incurred are highest during the execution stage because the hours worked by team members are usually highest during the execution stage. Most of the purchases for the project occur during the execution stage.
98	C	You can submit the resume. But you must let all stakeholders and hiring manager know that the candidate is your relative. You must also not participate in the decision-making process because it would create a conflict of interest.
99	A	The outline is for the Ishikawa diagram. It is also known as cause-and-effect or fishbone diagram.
100	D	A cause-and-effect diagram cannot develop a timeline for resolution of issues. It helps to identify the root cause of problems as well as effects, arising due to certain errors or defects.
101	C	A histogram shows the number of events or products that have a particular characteristic (such as number of defects produced each day in the month). Another example is a resource histogram that shows the resource requirements by time period.
102	D	A scatter diagram shows the correlation between an independent (X-axis) variable and a dependent (Y-axis) variable.
103	B	A fishbone diagram (also called a cause-and-effect diagram) is the best way to break down the causes of a particular problem into branches and identify the root cause(s).
104	D	Stakeholders, with high power within the organization and low interest in the project, must be kept satisfied by providing project information and status that they may require.

105	D	Total price for the FPIF contract
		= fixed fee + incentive for completing 6 months in advance
		      = \$2M + (\$200,000/month * 6 months)
		      = \$2M + \$1,200,000
		      = \$3,200,000
		The answer is \$3,200,000 or \$3.2M.

106	A	Risk register contains the responses for individual risks. Risk report contains the responses for overall project risk and high-priority risks. These two documents also contain the nominated owners to contact for implementation of the risk response plans.
107	C	Exploit is a risk response when the organization wants to make sure that the opportunity is realized.
108	D	Change requests are an output of **Implement Risk Responses** process. In this process, you implement the response plans in the risk register or report. This may lead to change requests to the baselines and other project management plans.
109	B	Bidder conferences are held during the **Conduct Procurements** process. It is a meeting between the buyer and all prospective sellers to clarify doubts and answer questions. It ensures fairness in providing information.
110	B	The project manager needs to establish professional relationships with the skilled resources and win their trust. It is best to use verbal and informal communications.
111	B	All the choices are required for successfully working with a multi-cultural team. But the most crucial requirements are good interpersonal and communication skills, which can help improve trust and cooperation within the team.
112	B	Since the two resources have some animosity, it is best to have an in-person and private discussion with the two resources. They need a secure environment to openly discuss their differences and arrive at a consensus.

113	C	All the stated choices are things that Kevin should do. But the question asks for "…the first thing..". The first thing to do is to understand the reasons for the strong resistance and address those.
114	A	Project progress report provides a summary of the project status. The other choices do not provide a quick status: • The variance report only compares the planned with the actuals. • The status report is usually too detailed. • The project schedule and work completed is limited to the completed scope. It does not tell whether the project is under or over-budget and if the stakeholders are satisfied with the progress.
115	D	Again, watch for keywords such as not, always or must in the question! An email by itself is not a formal tool for documenting a project decision. It is just a mechanism to send formal information such as meeting minutes, reports, etc.
116	D	Theory Y and Herzberg's Motivation-Hygiene Theory are correct answers. Resources nowadays are very informed and willing to accept new roles and challenges. The best way to motivate them is to let them exercise their self-control and self-direction to complete their work. Theory Y advocates a participative management style. Herzberg's Motivation-Hygiene Theory states that hygiene factors must be properly implemented to remove job dissatisfaction. In addition, motivational factors must be implemented to improve job satisfaction.
117	D	A good project manager is usually one who has worked in different project roles earlier.
118	C	This conflict resolution style is by compromising or reconciling the differences. The final solution consists of proposals from each side. This brings some satisfaction to all parties but may not be the optimum or most suitable solution for the organization.
119	A	Total productive maintenance (TPM) is a system of maintaining the production and quality systems with a goal to improve their value to the organization.
120	D	The description is for cause-and-effect diagrams. These are also known as why-why, fishbone or Ishikawa diagrams.
121	B	Lessons learned register is an output of **Manage Project Knowledge** process. It is updated by the other processes mentioned in the choices.
122	D	The most likely estimate is independent of the pessimistic and optimistic values. It is not possible to compute the most likely estimate, given the optimistic and pessimistic values.
123	C	Active is not an engagement level. The engagement levels are: • Unaware • Resistant • Neutral • Supportive and • Leading The gap between the current (existing) and desired levels of engagement help determine the amount of communications required to effectively engage each stakeholder. See Page 521 of the PMBOK®.
124	B	Risk report has a status, probability of occurrence, impact and mitigation plan for all risks. See Page 418 of the PMBOK®.

125	A	A Kanban board shows the work at each stage (such as to-be-done, in-progress and done). It: ■ enables the team and stakeholders to direct their resources towards completing the activities that are in-progress or stalled, ■ limits the amount of work at each stage and thus improves quality and productivity, and ■ improves the flexibility for prioritizing tasks.
126	B	This question asks for variance, which is $\{(P-O)/6\}^2 = \{(100-60)/6\}^2 = 6.66^2 = 44.44$ days. The closest answer is 45 days and is the correct answer.
127	C	A Kaizen event is a session to discuss and make improvements to the process. The goal is to improve profitability, safety, and quality of service. The foundation of these events is 5S, which stands for: 1) Sort – remove unnecessary items from the workplace 2) Set in order – keep things in their place 3) Shine – keep the workplace and tools clean 4) Standardize – make and follow rules 5) Sustain – make those a daily habit and do not slip back to the old ways. It helps establish a lean manufacturing environment.
128	C	Force/direct technique of resolving conflicts often leads to a win-lose situation, because the viewpoint of one party is upheld at the expense of viewpoints of others. Compromise/reconcile and smooth/accommodate can also create win-lose situations but force/direct is the best answer.
129	D	All the choices, except for A, seem like good answers, but could increase the project budget and timelines. Getting an external vendor resource is best answer because it would be less expensive and quicker than the other options.
130	A	Individual and team assessments are techniques used in the **Develop Team** process.
131	D	When you use collaboration and problem solving, you include multiple viewpoints to reach a consensus that is acceptable to all. This leads to a win-win situation.
132	D	Change in product features is a modification of the scope baseline and will likely impact contract terms cost, schedule and required resources. Therefore, it is essential to have written and formal communications.
133	C	A written formal communication is good for all the choices. The best answer is C because it deals with a change in the contract terms.
134	D	You are mitigating the risk by reducing the probability of occurrence.
135	C	This is cost for internal inspection or appraisal. The cost is being incurred before the cars reach the customers. Therefore, it is not an external failure cost.
136	C	All the stated choices are right things to do. But notice that the question asks for " .. the first thing ...". The first thing is to inform the client, sponsor and stakeholders.

Answers for Monitoring and Controlling Process Group (Questions 137 – 186)

Question Number	Correct Answer	Explanation
137	D	All the 3 processes in the **Procurement Management** Knowledge Area have change requests as an output.
138	C	Internal failure cost is the cost of failure found by the inspection team. Inspection may result in "no failures found" and hence there would be no cost related to failures. What about Choice D, which is cost for calibrating the test instruments. This is maintenance cost. In case, the test equipment has defects, the cost for fixing the defects would also be part of maintenance or prevention cost. It is not a failure cost because the cost is not related to fixing defects in the deliverables.
139	A	The attention should be on meeting the requirements. There is no need to exceed the requirements or gold-plate the product. Quality levels are achieved once the requirements are met.
140	A	Variance at completion (VAC) = BAC – EAC = $75,000 - $100,00 = - $25,00
141	B	A Pareto diagram depicts the distribution or frequency of occurrence (like a bar graph or histogram) in descending order from left to right. It separates the vital-few causes (that lead to 80% of the problems) from the trivial-many.
142	D	All the 4 choices seem correct, but the best answer is D. A checklist is a list of action items or activities to be done in a structured manner. A check sheet is used to document the findings (for example inspection readings) and later used to identify trends or defects.

143	D	The funding is part of internal failure cost (or cost of non-conformance) because the defects have been identified and must be fixed.
		
		There are two costs related to quality:
		   ■ Cost of conformance: Prevention, inspections and appraisals are all part of cost of conformance. These aim to correct the processes and thereby reduce defects in the end-products.
		   ■ Cost of non-conformance: This is incurred after you have found defective parts (before or after sending to the customer) and must fix the defects.

144	B	The questions refer to liabilities and warranty cost, which is part of cost of non-conformance. See Page 283 of the PMBOK®.
145	C	Crashing is reducing the project duration by adding resources, overtime hours, expedited delivery, etc. All this leads to increased costs and risks.
146	A	CV is EV (earned value) minus AC (actual cost). In this case EV=$100,000 and AC = $125,000 CV = $100,000 - $125,000 = - $25,000

147	A	The correct answer is resource leveling, which is a technique to adjust resources in order to optimize their utilization.
		   ■ Schedule compression is used to decrease the project duration.
		   ■ Resource smoothing uses free and total float to adjust the schedule so that it aligns with resource availability.
		   ■ Fast tracking is a schedule compression technique, where activities that were previously scheduled to be in sequence are overlapped.

148	D	Before fast tracking, the critical path is A-B-F which adds to 18 weeks. If you fast track all activities (except for A) the critical path will be A-F which adds to 12 weeks. That is a reduction of 18 – 12 = 6 weeks. Hence a reduction of 8 weeks is not possible.
149	D	In these problems, you need to first write whatever has been provided. ▪ BAC (budget at completion) = $50,000 ▪ PV (planned value) = 50% (halfway) of $50,000 = $25,000 ▪ EV (earned value) = 20% of $50,000 = $10,000 ▪ AC (actual cost) = $20,000 ▪ The question asks for CPI = EV/AC = $10,000/ $20,000 = 0.5
150	D	CCB provides approvals for changes in the project baselines.
151	C	Crashing is reducing activity duration. Crashing introduces additional expenses such as for overtime rates, expedited delivery of equipment, additional manpower and equipment requirements, etc. Crashing is not an option in this case because expenses cannot be increased.
152	D	Reviewing quality of a selected set is an example of statistical sampling and inspection. This is part of appraisal cost (not prevention cost) But choices A, B and C are examples of prevention cost which is incurred to improve quality while the product is being produced. It is not about post-production assessment or inspection.
153	A	There are three ways to get a reduction of 4 weeks: (1) Crash A and B which will cost an additional $14,000 (2) Crash B and C which will cost an additional $30,000 (3) Crash A and C which will cost an additional $24,000 The least expensive way will cost an additional $14,000. Therefore, A is the correct answer.
154	A	Draw a quick critical path diagram. You will need to reduce the project duration by 2 weeks. Note that both the paths (A-B-C-E and A-D-E) are critical paths. Crashing activities, A or E, would be an easy solution but the additional crash cost per week would be very high compared to that for B, C or D. You will need to crash the paths B-C as well as activity D. You need to ▪ crash either B or C by 2 weeks .. crashing C is cheaper and costs an additional **$1,000** for 2 weeks and ▪ crash D by 2 weeks, which costs an additional **$2,000** for 2 weeks The total additional cost is $3,000 for 2 weeks. Crashing A by 2 weeks or E by 2 weeks would meet the objective but would be more expensive.
155	A	Since these are discretionary dependencies, they can be removed, and the activities can be fast tracked (overlapped or done in parallel).

156	D	The control limits are different from specification limits. Control limits are determined using statistical calculations and reflect the natural capability of a stable process. Specification limits are based on requirements and reflect the allowable range.
157	D	The TCPI that must be maintained to complete the remaining work using the remaining funds is the second formula for TCPI on Page 267 in the PMBOK®. ▪ TCPI = (remaining work) / (remaining funds) = (BAC – EV) / (EAC – AC) ▪ In this case, BAC (budget at completion) = $500,000 ▪ The work completed = earned value (EV) = 20% of $500,000 = $100,000 ▪ AC (actual cost) = $400,000 ▪ EAC (estimate at completion) = $500,000 + $300,000 = $800,000 TCPI = (BAC – EV) / (EAC – AC) = ($500,000 - $100,000) / ($800,000 - $400,000) = $400,000/400,000 = 1.00 Now let us analyze this further. The future work must be done at performance index of 1.00 ▪ But in the past the CPI (cost performance index) has been EV/AC = $100,000/$400,000 = 0.25 ▪ Also, in the past the SPI (schedule performance index) has been EV/PV = $100,000/(0.50 * $500,000) = $100,000/$250,000 = 0.40 The CPI and SPI so far, have been 0.25 and 0.40. But for the future work, you need to maintain a TCPI of 1.00. This implies that the project team needs to be more efficient for the remainder of the project.
158	D	All the processes, given in the choices, have change requests as an output. There are other processes (such as **Control Costs**, **Control Quality** and **Identify Stakeholders**) that also have change requests as an output.
159	C	ETC = EAC – AC = $100,000 - $80,000 = $20,000 ETC is the expected cost to complete the remaining project work.
160	A	**Perform Integrated Change Control** is the only process, where change requests are reviewed and approved by the change control board (CCB) or stakeholders.
161	B	▪ SPI is EV/PV. In this case EV=100 and PV=200 hours ▪ SPI = 100/200 = 0.5
162	A	Since one person decided for the group, it is autocratic decision. The different types of decision-making are: ▪ autocratic (decision made by one person), ▪ plurality (a decision that is supported by the largest group, even if the largest group has less than 50% of the total population), ▪ majority (supported by more than 50% of the total population), and ▪ unanimity (supported by 100%).
163	B	If you fast track all the 4 activities (execute all in parallel) the project duration would therefore be equal to the duration of the longest activity, which is 40 days.
164	D	In this case, the required skills are related to communication, negotiation and conflict management. Scheduling management skills are not a concern in the situation.
165	C	Before fast tracking, the critical path is A-B-C-G and the project duration is 80 days. If B and C are fast tracked, the critical path then becomes A-D-E-F-G and the project duration is 75 days. The reduction in project duration = 80 – 75 = 5 days.

166	C	All the provided choices appear to be correct. But the best answer is achieving stakeholder satisfaction. Satisfaction of stakeholders includes many criteria such as meeting product requirements, sticking to the project baselines, fitness of use, and effective training for the end-users.
167	A	SV = EV – PV. In this case EV=100 and PV=200 SV = 100 – 200 hours = -100 hours
168	A	A control chart is used to determine if a process is stable and has predictable performance. It has upper and lower control limits that are based on statistical calculations. The limits are used to identify if and when a process becomes unstable.
169	D	TCPI is the efficiency that must be maintained to complete the remaining work within the remaining funds.
170	D	The best answer is D. A retrospective meeting is where execution-related issues are identified and discussed along with resolutions and improvements for the project. See Page 305 in the PMBOK®.
171	D	Quality control must be done during all stages of the project. A record must be maintained, which would serve as proof that the acceptance criteria have been met.
172	C	In these problems, you need to first write the information that has been provided. There are 4 formulas for EAC as shown on Page 267 in the PMBOK®. Depending on the question, you need to select and use the applicable formula. In this case the relevant formula is EAC = BAC/CPI<ul><li>BAC (budget at completion) = $50,000</li><li>PV (planned value) so far is 50% (halfway) of $50,000 = $25,000</li><li>EV (earned value) is however only 20% of $50,000 = $10,000</li><li>AC (actual cost) so far = $20,000</li></ul>The question asks for EAC which is BAC/CPI. CPI = EV/AC = $10,000/ $20,000 = 0.50 Hence EAC =BAC/CPI = $50,000/0.5 = $100,000
173	C	An iteration burndown chart is one that tracks the completed work (done) and compares that to the planned (or committed) burndown, developed during iteration planning. See Page 226 in the PMBOK®.
174	C	<ul><li>The critical path is A-E-F-G-H.</li><li>To reduce the project duration by 8 weeks, you need to crash the activities that have the least additional cost per week, when crashed, in the critical path.</li><li>By reviewing the last column in the table, you see that the least crash cost/week is for activities A, E and G and that is $2,500 per week.</li><li>To crash by 8 weeks (crash A by 4 weeks and E by 4 weeks), you would incur an additional cost of $2,500 x 8 = $20,000.</li></ul>Why are A and E crashed (and not G)? This is because A and E are earlier in the schedule. It is better to crash activities that occur earlier, so you have time later to address issues, if any.
175	C	You can fast track activities that have discretionary dependencies. Since A1 and E1 have discretionary dependencies, you can fast track those (or execute in parallel) thus saving 30 days. You can also fast track G1 and H1, thus saving 80 days. The total reduction, therefore, is 30 + 80 = 110 days.
176	D	The figure has burnup and burndown charts, which are graphical representations of the work completed as compared to the planned work towards completing a project deliverable or project. Burnup charts have a line that shows the completed work (done), which starts at zero and moves up. Burndown charts show the remaining work as the iterations (project activities) progress.

177	B	Cost variance (CV) = EV – AC. The earned value (EV) is $3.8M. The actual cost (AC) is $5M. Hence CV = $3.8M - $5M = -$1.2M
178	D	A process is considered as being out of control if any of the 3 conditions (A, B or C) are met. Corrective actions must be taken to bring the process or deliverables within the control limits.
179	D	The project is behind schedule and over-budget. When a question is about a project being ahead or behind schedule, compute the SPI (schedule performance index) which is EV/PV = $3.8M/$4M, SPI is less than 1 and therefore, the project is behind schedule. For a project being over or under-budget, compute the CPI, which in this case is EV/AC = $3.8M/$5M. This is also less than 1 and hence, the project is over-budget.
180	C	While all the options are valid and right actions, the most important action is to observe the unspoken, non-verbal communication or body language. That will tell you a lot if the disagreement is due to the proposed solutions or with the 'chemistry and getting along' between those two resources. Also it is important to focus on the merits /demerits of the proposed solutions.
181	C	The **Validate Scope** process helps you formalize the acceptance of the completed deliverables. The deliverables are reviewed with the customer or sponsor to make sure they meet the requirements and acceptance criteria.
182	D	CPI is EV (earned value)/AC (actual cost). In this case EV=$100,000 and AC = $75,000 CPI = $100,000/$75,000 = 1.33
183	D	**Control Quality** usually happens prior to Validate Scope and is about meeting the pre-specified requirements about the quality of the deliverables. The **Validate Scope** process is about acceptance of project deliverables by the sponsor or customer.
184	A	Note the keyword **first** in the question. Watch out for keywords such as first, must, never, always, not, in the questions. All of the stated choices are valid things to do, but the first thing would be to have a private 1:1 discussion with the resource.
185	A	The **Validate Scope** process has change requests as an output. The last three listed processes are part of Planning Process Group. Remember that change requests are **usually** part of the **Executing** and **Monitoring and Controlling** Process Groups. There are some exceptions. Some processes (such as **Define Activities**, **Develop Schedule**, **Plan Risk Responses**, **Plan Procurement Management** and **Identify Stakeholders**) are part of the **Planning** Process Group but have change requests as an output.
186	C	This is a difficult question. Since the project is in execution mode, the planning processes such as **Develop Risk Responses** and **Develop Stakeholder Communications** have been completed. It is likely that the lessons learned document is started because it is an output of the **Manage Project Knowledge** process (part of the **Executing** Process Group). Thus, we can eliminate three options. The only remaining activity is getting signoff for completed deliverables. This activity has not been started because the project is in executing stage.

Answers for Closing Process Group (Questions 187 – 200)

Question Number	Correct Answer	Explanation
187	D	All the lessons learned, and experience gained from completed projects cannot be explicitly documented. Many lessons learned are tacit and are usually not documented simply because those are difficult to explain and validate. However, those lessons could be valuable for similar projects in the future. See Page 100 in the PMBOK®.
188	A	Recording lessons learned and using those for future projects is not a recent or emerging practice.
189	C	The lessons learned document is updated by the project team throughout the project.
190	D	Al the choices are correct. This natural point is a transition from one project phase to another. Note that a project life can be split into phases (such as design, factory setup and go-live). The transition from one phase to another is referred as kill point, stage gate, phase gate or milestone phase review.
191	C	The best answer is that she needs to complete lessons learned document. It is usually the last document to be completed. Choice A is not a good answer because completing vendor contracts may continue long after the project is closed. Besides, there is no reference that this project has any vendor engagement. Choice B is also not a good answer because the project manager is already in the process of getting approvals from the sponsor. Requirement documentation must already be completed and signed off.
192	B	It is important to take actions that help protect the environment and are in the interest of public safety. Giving the toxic liquid to local recyclers or leaving it behind for the operations team could result in improper disposal.
193	A	The **Initiating** and **Closing** Process Groups usually have no overlap. An overlap between these two Process Groups can happen only in exceptional situations when a project is canceled soon after you start developing the stakeholder register and project charter.
194	B	The best answer is there must be formal acceptance of the project deliverables before project closure can start. All the other mentioned choices are activities to be done during project closure.
195	B	A review or assessment of the completed activities and understanding of what went right or wrong provide important inputs for the lessons learned document.
196	C	Cost-benefit analysis (CBA) is usually done during the project intake stage to assess if the project should be selected for initiation or not.
197	A	Getting signoff from stakeholders (that the deliverables meet acceptance criteria) must be done prior to **Close Project or Phase** process If stakeholders identify gaps or issues with the deliverables, the project team needs to remediate or fix the deliverables, which could require new change requests.
198	D	Paying the vendor invoices could be the last activity. There is a procurement team to do the administrative work and close the purchase orders, with help from the project manager.
199	D	Accepted deliverables are an input to **Close Project or Phase** process. Accepted deliverables include approved specifications of products, work performance documents, etc.
200	C	If a project is terminated early, an essential activity during closure is to investigate and document the reasons for the early termination and other decisions.

Acronyms

AC – Actual cost

AOA – Activity on arrows

AON – Activity on nodes

BAC – Budget at completion

BRD – Business requirement document

CA – Control account

CCB – Change control board

COQ – Cost of quality

CPAF – Cost Plus Award Fee contract

CPFF – Cost Plus Fixed Fee contract

CPI – Cost performance index

CPIF – Cost Plus Incentive Fee contract

CPM – Critical Path Method

CV – Cost variance

DfX – Design for X

EAC – Estimate at completion

EEF – Enterprise environmental factors

EF – Early finish

EI – Emotional Intelligence

ES – Early start

ETC – Estimate to complete

EV – Earned value

EVA – Earned value analysis

EVM – Earned value management

FFP – Firm Fixed Price contract

FPAF – Fixed Price Award Fee contract

FPEPA – Fixed Price with Economic Price Adjustment contract

FPIF – Fixed Price Incentive Fee contract

FR – Functional requirements

ID- Identifier

IFB – Invitation for Bid

KPI – Key performance indicator

LF – Late finish

LoE – Level of effort

LS – Late start

MOU – Memorandum of understanding

MSA – Master services agreement

NFR – Non-functional requirements

OBS – Organizational breakdown structure

OCM – Organizational change management

OPA – Organizational process assets

OPM - Organizational project management

OPM3 – Organizational project management maturity model

PBO – Project-based organization

PBP – Payback period

PDCA – Plan-do-check-act

PDM – Precedence diagramming method

PDPC – Process Decision Program Chart

PMB – Performance measurement baseline

PMBOK – Project Management Body of Knowledge

PMI – Project Management Institute

PMO – Project Management Office

PO – Purchase order

PV – Planned value

RACI – Responsible, accountable, consult and inform

RAM – Responsibility assignment matrix

RBS – Risk breakdown structure

RCA – Root cause analysis

RFI – Request for information

RFP– Request for proposal

RFQ – Request for quote

ROI – Return on investment

RTM – Requirements traceability matrix

SLA – Service level agreement

SME – Subject matter expert

SOW – Statement of work

SPI – Schedule performance index

SV – Schedule variance

SWOT – Strengths, weaknesses, opportunities and threats

T&M – Time and Material Contract

TCPI – To-complete performance index

TOC – Theory of constraints

VAC – Variance at completion

WBS – Work breakdown structure

WIP – Work in progress